PEACE ON OUR TERMS

COLUMBIA STUDIES IN INTERNATIONAL AND GLOBAL HISTORY
Cemil Aydin, Timothy Nunan, and Dominic Sachsenmaier, Series Editors

This series presents some of the finest and most innovative work coming out of the current landscapes of international and global historical scholarship. Grounded in empirical research, these titles transcend the usual area boundaries and address how history can help us understand contemporary problems, including poverty, inequality, power, political violence, and accountability beyond the nation-state. The series covers processes of flows, exchanges, and entanglements—and moments of blockage, friction, and fracture—not only between "the West" and "the Rest" but also among parts of what has variously been dubbed the "Third World" or the "Global South." Scholarship in international and global history remains indispensable for a better sense of current complex regional and global economic transformations. Such approaches are vital in understanding the making of our present world.

For a complete list of books in the series, see page 323.

Peace on Our Terms

THE GLOBAL BATTLE FOR WOMEN'S RIGHTS AFTER THE FIRST WORLD WAR

Mona L. Siegel

Columbia University Press

New York

Columbia University Press
Publishers Since 1893
New York   Chichester, West Sussex
cup.columbia.edu
Copyright © 2020 Mona L. Siegel
All rights reserved

Cataloging-in-Publication Data is available from the Library of Congress.
ISBN 978-0-231-19510-2 (cloth)
ISBN 978-0-231-55118-2 (e-book)

LCCN 2019025533

∞

Columbia University Press books are printed on permanent and durable acid-free paper.
Printed in the United States of America

Cover photos: (top) Women on the streets of Cairo demonstrating for national liberation during the Egyptian revolution of 1919. ©gettyimages; (bottom) Group of delegates to the Zurich Congress, enjoying the sunshine between meetings. *WILPF Papers, Special Collections and Archives, University of Colorado Boulder Libraries.*

For Braeden and Amelie

Contents

Timeline of International Women's Activism in 1919

JANUARY 18 Paris Peace Conference officially opens; Marguerite de Witt Schlumberger writes to Woodrow Wilson asking for women's representation in negotiations and an endorsement of women's suffrage in peace treaty

JANUARY 25 French women meet with Wilson to offer support for a just peace

JANUARY 27 French feminists meet with Wilson to discuss support for women's suffrage in peace negotiations

FEBRUARY 10–APRIL 10 Inter-Allied Women's Conference runs concurrently with peace conference in Paris

FEBRUARY 10 Inter-Allied delegates meet with Wilson to request creation of a Women's Commission to peace negotiations

FEBRUARY 13 Wilson brings proposal to form a Women's Commission before Supreme Council but retracts it in face of unanimous opposition

FEBRUARY 19–21 Pan-African Congress convenes in Paris, organized by Ida Gibbs Hunt; Addie Waites Hunton addresses the congress regarding women's role in global reconstruction

MARCH 11 Supreme Council agrees to allow women to address peace conferene's Labor Commission and League of Nations Commission

MARCH 16 First women's demonstration against British Protectorate in Cairo, Egypt, organized by Huda Shaarawi

MARCH 18 Delegation of Inter-Allied Women's Conference and other feminists present resolutions to Labor Commission

MARCH 20 Second women's demonstration in Cairo, Egypt

APRIL 6 Chinese peace delegate Soumay Tcheng arrives in Paris

APRIL 10 Delegation of Inter-Allied Women's Conference and other feminists present resolutions to League of Nations Commission

MAY 4 Mass protests in Beijing, China, in opposition to decision to grant Shandong Province to Japan; Soumay Tcheng begins organizing overseas students and workers in Paris

MAY 9 Soumay Tcheng addresses mass meeting in Paris opposing Shandong decision

MAY 12–17 Congress of the Women's International League for Peace and Freedom meets in Zurich, Switzerland, under the leadership of Jane Addams

MAY 13 Zurich Congress resolutions condemning Versailles Treaty and Allied blockade of Central Europe telegraphed to Paris

MAY 15 Zurich Congress unanimously adopts Mary Church Terrell's racial equality resolution

MAY 17 Jeanne Mélin from France and Lida Gustava Heymann from Germany embrace at Zurich Congress and join others in pledge to work for lasting peace

MAY 20 Formation of Society for the New Woman in Egypt is announced

JUNE 27 Soumay Tcheng organizes overseas Chinese students and workers to stand guard outside Lu Zhengxiang's residence in St. Cloud, preventing him from attending treaty signing ceremony at Versailles

JUNE 28 Versailles Treaty signed

OCTOBER 28–NOVEMBER 6 First International Congress of Working Women meets in Washington, D.C.

OCTOBER 29–NOVEMBER 29 First Conference of the International Labor Organization convenes in Washington, D.C., with twenty-three female nonvoting delegates

NOVEMBER 28 ILO Conference adopts Night-Work (Women) Convention of 1919

NOVEMBER 29 ILO Conference adopts Maternity Protection Convention of 1919

DECEMBER 12 Mass meeting of Egyptian women at the Coptic Church in Cairo to protest Milner Commission and British Protectorate

DECEMBER 23 After concerted campaign by Indian feminists, Government of India Act 1919 allows provincial governments to decide whether to enfranchise women

Illustrations

PEACE ON OUR TERMS

Prologue

The Closing Days of the First World War

B y October 1918 an end to the nightmare was finally in sight. After more than four years of ruinous war, the Allied armies had broken through the seemingly impregnable trench lines of the Western Front, and the Germans appeared on the verge of surrender. More rapidly than many could imagine, the authority of generals gave way to that of statesmen, who began the mad scramble to determine the terms of the final armistice and to arrange for the peace negotiations to follow. In stunned disbelief, the suffering peoples of the warring nations—some joyous, others anxious—allowed themselves to indulge in a near-forgotten luxury: hope.

Far from the devastated battlefields of Western Europe, in late October 1918 American suffrage leader Carrie Chapman Catt lay sick in bed in her adopted state of New York. Suffering from both a terrible case of influenza and the U.S. Senate's disappointing rejection of a women's suffrage amendment a few weeks earlier, Catt was too worn down to maintain her usual packed schedule of political crusading. Instead, she read the newspapers and caught up on the rapidly changing international news. The Belgian city of Bruges had been liberated, the Austro-Hungarian and Ottoman armies were in open retreat, and the German government had appealed to President Woodrow Wilson of the United States to negotiate an armistice. As the leader of the major American and international women's suffrage societies of the era, Catt absorbed this last piece of information thoughtfully. Statesmen were clearly beginning to prepare for war's end. Should women be doing the same?[1]

This question was on the minds of many politically engaged women in the waning days of autumn 1918. Five had come personally to Catt's bedside the preceding week alone, asking her to appeal to President Wilson to appoint a woman to the American delegation to the peace negotiations. Catt admitted she had dreamt of this possibility for quite some time. Only recently, however, had she come to think of it as a "reasonable and sensible" proposition. "The combined services of the women of the world have been sufficient to warrant some kind of representation at the peace table surely," Catt asserted in a letter to her friend and counterpart in Great Britain, Millicent Garrett Fawcett, and she asked if the British suffrage union was planning to ask Prime Minister David Lloyd George to appoint a female delegate to the negotiations. In fact, British women had already made such a request. By mid-November American women followed suit. "Never," reported the New York Times, "had the National Suffrage Association offered any suggestion which had received such strong and immediate response as this one for having women represented at the Peace Conference."[2]

Neither appeal got very far. The British prime minister told Fawcett he had no time for such matters, and Catt's entreaties to Wilson went unanswered. Once again, mustached and bespectacled men in starched collars and neckties would gather in stuffy staterooms to hammer out the fate of the world. History has not been kind to these men, who would see their noble ideals washed away two decades later by the rising tide of militarism and fascism and the outbreak of the Second World War. "When I hear that women are unfit to be diplomats," British pacifist Helena Swanwick would later reflect, "I wonder by what standards of duplicity and frivolity they could possibly prove themselves inferior to the men who represented the victors at Versailles."[3]

Wilson's and Lloyd George's refusals to appoint a female delegate were infuriating; they did little, however, to alter women's resolve to play a part in the historic negotiations. On the contrary, the Paris Peace Conference unleashed an unprecedented wave of female activism, drawing women from far-reaching corners of the world onto the international stage in a simultaneous and spirited defense of democracy, peace, and women's rights. Denied a seat at the negotiating table, women organized separately and prepared diligently to demand gender equality and social justice in the postwar world. Whether they would do so as men's partners or adversaries remained to be seen.[4]

A New World Order

With the armistice of November 11, 1918, which ended the fighting of the First World War, the elated populations of France, Britain, the United States, and their allies had the most to celebrate, but even subjects of the defeated German, Austro-Hungarian, and Ottoman Empires could take heart. The Allies, and especially Woodrow Wilson, had insisted they had no interest in imposing a vindictive peace. The end to secret diplomacy, the enforcement of freedom of the seas, a global reduction in armaments, the establishment of equitable trade relations, the recognition of national claims to autonomy, and the creation of a new world government: these, Wilson said, in his famous "Fourteen Points" speech, were the principal goals for a peace settlement. Equally important was Wilson's proclamation in April 1917 when he first led his nation into the conflict: "The world must be made safe for democracy." The peacemakers, Wilson implied, would not be satisfied with a treaty that merely ended a war. Their goal was to open a new chapter in world history, one in which global leaders would pay heed to the weak as well as the powerful, where national borders would be determined by those who lived within them, and where the rule of law would be established on the basis of popular will.[5]

For women from the belligerent nations who had largely suspended their campaigns for women's rights during the hostilities, these promises spoke directly to their most heartfelt aspirations. In Wilson's own backyard, Catt was already asking: "But what is this democracy for which the world is battling and for which we offer our man power, our woman power, our money power, our all? Government of the world by consent of the individual states; government of the nations by the individual people. Nothing more. Nothing less." Wilson's gradual warming to the idea of women's suffrage during World War I suggested a willingness on the president's part to finally act on his convictions at home in the United States. During the war, however, Wilson spoke not only to Americans but also to the world. He called for a new liberal international order: one in which governments would be beholden to the consent of those they governed and constrained by a new international body, the League of Nations. His principled vision sparked imaginative fires in corners he could scarcely imagine.[6]

It would not take long for foreign women to seize on Wilson's rhetoric. In early 1918 French suffrage leader Marguerite de Witt Schlumberger was so inspired by what she read in the papers that she wrote to Wilson personally to thank him for his "strong and beautiful" words. In her letter, Schlumberger also implored Wilson to state publicly what she and fellow suffragists presumed to be inherent in his declarations: that the principle of national self-determination implied women's inclusion in political life once the war had ended. "No one," the French woman insisted, "can speak in the name of the people as long as women are excluded from the political life of nations." To the amazement of American suffragists, Wilson responded to Schlumberger's entreaty, issuing a public statement that implied his support for women's political enfranchisement around the world. Schlumberger rejoiced. After the war finally ended, she would write to Wilson again asking him to make good on his words at the peace conference.[7]

The year 1919 promised to be a watershed in the establishment of global democracy, but concerned female activists were certainly not going to leave anything to chance. In parlors and meeting halls, through letters and telegrams, women plotted out strategies, defined their agendas, and prepared to act. Political rights were foremost on the minds of suffragists like Catt, Fawcett, and Schlumberger, but women's vision did not end at the ballot box. The torrent of female activism in 1919 was built of the overlapping aspirations of women from widely differing backgrounds across the globe. Colonized women from Asia and the Middle East, civil rights activists in the United States, peace activists from both sides of enemy lines, and female trade unionists throughout the industrialized world joined Western suffragists in lodging their demands. National sovereignty, military disarmament, racial justice, international governance, sex trafficking, educational opportunities, marital rights, maternity benefits, and wage equality: these issues and others drew women across oceans and into the public square to demand social, economic, and political equality in a new world order. What these women from different continents, religions, social classes, and ethnic backgrounds all shared was the firm belief that a lasting peace could neither emerge nor endure without their active collaboration, and that the peace terms needed to address the rights of individuals as well as nations. To the Allied leaders gathering in Paris, to the colonial nationalists preparing to confront them, and to the international journalists who amplified their claims, these women reached out, asking to join in the construction of a better world.

Great Statesmen and Grateful Women

Women had their work cut out for them. From January until June 1919, statesmen and diplomats poured into the French capital hoping to have a hand in shaping the peace settlement. Only the victorious Allied nations were invited, but given the international scope of the First World War, this still meant that thirty-some countries participated in the negotiations, including the major powers of France, Great Britain, the United States, Italy, and Japan and two dozen "minor" powers including Belgium, Greece, China, and Brazil. Uninvited delegations showed up too, including a group of Egyptian nationalists determined to put an end to the despised British Protectorate. The most important members of these delegations were the plenipotentiaries, the handful of representatives from each country charged with the full power to represent their governments in the negotiations. Although they possessed widely differing degrees of status and power, the plenipotentiaries had one important trait in common: they all were men. If the Paris Peace Conference was a parade of international diplomacy, men clearly expected women to applaud from the sidelines.

In fact, women had been doing a fair amount of that ever since the war's end. In newspaper articles describing the jubilant Allied celebrations that marked the armistice and the buildup to the peace conference, journalists repeatedly described women as spectators to men's heroic achievements. Woodrow Wilson's arrival in Paris on December 15, 1918, was one such occasion. Stepping off the train under unseasonably blue skies, Wilson was greeted by the French president and prime minister as well as the former commander-in-chief of French forces. Wilson, however, was the man of the hour, waving appreciatively to the cheering crowd.

Men and women had turned out en masse to greet him that morning, but as Wilson stepped into the carriage that would carry him down the Champs-Elysées, one of the throng of well-wishers broke through the cordon. "At the station," the *New York Times* reported, "a young woman in the peasant costume of Alsace got through the lines, and carried a big bunch of roses to the President's carriage." It was a "pretty incident" echoed the *Manchester Guardian*. It is easy to see why the young Alsatian woman captured journalists' imagination. In her lace-trimmed bodice, bright red skirt, and elaborately bowed headdress, she undoubtedly seemed like a living embodiment of the victorious French nation, which had recovered the "lost" provinces of Alsace and Lorraine from Germany as a condition of the armistice. More than that, after a war that had upended women's traditional roles in society and in the economy, the folkloric apparition of the young Alsatian provided reassurance that now that the war was over, women would return to their families and homes. In news stories of Wilson's arrival in France, this young woman stood as a colorful symbol of female gratitude to a great statesman. Women, the subtext of these articles implied, greeted powerful men with flowers and curtsies, not with petitions or demands.[8]

Such portrayals of grateful womanhood seem positively benign compared to other descriptions of women's place in the festivities marking the end of the First World War. Upon hearing the news of the armistice on November 11, 1918, for example, young male university students in Paris poured out of their classrooms to celebrate. One of them (a future military general) wrote of that day: "I remember one twenty-year-old youth who ran from one side of the street to the other whenever he saw a woman and whipped her skirt up, dropping it again to hurry off to another victim. . . . The girls of course had a rough time but they laughed and put up with it."[9] Perhaps. But there was a lot that women were no longer willing to put up with by 1919, and for good reason.

World War I—a war of attrition that had demanded the full human and economic resources of the participant nations—had encouraged, even demanded, that women step up and "do their bit." From 1914 to 1918 women had learned new jobs, taken on new responsibilities, and developed a new sense of confidence. The hard work and sacrifice had taken its toll, but for those paying attention, it was impossible not to notice women's altered disposition.

On November 12, 1918, immediately adjacent to a long article about the armistice (blaring "Germany Surrenders" in oversized print), the British *Daily Mail* featured an article by novelist Flora Annie Steel with the intriguing headline, "Woman Makes a New World." Steel began, "East, west, north, and south we have seen woman, with a curious calm, turning her hand, heart, brain and eye to tasks which but four years ago she would have [dismissed] as unwomanly." Steel proceeded to outline some of the responsibilities women had skillfully undertaken during the war: "To parade the [streets] at night in police uniform, keeping order among the rowdy, to fell mighty trees, to handle huge horses, pitch hay, plough . . . to brave death by violence even as men brave it—all of these the women who by tradition were bound to squeal at a mouse have learnt to do, soberly, quietly, calmly." Women had accomplished great things, the article insisted, and they were better for the experience. "Indeed," Steel wrote defiantly, "if we women have done something in this war, the war has done more for us women. It has taught us to recognise ourselves, to justify our existence. . . . It is not possible for us to go back to what we were before the flame of war tried us   And why should we?" On both sides of enemy lines, and in many neutral countries as well, World War I upended traditional ideals of womanhood. Having contributed and suffered so much during the long years of fighting, women looked to the peace conference fully expecting to receive their due.[10]

Women and the Peace of 1919

The Paris Peace Conference catalyzed women across the globe in a concerted bid to secure political equality and advance women's rights, both within the redrawn boundaries of sovereign nation-states and in the newly emerging international order. Their activism was broadly global in scope. In the colonized states of Asia and the Middle East and in subjugated countries like China (where independence movements blossomed in 1919), women were radicalized alongside men. Together they fought for national liberation, but women were also awakened to the necessity of battling gender inequality at home lest freedom be won for men alone. In 1919 in India and Syria, Korea and Japan, women led demonstrations, headed delegations, and founded new organizations. Most dramatically, in Cairo, upper-class Egyptian women, led by the emerging nationalist leader Huda Shaarawi, dispensed with the proscriptions of harem culture to stage their own public demonstrations against the British Protectorate. The experience of organizing female protesters in 1919 would lead Shaarawi to found Egypt's first feminist organization after (partial) independence was won four years later.[11]

In Beijing and Shanghai, popular disillusionment with the peacemakers' refusal to return formerly German-held territory to the Chinese state led to mass protests known as the May Fourth Incident. Thousands of female students helped lead demonstrations in opposition to the peace terms. At the same time in Paris, Chinese feminist and peace delegate Soumay Tcheng—the only Allied woman officially appointed a member of a national peace delegation—would lead fiery protests against the peacemakers' unjust treatment of her nation and, in a dramatic series of cloak-and-dagger events, would coordinate an eleventh-hour push to block the Chinese plenipotentiaries from signing the Versailles Treaty.

Also in Paris, experienced Western suffragists turned to the peacemakers directly to advance their agenda. When the initial goal of winning a seat at the negotiating table failed to materialize, French woman Marguerite de Witt Schlumberger rapidly organized an Inter-Allied Women's Conference, which brought together several dozen prominent suffragists to defend women's interests in the drawing rooms of the peace delegates. In the meantime, female peace activists, angered by the exclusion of the Central Powers from the Paris negotiations, congregated in neutral Zurich under the masterful leadership of American progressive reformer and future Nobel Peace Prize winner Jane Addams. After a week of emotional debate, the assembled women in Zurich denounced the Versailles Treaty (the first organization anywhere in the world to do so), drew up a "Women's Charter," which they saw as a prerequisite to a sustainable peace, and deputized Addams and several other women to deliver it in person to the peacemakers in Paris.

Upper- and middle-class white women dominated both the Inter-Allied and Zurich Conferences in Europe, but in 1919 women of color and working-class women were no less determined to shape the peace terms. African American women—including pan-Africanist Ida Gibbs Hunt and women's and civil rights activist Mary Church Terrell—traveled to Paris and Zurich in 1919 to lobby for a peace settlement that would advance racial as well as gender equality throughout the world. At the same time, female trade unionists—including the young New York garment industry organizer Rose Schneiderman and her French counterpart Jeanne Bouvier—crossed the Atlantic in both directions to ensure working women's concerns would get a fair hearing. In October 1919 they would convene the First International Congress of Working Women in Washington, D.C., to demand paid maternity leave and protective labor legislation for vulnerable female wage earners as a baseline standard of social justice in a new world order.

Hailing from different backgrounds and continents, these women all shared the firm conviction that an enduring peace could not be built to the exclusion of half of humanity. By the time the peace conference was over, they and women the world over would be able to celebrate some notable victories; overall, however, the peacemakers refused to address many of women's most pressing concerns. Contrary to the pleas of female activists, the peacemakers declined to take any principled stance on behalf of global female enfranchisement or to recognize that the establishment of lasting peace depended on protecting the rights of *individuals* as much as achieving an equitable balance of power between *nations*. The peacemakers' reluctance to empower women in the negotiations or to integrate the majority of their policy ideas into the peace settlement was one of their major failings in 1919. Male statesmen's shortsightedness perpetuated the belief that democracy could be built in women's absence and that gender equality was somehow peripheral to global stability. Today, over a century and innumerable bloody conflicts later, international relations scholars and global policy makers soundly reject such myopic assumptions and assert that "diverse, equal, and meaningful participation of women in peace processes, reconciliation processes [and] post-conflict reconstruction" is one of the surest means of creating and safeguarding conditions that promote lasting peace.[12]

In other ways, for women the inheritance of 1919 has been considerably more positive. Over the course of the peace negotiations after the First World War, male political leaders (both those seated at the table and those insistently knocking at the door) raised women's hopes by endorsing a new world order rooted in democratic governance, self-determination, and social justice. When these same men sought to marginalize women's concerns in the eventual peace settlement and to defend foreign relations (if not all political decision making) as a masculine domain, they set the stage for the development of global feminism, which is to say, for the comprehensive, sustained, and overlapping transnational campaigns for women's rights and gender equality across the world, which emerged in the aftermath of the First World War and have multiplied exponentially ever since. From its inception, global feminism has had worldwide reach and a universal appeal. In 1919 it drew inspiration from the leadership of women from Europe, Asia, the Middle East, and North America, from white women and women of color, from women steeped in the traditions of nearly all of the major world religions, from women raised in poverty as well as those privileged with wealth and titles, from women happily married to supportive husbands and others engaged in lifelong same-sex relationships, from among the colonized as well as the colonizers.[13]

Paris and the peace conference served as an incubator for these women's sharpening feminist consciousness, even for those women—like demonstrators in Egypt and China—who could only protest from afar. Appropriating the universal principles touted by the peacemakers for their own ends, female activists of 1919 organized, mobilized, and laid out their demands. While they undoubtedly achieved less than they hoped for, female activists drew inspiration from their experience in the global spotlight. Participation in this extraordinary political moment—when so much was simultaneously at stake in so many parts of the world—empowered women to speak out and allowed them to sharpen their ideas in dialogue with one another. Because of their efforts in the aftermath of the First World War, women would gain a toehold in new, influential institutions of global governance: the League of Nations and the International Labor Organization. Outside the halls of power, women would draw collective strength from the international networks they fostered in the heat of battle. Out of the experience of 1919, they would build not one international women's movement but many, all dedicated to battling women's subordination around the world.[14]

Peace on Our Terms provides a snapshot of this outpouring of female activism in 1919: the pivotal year when global feminism first began to take form. Proceeding chronologically through the year and geographically through the principal sites of female activism, the book follows women's extraordinary efforts to champion the interests of their sex and, by extension, all humanity. It opens in Paris in January 1919, as Allied suffragists threw down the gauntlet and demanded a voice for women in the peace negotiations. By February, predominantly white, elite, Western women were joined in the French capital by female pan-Africanists and civil rights activists. In March Egyptian women defiantly took to the streets of Cairo, joining in a national uprising that they fully anticipated would liberate the women of their country as well as the men. As winter gave way to spring, pacifist feminists from the Western nations shook off wartime animosities and flouted enemy lines to congregate in neutral Zurich, even as Chinese schoolgirls and women—including China's female peace delegate in Paris—proclaimed their allegiance to the May Fourth Movement and began staging protests in Beijing and around the world. The Versailles Treaty, signed in late June, failed to address most of women's insistent demands, but it did seek to forward "social justice" by establishing a new International Labor Organization, summoned to meet in Washington, D.C., before year's end. In late autumn female workers and their allies responded by convening the final international women's congress of 1919 on the banks of the Potomac in defense of women's economic rights.

By the time many of these activists would meet again four years later in Rome for the world's most diverse women's congress to date—the subject of the epilogue—global feminism had become an entrenched force to be reckoned with. Male leaders were still firmly in charge to be sure; indeed, the Rome Congress of 1923 would take place under the virile patronage of Italy's new Fascist leader, Benito Mussolini. But global feminists were resolute, organized, and already beginning to strategize about how to confront the challenges that lay ahead. One lesson they learned in 1919 was that international treaties and global bodies could serve as powerful leverage against recalcitrant governments in the battle to advance gender equality around the world. Another was that women were stronger when they banded together, even if this meant negotiating difficult ideological differences and continually challenging power imbalances that made some women's voices carry more loudly than others. The multiplication of national, international, and transnational women's organizations in the 1920s and 1930s was the immediate consequence. Today, over one hundred years after the historic peace negotiations in Paris concluded, the struggle for global women's rights continues unabated. Following in the footsteps of the brave women of 1919, a new generation may yet find its way to a more just and equitable global order in the century to come.

CHAPTER I

A New Year in Paris

Women's Rights at the Peace Conference of 1919

On January 18, 1919, as world leaders gathered for the opening day of the Paris Peace Conference, French philanthropist and feminist Marguerite de Witt Schlumberger was busy drafting a letter to the man who appeared most likely to become kingmaker of the negotiations: Woodrow Wilson. Writing as the head of the French Union for Women's Suffrage, Schlumberger described the debt that she and her sisters felt they owed the American president. "We desire," she wrote, "to express the deep admiration of French women for the policies that you inaugurated so nobly." International justice, national self-determination, and democratic governance: these were the principles that Wilson had repeatedly insisted must frame the peace terms. French women, Schlumberger stated, were eager to "help to vindicate [Wilson's] policies during the Peace Conference."[1]

Schlumberger's expression of gratitude was heartfelt, but like similar messages from the thousands of people who wrote to Wilson in the expectant months after the November 11 armistice that marked the end of the First World War, it came with a request. "We would beg of you," Schlumberger implored, "to use your immense influence for introducing Woman Suffrage together with the other world questions necessary to discuss at the Peace Conference." In the meantime, she asked the president to publicly affirm his sympathy for the "more than half of humanity represented by women who in many countries have been condemned to an unjust and cruel silence by the denial of the vote."[2]

Woodrow Wilson could hardly have missed the intent behind Schlumberger's letter: even having been denied a seat at the negotiating table, women had no intention of allowing the peace negotiations to unfold without their input. They expected, at the very least, that a war fought "to make the world safe for democracy" would lead to the enfranchisement of women from the victorious Allied nations and, ideally, in all states admitted to the new world government, the League of Nations. What is more, women were organizing to achieve such ends. In her letter, Schlumberger informed Wilson that on February 10, 1919, the French Union for Women's Suffrage would be convening an Inter-Allied Women's Conference to bring women's concerns directly to the peacemakers. With such a goal in mind, Schlumberger requested a "rendezvous" with Wilson at his earliest convenience.

Woodrow Wilson had a lot on his plate when Schlumberger's letter arrived. He and his primary counterparts—Prime Ministers Georges Clemenceau of France and David Lloyd George of Britain—still did not have a solid idea of the procedures they intended to follow, let alone an agenda of the issues they intended to broach, as they opened the peace conference on January 18. The formation of the Supreme Council—composed of the five "major" Allied powers of France, Britain, the United States, Italy, and Japan—was the first order of business. The establishment of advisory commissions on topics ranging from war reparations to the League of Nations to international labor legislation was the second. One meeting piled upon the next, and, given the rush of decision making, Wilson would certainly have been forgiven had he failed to respond to an appointment request from a French suffragist. Instead, he replied that he would be delighted to receive Madame Schlumberger and her delegation of French suffragists at his temporary Paris residence, the elegant Hôtel Murat, on Monday, January 27, 1919, at 6:00 P.M. sharp.[3]

Why did Wilson honor this request, when so many others went unanswered? Did he do so out of a sense of chivalry? The American president from Virginia had been raised, after all, to be a southern gentleman. Perhaps he was flattered by the women's praise. Still, he had reason to be wary. Back in the United States, suffragists had been a thorn in his side through much of his presidency. Who was to say this group of French women would be any different? It is possible Wilson thought that by granting the French women a personal interview before they had time to build expectations or formulate specific demands he could head them off at the gate. If so, he was sadly mistaken.

French suffragists' meeting with President Wilson on January 27, 1919, marked the beginning, not the end, of more than two months of intensive lobbying for recognition of women's rights at the Paris Peace Conference. From mid-February to mid-April over two dozen Allied women met continually to define women's vision of a just peace and to deliver their resolutions directly to the peacemakers. Their central message was straightforward and unwavering: a stable and democratic world order depended on women's political enfranchisement, and a lasting peace hung on international recognition of women's fundamental rights in the home, the economy, and society. Thinking strategically, the Inter-Allied women crafted Wilson's own words—the right of all people to self-determination, the justice of a "people's peace"— into a compelling argument for women's participation in the peace process and the postwar political order. Before it was all over, Schlumberger would meet face-to-face with Woodrow Wilson on four separate occasions, and the Inter-Allied suffragists would leave their mark directly on the Versailles Treaty, which brought a formal end to the First World War.

In 1919 French suffragists led a concerted international campaign for women's rights at the peace conference. More than most of the unenfranchised peoples who showed up in Paris that spring, Schlumberger and her collaborators managed to capture the ear of powerful statesmen. A century later, however, their efforts have been all but forgotten, a footnote in scholarly tomes at best. Why? History's tendency to celebrate the powerful at the expense of the weak can partially explain this omission. The longstanding bias that holds "women's issues" apart from the serious work of "real" politics is also at fault. In this case, however, tangible and powerful state actors bear part of the responsibility. Specifically, in the early months of World War II, as Germany occupied the defeated French state, the Nazis seized all the documents produced during the Inter-Allied Women's Conference (then in the possession of a Jewish French feminist) and carted them off to Berlin. There they remained until 1945, when the Red Army occupied the German capital. The Soviets confiscated the women's documents in turn, carrying them eastward and burying them in a Russian archive until the end of the Cold War. Only at the turn of the twenty-first century were the papers returned to France.

Now, a hundred years later, the full story of suffragists' campaign at the Paris Peace Conference can finally be told, and the French women who led the charge can be given their due. Together with women from other Allied states, these pioneering feminists stepped onto the diplomatic stage to demand international recognition of women's fundamental economic, social, and, most of all, political rights. What is more, they managed to extract meaningful (if limited) concessions from the peacemakers, transforming international treaties and organizations into powerful tools in the global fight for gender equality. Ironically, for the French suffragists who did the most to make women's voices heard in the peace negotiations, this victory would be bittersweet. Even as they helped establish women's right to participate in global governance, French women would remain stymied in their quest for the vote at home. In 1919 Marguerite de Witt Schlumberger worked tirelessly to capitalize on Woodrow Wilson's international stature to secure women's right to self-determination. Ultimately, her efforts would pay higher dividends outside French borders than within.

A French Woman and an American President

Marguerite de Witt Schlumberger's organizational prowess and raw determination may well have made her the most influential women's rights activist in Paris in 1919, but compared to many other suffrage leaders in the Western world, Schlumberger was a newcomer to the movement. She was also far from a radical suffragette. Her politics derived from a rich stew of Christian morality and republican patriotism.

Marguerite de Witt was born in 1853 into a devout, French Protestant family from the wealthy dairy lands of Normandy. Her father served as village mayor and later as a conservative legislator in the Chamber of Deputies. Her maternal grandfather was the illustrious historian and politician François Guizot, who wrote some of the first French laws mandating primary education. Marguerite's mother was a well-regarded woman of letters and philanthropist who helped her daughter develop a firm moral compass and an equally strong sense of social responsibility.

In her mid-twenties, Marguerite wed Paul Schlumberger, a wealthy industrialist from the border region of Alsace, which Germany had seized at the end of the Franco-Prussian War in 1871, six years prior to the couple's engagement. The Schlumbergers thus lived in German Alsace, and there, Marguerite gave birth to six children—five boys and a girl. As each of the boys reached the age of maturity, the parents faced a difficult choice. Either they could allow their sons to be conscripted into the German army or they could send them into exile. Ultimately, love of the French *patrie* exceeded all else, and one by one the boys were sent to live with their maternal grandmother in France. In 1902 the whole family moved to Paris for good.[4]

Wealth afforded a life of comfort, and, like many women of her class, Schlumberger devoted herself to raising a family and engaging in works of charity. Following in her mother's footsteps, she dedicated some of her earliest efforts to serving the needs of poor women, and she spent many hours visiting female prisoners and aiding their children. In addition, Schlumberger lent her energies to organizations battling prostitution, alcoholism, and the "White Slave Trade" (as sex trafficking was often described in the early twentieth century).

These various crusades gradually drew Schlumberger into the organized women's movement, where she headed both national and international committees on issues of social morality. Her suffrage work arose organically from there. As she would later explain, "Many people of our generation . . . once thought women were destined solely to be mothers, and their role was limited to good deeds, simple charity, and gifts to the poor. Today we still believe in these things, but we also believe that women have a larger role to play. . . . To me, [suffrage] is intimately connected to the moral and social reform we hope to achieve." In 1913 Schlumberger was elected president of the French Union for Women's Suffrage, then only in its fourth year of existence but already emerging as the primary suffrage organization in France.[5]

Although French women were more ideologically splintered and less well organized than their American or British counterparts, on the eve of World War I their suffrage movement was gaining momentum. From its earliest days, the French Union affiliated with the International Woman Suffrage Alliance, the only major international women's organization at the time dedicated to winning women the vote. Presided over by American suffrage leader Carrie Chapman Catt, the Suffrage Alliance represented twenty-six affiliated national sections, virtually all in Europe, North America, or the British Dominions. In 1913 Schlumberger joined the executive board, becoming one of four vice presidents alongside women from Finland, Germany, and Great Britain. The last of these, Millicent Garrett

Fawcett, would become something of a political legend at home, helping British women (age thirty and over) finally achieve the vote in 1918. She would also become an instrumental ally in Schlumberger's endeavors at the peace conference.[6]

Like other suffrage societies associated with the Alliance, the French Union was reformist in its temperament and tactics. In other words, while Schlumberger and her collaborators were dedicated *suffragists*, they were decidedly not *suffragettes*. That label was reserved for female activists who embraced confrontation in the quest for the vote. Militant suffragette organizations in both Great Britain and the United States organized parades, heckled speakers, and, in some cases, courted arrest, all with the goal of drawing attention to the women's cause.[7]

The French were notably more subdued in their approach. As a group, they hewed closely to the law and relied on moral persuasion to reach their goal. Only in 1914 did they attempt their first mass public demonstration. On July 5 of that year several thousand French women, including

French suffrage demonstration, July 5, 1914. Marguerite de Witt Schlumberger is in the front row, center, in white blouse and feathered hat. (Collections Bibliothèque Marguerite Durand—Ville de Paris)

Schlumberger, marched through the Tuileries Garden in central Paris to deposit garlands of flowers before the statue of the Marquis de Condorcet, a French Revolutionary hero who had advocated granting women the vote over a century earlier. The mood was upbeat, the press was positive, and French suffragists emerged energized. Four weeks later their country was at war.[8]

The general mobilization of August 1, 1914, and the German invasion of northern France brought the suffrage movement to a screeching halt. As the army called men to their barracks, the French president called on women to rally in defense of the fatherland. For the patriotic Marguerite de Witt Schlumberger, there was never a question whether suffragists would heed the call. "The (French) Union," she wrote in September 1914, "expects every member to do her duty with simplicity and generosity, helping her country in some way after speeding her loved ones on their way to the frontier." Aware that some pacifist-leaning women believed suffragists should demonstrate against a war they had no hand in causing, Schlumberger stated unequivocally, "[This] is not the moment to speak of it. Still less is it the moment for any sort of feminist demonstration against the war." Although she could imagine a time when international feminist collaboration would again become necessary, for the time being French women had only one calling: to "show by our calm and courageous attitude, by our devoted hearts and hands . . . that we are worthy to help direct our country since we are capable of serving it."[9]

During the years of war that followed, French suffragists continued to devote their energies to family and nation. For her part, Schlumberger saw all five of her sons and her only son-in-law off to war. One son, Daniel, fell in the line of duty while leading an artillery regiment in 1915. Donning the black crepe of mourning, Schlumberger sought solace in activity and redoubled her efforts to aid her nation at war. While peasant women learned to drive a plough and working-class women entered munitions factories, Schlumberger joined with other wealthy women in philanthropic work designed to sustain national morale. She founded a series of "soldiers' homes," devised to give men stationed far from their families a pleasant (and liquor-free) retreat during their time on leave. She also established an organization to aid refugees from German-controlled Alsace and Lorraine.

Finally, as the unflinching death count of World War I mounted, Schlumberger offered her support to the powerful French pronatalist movement, which promoted childbearing through positive steps (like state support for maternal health) and punitive measures (like the criminalization of contraception and abortion). To many French people in the early twentieth century, family size was a matter of national security. Ever since France's disastrous defeat in the Franco-Prussian War, pronatalists had been looking fearfully over their shoulders at the much larger German population on their eastern border. World War I exacerbated these concerns. During and after the war, Schlumberger openly encouraged French women to embrace their patriotic duty and raise large families. In 1919, she published a pamphlet spelling out women's choice in stark terms: "Mothers to the Fatherland or Traitors to the Fatherland." To Schlumberger, there was no inherent conflict between pronatalism and feminism. In her perspective, women's service as mothers was one of the strongest arguments for granting them the vote.[10]

If Schlumberger's overriding concern with large families was particularly French, the emphasis she placed on motherhood as women's primordial calling was quite typical of feminists of her generation. To politically engaged Western women of the early twentieth century, feminism (a word just coming into fashion outside France) implied the rejection of women's subordination to men in the family, in the economy, and in politics, not a repudiation of their unique social roles or qualities as mothers. As feminists, they demanded equal relations between the sexes, not the erasure of distinctions between them. For French suffragists, mothering the nation through the difficult war years was both a patriotic and a feminist act.[11]

Convinced women's wartime sacrifices had more than earned them the full rights of citizenship, French suffragists recovered their voices in the last year of the war. From late 1917 onward they began looking strategically toward an eventual Allied victory and the opportunities that it might create for women. Allied leaders were talking openly about the global reckoning that would take place at war's end and the democratic international order that would replace the old. Women would need to be prepared if they wanted to ensure women's rights were squarely on the table. Most important, women needed a powerful ally to champion their cause in the eventual peace negotiations. In late 1917 Schlumberger set her eyes on President Woodrow Wilson.

At first glance, Wilson may seem an unlikely target for Schlumberger's attention. For much of his adult life, he had been resolutely against women's suffrage: opposing any expansion of the voter rolls while he was governor of New Jersey and sidestepping the issue once elected to the presidency in 1912. American suffragists kept up the pressure, and in 1915 Wilson began to revise his views. For the next two years he maintained the position that each state should be allowed to decide the matter of women's suffrage based on its own needs and interests. Such a view conveniently placated the racist, antisuffrage southern bloc of his own Democratic Party, which was determined to keep both women and African Americans out of the polling booth. In 1917, disgusted by the president's refusal to endorse a federal suffrage amendment even as he led his nation into a war in defense of democracy, militant suffragettes staged pickets in front of the White House, bearing signs comparing Wilson to the despised German kaiser.[12]

Most American suffragists distanced themselves from such confrontational methods and followed the lead of Carrie Chapman Catt, who in 1915 was elected to a second term as president of the National American Woman Suffrage Association (in addition to her position as head of the International Woman Suffrage Alliance). Catt pledged suffragists' support for the American war effort, seeking to impress Wilson with women's patriotic dedication and wartime service. Moderate and militant tactics worked on the president in tandem. When a suffrage referendum came up for a popular vote in New York in October 1917, Wilson offered his enthusiastic support. Saluting American women's willingness to serve the nation at war, he asserted, "It is time for the people of the States of this country to show the world in what practical sense they have learned the lessons of democracy." Across the Atlantic, Marguerite de Witt Schlumberger read about Wilson's change of heart in the French papers and began to wonder: might the president's willingness to endorse women's suffrage in recognition of their wartime service extend to America's allies as well? Schlumberger decided to find out.[13]

Over the next few months, Schlumberger drafted an appeal to Woodrow Wilson on behalf of Allied women asking him to issue a public statement endorsing women's suffrage as a pillar of an eventual peace settlement. Highlighting women's war efforts as well as their suffering, she urged the American president to see that the "participation of wives and mothers in the suffrage would be one of the best means of guaranteeing a future peace." She also reminded Wilson of his own recent defense of the "right of peoples to self-determination," and she argued, "No one can speak in the name of the people as long as women are excluded from the political life of nations." Female enfranchisement, in other words, would be necessary if Wilson hoped to achieve his vision of a new, liberal world order.[14]

By mid-December the text of the letter was finalized, and the French obtained endorsements from women in Britain, Italy, and Portugal as well as Russia (in the midst of revolution) and British South Africa. "To refuse to treat our social and political rights seriously would be the greatest of injustices and the greatest of crimes," wrote a Portuguese suffragist encouragingly. Schlumberger forwarded the letter to Carrie Chapman Catt, asking her to deliver it in person to Woodrow Wilson. The request was not unreasonable. Catt was in fairly regular contact with the president, and she was sympathetic to the French cause. Initially, though, she worried about how the Allied request would affect American women's bid for suffrage at home and she stalled for time. Finally, in late spring 1918, she delivered the letter as asked.[15]

The outcome could not have delighted Schlumberger more. Wilson's response to French feminists began: "I have read your message with the deepest interest and I welcome the opportunity to say that I agree without reservation that the full and sincere democratic reconstruction of the world for which we are striving . . . will not have been completely or adequately attained until women are admitted to the suffrage." French feminists blanketed the media with Wilson's endorsement. "All the papers," Schlumberger wrote happily to Catt, "were eager to print a letter coming from President Wilson." Catt too was thrilled at the response, not least because in his closing paragraph, Wilson publicly and definitively urged the U.S. Senate to endorse women's suffrage at the federal level. By all appearances, Catt leveraged the French letter to help gain a long-sought endorsement from Wilson of what would eventually become the Nineteenth Amendment to the U.S. Constitution.[16]

Against all odds, Marguerite de Witt Schlumberger won Woodrow Wilson's moral support for global women's suffrage. Six months later, the president set sail for Paris and the opening of the peace negotiations. "President Wilson's arrival," Allied suffragists proclaimed, "is felt on all sides to earmark the beginning of a new era in the world's history. . . . His messages are not only to Governments, they go right to the hearts of peoples." Schlumberger had more reasons to celebrate than most. On January 27, 1919, she would meet her powerful benefactor face-to-face. Whether the budding relationship between the French suffragist from Normandy and the American president would bear fruit, only time would tell.[17]

On Gratitude and Strategy

American foreign correspondent Constance Drexel broke the story of Schlumberger's upcoming meeting with Wilson, writing approvingly in the *Chicago Tribune*, "French suffragists have done even more than their American sisters by taking the bull by the horns." In fact, Drexel was not a dispassionate observer; she was an outspoken suffragist, as interested in shaping the peace terms as she was in reporting them. Upon arriving in France in 1919, Drexel immediately began giving French suffragists a primer on American-style political lobbying, counseling Schlumberger not to invite the president to tea as French women had initially proposed. "Ask him to receive a delegation and he will grant it as nicely as he does in Washington," Drexel coached. Backing up Drexel in this message was H. Bruce Brougham, an editor at the *New York Times* who further advised French women to deliberately leak news of their progress to journalists hungry for a story. "The press of the world will be agog with speculation to the outcome," Brougham insisted, and "the ingenuity of the entire corps of correspondents in Paris will be put into play in the process." Diplomacy, both Americans implied, was a high stakes game, and French women needed to learn to play it strategically.[18]

French suffragists responded readily to the journalists' advice, so much so that they ended up securing not one but two meetings with Woodrow Wilson in late January 1919. As it turns out, a French woman named Valentine Thomson had also arranged a meeting with Wilson two days prior to Schlumberger's own. Thomson was the editor of the women's magazine *La Vie Féminine* (Feminine life), and, like Schlumberger, was a committed suffragist and an avid Wilsonian. Unlike Schlumberger, however, Thomson did not seek an appointment with the American president for political reasons. Hers was a mission of gratitude. French women, she believed, longed to demonstrate their indebtedness to the "champion of Peace" and offer him their wholehearted support. Thomson invited a broad social cross-section of French women—journalists, actresses, laborers, nurses, social activists, poets, and suffragists—to join her in paying homage to the American statesman. Among the last of these, Schlumberger received an invitation, as did the secretary general of the National Council for French Women Ghénia Avril de Sainte-Croix. Thomson's meeting, though unexpected, offered Schlumberger valuable insight into Wilson's thoughts regarding women's rights and the peace negotiations two days prior to her own appointment.[19]

Stormy skies threatened overhead as the French women joined Thomson outside the offices of *La Vie Féminine* on January 25. The weather, however, did little to dampen their spirits, as they smiled for a quick photo and then set off for Wilson's Paris residence "with joy and pride filling their hearts and shining in their eyes." Once ushered through the door by an American military officer, the women arranged themselves in two rows and waited nervously to address "the man whose words had already transformed the world."[20]

Woodrow Wilson—"the great man, the Man of the Hour"—entered the room. Thomson spoke first, describing to Wilson "the immense hope that he incarnates in the eyes of all French women." Others spoke in turn. Georgette Bouillot and Jeanne Bouvier, both garment workers and trade unionists, spoke for the working class, offering flowers and thanks to the man whom they addressed as the "apostle of peace." Schlumberger spoke too, as did Avril de Sainte-Croix who thanked Wilson for all that he had done for women during the war. In different ways, each of the speakers cast themselves in a reassuring cloak of motherhood and femininity. Sparing no hyperbole, they compared the president to a medieval knight sworn to defend justice and honor. They emphasized their own emotional vulnerability, describing themselves as carrying the "hearts of all women in (their) trembling hands." As a memento of the occasion, they offered Wilson a bas-relief sculpture inscribed "To President Wilson. The Grateful Women of France. 25th of January 1919." The sculpture featured a woman in simple dress holding a young child aloft in her arms, defining women's gratitude in terms of the sons they sacrificed and those spared by the war's end.[21]

What did the American president, who greeted each speaker with a "friendly smile," make of the French women's offering? Wilson seems to have been quite moved by the tribute. He thanked the women and responding humbly that he hoped he would merit the great hope that they had placed in him. Then, although the women had studiously avoided making any political appeals, Wilson turned his remarks to address "the great matter" that he assumed to be on all of their minds: "the right of women to take their full share in the political life of the nations to which they belong." Women's suffrage, he warned, was a domestic matter and thus outside the bounds of discussion for the peace negotiations. Anticipating

Bas-relief sculpture inscribed "To President Wilson. The Grateful Women of France. 25th of January 1919," *La Vie Féminine*, February 15, 1919, 1283. (Collections Bibliothèque Marguerite Durand—Ville de Paris)

disappointment, he softened the blow by speaking warmly of his admiration for the women of France. He saluted the "unspoken sufferings of the heart" as the most pervasive of tragedies in wartime. "They have been borne at home," Wilson said, "and the center of the home is the woman." In one sweep, Wilson honored maternal sacrifice and put women on notice that he would do little to advance their cause at the peace conference.[22]

Schlumberger did not record what she thought about her first face-to-face meeting with Woodrow Wilson, but she undoubtedly departed with much to think about. Wilson's moving tribute to French women's suffering must have touched a deep emotional chord in the mother of five sons who served in the war. But Schlumberger was also a suffragist with a mandate to fulfill. That very week the French Union for Women's Suffrage had affirmed that the "essential goal" of their upcoming Inter-Allied Women's Conference would be to secure "women's participation in national and international political life." Wilson's remarks on January 25 seemed deliberately designed to dissuade suffragists from seeking this very objective.[23]

What Schlumberger concluded from this first meeting with Woodrow Wilson was that appealing for the vote on the basis of women's suffering and maternal sacrifice was not likely to be a winning strategy. Looking for a different point of rhetorical entry that might get through to the president, she noted a telling phrase that Wilson had begun to test out in recent public speeches and that he used when he spoke to the French women on January 25 as well. The Great War, he had said, had been a "people's war," dependent on the dedication of men and women alike, and as such, the peace must also be a "people's peace." Appealing to Wilson as mothers, French women had won his sympathy. Perhaps, Schlumberger thought, if French suffragists appealed to him as "people"—as half of the human race on whom the peace terms depended—they could win his support. With less than forty-eight hours to work, Schlumberger pulled out a notepad and began to write.[24]

At 6:00 P.M. on January 27, Schlumberger and a slightly smaller entourage of twenty-some French suffragists arrived at the Hôtel Murat prepared to make their plea. This time the women dispensed with elaborate displays of gratitude and cut to the chase. Taking note of his comments two days earlier, Schlumberger reassured the president that she and her delegation had not come to seek his help in obtaining the vote for women in France. Instead, she said, they were there to represent "women from all countries" whose "rights must not be forgotten in the plans for the future peace." She informed Wilson of the upcoming Inter-Allied Women's Conference and its intention to bring women's demands before the plenipotentiaries, the chief delegates to the peace conference. Finally, Schlumberger portrayed women's aspirations as an extension of Wilson's own. "Last Saturday," she told him, "you expressed with much clearness our feelings when you said this war had been a people's war and that peace had to be a people's peace. Surely it could not really be called a people's peace if women had no part in its framing." Schlumberger's logic was impeccable, and this time Wilson's response was more encouraging: "It would seem impossible to me to refuse to listen to women after the service they rendered during the war," he stated. "Whatever it is within my power to do for them, I will do."[25]

Having extracted the promise she desired, Schlumberger departed from the Hôtel Murat in high spirits and rolled up her sleeves. With just a few days to go, she and the French Union prepared to welcome Allied suffragists to the French capital.

The Inter-Allied Women's Conference

From the time Schlumberger mailed out invitations to the Inter-Allied Women's Conference on January 10, 1919, to the day it opened one month later, French suffragists were consumed in a flurry of planning. The problem of where to meet was solved when one of France's wealthiest feminists, the Duchesse d'Uzès (an heiress to the Veuve Cliquot champagne fortune), secured the use of the elegant Parisian Lyceum Club, just a few blocks off the Champs-Elysées. As for travel arrangements, French Union member Suzanne Grinberg took time out from her job as a lawyer at the Paris Court of Appeals to serve as a makeshift corresponding secretary, procuring rooms for twenty to thirty-five francs per day.[26]

In total, more than a dozen foreign women joined the French for the Women's Conference. Each participating nation was allowed three delegates, although several women left early and others took their place. Aside from the French, the British played the most active role in shaping women's demands and in pleading their case to the peacemakers. Millicent Garrett Fawcett—a protégé of the famous English political philosopher John Stuart Mill—led the British delegation and served as a sounding board for Schlumberger before, during, and after the conference. Fawcett was compelled to return home in late February, but her shoes would be amply filled by a younger, up-and-coming British feminist named Margery Corbett Ashby, who had run (unsuccessfully) for a parliamentary seat in 1918. Of the remaining Allied nations, the Belgians sent the largest delegation, headed by Jane Brigode, president of the Belgian Federation for Women's Suffrage, who had spent the war years living under difficult circumstances in German-occupied Brussels. Margharita Ancona, president of the Italian Suffrage Society, came from Milan. Difficulties of travel complicated efforts to recruit women from farther afield, but fortunately, volunteer organizations had attracted a large number of talented foreign women to

Europe during the war. Three Americans were recruited from this mix, including Florence Jaffray Harriman, who had directed the Women's Motor Corps for the American Red Cross. A delegate each from the British dominions of New Zealand and South Africa filled out the list. Schlumberger anchored the French delegation, while Grinberg served as conference secretary and wrote up many of the reports that would appear in the French and international press.[27]

The women who responded to the French invitation were, in many respects, representative of the organized international women's movement up until the First World War. The participants were all from "the West" broadly constituted. Similarly, they were all white, including the fraternal delegate from South Africa. Most of the women were also of comfortable

Millicent Garrett Fawcett, president of the British National Union of Women's Suffrage Societies and delegate to the Inter-Allied Women's Conference. (Millicent Garrett Fawcett Papers, 7MGF/B/11, Box 4, Women's Library Collection, London School of Economics Library)

Suzanne Grinberg, French lawyer, suffragist, and secretary of the Inter-Allied Women's Conference. (Collections Bibliothèque Marguerite Durand—Ville de Paris)

means, which is why one of the British delegates insistently referred to the gathering as a "ladies' conference." ("You *can't* call them women," she huffed, "they are *so* well dressed!") While some of the delegates inherited or married into wealth, others were professional women with careers of their own.[28]

Like most activists in the women's movement, the delegates veered toward middle age; some were verging on geriatric. Schlumberger was sixty-six and had fifteen grandchildren in 1919. The three female delegates still in their thirties were the exceptions to the rule. "Everyone is very kind and nice to me," thirty-seven-year-old Englishwoman Margery Corbett Ashby wrote home when she joined the conference in mid-March. "They refer to my extreme youth in touching terms. My father considers it so wise of me to prefer an international conference to dances where I should be considered most passé!"[29]

Finally, as suggested by the name chosen for the meeting, all the delegates hailed from the Allied states. Women from the Central Powers—principally Germany and Austria-Hungary—were not invited, regardless of their affiliation with the International Woman Suffrage Alliance. This omission was deliberate. Carrie Chapman Catt had briefly flirted with the idea of convening a full meeting of the Alliance to coincide with the peace conference. French, Belgian, and Italian women were flatly opposed. "It is morally impossible for us to conceive any such reunion," they avowed in a public statement, "unless we truly feel that a unity of feeling and conscience can exist between us and the women of the Central Powers." German women would need to disavow the "crimes committed by their country," they stated, before any such meeting could be considered. Most women whose countries had suffered years under German bombardment or occupation were far from prepared to lock arms with their former enemies. Brigode experienced the invasion of Belgium firsthand. Schlumberger had lost her son. As the latter explained in a letter to Catt, "If you could have been here among us, I am persuaded that you too would have shivered with indignation and sadness at the description of the horrors, the deportations of women, and of the deliberate cruelty that ravaged our unfortunate countries." It was the rare suffragist who was able to embrace the former enemy immediately after World War I. From beginning to end, women's lobbying efforts in Paris were strictly an Allied affair.[30]

Paris did not put on its most welcoming face for the delegates to the Inter-Allied Women's Conference as they began to arrive in early February. Ice and snow blanketed the streets. Paris, one of the British delegates described, was "very cold and very serious. . . . Everyone looks as if a great burden were gone, and as if a hundred other small burdens had taken its place." Food, coal, and clothing were all scarce. Workers seemed "unsettled." At the same time, "the Peace Conference with all its vast swarm of foreign delegates and foreign secretariats" made "a very noticeable mark on the life of the streets." Hotels, restaurants, and the Metro were all "filled to bursting"; prime ministers were "as common as blackberries."[31]

The Lyceum Club offered a welcome retreat from the winter bluster as the suffragists gathered on the afternoon of Monday, February 10, to begin their work. Flags of the Allied countries decorated the walls, lending the

Inter-Allied Women's Conference delegates standing in front of the Lyceum Club, February 1919. Marguerite de Witt Schlumberger is in the front row, center. (National Archives and Record Administration, War Department, 533768)

salon an official air, but as Suzanne Grinberg noted, the room was hardly devoid of female charm. "Faded rose silk armchairs were set out as if for the daily calls of socialites," and fresh flowers graced the tables. With a warm fire burning in the fireplace behind her, Marguerite de Witt Schlumberger looked out at the women taking their seats, "visibly satisfied to find them thus reunited," and officially called the Inter-Allied Women's Conference to order. "February 10, 1919," *La Vie Féminine* proclaimed, "will be remembered as a landmark date in the history of women's rights and in the history of humanity."[32]

Schlumberger opened the conference with auspicious news. In response to a request she had made days earlier, Woodrow Wilson had agreed to meet with conference delegates at 8:30 that very evening. With only a few working hours before nightfall, the gathered women needed to decide what they wanted to request of the president. American delegate Florence Harriman came armed with a proposal. The conference, she suggested, should request the peacemakers create an official Women's Commission (much like the Labor Commission, already established), to be staffed by competent female leaders and tasked with advising the peacemakers on all matters relating to women and children. A lively discussion followed, "sometimes in English, sometimes in French," and the proposal was adopted. With just time enough for a quick cup of tea, the women took leave of each other and prepared for their evening appointment.[33]

While the Allied suffragists came to rather quick consensus on what they wanted to say to President Wilson, the question of what to wear for the occasion seems to have produced no such unanimity. The three English delegates arrived at the Hôtel Murat in eveningwear. Florence Harriman wore her starched gray Red Cross uniform, while another American chose a "glittery dress" with a corsage of red roses. The discordant array of fashion must have been a bit shocking to the eye, but as the women well knew, in matters of diplomacy, appearance mattered. Their choices reflected different strategies for courting Wilson's good graces. Suzanne Grinberg and Jane Brigode opted for simple day dresses, covered by thick coats and warm hats: a fortuitous choice as the two women could not find a taxi and had to make their way to Wilson's residence on foot through the snow. Fortunately the distance was short, and the two women arrived just as the others were being shown into the parlor where President Wilson awaited them, his wife at his side.[34]

For some of the women—including Schlumberger—this was the third visit with Woodrow Wilson in just over two weeks. They greeted the American president almost as an old friend. The foreign delegates, however, found themselves face-to-face with Wilson ("the arbiter of so many destinies," cooed the French newspaper Le Gaulois) for the first time. Belgian delegate Jane Brigode, hailing as she did from a parliamentary monarchy, instinctively curtsied before the president. The others maintained their composure and shook his hand. Englishwoman Millicent Garrett Fawcett spoke for the group, reminding Wilson of his public response to Schlumberger's appeal eight months earlier, when he stated that "the full and sincere democratic reconstruction of the world for which we are striving" rested on women's enfranchisement. She assured him the suffragists convened in Paris wanted nothing more than to help him realize his own vision of a just and democratic international order, and she offered up the idea of a Women's Commission as a means of ensuring that the peacemakers take account of women's interests in the negotiations.[35]

As was his custom, Wilson listened attentively, and after a few minutes of reflection, he smiled and endorsed their proposal, although with some modification. In place of a body staffed by women, Wilson suggested creating a Women's Commission manned by plenipotentiaries. This commission, Wilson suggested, could consult with Allied women, charged in an official capacity with representing women's and children's interests. Wilson's proposal offered substantially less than the women had asked for, placing them in a consultative rather than a decision-making position. Nonetheless, the Inter-Allied delegates interpreted the suggestion as a "big step" toward the realization of their goals. "Delighted," they retired to their homes and hotel rooms for some well-deserved rest. "And *voilà*," concluded the article in *Le Gaulois*, "that is how the suffragists won a victory and why another commission will be counted among those of the Peace Conference several days from now." It should only have been so easy.[36]

In the Drawing Rooms of the Peace Delegates

The next morning the women returned to work. The first order of business was to drum up support for the president's proposal. Determined to win backing that was as broad as possible, the women decided to try to meet with all the national delegations to the peace conference. "I didn't realize the amount of work this would be," Suzanne Grinberg confessed, "until I saw the official list of all the plenipotentiaries. Were we really going to visit the delegates from Hejaz [Arabia], Liberia, Uruguay, China, and Siam?" The comment betrayed Grinberg's prejudices as well as the reality of power relations in the peace conference, which confined the "minor" powers to the margins of decision making. Nevertheless, the suffragists decided to omit no one. "This promised to be colorful," Grinberg quipped, with a whiff of condescension, "but so much work!" As secretary of the conference, Grinberg promptly sent off appointment requests to each of the national delegation headquarters.[37]

The first to reply was Eleftherios Venizelos, prime minister of Greece, who invited a delegation to call on him later that same day. At 6:30 P.M. seven women arrived at his Paris residence, although if we are to believe the *Manchester Guardian*, the female delegation almost didn't make it through the door: "The gorgeousness of the Greek guardsman, in black and white and scarlet uniform with huge pompons on his shoes and a silver scimitar across his chest . . . almost daunted the delegation when they called on M. Venizelos," the British paper reported. Fortunately, the women found the fortitude to enter. The Greek prime minister greeted them amiably, offering the petite Millicent Garrett Fawcett an enormous armchair, which all but enveloped her as she took her seat. After listening supportively while the women stated their case, Venizelos promptly declared himself a firm supporter of women's suffrage. "I will do everything in my power to support President Wilson's proposal," he declared. The women were elated.[38]

Over the next six days, Inter-Allied women's delegations called on nearly a dozen statesmen. They would nearly double that number, meeting with at least twenty-two delegates from sixteen different countries, in the weeks to come. The suffragists' reflexive Orientalism—rooted in the belief that Eastern cultures were universally more oppressive toward women than their own—led them to expect the greatest resistance from representatives of the Asian states. "Almost inevitably," the British delegates explained, "the Eastern nations have less advanced views on the feminist question." The Marquis Saionji Kinmochi, the chief Japanese delegate to the peace conference, did seem "less enthusiastic" than many others they met. The "young and cheerful" Chinese delegates, however, proclaimed their full sympathy with Wilson's proposal. Their support for the principle of women's rights reflected a recent and profound cultural shift among the intellectual elite in China. Indeed, although the Inter-Allied women did not know it, at the same time that they were trying to win the Asian plenipotentiaries over to their cause, a Chinese feminist by the name of Soumay Tcheng was packing her bags in Shanghai and preparing to head to Paris to serve as an official attaché to her nation's peace delegation. Her actions would change the course of diplomatic history in Paris that spring.[39]

The Inter-Allied women's limited encounters with African statesmen also proved encouraging. Suzanne Grinberg and one other woman were tasked with visiting the plenipotentiaries from Liberia, one of only two independent African nations in 1919, and the only one represented at the peace conference. "There were two of us," Grinberg reported, "before two black ministers!" Blackness represented backwardness in Grinberg's instinctively imperial worldview, which justified colonialism by casting it as a civilizing mission among less "evolved" peoples of the world. But to Grinberg's surprise, Liberian president and peace delegate Charles D. B. King assured the suffragists of his "complete devotion" to the women's cause. One reason King might have been receptive to the suffragists' pleas is that just days earlier he had participated in a historic Pan-African Congress in Paris. There, two female speakers argued that natural sympathies united opponents of racial and sexual oppression around the world. Over the course of the conversation, Grinberg realized she knew very little about women's condition in Liberia, but she hoped King's supportive stance toward women's rights would have positive repercussions back home.[40]

Each of the two dozen visits the Inter-Allied women undertook involved deliberate planning. If any of the suffragists had a personal connection to the plenipotentiary in question, she was appointed to lead the delegation. Each group was deliberately multinational, giving the statesman visual evidence of the far-reaching geographic scope of the constituency the women represented. In their request for an appointment, the women leaned heavily on Wilson's authority, pointing out that the president "approved fully of the principle of feminine representation." Once face-to-face with the statesmen, the women injected their pleas with the weight of Wilson's rhetoric, reminding the male diplomats that the "peace they are preparing will never merit the beautiful name of a 'People's Peace' if half of humanity . . . is not able to make its voice heard."[41]

Careful diplomacy paid off, and the women who traveled from one meeting to the next garnered sympathetic words of support. It remained to be seen, however, whether the male peacemakers would be willing to translate their sympathy for women into tangible power in the negotiations. Despite the vast cultural differences that separated statesmen from Europe, the Americas, Africa, and Asia, all came from paternalistic societies in which fathers ruled families and men governed states. Men's power could be benevolent or tyrannical, but to nearly all, it seemed *natural*. Men, they assumed, had always been charged with protecting women's welfare. Why should these negotiations be any different?

In combatting this paternalistic mindset, the Inter-Allied women found that they had one particularly powerful argument on their side: the need to combat violence against women in wartime. As British suffragists explained, "Certain aspects of human life and tragedy—the deportation of women in war time is a glaring and horrible example—will never receive the attention they deserve till women have their say in the matter. It is only the very exceptional man who regards this kind of crime as anything but the inevitable outcome of war. It is only the very exceptional woman who now regards it as a thing to be suffered . . . in silence." Allied propaganda had drawn attention to violence against women, feeding up a steady stream of heartrending reports of French and Belgian women deported, raped, and killed by German soldiers (some real, others exaggerated). Such atrocity stories worked effectively to foster animosity toward the enemy and strengthen national resolve. When the Inter-Allied suffragists spoke of female victims and called for justice, male peacemakers took notice. This argument for female empowerment in the peace conference took on particular urgency in mid-February, when an Armenian woman named Zabel Yesayan tracked down the Inter-Allied suffragists in Paris and told her story.[42]

A Cry from Armenia

Exactly how Zabel Yesayan found her way to the Inter-Allied Women's Conference is unclear; certainly, she traveled a hard journey to get there. Born in Istanbul to an Ottoman Armenian family that believed in educating girls, Yesayan grew up harboring literary ambitions well beyond the aspirations of most women of her age. In 1895, at age seventeen, she moved to Paris, enrolled at the Sorbonne, and launched a writing career. In 1908 she returned to the Ottoman Empire (then undergoing a constitutional revolution) and began publishing essays in defense of girls' education. The following year she witnessed a brutal massacre of thousands of Armenians (punished by counterrevolutionary Turks for supporting reform) in the southeastern region of Cilicia. Yesayan described the horrors in several books and short stories, giving voice to the imperiled Armenian ethnic and Christian minority in an increasingly nationalistic Turkish state.[43]

During World War I Yesayan's notoriety nearly cost her her life. Under the cover of war, in April 1915, the Ottoman government launched a vicious campaign against its Armenian citizens. In the year that followed, Ottoman troops rounded up much of the Armenian Turkish population, killing many able-bodied men on the spot and driving the rest—primarily women, children, and older people—into exile in the Syrian desert. Deprived of food and water, and subject to repeated assaults en route, hundreds of thousands—some suspect well over a million—died on the genocidal march. Zabel Yesayan was the sole woman to appear on a government list of Armenian intellectuals and community leaders to be targeted for immediate execution. Narrowly escaping her persecutors, she first went into hiding in Bulgaria and then (when Bulgaria declared war on the side of the Turks) fled eastward to work with Armenian refugees, setting up orphanages and recording victims' stories.[44]

Somehow, in early 1919, Yesayan made her way back to Paris and to the doorstep of the Inter-Allied Women's Conference where she appealed to the congregated women to come to Armenia's aid. Her descriptions of targeted attacks on Armenian girls and women were horrifying. Reading a studiously prepared report aloud in a "soft and monotone voice," Yesayan told the Women's Conference about Armenian girls who were torn from their families and distributed to Turkish men as slaves. Those who escaped this fate, she said, were marched into the desert. When a caravan would reach a spring or water source, the Turkish guards would allow the parched and starving refugees to drink only if they turned over a certain number of girls for the guards' pleasure. In many cases, the Turkish guards raped the victims, "in plain daylight, in front of numerous spectators." Many Armenian girls and women died or committed suicide. Others remained confined in Turkish homes against their will and desperately needed the international community—and especially women—to come to their aid.[45]

Horrified by Yesayan's account and determined to take action, the members of the Inter-Allied Women's Conference quickly drew up a petition to present to the Commission on War Responsibilities, demanding that it establish a mixed-sex body that could investigate the report and demand the liberation of all female war victims still held against their will. The plenipotentiaries declined to act on the request. At the same time, the women began raising the matter in individual meetings with peace delegates. There they gained more traction. With French plenipotentiary Jules Cambon they offered "the distress and suffering of Armenian women" as evidence of the need for a Women's Commission. Cambon responded viscerally. "When he heard of the sufferings and martyrdom of the Armenian and Serbian women," Grinberg reported, "he replied that he understood perfectly that Women Suffragists should desire to have women's interests protected." Cambon also offered the women "good advice" about "raising the question of the enslaved Armenian women" in their upcoming meeting with Prime Minister Georges Clemenceau of France. Over the weeks that followed, the Inter-Allied delegates repeatedly pled the cause of captive Armenian women as part of their general campaign to win support for a Women's Commission.[46]

Through such discussions, Western feminists learned a vital lesson. Playing on male peacemakers' sense of moral outrage worked to strengthen their own case for representation. Even those men unmoved by abstract appeals for gender equality could be chastened by reports of female victimhood. The fact that the women in question were "Eastern," in the broad sense of the term—and Christian victims of a predominantly Muslim state—only made the appeal more persuasive. While they agreed on little else, male statesmen and female suffragists from imperial nations were generally united in their belief that women of the "East" needed to be saved and that Western women were uniquely positioned to play the role of rescuer. The plight of Armenian women confirmed Western suffragists in the belief that their role at the peace conference was to speak for *all* women, even those from faraway lands whose circumstances they understood imperfectly, if at all. Gender solidarity and Western superiority fed their ambitions in equal measure.

For the time being, however, the male plenipotentiaries seemed won over to the women's arguments, with most endorsing the concept of a Women's Commission when meeting with the Inter-Allied suffragists face-to-face. The question remained: How would they respond when they debated women's fate behind closed doors?

"These Ladies Did Not Only Ask to Be Heard"

The Inter-Allied delegates were not the only representatives of their sex seeking the attention of the plenipotentiaries in the winter of 1919. Russian women in exile, Scandinavian pacifists, and even American female antisuffragists all sent letters and petitions to Paris in the hopes of influencing the peacemakers. Male diplomats viewed most of these requests as irrelevant to the work at hand, even those sent by as prominent and well connected a woman as Ishbel Maria Hamilton-Gordon, Marchioness of Aberdeen and Temaire (Lady Aberdeen for short). Lady Aberdeen's husband, a Scottish member of the House of Lords, had served as both governor general of Canada and lord lieutenant of Ireland. Lady Aberdeen was no less accomplished, having presided for decades over the International Council of Women, the oldest and largest international women's organization in the world. In late January, having received word that "women from the Suffrage Societies" were to be heard in Paris, Lady Aberdeen submitted her own request to meet with the peacemakers. British Foreign Office staff decided to delay responding to her appeal until after the Supreme

Council had decided whether it would create a Women's Commission, noting cynically that "the end will be that nothing will be done, because no such commission will ever be appointed."[47]

Sadly, such skepticism proved warranted. On February 13, just three days after meeting with Schlumberger and the members of the Inter-Allied Women's Conference, President Wilson brought a proposal to create a Women's Commission before the Supreme Council. Wilson told his colleagues that he "sincerely desire[d]" to satisfy the women's request, but he qualified his comments by adding that "he did not wish to urge this against the opinion of the Conference." Wilson, in other words, was happy enough to appear as women's champion, but he did not want to waste any valuable political capital on their behalf. The proposal was promptly dismissed.[48]

Left to deliver the bad news, Wilson wrote apologetically to the Inter-Allied Women's Conference, explaining that most of the statesmen who decided the issue were "entirely sympathetic with the cause of woman suffrage." In confidence, however, he stated that the Women's Commission had run up against "the objections raised by representatives of India and Japan to a world wide investigation, which would raise questions most unacceptable to them." This was a half-truth at best. As American minutes of the meeting show, the Indian and Japanese delegates did object to forming a Women's Commission. The Maharaja Gangha Singh of Bikaner stated explicitly that the proposal "would present considerable difficulties in all oriental countries." Japanese Baron Sonnino professed to be personally in favor of women's suffrage, but "he thought interference by the Peace Conference would hardly lead to good results." What Wilson conveniently omitted from his letter to the women, however, was the fact that the European statesmen in the room were scarcely more enthusiastic. Prime Minister Clemenceau stated he would "strongly object to any enquiry being held into the political status of women," while British foreign secretary Arthur Balfour expressed "considerable alarm" at the idea that women's suffrage might be raised at the peace conference. In the end, no formal vote was taken; Wilson simply withdrew his proposal.[49]

Why did Wilson mask the truth? Most likely, the American president found it more expedient to attribute the failure of the motion to the "backward" Asian nations than to expose his Western colleagues to the wrath of their female populations. For that matter, Wilson was far from enlightened on matters of race. Pinning the blame on the nonwhite delegates in the room fit comfortably into his worldview. In any case, the matter had been settled, and Wilson considered his promise to the suffragists fulfilled. Soon after, he departed for the United States for a monthlong midwinter break from the negotiations, leaving women's fate in the hands of his fellow plenipotentiaries.

In the meantime, a delegation of Inter-Allied women called on Prime Minister Clemenceau. He had not been a particular friend of female enfranchisement prior to World War I, and French suffragists went into the meeting with low expectations. They emerged delighted. Clemenceau, reported *La Vie Féminine*, "offered the delegation more than it could have hoped for." For the first time, he went on record approving some measure of female enfranchisement in France (only the municipal vote, but a step in the right direction). Equally important, he offered a new proposal for securing women's representation at the peace conference. "Competing zealously with the foreign plenipotentiaries," Clemenceau suggested seating a female delegate on existing commissions likely to address subjects of special interest to women. With this suggestion, remarked English delegate Millicent Garrett Fawcett, "he went one better than Wilson, which was, I think, rather agreeable to him." More likely, the French prime minister merely saw his proposal as a way of satisfying women's demands for representation without according them any real power. A lone female voice on a committee could easily be drowned out.[50]

It would be nearly three weeks before Clemenceau (laid up temporarily by a botched assassination attempt) would bring the issue of women's representation back before the Supreme Council. On March 11 he finally broached the issue, asking his male colleagues if they would be willing to allow the "ladies" who had requested "to take part in the work of the Conference" the possibility of being heard "by the various Commissions of the Conference dealing with questions in which they were interested." French foreign minister Stephen Pichon, who had also received a visit from a delegation of Inter-Allied women, quite reasonably "pointed out that these ladies did not only ask to be heard, but they also wished to form part of the Commissions in question." Pichon's observation fell on deaf ears. The statesmen in the room agreed to invite the Inter-Allied women to "state their case" before both the Labor and League of Nations Commissions of the peace conference. With that, the meeting adjourned.[51]

The peace conference secretary wrote to Marguerite de Witt Schlumberger to inform her of the Supreme Council's decision, but the sluggish French mail system couldn't keep pace with international news. On

March 14 one of the American delegates showed Schlumberger a copy of the secretary's letter, printed in the *Chicago Tribune*. Did Schlumberger find it dryly fitting to receive the news that women would finally be heard at the peace conference secondhand? From their initial refusal to seat women as peace delegates, to their rejection of a Women's Commission, to their final decision not to appoint women to existing commissions, the male peacemakers had done their utmost to minimize women's influence in the negotiations. Inter-Allied suffragists would have been justified in interpreting the offer to speak before the Labor and League of Nations Commissions as little more than a fig leaf.[52]

Schlumberger and her collaborators viewed it otherwise. "Women's hour has struck," announced Constance Drexel in the *Los Angeles Times*, "perhaps not with the resounding whack for which some of us had hoped, but it struck men's hearts." Women—who in most of the world had limited education and no political voice—would be heard in the most influential international policy arena in the world. The Inter-Allied women saw their intervention in the peace negotiations as "an audition" of sorts. Appearing on the stage of the peace conference, even in a supporting role, felt like a "great feminist victory." "Statesmen from East and West," claimed the international feminist newsletter *Jus Suffragii*, "are not being allowed to forget the female half of the nations they represent. . . . It may help them to the tardy recognition of the true meaning of democracy, and the principles of which they have been readier to profess than to carry out." Thanks to coverage of the peace conference in the international media, moreover, even a small opening would allow women to air their views before the entire world. After weeks of tireless preparation, they were ready.[53]

"The Right of Peoples to Free Self-Determination"

Of the two commissions the Inter-Allied women had been invited to address, the Labor Commission acted with the greatest speed. On March 18 the women's delegation arrived at the French Ministry of Labor where commission chair (and American Federation of Labor president) Samuel Gompers extended a warm welcome. The women spelled out their basic demands: identical work conditions and labor laws for both sexes (except in the case of maternity), the application of the principle "equal pay for equal work," and the recognition of women's right to help shape national and international labor legislation. Gompers congratulated the women for their "methodical" approach, promising to take their concerns under consideration. Seven months later, female labor activists would take their fate in their own hands and convene an International Congress of Working Women in Washington, D.C., to refine their demands and present them to the newly established International Labor Organization. Their spirited defense of working women's economic rights, as we will see below in greater detail, formed an integral component of women's international activism in 1919.[54]

The Inter-Allied women had considerably more time—a full month, in the end—to prepare for their appearance before the League of Nations Commission. The long delay made it difficult for some of the foreign women to remain in Paris, including the head of the British delegation, Millicent Garrett Fawcett, who left for home optimistic about women's prospects going forward. In mid-March the youthful Margery Corbett Ashby took her place. Four years after the Paris Peace Conference, Corbett Ashby would succeed Carrie Chapman Catt at the head of the International Woman Suffrage Alliance and come to play a central role in the expanding women's movement. For the time being, she was fairly giddy at the prospect of taking part in such an important global event. "I am tremendously glad of the chance of being here," she wrote home to her father, "and am having a most amusing time being entertained at the Ritz in private apartments of great splendor." Corbett Ashby's husband, not yet discharged from the army, was less excited at the idea of his wife running loose in the French capital. "As to Paris," he wrote her, "I am told the prices are appalling. . . . Also, it is none so peaceful with a good sprinkling of highly barbarian colonials about, so . . . don't dangle your money in the streets." Whether out of conviction or to preserve the domestic peace, Corbett Ashby let the comment pass, simply reassuring her family the *agents de police* had matters well under control.[55]

In mid-March Lady Aberdeen of the International Council for Women finally arrived in Paris as well. Once there, she dropped any adversarial stance she had once had toward the "suffragists," approved of the work the Inter-Allied Women's Conference had accomplished to date, and began throwing her name around to ensure women's representation in the negotiations. Lady Aberdeen's stature allowed her (in Corbett Ashby's words) to "get easy access to the big folk." In no time, she lined up appointments with a full global expanse of plenipotentiaries, from Brazil to Australia by way

PHOTOGRAPH OF BEARER.

Margery Corbett Ashby, British delegate to the Inter-Allied Women's Conference, in her 1919 passport photo. (Margery Corbett Ashby Papers, Women's Library collection, London School of Economics Library)

of Romania, Japan, and South Africa. The other women were impressed. "Lady Aberdeen . . . is bossing the show pretty completely out here!" one wrote home.[56]

For all her worldly connections, Lady Aberdeen's most important meeting brought her face-to-face with an old friend from home: Lord Robert Cecil, a Conservative member of Parliament, longtime supporter of women's suffrage, plenipotentiary to the peace conference, and one of the principal architects of the League of Nations. On March 26 Lady Aberdeen and Corbett Ashby met with Lord Cecil and spelled out the various resolutions the Inter-Allied Women's Conference planned to bring before the League of Nations Commission. Most important, they informed him of their intent to demand women's right to full participation in the new world government. Cecil heard them out and promptly "volunteered to propose a new clause in the Covenant of the League of Nations which would have the effect of opening all posts under the League to men and women alike." Two days later he followed through on his promise, and the amendment was "accepted enthusiastically."[57]

More weeks dragged by, but just as the women began to despair, a summons to appear before the League of Nations Commission finally arrived. The Inter-Allied women were cordially invited to appear at the Hôtel Crillon on April 10, 1919, at 8:00 P.M. One last time, the Inter-Allied suffragists prepared to lay their case before the gatekeepers of the new world order. As the seventeen female delegates (French, British, American, and Italian) filed into the salon, they were surprised by the disorder around them. Papers were "strewn everywhere," French delegate Suzanne Grinberg observed. Margery Corbett Ashby found it a "curious scene, the big lofty room all white but for blazing scarlet curtains." Statesmen from the major powers sat at a big table at the center of the room. The "lesser fry" (Corbett Ashby's phrase), were relegated to tiny tables in the corners. President Wilson, serving as chair of the commission, rose to shake each woman's hand as she entered. Lord Cecil smiled knowingly. The other statesmen, unsure of protocol, "looked profoundly embarrassed."[58]

The women had been granted half an hour of the commission's time, and they stuck to it like clockwork. Lady Aberdeen introduced the delegation members. President Wilson then gave Margery Corbett Ashby a small nod of encouragement and asked her to begin the presentation. This gesture of personal attention from the famous statesman left the British suffragist dumbstruck. "I lost my head," she later admitted, "and nearly the rest of my speech!" Regaining her composure, Corbett Ashby formally requested that which Lord Cecil had already promised: the full and equal collaboration of women and men in all the offices and bodies of the League of Nations. The other women spoke in turn, presenting a full range of resolutions. They spoke with the confidence that came from firm research and personal experience, a fact not fully appreciated by all the men in the room. For example, when another member of the women's delegation, Dr. Nicole Girard-Mangin, rose to address the commission on the importance of public health to global peace, one of the statesmen "looked at her through his glasses and murmured, 'A nurse, she is pretty.'" In response, the women fired back that Girard-Mangin was not a nurse but a doctor and an army officer at that (the French Army had mistaken her name for a man's, drafted her, and retained her for the entirety of the war). After all they had been through during and after World War I, the women had little tolerance for casual sexism. At the very least, they expected to be treated with respect.[59]

French feminists Suzanne Grinberg and Ghénia Avril de Sainte-Croix addressed the commission next, speaking not for Western women but for women from those countries where "the law of man, the stronger, is exercised in all its horror." Remaining carefully vague, so as not to "offend the plenipotentiaries belonging to the countries that still have such customs," Grinberg outlined a whole series of practices and laws that restricted women's freedoms and put their lives in danger around the world. These included marrying off daughters without their consent or binding them into slavery to pay off a debt. They also included marriage laws that allowed husbands to repudiate their wives and seize guardianship of their children. In raising these issues, Grinberg admitted, "It is true that we have received no mandate to plead this cause by those whom it concerns," but she and the other Western suffragists felt it to be the duty of "every human being who knows these injustices and inequities to denounce them." In her conclusion, she boldly suggested that only those nations that "undertake to give the women of their country new and better conditions" be admitted to the League. To this, Avril de Sainte-Croix added the demand that the League accept responsibility for repressing the international sex trade, which resulted in the forced prostitution of women and children around the world.[60]

Finally, although Wilson had put women on notice from day one that the peace conference would not take up the issue of suffrage, the Inter-Allied delegation was not about to simply let the matter drop. "Nobody," they reiterated one last time, "can speak in the name of the people as long as women, who represent half of humanity, are excluded from the political life of nations." As a formal resolution, the women demanded, "the well-founded principle of women's suffrage be proclaimed by the Peace Conference and the League of Nations so that it will be applied throughout the world as quickly as the degree of civilization and the democratic development of each country allows."[61]

At every turn, the delegates drove home the central point that a world order shaped by national self-determination and popular sovereignty would be an empty shell without women's active participation. Marguerite de Witt Schlumberger, whose determination and resourcefulness had done so much to put women's democratic rights on the table in 1919, reminded the plenipotentiaries that the peace conference "concerns the whole human race," women as well as men. As such, "from this Conference we trust that there will issue the reign of lasting peace and the recognition of the right of peoples to free self-determination." Suzanne Grinberg echoed the theme: "After having established the first principle of human justice, that the peoples have the right to free self-determination, do you not feel the higher duty affirming that every human being, man and woman, has the right to freely choose his own destiny?" With such arguments, the Inter-Allied Women's Conference delegates transformed the debate surrounding the right to national self-determination into an argument in favor of individual sovereignty, placing women's rights at the center of the new world order. Finally, in concrete terms, the delegation demanded that all countries whose new boundaries were to be settled by referendum include women in the voting process.[62]

For once, President Wilson could offer the women tangible results. Thanking them for their meticulous preparation, for their competence, and for their brevity (no small matter for a meeting that did not begin until 8:00 P.M.), Wilson officially informed the delegation that all League of Nations positions would be open to men and women on equal footing, a promise that would be encoded in article 7 of the Covenant of the League of Nations, itself incorporated into the Versailles Treaty. Referendums regarding future border decisions would similarly be open to both sexes. As for the recognition of female suffrage or the protection of women's individual rights, those were "details to be filled in by experience rather than by our forecasting of what is wanted." With that, the statesmen once again tendered their hands and shepherded the women out the door. As she passed Lord Cecil, Margery Corbett Ashby murmured quietly, "Don't you wish all your troubles were over so quickly?" Lord Cecil smiled, and the women's hour at the peace negotiations drew to a close. Both by cracking open the door of international governance to women *and* by refusing to address women's broader demands for equality, the peacemakers set the parameters of many battles to come.[63]

The League of Nations and Global Women's Rights

Journalist Constance Drexel, who had been championing the Inter-Allied Women's Conference from the beginning, cabled news of its achievements across the Atlantic, shaping the story as it would appear in the *New York Times*, *Chicago Tribune*, and *Los Angeles Times*. Drexel's lead-in paragraph merits a moment of reflection: "One of the greatest compliments ever paid to women was given Thursday evening," she wrote, "when the full Commission of the League of Nations received a delegation of seven [*sic*] women representing the International Council of Women and the Conference of Women Suffragists of Allied Countries. It was the first time women had actually been called upon to help remake the world." What is odd about this particular telling of the events is that even though Drexel was an outspoken feminist and had played a personal role in bringing about the historic meeting, in her story, men appear as the central protagonists. *Men* paid women a compliment. *Men* called upon women to help shape the new international order. Never mind that it took women two months of persistent lobbying to get a foot in the door. Drexel's framing of this story serves as a vivid reminder that in 1919, everyone assumed international statecraft to be a man's affair. It is in this context that we need to weigh our assessment of the suffragists' achievements.[64]

Did the concessions that Inter-Allied Women's Conference wrung from the peacemakers constitute a victory? Absolutely. By force of their own will, women stepped onto men's stage and performed admirably. As the *Sydney Morning Herald* proclaimed in faraway Australia, "It is a step in advance for women to have secured even so small a share in momentous decisions on which the fate of the world depends." American feminists took time out from their fevered effort to push a women's suffrage amendment through the U.S. Senate to hail the news from Paris. "It is splendid," declared movement leader Anna Howard Shaw. "People of the United States will understand what democracy means by the time the Peace Conference gets through." Suzanne Grinberg, who had been at the center of the Inter-Allied women's lobbying effort throughout, proclaimed unabashedly, "February 10–April 10. These two dates will be celebrated in the history of feminism. The first marks the beginning of our efforts to participate in international politics, the second, the result."[65]

Such celebratory comments were overly optimistic; nevertheless, the Inter-Allied Women's Conference of 1919 set important precedents that would help guide global feminism for decades to come. Most centrally, by demanding a seat at the negotiating table, Marguerite de Witt Schlumberger and her Allied collaborators advanced the idea that women's cooperation was vital to building a just and democratic world order and to securing a lasting peace. This demand largely fell on deaf ears in 1919, but it reverberated across the twentieth century and has spilled over into the twenty-first. In the aftermath of the Second World War in 1945, a new generation of international feminists would unabashedly issue the same demand. Their call would meet with greater success, and a handful of determined women were able to travel to San Francisco to help shape the agenda of the nascent United Nations and the parameters of the postwar international order. Today scholars of international relations and international policy makers have begun to revisit both the history and the claims of World War I–era feminists and to argue that women's participation in postconflict negotiations is vital to the success of peace-building efforts.[66]

Second, by seeking to inscribe official recognition of women's rights— social and economic as well as political—in the Versailles Treaty, Allied suffragists proposed that international agreements and conventions could become a powerful tool for pressuring recalcitrant governments to reform national laws in women's favor. Having made some headway down this path in the spring of 1919 in Paris, female activists would deploy a similar strategy several months later in Washington, D.C., were they would lobby for women's economic rights at the inaugural conference of the International Labor Organization. In the 1920s and 1930s feminists throughout the Americas would work from the same playbook by lobbying for the adoption of a Pan-American Equal Rights Treaty, calling on all signatory states to mandate women's civil and political equality with men.[67]

The League of Nations' embrace of women was similarly no small accomplishment. In the male-dominated world of international relations, this opening would afford women their most effective means of legitimizing international female policy-making expertise in the interwar decades. Even as most avenues to national diplomatic service remained barred to women, the League of Nations Secretariat opened exciting new international career opportunities to a small number of enterprising female diplomats, activists, and experts.

In particular, the section of the League charged with developing policy on social issues would attract talented women with vast stores of knowledge and experience. From 1919 to 1931 the Social Section would be headed by Dame Rachel Crowdy (who cut her administrative teeth managing thousands of British nurses enlisted in the Voluntary Aid Detachment during World War I). As section chief, Crowdy was responsible for overseeing all League work related to sex trafficking. This issue, of course, had been a major preoccupation for women at the peace conference who had wanted the League to accept responsibility for halting the traffic in women and children. Instead, the peacemakers inserted more ambiguous language in the League Covenant, indicating the body had license to oversee international agreements on the issue. "With this," grumbled a prominent French feminist and lawyer, "you can be sure that nothing will change in the actual situation." Instead, female policy makers would demand the League of Nations take the obligation seriously. From 1923 to 1931 Ghénia Avril de Sainte-Croix would serve on the League's Advisory Commission on the Traffic in Women and Children, establishing a reputation as an international expert on the topic and keeping the problem in the public eye.[68]

Only a small handful of countries appointed women as delegates to the League's General Assembly during the interwar years, but those chosen were often prominent feminists, like Soviet representative Alexendra Kollontai (who also held the distinction of being one of the first female ambassadors anywhere in the world). The League tackled other issues of particular importance to women, including the citizenship status of married women, challenging the widespread requirement that women assume the nationality of their husbands upon marriage. And while women struggled to gain entry into the more prestigious sections of the League, their relentless push to encode women's rights as a matter of international law helped lay the intellectual groundwork for the United Nations Charter and the Universal Declaration of Human Rights after World War II.[69]

In 1919 suffragists also hoped the decision to open positions in the world government to women would inspire member states to follow suit, thus spurring women's enfranchisement at the national as well as the international level. "The League of Nations will be the first political body in the world," proclaimed British feminists. "It is hard to see how any of the nations under it will be able to refuse to follow the example which it sets them. We take it then, that in the near future all political positions in all civilized countries in the world will be open to women." In this prediction, they were sadly mistaken. The failure of the peacemakers to offer even a simple moral endorsement of female enfranchisement, let alone require universal suffrage as the basis of membership in the League of Nations, reinforced the idea that democracy could be built in women's absence. The consequences of global statesmen's shortsightedness would be felt for decades. In some corners of the world, they are still felt today.[70]

Of the women who participated as delegates in the Inter-Allied Women's Conference, only the Americans gained the right to vote and hold office in the immediate aftermath of the peace conference. The delegates from Great Britain and New Zealand possessed the vote already (although not until 1928 would British women gain suffrage on equal terms as men). In 1919 Belgium did grant some women the vote, but only those who were widows or mothers of servicemen killed in World War I. In this patriotic scheme, termed the "Widow's Vote," women could cast a ballot only as surrogates for their (absent) male relations, not as individuals endowed with political rights of their own. Italian suffragists fared no better. While they were temporarily heartened to hear Prime Minister Benito Mussolini proclaim himself open to the idea of women's suffrage in 1923, three years later his Fascist Party would seize dictatorial power and abolish elections altogether.[71]

Like Italy, France proved one of the stubborn "civilized" countries that resisted opening both elected office and the polling booth to women throughout the interwar decades. Between 1919 and 1936, while the Chamber of Deputies passed some version of female suffrage on five separate occasions, the French Senate defeated it every time. French women would not be granted the vote until 1944. Marguerite de Witt Schlumberger, who had worked tirelessly to secure women's political rights at the Paris Peace Conference, would die in 1924 having never cast a ballot. Other French suffragists would carry the battle into the interwar years, or at least until the late 1930s, when the saber rattling of France's fascist neighbors diverted everyone's attention. In the international suffrage movement, however, the French soon found themselves relegated to the unenfranchised fringe, falling behind women from some of the purportedly "uncivilized" countries (like Turkey, where women began voting in parliamentary elections in 1934) that the Allied women had confidently spoken for at the Paris Peace Conference.[72]

Which leads us to a final question: How effectively did Western suffragists represent the interests of women from the rest of the world? After all, the Inter-Allied Women's Conference addressed the peacemakers in the name of "half of humanity," not just women like themselves. French women and their collaborators were quite aware they had assumed this responsibility without any real mandate from women from outside the Western world. They stated so explicitly before the League of Nations Commission.

But their language also rested on an assumption of Western superiority that was near pervasive in international feminist circles in the early twentieth century.

Inter-Allied suffragists' limited knowledge of other cultures does not mean that they got everything wrong. Marital subjugation (including child betrothal and polygamy) and sexual servitude (including prostitution, concubinage, and slavery), both issues Inter-Allied suffragists raised with the League of Nations Commission, were real and pressing concerns for women in many parts of Asia and the Middle East. What the Western women did not fully see, however, was that some of these women—including women from Egypt and China—not only were capable of raising these issues on their own terms but were beginning to do so, and at the doorstep of the peace conference itself. But for the non-Western (or, for that matter, non-white) women who spoke out, organized, and took to the streets in 1919, male intransigence was not the only or primary obstacle to women's independence. Western imperialism abroad and (in the American case) entrenched racism at home were equally limiting factors. The global events of 1919 brought all these grievances into the public eye. At the time of the Paris Peace Conference, as we will see in the pages that follow, female political activists of widely differing backgrounds formulated their demands and fought their battles largely independently of one another, but the events of 1919 would start to bring them together and encourage them to bridge the wide gulf of female experience to confront women's oppression around the globe.

CHAPTER II

Winter of Our Discontent

Racial Justice in a New World Order

E ven as the delegates to the French-sponsored Inter-Allied Wom-
en's Conference were wrapping up their business in April 1919,
other female activists were boarding trains and ships, preparing to
make their entrance onto the diplomatic scene. Among them were a dozen
or so American women led by the intrepid social worker and peace activist
Jane Addams. Addams's group was headed to Zurich for the inaugural
meeting of the Women's International League for Peace and Freedom
(WILPF), a separate women's conference convened in response to the peace
negotiations, this one deliberately designed to unite women across former
enemy lines. Addams and her travel companions arrived in the French port
of Le Havre a couple of weeks before the Zurich Congress was scheduled
to begin. No matter. A short stopover in Paris, the women all agreed, would
allow their party to recuperate and catch up with the latest developments
in the peace negotiations. And then there was the trip they were hoping to
make before continuing on to Switzerland: a tour of the devastated region
of northern France.[1]

The battlefields of the First World War had an oddly seductive appeal
to visitors to France and Belgium in 1919. Throughout the long years of
the war, those spared the experience of combat had struggled to understand the immensity of the conflict that had engulfed so much of the world's
attention, manpower, and resources. Once the guns were silenced, the
Western battlefields became sites of pilgrimage and tourism, and foreigners

flooding into France for the peace negotiations were among the first wave of visitors. These men and women came to bear witness to the European cataclysm and to connect viscerally with the places that had so recently played host to human tragedy.

Because northern France was still considered a military zone in the winter of 1919, prospective visitors needed advance permission to tour the battlefields. The WILPF women did not waste time putting in a request with the American Visitor's Bureau in Paris, and fortunately the Red Cross came through in short order with a five-day motor tour. By all accounts, the experience was deeply moving. WILPF delegate Dr. Alice Hamilton described her impressions in a letter home to her family: "We saw villages pounded to dust and great towns reduced to ruins and miles and miles of battlefields. One can't possibly imagine it, one has to see it and even then it is hard to believe." The desire to experience the reality of war—or at least its aftereffects—was compelling, and nearly all members of the American WILPF delegation in Paris made the trip. All, that is, but one: Mary Church Terrell, who was not invited.[2]

Terrell did not blame the snub on Addams, who had invited her to join the delegation to Europe and had fully included her in all planning sessions on the ship over. Instead, she attributed the rebuff to the women's desire to spare her the embarrassment of rejection by the American agency arranging the tour. "They probably took it for granted," Terrell would later write in her memoir, "that the discrimination against colored people in the United States under similar circumstances would quite likely be displayed by its citizens in France. In other words a taboo on anything that might be twisted to mean 'social equality' for Colored Americans would undoubtedly 'follow the flag.'" Whether the women actually asked if a mixed-race party would be a source of contention for the segregated American military mattered little in terms of the outcome. As the only nonwhite member of the American WILPF delegation, Terrell alone was preemptively excluded.[3]

Already a prominent civil rights and women's rights activist in 1919, fifty-eight-year-old Mary Church Terrell was not one to suffer discrimination quietly. Instead, Terrell would wage a one-woman battle for the right to tour the battlefields of France like any other American abroad. The incident mattered, not only because of Terrell's desire to see the hallowed landscape of the recent conflict, but also, and more important, because it spoke to the inescapable curse of racial discrimination that had hounded her throughout her adult life in Jim Crow America, shadowed her as she collaborated with (predominantly white) women's organizations in the pursuit of gender equality, and now threatened to undermine global relations owing to the racial biases of the peacemakers.

As Terrell's presence in Europe indicates, African American women were among the dozens of female activists who flocked to Paris in 1919. No less than the white suffragists who organized the Inter-Allied Women's Conference, these women seized on the international stage of the peace conference to demand that the peacemakers fulfill President Woodrow Wilson's wartime pledge to make the world safe for democracy. Unlike their white counterparts, however, African American women could not easily ignore the hypocrisy behind Wilson's calls for a peace rooted in justice, self-determination, and popular sovereignty at the same time that he was reaffirming racial segregation as the basis of American social, political, and economic life. If the new world order wrought in Paris were going to benefit people of color, they believed, it would more likely do so in spite of the American president than because of him.

This chapter recounts the experiences of the women who came to Europe in 1919 to pursue equality and justice for the African American population of the United States, for Africans and their descendants throughout the world, and, most specifically, for women of color like themselves, who suffered under the double affliction of racial prejudice and gender discrimination. It focuses on two women in particular: Mary Church Terrell and her longtime friend, Ida Gibbs Hunt. Both were among the first generation of college-educated African American women. Both were stalwart champions of racial justice and gender equality in the United States and abroad.

For all their similarities, however, Terrell and Hunt brought different perspectives with them as they entered the political arena in 1919. Having spent the prewar and war years in Washington, D.C., Terrell had America's pernicious affair with segregation and racial violence foremost on her mind. While abroad in 1919, she divided her time between networking with powerful African and Asian statesmen in Paris, imploring white feminists to recognize racial inequality as an impediment to peace and freedom in Zurich, and fighting with the segregated American military for the right to visit the battlefields of the Great War.

Ida Gibbs Hunt, for her part, had lived abroad with her diplomat husband for nearly two decades by the time of the peace conference. Posted first to the French colony of Madagascar and then to St. Étienne in south-eastern France, Hunt had a more global perspective on race relations than her longtime friend. Unlike Terrell, who came to Europe to lobby along-side female peace activists, Hunt traveled to Paris to help organize what became known as the Pan-African Congress of 1919. Convened in mid-February of that year by the esteemed African American intellectual and Hunt's personal friend W.E.B. Du Bois, the congress was a historic initia-tive designed to ensure that the voices of "the children of Africa," both at home and scattered throughout the diaspora, were heard during the Paris Peace Conference.[4]

Both women were destined for disappointment: the peacemakers did little to address racism in the United States or around the world at the end of the First World War. The experience of championing racial equality in 1919 nonetheless expanded both Terrell's and Hunt's political horizons and emboldened them, and many other African American women, to fight for the rights of those they referred to as the "darker races." At the same time, male civil rights leaders' refusal to accord female activists the respect they deserved sharpened Hunt's and Terrell's feminist consciousness. Adopting racial justice and gender equality as their dual battle cry, Hunt, Terrell, and a growing body of like-minded women began to organize. Unwilling to give in to despair in the face of intractable racism and sexism, African American women responded by enlisting in the long-term struggle for a democratic world order worthy of its name.

Two Daughters of the "Talented Tenth"

Mary Church Terrell and Ida Gibbs Hunt owed much to their upbringing. Although born in different circumstances, each came from an affluent fam-ily, acquired the very best of schooling, and married well. Daughters of what W.E.B. Du Bois termed the "Talented Tenth" (the "exceptional men" of the "Negro race" distinguished by their intelligence, education, and worldliness), Terrell and Hunt enjoyed the rare advantages and carried the particular burdens that fell to the African American social elite of the post–Civil War era.[5]

Mary Eliza Church was born on September 23, 1863, just months after Abraham Lincoln issued the Emancipation Proclamation. Her mother and father had both been enslaved from birth. Robert Church bore the fair skin of his father and master, which he passed on to his daughter. After gaining his freedom, he made a fortune in Memphis real estate and became a prominent philanthropist in the local African American community. It was Mary's female relations, however, who had the greatest influence on her young life. Her mother, Louisa Ayers Church, had an unusually liberal-minded master who taught her to read and write as well as to speak French. As a young woman, once freed and married, she opened a hair salon that quickly became a Memphis institution. Mary's parents were thus both successful businesspeople, but their shared entrepreneurialism did little to smooth over differences between them, and they divorced when she was a young girl.

Like many children, Mary was curious about her parents' lives before she was born. Having "made it" in the post–Civil War era, Mary's mother was hesitant to talk to her daughter about life in bondage. It fell to Mary's maternal grandmother to answer the young girl's persistent questions, telling her "tales of brutality perpetrated upon slaves who belonged to cruel masters." Such stories were difficult to hear and even harder to tell, often leaving both grandmother and granddaughter in tears. "It nearly killed me," Terrell would later write, "to think that my dear grandmother, whom I loved so devotedly, had once been a slave." Not wanting to burden her granddaughter with the weight of the past, her grandmother would comfort her saying, "Never mind, honey . . . Gramma ain't a slave no more." Such stories left Mary cognizant of how narrowly she missed being born into slavery herself, and she would fight against the institution's pernicious legacies throughout her adult life.[6]

One thing Mary's parents agreed on was the importance of providing their daughter with the best education available to a young African American girl in the final third of the nineteenth century. At the tender age of six, Mary was sent to board with a kindhearted family in Yellow Springs, Ohio, where she was able to attend integrated schools. Pleased with their daughter's academic progress, Mary's parents eventually moved her to Oberlin, Ohio, to advance her studies. In 1880 she entered Oberlin College, one of the first coeducational institutions of higher education in America and one of the first to embrace racial integration as well. Mary opted for the Classical Course of training, which required the study of Greek as well as Latin. Such an academic path was rare for a woman and almost unheard of for an African American woman. Friends warned Mary against it, telling her that if she became too educated she would never find a husband. Terrell persisted, graduating in 1884. She was among three African American women to receive a bachelor's degree from Oberlin that year (bringing the total of black, female bachelor's degree holders in the United States to five). One of her few classmates of color was Ida Alexander Gibbs.[7]

While Mary followed a path northward from Memphis to Yellow Springs to Oberlin, Ida traveled southeast. She was born in the British colony of Vancouver on November 16, 1862. There, her father, Mifflin Wister Gibbs, made his fortune as a land speculator and commercial partner in a successful store outfitting prospectors. Ida's mother, Maria Alexander, had been born in slavery in rural Kentucky, most likely as both the daughter and property of the man who had once served as vice president under Martin Van Buren. By the time she was a young woman, however, Maria had gained her freedom, and, after marrying in 1859, she traveled with Mifflin to Vancouver where she was able to live in high style and gave birth to six children, five of whom survived infancy. Ida was the third of her children and the first of two daughters.[8]

Despite the comforts of her married life in Vancouver, Ida's mother was not happy. After the American Civil War, she dreamt of returning home, eventually moving to Oberlin, Ohio, to raise her children. Ida's mother and father would remain separated, though on amicable terms, for the rest of their lives. Ida's father also returned to the United States, where he continued to build his fortune and became the first African American judge to be elected to office. Later he would be appointed U.S. consul to the French colony of Madagascar.[9]

Once settled in Ohio, Ida and her siblings were enrolled in public school. A good student, Ida entered Oberlin College's preparatory academy, where she met Mary Church. The two became inseparable friends and, later, college roommates. She too opted for the Classical Course at Oberlin, and the two friends devoted themselves to their studies, although not without a little dancing and socializing mixed in.[10]

College expanded the young women's intellectual and political horizons, and before Ida and Mary graduated, they were introduced to the radical idea that American women, no matter their skin color, should be allowed to vote. During her freshman year at Oberlin, Mary recorded her opinion on the matter in a school ledger in terms quite similar to those that would be used by the Inter-Allied suffragists at the Paris Peace Conference a full four decades later: "Is it fair," she wrote, "that one half of the citizens of this free land should be totally denied the privilege of expressing their opinion by the ballot? We ask, is it justice?" Both Mary and Ida thought not. Armed with college degrees, they were also ready to set out and make a difference in the world.[11]

The Racial Uplift Activism of Mary Church Terrell

After college graduation, Mary's father expected her to live with him in Memphis and take up the life of a proper young lady in middle-class African American society. Mary had other ideas. All during college, she said, "I had dreamed of the day when I could promote the welfare of my race."[12]

Such desires marked Mary Church as a true daughter of the Talented Tenth in late-nineteenth-century America. "Racial uplift" was their credo: a service ethos that called on members of the black elite to help fellow African Americans—so recently released from the fetters of bondage—develop the habits of hard work, social purity, economic prudence, and sexual virtue. Proponents of racial uplift generally emphasized the importance of the patriarchal family, in which mothers stayed at home and fathers ruled the roost. On the positive side, such ideals sought to undo the ravages that centuries of slavery had wrought on black families, when men and women were prohibited from marrying, and children could be sold away from parents at the master's whim. Less ideally, racial uplift tended to insist that all African Americans, many of whom were uneducated and impoverished, adhere to the ideals of the white middle class to prove their worthiness of citizenship. It also complicated black women's efforts to carve out a role outside home or church.[13]

Mary was nonetheless determined to help her community and start a career. She began by accepting a teaching position in Ohio at Wilberforce University, the first college in America both owned and operated by African Americans. Two years later she began teaching at the prestigious M Street High School in Washington, D.C., one of the first public high schools for African Americans in the country that was known for its rigorous curriculum. There she refined her teaching skills and developed a soft spot for the head of the Latin department, a handsome, young Harvard graduate by the name of Robert Terrell.

Despite the budding romance, Mary left Washington for a summertime tour of Europe with her father, followed by two years of study abroad. She spent much of her time in Germany, where she gained fluency in the language and experienced a newfound freedom from the burden of racial prejudice. In Europe, America's "one drop of blood" standard (by which any person with "one drop" of African blood was branded a Negro) did not hold weight. Her relatively fair complexion and her middle-class manners translated into social acceptance. Before the year was over, she turned down marriage proposals from several white suitors, any one of which would have allowed her to "pass" into white society. Mary, however, was uninterested. At the end of two years, she returned home, alone.[14]

Mary's resistance to the pleas of her European suitors worked out well for Robert Terrell. In 1891, shortly after she returned to the United States, the two were married. Robert Terrell would later become the principal of M Street High School and then the first African American to serve on the Municipal Court of Washington, D.C., a position he managed to retain through four different administrations.

As married women were prohibited from teaching, Mary Church Terrell applied herself to becoming the ideal housewife and giving birth to three children, all of whom, tragically, died in infancy (a later arrival, Phyllis, would survive into adulthood, and Mary and Robert would adopt a second daughter as well). Generally restless keeping house, Terrell began searching for ways to combine married life with racial uplift work. In 1895 she was appointed to the Washington, D.C., Board of Education, becoming the first African American woman to serve in such a position anywhere in the country. In 1909, upon the invitation of W.E.B. Du Bois, she became a charter member of the National Association for the Advancement of Colored People (NAACP, an interracial civil rights organization committed to seeking justice for African Americans). At her husband's prompting, Terrell also embarked on a career as a public speaker. She hired an agent and went out on the lecture circuit, speaking on "The Progress of Colored Women" and similar topics. Finally, Terrell tried her hand at writing, publishing articles and essays in both black and mainstream white newspapers, most addressing (as it was known at the time) the "Race Problem."[15]

Dedicated to improving the lives of black women and to fostering interracial understanding, Terrell also began attending meetings of the National American Woman Suffrage Association (NAWSA), where she befriended pioneering suffragist Susan B. Anthony as well as her successor, Carrie Chapman Catt. Already convinced of the justice of women's suffrage, Terrell embraced the "great cause." The suffrage movement, she would later insist, brought her into "direct personal contact with some of the brainiest and finest women in the country."[16]

Terrell's collaboration with white feminists was not without its difficulties. Race was a fraught issue in the American suffrage movement. On the one hand, in the early twentieth century white women seeking the ballot needed all the friends they could muster. Their movement could also claim a long history of interracial cooperation, dating back to abolitionist Frederick Douglass's endorsement of female suffrage at Seneca Falls in 1848 and stretching through Du Bois's outspoken endorsement of a women's suffrage amendment in the years before the First World War. On the other hand, many white suffragists were not particularly enlightened on racial matters. Even those in the North who genuinely welcomed black women's activism feared antagonizing outspokenly racist southern suffragists. Despite the ambivalent embrace of white women, however, a fair number of well-off African American women joined the national suffrage movement, believing that black women needed the vote to protect their communities from racially motivated violence, to champion their own economic interests, and to effectively challenge segregation.[17]

Terrell, who was often asked to address suffrage meetings about "the" viewpoint of African American women (as though there were but one), saw her suffrage work as an extension of her racial uplift goals. She used her appearances to exhort white women to "stand up not only for the oppressed sex, but also for the oppressed race." At national suffrage meetings, and once, speaking in German at a 1904 international meeting in Berlin, Terrell garnered white suffragists' respect and encouraged them to reflect on "the condition of the race problem in the United States, as it really is."[18]

While Terrell saw much to be gained from collaborating with white women, she also recognized that there were limitations to what could be accomplished in such interracial settings. As such, she reserved a good part of her energy for work with other women of color in the pursuit of racial progress. In 1896 Terrell was elected the first president of the newly formed National Association of Colored Women (NACW). The organization, which adopted the slogan "Lifting as We Climb," engaged in classic racial uplift projects: raising money for kindergartens and promoting household management, for example. It also readily entered into the political fray, decrying the segregation of train cars, protesting the convict-lease system, and demanding an end to the lynching of African Americans (over one hundred of whom were murdered in brutal attacks every year). Terrell's work on behalf of the NACW eventually brought her to the attention of Jane Addams. Years later, having committed herself to peace work, Addams would invite Terrell to join the delegation of American women heading to the Zurich Congress in 1919. Eager to carry her message of racial equality to the doorstep of the Paris Peace Conference, Terrell accepted. She also hoped that the trip to Europe would give her the occasion to reconnect with her college friend Ida Gibbs, who had long since moved abroad.[19]

The Diplomatic Career of Ida Gibbs Hunt

Back in 1904, when Mary Church Terrell was preparing to travel to the international women's conference in Berlin, by sheer coincidence, her dear friend Ida was also packing her bags for a voyage across the Atlantic. Ida's trip, however, amounted to the bigger and longer adventure of the two. That spring, Ida had finally agreed to marry her longtime beau, William Henry Hunt (Billy, to his family and friends). According to *The Colored American*, their April wedding was "the most brilliant social function of the season." Following the nuptial festivities, the couple set off on a Parisian honeymoon and then proceeded onward to their final destination: Tamatave (Toamasina), Madagascar, the French colonial island in southeastern Africa where Billy Hunt had replaced Ida's father as the American consul. Somewhere buried in her bags, Ida carried a photograph Terrell had given to her, inscribed (using her nickname) "Bon Voyage—Your old college mate, Mollie, April 12, 1904."[20]

Much like Terrell, though in vastly different surroundings, Ida struggled to adjust to domestic life. The intervening two decades between college graduation and marriage had hardly been idle ones for her. She too had found her way to Washington, D.C., teaching at M Street High. With Mary, she helped to found the NACW. Together they attended suffragist meetings of the NAWSA, believing (as Ida later explained) "that women needed the ballot to correct many of the injustices to which women of the day were subjected."[21]

Arriving in Madagascar in 1904, Hunt traded her teaching career for *la vie large coloniale* (the colonial good life). The palm trees and Indian Ocean breezes were pleasant, and the view of the harbor from her balcony was lovely as well. The red mud streets of Tamatave, however, became a sludgy

Bon voyage—
Your old College mate
Mollie
April 12, 1904

Studio portrait of Mary Church Terrell given to her college classmate Ida Gibbs Hunt upon Hunt's departure for Madagascar. (William Henry Hunt Papers, Box 3, Folder 69. Moorland-Spingarn Research Center, Manuscript Division, Howard University, Washington, D.C.)

mess in the torrential tropical rains. Housekeeping under such conditions was challenging, but Ida had three live-in servants, including a French chef, to handle the workload. Transported about town by rickshaw or carried in a sedan chair, Ida paid visits to the other colonial wives. Her French language skills served her well. To her sister Hattie she wrote, "I am quite happy here and enjoy my home."[22]

Despite the comforts of the diplomatic post she now shared with her husband, Hunt was not an uncritical observer of the racial power dynamic at work in France's African colony. Whereas Billy Hunt fully adopted the French view of colonialism as a civilizing mission (undertaken primarily to advance the moral and economic well-being of the indigenous inhabitants), Ida was skeptical. During her first long visit back home in 1906, she was already voicing concerns. Speaking to a chapter of the NACW in Detroit, Hunt discussed "the conditions women in Africa had endured."

Ida Gibbs Hunt riding in a rickshaw in Tamatave (Toamasina), Madagascar, ca. 1904, *Negro History Bulletin*, October 1947, 7. (Moorland-Spingarn Research Center, Manuscript Division, Howard University, Washington, D.C.)

She informed her audience that because of the abuse Africans suffered at the hands of European colonists, they were increasingly advancing the cry, "Africa for the Africans." At the meeting, Hunt suggested the need for some kind of international women's organization that could unite African American and African women to advance their common interests.[23]

Soon after, Ida began composing a speech or essay titled "Peace and Civilization: The Other Side of the Shield." Although only fragmentary notes survive, the essay paints a clear picture of the radical nature of Hunt's evolving ideas on racism and colonialism and her developing interest in global affairs. In it she denounced, first, the virulent anti-Japanese sentiment that had been capturing headlines in the United States in 1906 after Japanese children in San Francisco were barred from attending school with their white peers. The bulk of the essay, however, dealt with matters closer to her diplomatic home. Harboring little patience with Europe's professed civilizing mission in Africa, and outraged by reports of Belgian exploitation of indigenous workers in the Congo, Hunt wrote, "The sooner the Caucasian race learns to believe in the brotherhood of man and in the essential equality of all races, however backward, and that colonial expansion by brute force and by bullying is not an evidence of the highest civilization, the better it will be for the world." When white men spoke of advancing "civilization" in Africa, Hunt continued, they were really only disguising their interest in "commercializing other countries." But Africans and Asians, she felt, were growing wise to the white man's ways. "The darker races are already realizing that this boasted Western Civilization does not mean more justice and humanity." Hunt rounded out her argument with words of warning to the leaders of North and South America, Asia, and Europe who were gathering at The Hague in 1907 for the second of two famous peace conventions. "The Peace Conference fails to fulfill its purpose," she cautioned, "if it fails to see that the great menace before the world today is that the darker races will openly resent the disparagement, the injustice, and scorn with which they are long being treated. The Congo and other African adventures cannot be forever repeated with impunity." Racism and imperialism, she foretold, would push the people of color to rise up in their own defense.[24]

Did Hunt speak these prophetic words aloud to an American audience or commit them to print prior to World War I? It seems unlikely. As the wife of an African American diplomat, Hunt would have known that such a direct condemnation of American and European foreign policy would almost certainly have cost her husband his job. For the time being, it appears, Hunt kept her most radical ideas to herself or shared them only with sympathetic friends. (Much later, in a published article titled "The Price of Peace," she would give full voice to her cynical assessment of international relations, warning, "The darker races are restless and seething, and all realize as never before that their rights are not to be respected if they conflict with the greed or selfish interests of the white man.") Already in 1907, Hunt's "Peace and Civilization" showed the depth and sophistication of her anti-imperialist vision. When W.E.B. Du Bois would tap her to help plan a Pan-African Conference in 1919, just over a decade later, Hunt would bring much more to the table than her linguistic and organizational skills. When it came to anti-imperialism, Hunt was an intellectual heavyweight in her own right.[25]

By the time Hunt was ready to rejoin her husband at his diplomatic post in the summer of 1907, it was not to Madagascar that she would sail but to France. Billy Hunt's faithful defense of American interests in the French colony helped him obtain one of the rare postings in Europe offered to a diplomat of color: a notable achievement, but perhaps not as glamorous as it might seem at first glance. Hunt was appointed consul general in St. Étienne, a fairly grimy center of coal mining, arms manufacturing, and textiles production in central-eastern France. If St. Étienne was not terribly picturesque, however, its citizens were welcoming, and Consul Hunt thrived at his new post. When his wife Ida arrived to join him, she was similarly granted a stately reception. Altogether, the Hunts would remain in St. Étienne for twenty years.[26]

In France, and particularly during lengthy visits stateside, Ida maintained contact with her African American friends, many of whom were growing frustrated with the deteriorating state of race relations in the United States. Mary Church Terrell kept her abreast of the news. So too did Du Bois, who had befriended Ida sometime in the late nineteenth century (and apparently based one of the admirable female characters in his first novel on her as well). While home in 1910, Hunt joined the newly constituted NAACP, just as Du Bois was launching its monthly magazine, the *Crisis*.[27]

In France, Hunt also had new opportunities to nurture her interest in women's rights. In 1911 she began following the work of the recently founded French Union for Women's Suffrage. Hunt attended local meetings, including one at which she heard a French legislator who favored suffrage speak about "Woman and Voting Rights" while Hunt scribbled notes on the back of the program: "Press—ridicule, silence . . . Devoted women, men." In the early summer of 1914, Hunt seems to have attended the French Union's annual meeting in nearby Lyon, which was presided over by Marguerite de Witt Schlumberger (who, less than five years later, would convene the Inter-Allied Women's Conference). Before Hunt could nurture these ties to French suffragists, however, German troops crossed into Belgium, and France was at war.[28]

World War I and the Color Line

Life grew busier for Ida Gibbs Hunt with the outbreak of the Great War. Working with the French Red Cross, Hunt helped settle Belgian refugees in southeastern France, paid visits to wounded soldiers at the local hospital, knit warm clothes for those at the front, and gathered up linens for bandages. Like most Western Europeans in 1914, Hunt found Germany's invasion of Belgium and the "outrages" perpetrated against the fleeing population particularly galling. "It's enough to make one's heart sick to read of them," she wrote in a long, emotional letter to Terrell in April 1915, "and to hear of them first hand, as I often do, it's worse." But Hunt also recognized the irony of Belgium's new international status as the chief victim of German aggression. "I can't help but notice this inconsistency in protesting against the overrunning and annexing of weaker nations when that is what they all have been doing in Africa and other countries for nearly a century," she confessed. "Even poor Belgium is reaping what [King] Leopold sowed."[29]

What moved Hunt more than the fate of the German-occupied Belgian kingdom was the far-reaching global effort under way to rescue it. In a heartfelt but somewhat clumsy poem titled "To Belgium," written in 1914, Hunt likened Belgian war victims to the homeless baby Jesus, who began his life a refugee of sorts. But just as Jesus had been welcomed into the world by "Wise Men come from every clime," Belgium had attracted, in her defense, soldiers from across the world: "The dusky sons of Afric's soil / And India's mosque-clad hills, / And Asia's incense laden crests, / From mountain, plain and sea, / In mingled ranks with Europe's best, / Offer their all to thee." Hunt echoed this observation, in less poetic terms, in a 1915 letter home to Terrell. Colonial soldiers' participation in the Great War, she wrote, "must change things somewhat for the darker races. [The imperial powers] must recognize and recompense some of those who fought with and for them."[30]

Hunt's observations were apt. When the European imperial powers declared war in 1914, they did so in the name of their colonial subjects as well as their own citizens. The British sent over 130,000 Indian troops to the Western Front. The French relied even more heavily on *troupes indigènes*, nearly half a million of whom were recruited (under widely differing degrees of coercion) from North and West Africa, Madagascar, and Indochina. Hunt's poem "To Belgium," written early in the conflict, drew attention to colonial soldiers' sacrifice and to the war's potential to foster interracial cooperation and equality.[31]

By late 1917 Hunt had a personal as well as a humanitarian interest in the well-being of Allied soldiers. Her brother-in-law, Napoleon Marshall (the husband of her beloved sister Hattie), had enlisted as an infantry captain in the all-black 369th Regiment out of New York, which shipped out to France in December 1917. That winter, the Allies were desperate for reinforcements, but when Napoleon Marshall and the 369th arrived in

Europe, the general in charge of the American Expeditionary Force refused to send the regiment into battle. He, like much of the U.S. Army brass, was opposed to arming black men to shoot white soldiers. Most of the 200,000 African American troops sent overseas in World War I were restricted to grueling heavy labor far from the front lines. The 369th was an exception. Attached directly to the French Army (and thus circumventing the American military's segregationist policies), the soldiers of the 369th saw more action than any other American unit during the brutal spring offensives of 1918. Celebrated for their courage (as well as for their band, led by the incomparable jazz musician James Reese Europe) the 369th was immortalized as the Harlem Hellfighters.[32]

Hunt's brother-in-law fought bravely with the 369th. He was among the countless African Americans who saw in the First World War a means of demonstrating black men's courage, responsibility, and leadership: in other words, of reclaiming their manhood in a racist society that demeaned, infantilized, and, in the most extreme cases, murdered them. Soldiers like Marshall also hoped desperately that their loyalty and bravery would convince white Americans to dismantle the laws and customs that prevented African American men from exercising their democratic rights. The American military wasted little time dashing such hopes. Not only did it keep black and white units segregated, it also issued a secret memo to French officers (who were effusive in their praise of the 369th), reminding them, "the black man is regarded by the white American as an inferior being." Intimate contact with or commendation of black soldiers was not advised.[33]

Racial discrimination was no less pronounced back in the United States during World War I, as Mary Church Terrell discovered when she went looking for a wartime job with the federal government. Despite the fact that Woodrow Wilson had managed to woo a sizable number of African Americans during his first presidential run, after taking office, Wilson remained true to his southern Democratic origins and authorized the segregation of federal office buildings. Throughout his presidency, Wilson proved stubbornly resistant to addressing America's festering racial wounds. Instead, he stripped most high-level black government appointees of their jobs (Terrell's and Hunt's husbands counting among the few survivors), endorsed the racist film *The Birth of a Nation* (with its heroic representation of the Ku Klux Klan), and ordered American troops to occupy the black Republic of Haiti. He also resisted authorizing federal troops to check the lynch mobs and racially motivated rioters hounding African American citizens. Terrell harbored few illusions about Wilson or his administration, but she also knew that with American boys shipping off to war, the government needed clerks and typists. Terrell applied.[34]

At first, Terrell's federal employment seemed to go smoothly. As requested, Terrell reported for work at the War Risk Insurance Bureau. The office, she observed upon arrival, seemed to be staffed exclusively by white women. It took Terrell's distracted boss two months to notice that his new employee's complexion was somewhat darker than that of her coworkers, at which point he abruptly fired her. Terrell was angry and humiliated, but fearful of costing her husband his judicial appointment, she (uncharacteristically) held her tongue. Assigned next to the Census Bureau with other "colored" female clerks, she enjoyed her work until an order was issued banning African American women in her hall from using the nearest women's bathroom, which had been redesignated as "whites only." Fed up with the federal government, Terrell resigned, taking a job instead teaching French to young black men at Howard University. After the armistice, she agreed once again to sign on to the federal payroll, this time accepting a job with the War Camp Community Service, which had money to organize recreation centers for working-class girls, including in African American communities.[35]

Terrell was settling into her new position when she received a letter from the American Women's Peace Party, formed during World War I and affiliated with the Women's International League for Peace and Freedom. The WILPF, the letter informed her, was working diligently to gather women together at an international meeting to coincide with the Paris Peace Conference. The Women's Peace Party wished to invite Terrell to join the American delegation. Much was still up in the air, including the place of the meeting (somewhere in Europe) as well as the date ("either the first week in February, or early in May, or at some date between these two," the letter helpfully suggested). Appealing to Terrell's "love of humanity," the Women's Peace Party secretary politely requested her rapid reply.[36]

Terrell probably knew little about the WILPF before receiving the invitation, although she already had a decade-old relationship with Jane Addams, who was heading the American delegation. The WILPF had been born out of a meeting of Western suffragists during World War I. Against all odds, these women had managed to overcome wartime animosities and unite at The Hague in 1915 to reaffirm their commitment to women's rights and to demand a negotiated peace. At The Hague, feminist pacifists also pledged to reconvene at war's end to allow women a voice in the peace settlement. When the Allies decided to locate the postwar negotiations in Paris, however, the WILPF decided to move its meeting to neutral Zurich so that women from the defeated powers could participate. Unlike the Inter-Allied Women's Conference in Paris, the WILPF Congress in Zurich deliberately sought to challenge wartime animosities and reintegrate women from Germany and Austria-Hungary into the international women's movement.[37]

Although the invitation to join the American delegation warned, "this is not an easy journey which we are inviting you to undertake under crowded conditions, in winter, to war-worn countries," Terrell jumped at the opportunity. African Americans, she well knew, had done as much as anyone to make certain the Allies prevailed in the war for democracy. Now that victory was won, it was time to demand that the peacemakers make good on their promises. The next several months were consumed in a flurry of planning, even as the U.S. State Department (nervous about what the women were up to) shrank the number of passports it would authorize from thirty down to fifteen. Terrell made the short list. Her white collaborators felt that Terrell's participation was "terribly important for the colored people of America . . . for the women of America and for the cause of Permanent Peace."[38]

Over the next three months, Terrell scrambled to finish her work for the War Camp Community Service, arrange for care for her children (her mother came to the rescue), purchase a berth on a steamer, and apply for a passport. The last of these was no small task. The WILPF sent a letter in late March 1919 warning her, "Don't delay half a day," and reminding her to bring to the passport office a signed letter from Jane Addams attesting to her participation in the conference and her husband, Judge Terrell, "for identification purposes and to prove your citizenship." On April 2 Terrell cleared her schedule, waited in line, and, by day's end, counted herself among the rare recipients of a passport and visa to Europe in 1919. Today Terrell's 1919 passport sits in the Library of Congress in Washington, D.C.: a relic of a remarkable woman in a remarkable era. A collage of stamps and visas traces Terrell's journey across France, Switzerland, and England, while the worn pages and chaotic collection of signatures serve as a vivid reminder of the practical difficulties and sheer adventure of traveling to Europe at the end of the First World War.[39]

Mary Church Terrell, American delegate to the Zurich Congress, in her 1919 passport photo. (Mary Church Terrell Papers, Library of Congress, Manuscript Division)

The photo affixed to Terrell's passport is an amazing artifact unto itself. As a public figure, Mary Church Terrell took any number of studio portraits. In all these other, better-known photographs, Terrell is impeccably dressed in high-buttoned collars, delicate lace, and rich velvet; her poses are stiff and formal, and every hair on her head is carefully tamed. Such professional photographs were an important means by which members of the black elite (including Terrell) embodied respectability and countered racist caricatures of African Americans in popular culture. What these portraits seldom reveal, however, are the personalities behind the image. Terrell's passport photo is different. She is dressed in a practical, unadorned jacket with wisps of hair betraying whatever style she had sought to impose at the start of the day. Only a simple strand of pearls hints at her class status. Terrell stares directly into the camera and looks, frankly, tired: like a woman who has just moved heaven and earth to cut through all the necessary red tape to board a ship to Europe. Seven days later that is exactly what she would do. Catching the *Noordam* in New York with her fellow WILPF delegates, Terrell steamed off across the Atlantic.

The Pan-African Congress of 1919

In late 1918, as Mary Church Terrell was exchanging letters with American WILPF members about joining their delegation to Zurich, Ida Gibbs Hunt was engaged in a separate, cross-Atlantic correspondence, similarly designed to ensure that people of color would be represented at the peace negotiations. From her diplomatic residence in southeastern France, Hunt took out a yellow notepad and shaped an appeal to her friend W.E.B. Du Bois.

With the passing away of Du Bois's primary rival, Booker T. Washington, in 1915, and with the circulation numbers of the *Crisis*, the monthly magazine Du Bois edited for the NAACP, edging over the fifty thousand mark, Du Bois's authority among African Americans was arguably unmatched as World War I drew to a close. His appeal to black Americans to "close ranks" with whites and support the war effort had, admittedly, been controversial, but now that America had won the war, Du Bois was in an unparalleled position to leverage the patriotism of African Americans for tangible progress toward racial equality. To do so effectively, he thought, he would need to deliver the demand for racial justice in person to the peacemakers.

Ida Gibbs Hunt was fully on board with this plan, and she wrote to Du Bois to tell him that his presence was needed in Paris not only to champion the interests of African Americans but also to ensure that the peacemakers resolve the "colonial side" of global relations "in the interest of the natives as well as of Europe." Acutely aware of how rapidly plans for a peace conference were progressing, she urged Du Bois to "act quickly" and "come over soon." She also pledged her unqualified assistance once he arrived.[40]

Scarcely a week after Hunt posted her letter (and almost surely before it reached New York), Du Bois boarded a ship to cross the Atlantic. With the blessings of the NAACP, he departed for Europe with three vaguely defined goals in mind: to collect documentation on the experiences of African American troops in the Great War, to represent people of African descent at the peace conference, and to convene a separate Pan-African Congress to unite the "darker races" of the world around a common agenda.

On December 11, 1918, when Du Bois arrived at the Montparnasse train station in Paris, Ida Gibbs Hunt was waiting on the platform.

For Hunt, who had quietly nurtured anti-imperialist sentiments for over a decade, the Paris Peace Conference was a transformative moment: a catalyzing event that propelled her onto the global stage as a political actor in her own right. No longer relegated to the secondary status of a diplomat's wife, Hunt threw herself into making Du Bois's dream of a Pan-African Congress a reality. But what role, exactly, did Hunt play in shaping the Pan-African Congress of 1919? Most accounts of the congress mention her in passing, if at all. Yet W.E.B. Du Bois depended on Hunt's linguistic skills, her knowledge of the French capital, her political connections, and her tireless capacity for organizational work. Although the documentary record is spotty, a strong case can be made that without Ida Gibbs Hunt, the Pan-African Congress of 1919 might never have occurred at all.[41]

To begin with, despite Du Bois's bold proclamation in the *Crisis*, "Every Negro should speak French," he himself spoke the language poorly. Time and again, Du Bois was saved by Hunt's fluency in the diplomatic language *du jour*, beginning on the day he arrived, worn out from travel and without a place to lay his head. Parisian hotels were filling rapidly in December 1918, but Hunt proved an adept travel agent, finding them both lodging at a reasonably priced hotel near the center of the city.[42]

With rooms secured, the two got down to work. Planning an international conference in short order was no simple task, not least because the governments of France, England, and the United States were united in their opposition to providing Africans and African Americans any kind of political platform in Paris. The American State Department, which was determined to prevent the issue of American racial segregation from being raised in the peace negotiations, had already begun denying passports to anyone who declared his or her intention to attend the Pan-African meeting. In Paris, the Secret Service trailed Du Bois dusk to dawn. By Du Bois's own account, "had it not been for one circumstance, [the Pan-African Congress] would have utterly failed."[43]

The circumstance to which Du Bois alluded was the timely offer of help from France's black legislator from the African colony of Senegal, Blaise Diagne. During the war Diagne had cemented the trust of French political elites by recruiting hundreds of thousands of colonial soldiers and laborers for the war effort, earning for himself the title of high commissioner of colonial troops. Now, upon Dubois's request, Diagne capitalized on his influence with Prime Minister Georges Clemenceau to secure permission to hold a Pan-African Congress.

Diagne's collaboration was critical to the congress's success, but how did Du Bois meet the Senegalese deputy in the first place? In one of Du Bois's accounts, Diagne seems to appear out of nowhere: a gift from providence. In another, Du Bois claims he simply knocked on Diagne's door. More likely, Ida Gibbs Hunt brought the two men together. Hunt's husband had befriended Diagne years earlier in Madagascar, when the young Senegalese was serving with the French-Malagasy customs service. Hunt may well have drawn on that friendship on Du Bois's behalf. It is certainly the case that after the Pan-African Congress was over, Hunt would often serve as an interlocutor between Du Bois and Diagne, not only because of her fluency in French but also because the two men firmly disagreed about what was in Africa's best interests, and each expected the other to bend to his will.[44]

Once the French government granted authorization for the Congress, the real work began: lining up meeting space, recruiting participants, and defining an agenda. On January 1, 1919, Du Bois drafted a two-page memo outlining what he saw to be the "chief work" to be undertaken: study the "condition of Negroes throughout the world," gather policy statements regarding "the Negro race from the Great Powers," make certain Africans' needs were met by the emerging League of Nations, and champion the "future development of the Negro race." Having drafted this broad outline of a plan, Du Bois promptly left Paris for the military front to meet with African American troops. By and large, the Pan-African Congress would come together in his absence. Du Bois would later admit to receiving vital aid from a female collaborator in planning the Congress, but the woman he named was not Hunt but a French woman named Madame Paul Calmann-Lévy, "a quiet, charming woman" and the widow of a prominent Parisian publisher who championed the Congress among French and Belgian officials who attended her Parisian salon. As for Ida Gibbs Hunt's indispensable labors, he hardly mentions them at all. It is a curious oversight, for as Hunt's biographer notes, "during Du Bois's intermittent excursions away from Paris that winter, Gibbs Hunt staffed the organization's new offices herself, handled its correspondence, contacted and cajoled potential supporters, confirmed participants and facilities, and otherwise kept the reigns of control in her own capable hands."[45]

It was thus in no small part due to Hunt's efforts that the three-day-long Pan-African Congress was able to open on February 19, 1919, at the Grand Hotel in Paris with just shy of sixty participants in attendance. The largest contingents hailed from the United States, Europe, and the Caribbean, but a handful of African delegates participated as well. The mood was upbeat and the tone decidedly moderate. Diagne opened the Congress by praising the French civilizing mission in Africa, proposing it as a model for the gradual emancipation of the continent. Many spoke expectantly of a future of racial unity. The delegates called on the League of Nations to protect the peoples of Africa from exploitation and to allow them a "voice in government to the extent their development permits." They also agreed to establish a Pan-African Association to continue the work of the congress. Four delegates were appointed to the executive board: Du Bois, Diagne, an official from the London-based African Progress Union, and Ida Gibbs Hunt. They planned to meet again in two years' time.[46]

Indispensable in the planning stages (and counted on for her ongoing work after it was over), during the three days of the Pan-African Congress

A session of the Pan-African Congress, Paris, February 1919, published in the *Crisis*, May 1919, 32. Ida Gibbs Hunt is in the foreground in a dark dress with a white collar. W.E.B Du Bois is seated in front of her in the center. Blaise Diagne is seated at the table (*second from the left*). (Moorland-Spingarn Research Center, Manuscript Division, Howard University, Washington, D.C.)

itself, Ida Gibbs Hunt faded into the background. She offered running translation for the illustrious men who ran the show, but she did not address the congress itself. Was it Hunt's status as a woman that prevented her from playing a more prominent role?

Relatively few women attended the Pan-African Congress of 1919, although not for want of trying. Ida B. Wells-Barnett, the famous anti-lynching activist, and the entrepreneur and philanthropist Madame C. J. Walker (by some accounts, the wealthiest self-made woman in America) both were denied passports by the U.S. State Department. The latter was purportedly told her application had been rejected "because she was a woman," although race was clearly a factor in the State Department's refusal to authorize travel. Several other African American women already in France in 1919 did manage to attend, most notably Addie Waites Hunton and Helen Curtis. Hunton and Curtis constituted two of the three African American women brought to France during the war by the Young Men's Christian Association (YMCA) to oversee recreational activities for the tens of thousands of African American soldiers during their time on leave. For over a year the three women worked tirelessly to ease the burdens of service for African American men in France, while proudly representing "the womanhood of our race." Now, after the war, they were eager to contribute to the Pan-African battle against racial oppression. Hunton even managed to secure a spot on the program, speaking "of the importance of women in the world's reconstruction and regeneration of today, and of the necessity seeking their cooperation and counsel."[47]

One last woman was accorded the opportunity to speak to the Pan-African delegates: Julie Siegfried, a prominent French suffragist, president of the National Council of French Women, and a close collaborator of Marguerite de Witt Schlumberger during the Inter-Allied Women's Conference (which, in mid-February 1919, was just getting under way on the opposite bank of the Seine). Siegfried brought "words of encouragement" from the white Allied suffragists. Speaking for her sex, Siegfried affirmed to the Pan-African delegates, "no one could appreciate better than women the struggle for broader rights and liberties."[48]

Little did she know that sitting in the very room was a woman who had overseen much of the work and yet received none of the credit for the congress in session. Did Ida Gibbs Hunt resent her exclusion from the limelight of the Pan-African Congress? It is possible that Hunt was content to take a backseat to Du Bois, Diagne, and the other dynamic male leaders running the show in Paris that winter. But Hunt was a feminist as well as a pan-Africanist. If she did not seek glory, she did demand respect, as Du Bois would learn the hard way in the months and years ahead. In the meantime, Du Bois sailed back to America "full of regret that [he] did not get to St. Etienne" before departing. For the time being, the future of pan-Africanism would be distributed between the two sides of the Atlantic, a piece of it in Ida Gibbs Hunt's capable hands.[49]

"The Only Delegate Who Represented the Darker Races of the World"

On Easter Sunday, April 20, 1919, well after W.E.B. Du Bois had returned to New York and Ida Gibbs Hunt to St. Étienne, Mary Church Terrell arrived in France with the American WILPF delegation. Owing to this unfortunate timing, Terrell missed the opportunity to join in the history-making Pan-African Congress; nevertheless, in April the peace negotiations were still going full swing. Terrell's time in Europe would not be wasted.

Setting foot on French soil, Terrell breathed a palpable sigh of relief. "How I love France and the French people!" she would declare to anyone who would listen. For Terrell, the indignities of daily life in Jim Crow America seemed to magically melt away in *la belle France*: "Goethe says that everybody has a fatherland and a motherland," she would later reflect. "My motherland is dear, broadminded France, in which people with dark complexions are not discriminated against on account of their color." Although Terrell was particularly rhapsodic in her celebration of French inclusiveness, she was hardly alone: African Americans who came to France during and after World War I commonly sang the nation's praises. Du Bois had similarly declared France to be "the only white civilization in the world to which color-hatred is not only unknown, but absolutely unintelligible." Inspired by such proclamations, in the 1920s a small but visible African American community of jazz musicians, writers, and artists (including music hall legend Josephine Baker and poet Langston Hughes) would flee America's oppressive racial politics and seek refuge in "color-blind" France.[50]

If such a national portrait seems too good to be true, it was. Even at the time, Terrell recognized that France's embrace of talented African Americans might not extend equally to the millions of black African subjects of the French Empire. To check her impressions, Terrell resolved to ask any black man she met on the street how the French treated him. Those she spoke to seemed confused. One explained patiently: "Mais, Madame, les Français nous aiment!" (But Ma'am, the French love us!). Blaise Diagne further reinforced Terrell's idealistic view of the republic when he invited her to attend a session of the French Chamber of Deputies during her stay in Paris. There she witnessed France's five or six legislators from Africa and the Antilles "mingling indiscriminately" with their white colleagues, noting, "every now and then one would place his hand familiarly on the other's shoulder, just as though there were no difference in race or color at all." Coming from the United States, where African Americans had been effectively chased from the House of Representatives decades earlier, this must have been a remarkable sight.[51]

But while France widely touted the ideals of liberty, equality, and fraternity in its armed forces, and while it allowed a small percentage of its colonial subjects to elect representatives, in fact, France's ideals were routinely compromised by racial and cultural prejudice. Most indigenous officers were prevented from rising very far in military ranks, and only a tiny portion of African troops found their service to the republic rewarded with citizenship. Conscription, moreover, had provoked rebellion in parts of the empire, which the French suppressed with a firm hand. Despite these limitations, in the eyes of African American visitors in 1919, France's assimilationist ideals, its willingness to accord men like Diagne the highest honors, its open embrace of African American soldiers (even, or perhaps especially, by white French women), and its atmosphere of racial tolerance all stood in stark contrast to overt American racial prejudice and violence.[52]

Given this background, it was all the more galling when Terrell landed in France, only to realize that her white American travel companions were departing for the battlefields of northern France without her. Had American racial discrimination followed her across the Atlantic? Terrell, who was acutely aware of her minority status in the international women's movement, was careful not to hold the white WILPF delegates accountable for their rebuff, either at the time or in her memoir years later. Instead, she chose to believe that delegates had unintentionally raised a red flag by asking "the officials of the Visitors' Bureau in Paris whether there would be any objections to having a colored woman accompany them on the trip." Whether this inquiry was actually made or the white women simply assumed that Terrell's presence might raise eyebrows made little difference. Terrell was excluded.

Although the rejection hurt, Terrell put her time alone in Paris to good use, securing an appointment with one of the Japanese plenipotentiaries to the peace conference: Baron Nobuaki Makino. On his way to Paris in early January 1919, Makino and the other Japanese delegates had met with African American community leaders who urged the Japanese to use the peace negotiations as a forum "to remove prejudice and race discrimination in all nations of the earth." Among those forwarding this argument was an outspoken black journalist named William Monroe Trotter who, though denied a passport to travel to Europe in 1919, managed to sneak across the Atlantic by hiring himself out as a cook on a steamship. Once in Paris, Trotter met up with the Japanese, extracting a promise that they would aid black Americans in getting their concerns before the peace conference. Terrell tracked Trotter down in Paris, and most likely it was he who set up her meeting with Makino. The highly unusual tête-à-tête that ensued brought together the diplomatic son of a once-great samurai family and the feminist daughter of once-enslaved parents to discuss the prospects of racial equality in a new world order.[53]

In the early weeks of the peace conference, Makino and the Japanese delegation had proposed that the peacemakers include a clause in the covenant of the new League of Nations prohibiting member-states from discriminating on the basis of race. From the beginning, the Japanese "racial equality clause" was highly controversial. Representatives of the British Dominions were firmly opposed, with the Australian prime minister proclaiming it more likely that he would walk into a French cabaret buck naked than attach his signature to such a provision. Woodrow Wilson was no less opposed. In April, just days before Terrell's arrival in Paris, Wilson overrode a majority vote of the League of Nations Commission in favor of the Japanese amendment, insisting (without any supporting evidence) that because of the potency of the minority opposition, the question of racial equality had to be shelved. Terrell shared Makino's frustration at Wilson's diplomatic sleight of hand, and she told him personally "how shocked and sorry I was that racial equality . . . had been denied Japan." The peacemakers' refusal to encode racial equality in the covenant of the new world government further strengthened Terrell's resolve to ask fellow feminists to address the "race problem" when they met in Zurich a few weeks later.[54]

Terrell also decided racism would not stand in the way of her desire to visit the battlefields of the First World War. Jane Addams's description of the devastated region of northern France, recounted at a luncheon Terrell prepared for the white women upon their return to Paris, only emphasized the galling unfairness of her exclusion from the trip. "There had not been time to gather the dead into cemeteries," Addams reported, "but at Vimy Ridge colored troops from the United States were digging rows of graves for the bodies being drawn toward them in huge trucks." If the segregated military was willing to entrust African Americans with the laborious work of burying the dead, surely America's black delegate to the WILPF Congress should be able to pay her respects. "I made up my mind," she said, "that I would do my level best to get a chance to go." Terrell went to the American Visitors Bureau in person to submit a request for a tour, and an obliging redheaded army captain told her to be prepared to leave on the first day of May. When the date for departure came, however, Terrell received a message that the trip had been canceled. With the WILPF Congress about to open in Zurich, Terrell laid aside her plans for the time being, frustrated but undeterred.[55]

The WILPF Congress, which met in Zurich from May 12 to 17, 1919, was a historic event. Although the end of the war had released international energies of all sorts, virtually all the conferences, congresses, and

American delegation to the WILPF Congress in Zurich, May 1919. Mary Church Terrell is standing in the center back (*seventh from right*) in a dark coat with a white collar. Jane Addams is seated in the front row (*third from right*). (WILPF Papers, Special Collections and Archives, University of Colorado Boulder Libraries)

meetings of that year involved the Allied powers or neutral supplicants coming to seek the Allies' favor. In Zurich, women of the Central Powers (Germany, Austria, Hungary, and Bulgaria) were able to meet with women from the Entente (Great Britain, the United States, France, Italy, Romania, and Australia) as well as neutral countries to craft a common agenda for a just and sustainable peace. The congress rippled with expectation and delivered its share of drama. "Attending this Congress," Terrell would later write, "was as interesting, as illuminating and as gratifying an experience as it falls to the lot of the average woman to enjoy."[56]

But while most who reported on the WILPF Congress either celebrated or condemned the international spectrum of its participants, what struck Terrell most was the congress's homogeneity. "I was about to say that women from all over the world were present," Terrell would later write, "But on sober, second thought it is more truthful to say that women from all over the white world were present." Referring back to the international women's meeting she had attended in Berlin in 1904, she further stated, "For the second time in my life it was my privilege to represent, not only the colored women of the United States, but the whole continent of Africa as well." Indeed, given the absence of women from China, India, or Japan, Terrell ultimately saw it has her responsibility to represent "the women of all the non-white countries in the world." A daunting prospect, to be sure, but by 1919 Terrell had established a long record of enlightening white audiences about black Americans' travails and achievements. At the WILPF Congress of 1919, Terrell again served as an ambassador for her race, both to the congregated representatives of white womanhood and to the international journalists who had come to report on the spectacle.[57]

Terrell spoke twice before the Zurich Congress, both times to insist on the centrality of racial equality to the broader goals of peace and freedom. The first opportunity came midway through the congress, when Jane Addams asked Terrell if she would be willing to address the assembled body of women on behalf of the American delegation the following night. Why the American women chose Terrell for this honor is not clear (although it seems entirely possible that they were nursing guilty consciences for having excluded her from their battlefield pilgrimage). In any case, Terrell accepted the offer, determined to make the most of a rare public platform to advance the cause of racial justice within the international women's movement. Knowing that much goodwill could be gained from delivering her speech in the language of the host city, Terrell immediately began drafting the second major speech of her life in German. "Wednesday night," she says, "I did nothing but read and reread that speech until dawn."[58]

Still hard at work on Thursday morning, Terrell was obliged to set her speech aside for several hours when she learned that a resolution she had submitted for consideration by the congress had been placed on the agenda. The WILPF delegates debated two different types of resolutions that May. The first included recommendations for restoring justice and maintaining peace, to be delivered to the peacemakers in Paris as soon as the congress was over. Terrell's was one of a second set of resolutions designed to serve as general policy positions for the infant WILPF organization. Her resolution read: "We believe no human being should be deprived of an education, prevented from earning a living, debarred from any legitimate pursuit in which he wishes to engage or be subjected to humiliation of various kinds on account of race, color, or creed." In stark contrast to the Japanese racial equality clause, rejected in Paris, Terrell's race resolution evoked little controversy among the radical WILPF women and passed by a unanimous vote. "It was a proud and gratifying moment in my life when I read that resolution in person in Zürich, Switzerland," Terrell would later recount. "The only delegate who represented the dark races of the world had a chance to speak in their behalf."[59]

Later that same night, Terrell delivered the plenary address to a packed house "in a magnificent old cathedral [St. Peter's Church] in which women had never been allowed to speak before." From a raised pulpit looking down at the arrayed female delegates, curious Zurich residents, and international journalists, Terrell drew a deep breath and in her practiced German, opened by drawing the crowd's attention to her racial status: "I am the only woman at this congress," she stated, "who has a drop of colored blood in her veins." As such, Terrell's speech would emphasize different themes from those raised by earlier speakers, such as reconciliation, suffrage, and disarmament. Instead, Terrell commanded the congress to recognize that the principles it claimed to profess—peace and freedom—could not be understood in the absence of a consideration of race. Offering herself up as an example, she told the gathered crowd that were it not for the American Civil War, she would most likely not have found herself in Zurich speaking to them as a free woman but instead would be "forced to live out the miserable existence of a slave." Terrell's rhetorical approach was smart and deliberate. By identifying immediately as a black woman, subject to all the risks inherent in living in nonwhite skin, Terrell forced her white listeners to confront their own racial biases and preconceptions. And by simultaneously embodying the ideals of civilized womanhood—refined manners, eloquent speaking, and fashionable clothing—she also disrupted their understanding of black racial identity, both in America and around the world.[60]

The primary theme of the congress was peace, and Terrell assured her audience that despite the importance of the Civil War to the history of her people, "No women of the world hate war and seek peace more than the colored women, whether they are in America, Africa, or some island nation." But peace, she said, could not be measured simply by the absence of conflict. "A lasting peace is an impossibility as long as the colored races are subject to injustice." This statement represented the essence of the message Terrell delivered to the WILPF that night. She warned pacifists in the audience not to put much hope in the League of Nations now that the peacemakers had rejected Japan's racial equality clause. Africa, "which has been plundered so relentlessly," was no more likely to benefit from a white man's peace than were the black victims of lynching back in the United States.[61]

Terrell brought her speech to a close with an emotional appeal to women's sensibility and motherhood, imploring "white women of all countries" to "help the children of my race, as well as all the races who do not have white skin." Despite such reassuring maternalist rhetoric, Terrell's speech was not free of controversy. American delegate and incoming international WILPF secretary Emily Greene Balch quietly seethed as she listened to Terrell describe how she owed her freedom to a war. Even worse, Terrell used part of her speech to praise the African American soldiers "who with astonishing sacrifice and enthusiasm" crossed the ocean in 1917 and 1918 in defense of democracy, despite any assurance that "the sad circumstances under which they and their loved ones lived would ever be improved." To Balch, such statements constituted "too much militarism." Speaking "very sharply," Balch reprimanded Terrell the following day. In contrast to this unpleasant incident, however, the vast majority of the Zurich delegates greeted her speech with long and warm applause. "For once in my life I was satisfied with my effort," Terrell would later confess. To the best of her ability, she had stepped onto the white women's stage and defended the basic principle that peace and freedom, sovereignty and democracy, were empty words until they extended to all people regardless of the color of their skin.[62]

Upon the conclusion of the Zurich Congress, Terrell returned to Paris for a few more weeks, traveling by way of St. Étienne, where finally she was able to catch up with her old friend Ida Gibbs Hunt. The trip turned into something of an adventure. Terrell purchased her Zurich-to-Paris ticket on the understanding that she would be able to dismount the train midroute and take the planned side trip to St. Étienne. After boarding, however, the conductor told her it was strictly forbidden to leave the train before reaching her final destination. A group of French soldiers who overheard the dispute came to the rescue: "It was an outrage, they said, or words to that effect. The idea of the conductor daring to keep me from visiting the friend of my childhood!" When they reached the midway station, the soldiers "snatched up (her) two suitcases" and helped her rapidly dismount, telling her where and when she needed to catch the next train. It was 2:00 A.M. when Terrell arrived in St. Étienne. "The next morning," Terrell said, "I surprised my classmate and her distinguished husband." The two old friends had stories to share: from the Pan-African Congress in February to the WILPF Congress in May, Terrell and Hunt had been at the very center of the international battle for racial justice in 1919.[63]

Terrell was back in the French capital as the Allied leaders hammered out the final provisions of the Versailles Treaty. By that time, she had given up any hope that the peace conference would address the seemingly intractable problem of racial oppression, but she was all the more determined not to leave for home before concluding her own personal battle against American discrimination in France. Upon arriving back in Paris, she immediately returned to the Visitor's Bureau to reissue her request for a battlefield tour. Terrell encountered the same redheaded captain at the front desk, but this time the officer was rude and dismissive, according her none of the courtesy he had extended before she left for Zurich. "The moment I began to talk with him," Terrell wrote, "I knew the awful secret had leaked out. Either he was using his own eyes more effectively than he had at first, or he had learned from others the damning fact of my African descent." Told the Visitors Bureau was no longer arranging tours (a blatant lie), Terrell grew indignant, accused the officer in charge of discrimination, and followed up with a letter to his superior, steaming, "*Even* tho I am not white, I *like* to be treated with a little courtesy and consideration." By the following day, somebody had second thoughts. An African American officer was brought in to handle the situation, and he offered to give Terrell a personal tour of the devastated region of northern France. "I was glad I had struggled against the exhibition of race prejudice shown by my countrymen in France and finally had an opportunity to see [the battlefields] for myself. . . . It was an object lesson in the horrors of war which I can never forget."[64]

Mandates, Race Riots, and the Red Summer of 1919

Like most women who came to Europe in 1919, Ida Gibbs Hunt and Mary Church Terrell left Paris disillusioned with the peace process but empowered by the experience of championing their principles in the global arena. For both women, the failure of the peace settlement to address the question of racial equality was its greatest shortcoming. The peacemakers' refusal to include a "racial equality clause" in the Covenant of the League of Nations underscored a broader unwillingness to confront, let alone address, inequities stemming from the long history of slavery and imperialism that would continue to imperil global peace and stability for decades to come.

World War I did not make the world safe for democracy in Africa. It did not even live up to the moderate demands of the Pan-African Congress to protect indigenous populations from exploitation. The Mandate System, formalized in article 22 of the League of Nations Covenant, placed former German colonies in Africa under French, British, Belgian, or white South African tutelage. Despite treaty language insisting that the "well being and development of such peoples form a sacred trust of civilization," the diplomatic maneuver amounted to little more than an imperial land grab. Throughout the European colonies in Africa, white rule continued unabated. It was enough to lead Ida Gibbs Hunt—once hopeful that the war would usher in a more equitable world order—to sour on the League of Nations entirely. By 1923 she was declaring that the League of Nations was unlikely to settle the "great questions" of the day because "the Governments saw that the great questions did not get before it." In Africa, colonial nationalism would simmer below the surface, only to boil over after World War II.[65]

African Americans' patriotic service during World War I and advocacy on behalf of racial minorities at the peace conference did little to advance racial justice in the United States either. On the contrary, during the Red Summer of 1919, nearly a dozen American cities and counties were wracked by mob violence directed at black war veterans and civilians. Some of the worst attacks took place in July in Mary Church Terrell's own Washington, D.C. There, unsubstantiated rumors of the assault of a white woman by an African American man led the city's police chief to call up a posse of over a thousand white auxiliary forces to aid in the manhunt. White citizens' associations, unsatisfied by the police response, called for the suspect to be lynched. Over the next couple of nights, goaded on by the press, local white service men took to the streets with clubs, beating up black residents at random. The sizable black population of the District of Columbia—sick of daily abuse and radicalized by wartime rhetoric and experiences—fought back. By the time Woodrow Wilson called in federal troops, somewhere between thirty and forty people had been killed.[66]

Against this backdrop of ongoing violence against black Americans, Terrell returned to the United States and denounced the League of Nations and its purported promise of enlightened stewardship over oppressed people of color. We are told, she would write in 1920, "that Article 22 [creating the Mandate system] extends the Emancipation Proclamation of Lincoln to the whole world. I would like to ask . . . how any article can extend the Proclamation of Lincoln to the whole world when liberty, freedom, and equality of opportunities are not extended to colored people right here in the United States." The peace settlement did little to nothing for people of African descent, but it did help draw together American civil rights activists and European, Caribbean, and African colonial nationalists for the longer fight that lay ahead. Women—including Mary Church Terrell and Ida Gibbs Hunt—would play a central role in building this new, trans-Atlantic movement for racial justice.[67]

On Being a "Colored Woman in a White World"

The peacemakers' stubborn deafness to the pleas of the nonwhite world underlined the need for civil rights advocates to redouble their fight. Uplift work within the African American community no longer appeared a sufficient response to racial injustice. After 1919 Hunt and Terrell, along with hundreds of African American women, grew more radical and more internationalist in their outlook as they sought the most effective means of championing racial equality. Their activism is an important, if often overlooked, legacy of the peace conference.

The Pan-African movement provided a natural home for internationally minded activists like Ida Gibbs Hunt. The Pan-African Association, which Hunt helped to establish at the end of the 1919 congress, sought to champion the needs of people of color by linking the problem of racial discrimination in the United States to the broader exploitation of people of African descent at home and in the diaspora. Through periodic international meetings and ongoing propaganda, the leader of the movement, W.E.B. Du Bois, hoped to pressure the world's imperial powers to live up to their professed civilizing ideals and work toward self-government in their colonies. Looking back, this gradualist pan-African vision appears cautious, conservative even, especially when compared to the alternative being championed by Du Bois's chief interwar rival, Jamaican intellectual Marcus Garvey, who promoted black separatism and the return to mother Africa. Du Bois's Pan-African Association advocated a more romantic, assimilationist vision of an integrated global order in which racial harmony and social equality prevailed.[68]

It was a vision Ida Gibbs Hunt shared, and in the decade after the Paris Peace Conference, pan-Africanism became her driving passion. As one of the four members of the Pan-African Association's executive board, Hunt pledged her assistance in organizing future congresses. If 1919 had proved nothing else, it was that Du Bois needed Hunt if he wanted the meetings to succeed, but it was a lesson he was slow to learn. One can only wonder what led Du Bois, in the summer of 1921, to send an invitation to the Second Pan-African Congress to Ida's husband Billy Hunt but not to her. Was it the fact that Du Bois had begun depending on another talented woman (the accomplished writer and new literary editor at the *Crisis*, Jessie Fauset) that led Du Bois to overlook his loyal friend and collaborator? Ida certainly did not appreciate being given the cold shoulder, writing chidingly to Du Bois, "How is the Pan-African Congress coming on? I know very little about it except that Mr. Hunt received a notice some time ago."[69]

Du Bois wisely apologized, and a good thing too, as he needed Hunt's impressive set of skills to save the nascent Pan-African Association from implosion. Repeatedly in the early 1920s, Du Bois clashed with Francophone members of the executive board, and Hunt stepped in to mediate. After calmly defusing one such conflict in 1923, Hunt received a grateful letter from the incoming Pan-African secretary, Isaac Béton of Martinique, telling her, "You made such a strong impression on my compatriots last

Sunday. . . . After you left, we praised you to the moon . . . my comrades and I are of the same heart in hoping that you will take on a more active and less hidden role in the new association."[70]

Unknowingly, Béton put his finger precisely on the problem for female anti-imperialist and civil rights activists like Hunt. While their labor was often welcomed behind the scenes, their hard work was seldom rewarded with positions of responsibility, visibility, or power. Such attitudes were hardly unique to the Pan-African movement or civil rights organizations more generally, but the overriding emphasis that African American communities placed on reclaiming black manhood reinforced the widely shared presumption that men should lead and women should support them. Black women with leadership aspirations found their ambitions stymied time and again. Terrell had her own run-in with Du Bois years earlier, when he invited her to serve as a charter member of the NAACP but refused to offer her a public role representing the organization. "I don't care how they dislike me, how nasty, mean and small they are," Terrell huffed to her husband, "they shall not stand between me and the principles I believe with all my heart." Ella Baker would express similar frustrations when working with Dr. Martin Luther King, Jr., years later ("Someone's got to run the mimeographing machine," she would quip bitterly). The cult of the male leader was deeply engrained in the civil rights movement and proved a real obstacle to capable black female activists.[71]

Hunt did learn to speak up for herself more firmly as the years progressed. After having been snubbed in 1921, she debated whether to attend the Third Pan-African Congress two years later, writing to Du Bois, "If I am to be ignored, misunderstood, and mistreated as the last time, it is hardly worth my while." Hunt told Du Bois she was willing to meet with him in Paris in advance of the congress to talk things over: willing, that is, if Du Bois was able to "concede a woman's idea worth anything." Du Bois got the message. In 1923 he accorded Hunt a space in the congress program, affording her the opportunity to put forward her critique of the League of Nations. The problem of sexism, however, never really went away. Four years later she would write to a female friend: "I've worked hard for the P.A.C. [Pan African Congress] without receiving much thanks." Convinced, nonetheless, that she had her own "fine and far reaching convictions . . . on world problems," Hunt would look outside the Pan-African movement for organizations that valued women's ideas as well as their labor.[72]

Hunt's frustrating experience working within the male-dominated Pan-African Association reinforced her belief that women needed political rights and organizations of their own. In a 1922 speech to the students of Dunbar High School (formerly M Street High) in Washington, D.C., she stated bluntly, "[Woman] is no longer satisfied to be treated as a child. . . . She wishes to have a voice and a vote in settling public matters." Ticking off women's recent political gains in Europe and the United States, Hunt cast African American women's rights in a global context. "Even in countries like Egypt, India, and Turkey," she stated, "where women have been kept in seclusion and ignorance, we read that they are taking great interest in national independence and are holding meetings to advance the cause." Hunt spoke at length about French women who had yet to be accorded the vote but who were carrying on their battle for suffrage undeterred. She predicted French women's eventual victory, if for no other reason than because French men needed women's votes "to help establish permanent peace."[73]

This conviction (that men had brought the world to the brink of destruction and women would be needed to save it), as well as simmering frustration with the male leadership of the Pan-African Association, led Hunt to join the Women's International League for Peace and Freedom. In fact, the WILPF attracted a fair number of prominent African American women after World War I, helping solidify its reputation as the international women's organization most open to interracial organizing and most willing to confront questions of colonialism in the interwar decades. Nearly all the women of color who had been active in Paris in 1919 found their way to the WILPF in the years that followed. More than any other interracial women's organization, the WILPF directly tackled the problems of racial injustice and imperial exploitation in the 1920s and 1930s, for example, by sponsoring fact-finding missions to Haiti, Indochina, and China and by founding interracial committees in the United States. Nonetheless, even in this radical women's organization, women of color regularly faced situations where white women's deeply engrained racial biases stood in the way of true collaboration.[74]

Mary Church Terrell, who returned home from Zurich dedicated to the WILPF's mission, soon discovered how quickly WILPF members' high-minded principles could be smothered by racial stereotypes, as the organization got caught up in the notorious postwar "Black Horror on the Rhine" campaign. The news scandal arose in response to the French military's decision in 1920 to deploy colonial troops among the occupation forces in the German Rhineland (an occupation authorized by the peace settlement). German women's groups and journalists immediately denounced the colonial soldiers as black savages, accused them of wantonly raping innocent German *fraüleins*, and demanded they be withdrawn. Although the accusations were unsubstantiated, as tools of propaganda they were pure genius. Almost overnight, sympathetic Western journalists transformed the German people from barbarous Huns (as they had frequently been depicted during the war) into innocent victims of unchecked, black male lust.

Convinced by the propaganda, and distraught at the thought of German girls being thrown in harm's way, several national WILPF sections joined in the protest. The British section of the WILPF was particularly exercised, sponsoring a mass meeting in London on April 27, 1920, that featured the pacifist journalist E. D. Morel. Morel framed his argument for pulling colonial troops out of the Rhineland as a defense of "primitive peoples" forcibly militarized by the West. In fact, the far-from-hidden subtext to his speech was that dark-skinned men constituted a threat to the civilized world and especially to white women. Captivating the crowd with his provocative rhetoric, Morel thundered, "You cannot quarter tens of thousands of Africans, big, powerful, muscular men with fierce, strong natural passions . . . without subjecting thousands of European women to willing, or unwilling, sexual intercourse with them." Horrified, British WILPF members issued a resolution calling on the League of Nations to prohibit importing "primitive" troops into Europe "in the interests of good feeling between all the races of the world and the security of all women." Having taken this "principled" stance, the British WILPF called on other national sections to issue similar protests.[75]

A petition to demand the removal of colonial troops from the Rhineland eventually reached the executive board of the American section of the WILPF, a board on which Terrell sat as the lone woman of color. Many of the American WILPF board members were favorable to signing. Terrell was mortified. Pulling out her typewriter, she composed a lengthy letter to WILPF president Jane Addams explaining in as dispassionate a tone as she could muster: "I can not sign the petition asking for the removal of the black troops because I believe it is a direct appeal to race prejudice." "Because the women of my race have suffered so terribly and so long from assaults committed with impunity by men of all races," Terrell continued, she too felt deep sympathy for any victims of "brutal treatment." But she also saw no evidence that black troops were any more poorly behaved than others (and no such evidence has surfaced since).[76]

There was much Terrell did not put in her letter to Addams; nevertheless, we can imagine the searing memories swirling through her head as she wrote: the brutal lynching of one of her childhood friends in 1892; the vicious personal attacks made on her husband when he was up for reappointment (implying he used his judicial robes to facilitate "Negro" attacks on white women); and, most recently, the mob violence unleashed in Washington, D.C. ("The . . . papers over here gave the cause as attacks on white women," wrote a worried Ida Gibbs Hunt to Terrell. "Is that true? I doubt it.") Nothing in her experience as a black woman in America led Terrell to believe the accusations against French colonial troops, and she told Addams she would rather resign from the WILPF board than sign the petition.[77]

In the end, Addams agreed with Terrell, and the American section declined to endorse the petition. The issue nonetheless continued to fester. Although the WILPF took no stand on the subject at its international conference in 1921, league secretary Emily Greene Balch continued to express sympathy for the Germans "whose feelings have been wounded by what they feel as a studied insult." Terrell's impassioned defense of French colonial troops during the "Black Horror on the Rhine" campaign, much like her plenary speech and race resolution in Zurich in 1919, challenged white WILPF members to live up to their professed ideals.[78]

Neither the WILPF nor the Pan-African Association (both stepchildren of the Paris Peace Conference) provided African American women with the ideal organizational home. In their dual fight against racism and sexism, African American women eventually turned to one another and created new organizations to serve their needs. The International Council of Women of the Darker Races, founded in 1922 by many of the same women active in the Pan-African Association and the WILPF, became the most tangible expression of black women's post–World War I internationalist consciousness. In the 1930s the National Council of Negro Women would also take an avid interest in international affairs. After World War II this organization would work to resuscitate the moribund Pan-African movement and pass its ideals on to a younger generation of leaders. These would include a young Kwame Nkrumah, who would spearhead

Ghana's successful drive for independence in the 1950s and carry the pan-African dream into the postcolonial era.[79]

In the years leading up to the Second World War, as Terrell worked on her memoirs, she would reflect back on the rich, if often times frustrating, experiences that had framed her life up to that date. Trying to encapsulate her struggle for racial and gender equality for future generations, she began: "This is the story of a colored woman living in a white world. It cannot be like a story written by a white woman. A white woman has only one handicap to overcome—that of sex. I have two—both sex and race. I belong to the only group in this country which has two such huge obstacles to surmount." From 1919 to the end of her days (when, as an octogenarian, she would participate in sit-ins and lawsuits and successfully battle the segregation of Washington, D.C., lunch counters right up to the Supreme Court), Terrell did not just work to overcome those obstacles; she fought to demolish them entirely. She, Ida Gibbs Hunt, and so many women like them spent decades of their adult lives reminding the world that World War I had not, in fact, "made the world safe for democracy" and refusing to rest until it did.

CHAPTER III

March(ing) in Cairo

Women's Awakening and the Egyptian Revolution of 1919

A n icy cold front settled over Paris in the winter of 1919, driving peacemakers, suffragists, and pan-Africanists indoors to seek what comfort they could in coal-heated staterooms and warm cafés. To impatient observers, the weather seemed to mimic the glacial pace of the peace negotiations themselves. In the meantime, two thousand miles away and across the Mediterranean, the meteorological and political climate could hardly have been more different. There, Egypt simmered under the heat of an unrelenting sun and blistered with the passions of a nation that saw the distant peace negotiations as the key to its liberation from British rule. By mid-March enflamed nationalists were pouring into the streets of Cairo to voice their demands.

Standing among them on March 16, 1919, was Huda Shaarawi, a forty-year-old philanthropist, budding social feminist, and wife of a wealthy Egyptian landowner and nationalist political leader. Like many other women of her social class, Shaarawi had lived much of her adult life following the conventions of discreet seclusion in the family home. That morning, however, she and several hundred other upper-class Egyptian women had taken the extraordinary step of leaving their households to stage a demonstration on the streets of Cairo. The "revolutionary gentlewomen" made for an unusual spectacle, one that British authorities were eager to contain. They ordered the police to halt the women's march before it spun out of control. Armed British officers surrounded the women, while the Egyptian conscript police taunted them with insults. The show of force was meant to intimidate, but Shaarawi was not one to back down. Under a blazing sun, she stared across the police cordon, took in a breath, and dared the British to make her a martyr. "Let me die," she yelled, "so Egypt shall have an Edith Cavell!"[1]

Shaarawi's remark was perfectly calibrated to hit a raw British nerve. Edith Cavell—an English nurse executed by a German firing squad for helping Allied soldiers escape from Belgium—became, in death, the most famous heroine of the First World War. Cavell's execution was used as a centerpiece of Allied propaganda designed to defame the "barbarous Huns." By offering herself up on the streets of Cairo, Shaarawi goaded the British by suggesting that her death would similarly serve as fodder for the Egyptian nationalist cause and expose the British as oppressive colonizers.

Shaarawi was not shot that day, nor did she or the other female protestors retire to their homes, as the British had anticipated. Instead, the ladies of Cairo—along with peasant, working-class, and middle-class women from throughout the country—pledged themselves to the nationalist cause and assumed a place at the heart of the Egyptian Revolution of 1919. Shaarawi's actions marked the public debut of female nationalist activism, which would soon coalesce into an organized Egyptian feminist movement.

The uprising on the streets of Cairo in March 1919 was directly tied to political aspirations unleashed by World War I and the Paris Peace Conference. Egypt—which had been part of the Ottoman Empire from the sixteenth to the nineteenth centuries and had gained de facto autonomy under Muhammed Ali Pasha in 1805—had been occupied by the British in 1882. With the outbreak of World War I, the Ottomans joined forces with the Central Powers, and the Sultan called on Muslims around the world to side with the Ottoman Empire. The British used the war as an excuse to formalize their rule over Egypt, declaring the state to be a Protectorate of the British Empire and imposing martial law throughout the country. For the next four years, British imperial troops flooded into Egypt, wartime inflation drove the prices of consumer goods through the roof, and over a million Egyptian peasant-farmers, the *fellahin*, were drafted to perform forced labor for the British Army.

Such wartime indignities were made tolerable only by the promise implicit in the terms of the Protectorate of 1914 that British colonial rule would be temporary, encouraging Egyptian nationalist aspirations to flourish. In the final year of the war, President Woodrow Wilson fueled

Egyptian hopes further by calling for a peace built on the principle of national self-determination. Implicit in this ideal was the assertion that self-defined national communities, both weak and powerful, should be able to determine their own borders and governments. Immediately after the armistice was signed, a delegation of male Egyptian leaders presented British officials in Cairo with a formal request to travel to London to negotiate for Egyptian independence. The request was denied. Frustrated but convinced the British Protectorate could no longer be justified in a Wilsonian world order, Egyptian nationalists switched tactics and requested permission to travel to Paris to present the case for independence directly to the peacemakers. The British responded this time by rounding up several of the most prominent Egyptian nationalist leaders and banishing them to Malta. Ali Shaarawi, Huda's husband, was among the few left behind.[2]

Ali and Huda Shaarawi had not enjoyed a particularly close relationship prior to the outbreak of the revolution. The former had been betrothed to Huda, his cousin, when he was in his forties and she was not yet thirteen. It was a marriage she resented and sought to escape but eventually learned to tolerate. The 1919 revolution, however, united the couple's hearts behind a common cause. Down with colonial occupation! Freedom from oppression! Justice and liberty! These and similar battle cries transcended the classes and united the sexes in 1919, creating a sense of unity in purpose and vision.

Egyptian men and women shared a single, driving political goal—independence—but when it came to assumptions about appropriate gender roles within a newly independent state, Egyptian nationalist men shared many of the same prejudices as their British colonial opponents. Both saw Egyptian women's political activism as a transgression of gender norms: laughable to the British, expedient to Egyptian nationalists. Both expected that once the political tumult had subsided, the women of Cairo would willingly retreat back to their homes. Having won the right to draft a constitution for the (partially) independent state of Egypt in 1922, nationalist men deliberately excluded women from the halls of power.

Shaarawi was outraged. For her and like-minded Egyptian women, nationalism represented a call for a new social, economic, and political order rooted not only in complete political autonomy but also in greater gender equality. Upper- and middle-class Egyptian women—much like their contemporaries in Turkey and Syria—had nurtured such ambitions behind closed doors and in print since the end of the nineteenth century. In the revolution of 1919, they carried their aspirations into the public square and infused them with newfound confidence and organizational prowess. Egyptian women's activism in March 1919 signaled their arrival in national political life as well as on the international diplomatic stage. Given the colonized and traditional society in which they lived, Egyptian women—unlike Western suffragists and female pan-Africanists—could not travel independently to Paris to lay their demands before the peacemakers. Their actions in 1919 were nonetheless a part of the much broader global attempt by women to intercede in international affairs at the time of the peace conference.[3]

They also served as a prelude to the formation of an organized and public feminist movement in Egypt. In the aftermath of the Paris Peace Conference, and in the midst of an ongoing battle against colonial rule, Egyptian women would lobby tirelessly for policies that would liberate women of all classes from the gender-based oppression that restricted their freedom and limited their horizons. Expanding educational and work opportunities, revising family laws and customs, and gaining political rights were among their top priorities. By the 1920s, in the face of ongoing male hostility to their program and in recognition of the universal nature of gender oppression, Egyptian women began collaborating with international feminist organizations to achieve their goals. Huda Shaarawi worked actively with Western feminist allies, lending her own notoriety to help advance suffrage and gender equality in Europe and the United States, even as she sought to capitalize on her international connections to expand women's rights in Egypt and throughout the Arab world. The legacies of colonialism complicated these alliances, and by the 1930s Shaarawi and other Egyptian women began putting more emphasis on constructing international feminist networks closer to home. The multiplication of "Eastern" and pan-Arab feminist movements in the 1930s thus became one of the many unanticipated legacies of the peace conference of 1919.

Harem Years

Nearly all of the elite women who strode confidently onto the political stage in 1919 had to cast aside customs and traditions to assert their voices and demand their rights. This was certainly true for Huda Shaarawi, whose upper-class upbringing in late-nineteenth-century Egypt had destined her for a restricted life of domestic seclusion.

Born in 1879, Nur al-Huda Sultan was the daughter of an extremely wealthy Egyptian landowner, Sultan Pasha. Later in life Sultan Pasha moved into central government administration and, like many men of his standing, built a house in Cairo: a beautiful three-story home surrounded by an expansive garden. It was here that Huda spent much of her childhood. Sultan Pasha died when Huda was five years old, leaving the young girl and her brother to be raised by two women. The first was their mother, Iqbal, who was born in the Caucasus (the region between the Black Sea and the Caspian Sea) and raised in a Turco-Circassian harem in Cairo. The second woman was their father's wife, Hasibah, whom Huda referred to as Umm Kabira (Big Mother). Huda's mother was never formally married to her father. This relationship was not unusual, nor was the fact that Iqbal shared the harem quarters with another woman. In the early twentieth century many wealthy Egyptian men practiced polygamy (within the limits prescribed by juristic understandings of Sharia law) and/or developed long-lasting relationships with female consorts. Fair-skinned Circassian women were highly favored as concubines and wives and helped solidify family ties between native Egyptians, like Sultan Pasha, and the Turco-Circassian ruling class.

In her memoirs, Huda describes her childhood as tranquil, despite the sadness of living with two widowed mothers in a harem without a master. Being raised in a harem was viewed as a privilege among the Egyptian upper class in the late nineteenth century. It was an expression of the custom of seclusion, designed to protect women's chastity and honor by removing them from the gaze of unrelated men upon reaching maturity. In practice, this meant secluding women in their own quarters in the home (the domestic space allotted to women was thus also known as the harem). When wealthy women went out—whether to visit female friends, for feast days, or for some other special occasion—they covered their bodies with a long cloak (*izar*) and wore a face veil (referred to then as *hijab* and today as *niqab*) to protect them from strangers, effectively carrying their seclusion with them. Huda fondly recalls the mornings she spent in the harem quarters with Umm Kabira eating fresh fruit and bread slathered with clotted cream and evenings spent roasting chestnuts over the fire. She passed her childhood afternoons with her beloved younger brother, Umar, and their

Huda Shaarawi with her brother, Umar. (From the personal collection of Margot Badran)

companions in the family garden "amid the fruit and flower trees, and the birds, fish, and pet animals."[4]

Tutors came to the home to provide lessons to Huda and her brother. Formal education—beyond the very basic reading and math skills taught in traditional village schools—was available only to a relatively small number of girls in turn-of-the-century Egypt. In the 1870s the Egyptian ruler Khedive Ismail established the first state primary school for daughters of state officials, but these reached only a tiny portion of the population. When the British began to take over state institutions in 1882, their primary concern was with training young men to become low-level colonial administrators. Girls' education was not a priority. Some middle-class families made up for deficiencies in state-sponsored education by sending their children to foreign missionary schools, while the wealthiest elite generally hired private tutors to come to the home. Whether daughters were afforded these opportunities varied from family to family.[5]

Huda took to her lessons with a passion. "Of all the subjects," she recalls, "Arabic was my favourite." By the age of nine, she could recite the Quran from memory. When Huda asked to learn the rules of Arabic grammar, however, the eunuch who oversaw her schooling put a halt to the lessons. "The young lady has no need of grammar," he scolded, "as she will not become a judge." His word was final. "I became depressed," Huda says, "and began to neglect my studies, hating being a girl because it kept me from the education I sought." Her formal Arabic instruction remained rudimentary, but she continued her studies in French and took up piano. She also developed a love of poetry, stealing into her father's study to pore over his books. One day an itinerant poetess came and spent time with the family, reciting verses and discussing literature with the men. Observing her, Huda became convinced that "with learning, women could be the equals of men if not surpass them."[6]

Outside of lesson time, Huda had considerable freedom to play with her brother and their friends until she reached maturity, around the age of eleven. At that point, she remembers, "I was required to restrict myself to the company of girls and women. I felt a stranger in their world." Not long after, Huda's cousin Ali Shaarawi, who had been appointed as legal guardian over her and her brother upon their father's death, began appearing more frequently at the house. Ali Shaarawi was much older than Huda and had a wife and family of his own. Huda grew up regarding him "as a father or older brother deserving my fear and respect," but she felt "alienated" in his presence owing to his curt manner and his manifest preference for her brother.[7]

Only after some months was the reason for her cousin's recurring visits revealed: Huda's relations had contracted for the two of them to be married. Huda was inconsolable at the news, but she was told a refusal would disappoint her mother who had arranged the marriage when she heard a member of the royal family was interested in seeking her hand. Such an engagement would have broken up the family estate (Islamic law mandates girls inherit a share of family wealth). Determined not to let this happen, but nonetheless concerned about her daughter's interests, Huda's mother insisted on a prenuptial agreement stipulating Ali Shaarawi would renounce his first wife and accept a monogamous union.

The document was duly signed, and the two were betrothed. Part of the family garden was cleared of flowers and trees to make room for the many guests invited to the elaborate three-day-long wedding celebration. The morning after it was over, Huda looked out the window and reflected poetically on her fate. "I wept for my trees. I wept for my childhood and for my freedom. I saw in this barren garden a picture of life—the life I would live cut off from everything that had delighted me and consoled me in my melancholy childhood. I turned from the window with a heavy heart."[8]

Although marriage at such a young age was not uncommon in the late nineteenth century, at age thirteen, Huda Shaarawi struggled to adjust. She felt shy around her new husband and grew depressed when he tried to restrict her activities. Over time, moreover, his behavior grew furtive and odd. Before long, she discovered the cause. Ali Shaarawi had returned to his former wife, who was again with child. The prenuptial agreement came into play, and Huda and her husband were separated. "The seven years I remained apart from my husband," Huda would later reflect, "was a time for new experiences and for growing into adulthood." In those critical years, living comfortably with her mother and brother in her childhood

Huda Shaarawi at her desk, date unknown. (Collections Bibliothèque Marguerite Durand—Ville de Paris)

home, Huda experienced freedom from the strictest harem customs and from the responsibilities of childbearing and childrearing. The years of separation allowed her intellectual curiosity and spirit to blossom.[9]

Modern innovations of the late nineteenth century opened Shaarawi's horizons, as they did for other Egyptian women who were beginning to renegotiate the boundaries between seclusion and public space in an era of rapid change. Shaarawi began attending concerts at the Opera House (shielded from public view by wooden screens) and visiting the new, modern department stores just appearing in Cairo and Alexandria. Her first shopping trip "threw the entire household into an uproar." She set out, fully cloaked and veiled, accompanied by maids and a eunuch who "proceeded straight to the store manager and brusquely demanded a place for the harem." Screens were quickly erected to shield her from view, and an astonished female shop assistant brought Shaarawi whatever she requested. Shopping gradually became more commonplace (and less complicated) for women of her generation who sought out the latest trends from Paris and Istanbul. Some switched to using light, gauze-like face veils that became as much a fashion statement as a customary obligation.[10]

In these years Shaarawi also developed strong friendships with other women of her social class as well as with several foreign women who were among the Europeans flocking to Cairo and Alexandria in the late nineteenth century. In particular, she grew close to an older French woman named Eugénie Le Brun Rushdi, who had emigrated to Egypt to marry her love (and a future prime minister of Egypt), Husain Rushdi Pasha. After her marriage, Rushdi converted to Islam and positioned herself as a cultural mediator between East and West. She maintained a Saturday women's salon, inviting foreign and Egyptian women to her home to discuss literature, philosophy, and social questions, including Islamic attitudes toward veiling. Rushdi also read to Shaarawi pieces of a book she was writing titled *The Divorcees*, which argued that Egyptian social customs, rather than Islam, had fostered women's oppression.[11]

In this way, in the seven years of separation from her husband, Shaarawi grew into adulthood and cemented a critical spirit that she would never abandon. The kinds of questions that she was beginning to explore—regarding marriage and family, fashion and custom, men and women—mirrored issues of growing interest and debate in Egyptian intellectual life at the turn of the century. Shaarawi's period of self-discovery coincided with a broader culture movement in Egypt referred to as "women's awakening," which served as the immediate backdrop to the political events of 1919.

Women's Awakening

By the turn of the twentieth century, modern developments in Egypt were rapidly chipping away at gender conventions that had circumscribed the lives of upper-class women of earlier generations. While the opera house, department stores, and girls' schools drew more women out of their homes and into public spaces, tramways (with separate compartments for women) and motorcars facilitated their movement. Equally important, the expansion of the printing press and the spread of popular periodicals allowed literate women to engage in a public conversation about topics of widespread interest without overtly challenging the practice of seclusion. The spread of print culture, in turn, helped instigate a lively public debate about men and women's roles in Egypt and around the world.

Between 1892 and 1922 nearly thirty women's magazines appeared in Egypt. Supportive male collaborators helped female editors and writers step into this world by serving as business partners. Some presses established secluded quarters within their offices, while many contributors wrote from home. The possibility of publishing anonymously or under a pen name helped women accustomed to seclusion develop a public voice. A widening circle of female readers (some sixty thousand by 1907) eagerly waited for new editions to arrive in the mail. Many subscribers read stories and essays aloud to illiterate friends and female relations.[12]

Women's magazines, on the whole, shied away from national political topics, but this did not make them apolitical. The phrase female writers most often used to describe the literary and social movement in which they were engaging was *al-nahda al-nisa'iyya*: the women's awakening. The phrase indicates women's sense of newfound awareness about the social, economic, and political conditions governing their lives. Articles touched frequently on women's education, wage and domestic labor, maternal responsibilities, and family relations. Female editors and writers—coming from different ethnic, religious, and regional backgrounds—offered varying opinions regarding women's place in the family and social order. Together they fueled a new gender consciousness among the literate Egyptian middle and upper class.[13]

Such ideas remained on a low simmer through the final decade of the nineteenth century. Then, in 1899, a Muslim judge by the name of Qasim Amin threw the literary equivalent of gasoline on the fire with the publication of a book he titled *The Liberation of Women*, followed a year later by *The New Woman*. Together, Amin's two books argued that Egyptian progress—indeed, the nation's very survival—depended on elevating women's status in society. In making such a claim, Amin drew on arguments being forwarded by modernist Islamic reformer Shaikh Muhammad 'Abduh, who maintained that both the Quran and Islamic law granted women and men "an equal place in human society." In modernists' eyes, social practices that undermined this fundamental truth were rooted in ignorance and misinterpretation rather than religious orthodoxy. Many pages of *The Liberation of Women* were taken up with an Islamic defense of female emancipation.[14]

Amin also drew on Western thought in his arguments and offered direct comparisons between Western and Egyptian women in his books. Both intellectually and professionally, he sat astride the colonial divide. Amin had spent time studying law in France and admired the West, seeing in its development a model for Egypt's own. He argued that Egyptians would only be able to meet the challenge of a Darwinian struggle for global survival if their society evolved. While he did not propose a wholesale abandonment of traditional culture, he was convinced that "the inferior position of Muslim women is the greatest obstacle" to Egypt's economic advancement, preventing the country from taking its place among the major global powers.[15]

Amin believed an important reform for the state to undertake was the provision of equal primary schooling for boys and girls. Education, he argued, would elevate women's status in the family and in society and lift Egyptian civilization as a whole. Like most of his male and female contemporaries, Amin understood motherhood and domesticity to be women's natural calling, even if he readily admitted "the revealed law of God indicates that women were endowed with minds in the same manner as men." Still, Amin did not see women's secondary schooling—to say nothing of higher education—to be a priority. More pressing, he thought, was reform of laws regulating the practices of polygamy and unilateral male divorce. Even more controversially, Amin argued for abandoning the practices of domestic seclusion and face veiling, arguing neither was mandated by Islam and both impeded women's freedom and intellectual development.[16]

Amin's tracts unleashed a firestorm. Critics argued that his cry for reform was a Western plot designed to corrupt Egyptian morals and weaken society. These counterarguments carried considerable sway and would taint feminism as a colonial ideology for decades after. Yet for women like Huda Shaarawi, who had already begun to grapple privately and in print with the customs and institutions that inhibited their lives, Amin's arguments served as a wellspring of inspiration. After 1919 Shaarawi would hail Amin as a hero and the "liberator of Egyptian women."[17]

In the years between the publication of Amin's *The Liberation of Women* and the outbreak of the First World War, Egyptian women began pushing further against the walls of seclusion by seeking socially acceptable outlets for their energy and curiosity. Philanthropy proved one promising path into public service for upper-class Egyptian women (as it had for many women in the West), and a small number of them began to found and direct institutions that filled vital needs in the community. Shaarawi led one of the most substantial of these efforts, establishing a medical clinic for poor women and children in Cairo. That same year she also helped launch a lecture series for women at the newly opened Egyptian University (on Fridays, when male students were absent) as well as in other locations. The inaugural lecture, presented by a French acquaintance of Shaarawi's, compared the lives of Egyptian and European women. In time, Egyptian women—including graduates of the new women's teacher training college—began leading the discussions themselves.[18]

Among the most effective of these speakers was a woman by the name of Malak Hifni Nasif (who published under the penname Bahithat al-Badiyah, or Seeker of the Desert). Nasif was among the first graduates of the women's teacher training college in Cairo and an unflinching advocate of women's educational and professional rights. She had little patience for men who argued that women were not designed for exertion or hard work. "Nothing irritates me more," she said in one public lecture, "than when men claim they do not wish us to work because they wish to spare us the burden. We do not want condescension, we want respect." In matters of dress in particular Nasif advocated modesty and retaining the face veil for the time being, largely for expedient reasons. Such warnings stemmed from her belief that Egyptian men and women were not ready to mix openly in public as well as from a desire to retain Egypt's cultural distinctiveness. "If we pursue everything Western," she worried, "we shall destroy our own civilization and a nation that has lost its civilization grows weak and vanishes." Still, she believed, many customs were indefensible and due for reform. Polygamy was one of them. Co-wife, she wrote, "is a terrible word, laden with savagery and selfishness." Nasif knew from experience. Not until after she was married and followed her husband to his desert home did she discover he already had a wife.[19]

By the early twentieth century, middle- and upper-class Egyptian women began to establish intellectual societies of their own. Nasif and Shaarawi were active in several of these, including the Women's Refinement Union, the Intellectual Association of Egyptian Women, and the Ladies Literary Improvement Society. A third active member, Nabawiya Musa, was the first Egyptian girl to be allowed to take the state baccalaureate exam, which she passed with flying colors (in 1907), despite having to study on her own in the absence of any secondary schools for girls. It would be over two decades before another female student would be able to follow in her footsteps.[20]

Thus in print and in person, through works of public service and in pursuit of their own "awakening," educated Egyptian women pushed at the boundaries of acceptable gender roles and explored ways to establish themselves as legitimate public actors and intellectuals. Many knew and befriended European women, and the dialogue between East and West was part of the intellectual context of their budding feminist consciousness, but it in no way dictated the parameters of Egyptian women's aspirations or outlook. In their own way, Egyptian women were deeply concerned about preserving national culture and regaining national autonomy. Both these goals were catapulted to national prominence with the outbreak of the First World War.

Family, Nationalism, and War

The decade prior to World War I was a full one for Shaarawi, whose foray into intellectual and philanthropic work was accompanied by a return to married life and the birth of her two children. Shaarawi's cherished brother, Umar, engineered the reconciliation with her husband. Umar was engaged to a friend, but his marriage would require that he leave his sister and mother alone in the family home to set up his own household. Unwilling to do so, he refused to get married until Huda and her husband made amends. Huda's estranged husband simultaneously pleaded for Huda to return to him, resolving to live monogamously once and for all (and to walk away, again, from his first wife). Sensitive to the demands of family honor and cognizant of the pragmatic benefits of a union with a powerful man—and with few other options available to her—Huda consented. In 1901 she moved back in with her husband. Two years later she gave birth to a daughter, Bassna, followed by a son, Muhammed. Family came to play a larger role in her life. Both her brother and her husband were growing involved in nationalist opposition politics, and conversations with them fed Shaarawi's budding political consciousness.[21]

Shaarawi also began to travel abroad in these years, expanding her horizons. One summer, she and her mother took the children to Istanbul in the hopes of helping her daughter recover from malaria. She loved the views of the Bosporus and reconnecting with the Ottoman side of her family. In 1908 Shaarawi's husband brought her to Paris to help her recover from depression following the death of her friend Eugénie Le Brun Rushdi. In the French capital, Shaarawi marveled at the fashionably dressed men and women walking arm-in-arm in the public gardens. She also appreciated the French people's celebration of their collective past in architecture and monuments "raised to honour those who have died for the freedom and independence of their country." She was less taken, however, with the crowds and the cigarette-filled air hanging heavily in Parisian cafés.[22]

Shaarawi and her family returned to Paris in the summer of 1914. Their timing could not have been worse. On June 28, shortly after they arrived, a Serbian nationalist assassinated the heir to the Austro-Hungarian throne, and European leaders would begin to spin the tangled web that would lead to the outbreak of World War I. Caught in the lull before the storm, Shaarawi attended "a large meeting for women who were agitating for peace and the right to vote." Many prominent French suffragists spoke at the gathering, including Ghénia Avril de Saint Croix. Everywhere Shaarawi went, people spoke of the possibility of war. She found it hard to believe. "Europe seemed too civilized and too enlightened to resort to war," she thought.[23]

The family left France for Switzerland on August 1, 1914, the same day the French announced a general mobilization of their armed forces. From those frantic days, Shaarawi would remember train cars "filled with soldiers waving flags and singing patriotic songs" and "women with tears in their eyes . . . bidding them farewell." Anxious to escape, the family traveled overland from Switzerland to Italy and then by ship from Genoa to Alexandria. Their progress was hampered by repeated delays. When the ship finally docked in Alexandria on August 19, Shaarawi was met with the devastating news that her mother had died in Cairo earlier that same day.[24]

Their mother's death brought Shaarawi and her brother even closer together. They sought solace in each other's company, and, inevitably, their conversation turned to the world war and Great Britain's unilateral assumption of government and military control in Egypt, in place since 1882 but tightened upon the outbreak of war in Europe. Umar, who had long been a critic of British imperialism, deeply resented Egypt's status under the British Protectorate and had little sympathy for the Allies in the escalating conflict. "He called [the Allies] imperialists," Shaarawi would later write, "and blamed them for starting the war. He hoped for victory for the Turks and Germans." Such a position was not uncommon among Egyptian nationalists. Huda saw Egypt's stakes in the war as more complicated. She hoped that a quick Allied victory would hasten the moment when British government would relinquish its control over Egypt and allow the Egyptian people to establish a democratic state.[25]

In this family debate, her brother proved the more prescient, but he would not live to see the war's outcome. In 1917, at age thirty-seven, Umar died suddenly of an aneurism. Huda was inconsolable. A year later, in October 1918, she suffered another loss. Malak Hifni Nasif, her friend and fellow traveler on the path to "women's awakening," died of the Spanish flu. Upon hearing the news, Shaarawi ran distraught out of her home to join her friend's funeral procession. Shortly after, a group of women held a remembrance ceremony at the university hall where Nasif had given many of her lectures. That day, Shaarawi gave her first public speech, in celebration of her friend's life and legacy.[26]

Reeling from these losses, Shaarawi experienced another personal blow when her husband announced that he intended to seek the engagement of her fourteen-year-old niece (her brother's daughter) to his son by his first wife. Shaarawi, who had suffered so terribly from her marriage at a young age, bravely asked her husband to wait before binding the young couple to each other. He responded angrily to her questioning of his paternal privilege, and he began to hold her at a distance. "I would have separated from my husband," Shaarawi said, "if it had not been for the nationalist movement."[27]

In the final months of 1918, calls for Egyptian independence were mounting. Although British martial law had restricted nationalists' ability to air their grievances, members of the Egyptian political elite (including Ali Shaarawi) began meeting privately to discuss how to pursue independence once the war was over. They were encouraged in these efforts by Woodrow Wilson, who had begun calling openly for a postwar peace built on the principle of national self-determination. Wilson's suggestion that weak nations had as much right as the strong to shape their own governments received wide circulation in the Egyptian press, generating tremendous excitement. On the day the armistice was announced in Europe, the American consul general in Cairo reported to his superiors: "I have been made aware of a tendency in all classes of Egyptians to believe that President Wilson favors self-government throughout all the world and that he will champion the right of the people of this country to govern themselves."[28]

Ali Shaarawi and his friends were actively planning for that very reality. On November 13, 1918, two days after the armistice, Shaarawi and two others—including Saad Zaghlul, vice president of the Legislative Assembly—met with the British high commissioner in Cairo and requested permission to travel to London to negotiate for Egypt's independence. The answer came back a terse no. Shortly thereafter the peace conference opened in Paris, and Ali Shaarawi, Saad Zaghlul, and their fellow nationalists began to read in the newspapers about delegations from across Eurasia—including one headed by Prince Faisal of Arabia—heading to the French capital.

Fearful the window of opportunity to press for independence was narrowing, Egyptian nationalist leaders went on the offensive. First, they formed a new political party called the Wafd (Arabic for delegation) with the stated goal of achieving the complete independence of Egypt by peaceful means. Then, Wafd leaders took their case to the people, staging mass rallies and asking Egyptians of all classes and backgrounds to sign petitions of support. Wafd leaders also shifted diplomatic tactics, sidestepping the British government and demanding the right to travel to Paris to lay their claims before the peace conference. In preparation, they also sent a lengthy memo to each of the Allied delegations insisting that at no other moment in history had the Egyptian people given evidence of "such unanimity of opinion" as they had for the "sacred cause of independence."[29]

As popular expectations mounted, the British authorities in Egypt grew alarmed, and on March 8, 1919, they arrested Zaghlul (who had emerged as Wafd's popular leader). The following day he and three other Wafd leaders were deported to Malta. Ali Shaarawi escaped the dragnet, but his freedom was precarious. Knowing that he could be exiled at any moment, he turned to his wife. "My husband kept me informed of events," Huda later recalled, "so that I could fill the vacuum if he were imprisoned or exiled." Only a few weeks old, the popular uprising against the British was already chipping at the centuries-old walls that separated men and women, husbands and wives. Such unity of purpose—which transcended not only gender but also class and religious lines—worried the British deeply, and they hoped that by sending the movement's leaders into exile, they could stop the movement in its tracks. Instead, the deportation of the Wafd leaders fueled public anger, and men and women alike prepared to come to the nationalists' defense.[30]

The "Ladies' Protests" of March 1919

By mid-March Egypt's independence movement was looking more and more like a revolution, as the Egyptian people rose up en masse and clashed with the British colonial authorities determined to cling to power (as well as to control of the Suez Canal). Egyptian students in Cairo were the first to stage public demonstrations beginning on March 10, the day after the deportation of the Wafd leadership. The British met the students with a show of force, arresting several hundred by day's end. The protests and arrests, Shaarawi would later write, were like "sparks flying from the mouth of a boiling volcano ready to erupt."[31]

The next day the British responded by opening fire on the crowd, killing six students. Protests quickly spread to other cities and into the countryside. Some working-class and peasant women joined in the protests, and on March 14 Hamidah Khalil, a "woman of the people," was killed, becoming the first female victim of Britain's repressive tactics. In Cairo, anger boiled over. Shopkeepers shuttered their stores, and striking taxi and tramway drivers paralyzed transportation networks. Finally, on March 16, hundreds of upper-class women (estimates vary from three hundred to six hundred), shrouded in black cloaks with white veils covering their faces, left their harems and staged a march in central Cairo. It was a singular moment in the history of the Egyptian nation and in the history of women's emancipation.[32]

Egyptian women's demonstration, March 1919. (From the personal collection of Margot Badran)

The "ladies' protest," as some dubbed the event, was not spontaneous. It was meticulously planned by Huda Shaarawi and a cohort of politicized women who had access to up-to-date information on the uprising from Ali Shaarawi and were determined that women would play a part in Egypt's liberation. Initially eager to act within the confines of the law, Huda sent several women to the British police headquarters to request permission to hold a rally. The request was denied, but a local newspaper later printed that sanction had been granted for the following day. Upon hearing the news, Huda Shaarawi began phoning friends and acquaintances. Most responded enthusiastically, with some deciding to participate "in spite of the objections of the husbands."[33]

Shaarawi remembers the events that transpired next as follows: "On the morning of 16 March, I sent placards to the house of Ahmad Bey Abu Usbaa (a prominent nationalist who lived in central Cairo and whose wife helped plan the demonstration), bearing slogans in Arabic and French painted in white on a background of black—the colour of mourning. Some of the slogans read, 'Long Live the Supporters of Justice and Freedom,' others said 'Down with Oppressors and Tyrants' and 'Down with Occupation.'"

Arraying themselves in columns, with those in front bearing banners and flags, the women began marching, as planned, toward the foreign legation quarters of the United States, Italy, and France. Soon after departing, however, some of the younger women at the front of the procession made a detour, heading directly to the final destination: Bait al-Umma, the House of the Nation (the home of Saad Zaghlul, whose wife Safiya had stepped in as a party organizer and movement figurehead when her husband was exiled). The marchers, unsurprisingly, drew considerable attention. One male onlooker recalls that "crowds thronged the pavements to applaud and cheer them on and women leaned out from windows and balconies, ululating in jubilant support. It was a fantastic scene that stirred every heart!"[34]

The marchers were on their way to Bait al-Umma when, abruptly, they found themselves face-to-face with the British authorities. "No sooner were we approaching Zaghlul's house," Shaarawi recalls, "than British troops surrounded us. They blocked the streets with machine guns, forcing us to stop along with the students who had formed columns on both sides of us." A British soldier stepped into Shaarawi's path, pointed his gun at her, and ordered the women to halt. The show of British force angered her to the core. "As one of the women tried to pull me back," she says, "I shouted in a loud voice, 'Let me die so Egypt shall have an Edith Cavell!'" She tried to push her way past the police and soldiers, calling out to the other women to follow, but one of the marchers pulled her back, insisting, "This is madness. Do you want to risk the lives of the students? It will happen if the British raise a hand against you." And so, Shaarawi writes, "I came to my senses and stopped. We stood still for three hours while the sun blazed down on us. . . . I did not care if I suffered sunstroke—the blame would fall upon the tyrannical British authority."[35]

Thomas Russell, the British chief of police in Cairo, eventually arrived and demanded the Egyptian women disperse, claiming that no permission for the march had ever been granted. "Yielding in the face of force," Shaarawi says, "we made our way to our carriages. After departing from the scene, we called on some of the foreign legations to inform them of events and to register protest against the Protectorate. We received courtesy, but nothing more." The women left for home, vowing to return. Four days later the "ladies" staged another, equally large demonstration. For the next three years, until the British reluctantly granted Egypt partial independence, women would remain an active and vital part of the nationalist movement.[36]

Like Western suffragists pursuing women's emancipation in Paris at the exact same time, Shaarawi hoped that Egyptian women's public defense of national independence in March 1919 would bring broad attention to an issue global leaders would have preferred to sweep under the rug. She would not be not disappointed. Egyptian and foreign journalists covering the uprising, the British authorities confronting the protestors, and the women who risked their reputations and their lives to join the movement all would highlight the importance of women's participation in the Egyptian Revolution of 1919. What each thought women's actions meant for Egypt going forward, however, differed considerably depending on the perspective of the observer.

"A Nation Cannot Arrive at Full Emancipation If Woman Herself Is Not Free"

For upper-class women, March 16, 1919, marked the beginning of a long process of liberation from the oppression of imperialism *and* from restrictions stemming from a social system that denied women a role in public life. Over time Shaarawi and other demonstrators would come to define the March 16 protest as a foundational moment—their own, gender-specific July 4 or Bastille Day—when women learned to break free of the constraints placed on their sex and when men learned to accept women as their partners. As Shaarawi would explain to American feminists during a visit to Washington, D.C., some years later, "While serving her Fatherland, [the Egyptian woman] learned to despise prejudices, broke her chains, and intervened courageously in the general battle for the independence of her country. . . . Since this time, men, impressed by the courage, ability, and patriotism of their women, no longer dream of opposing their evolution. They have finally understood that a nation cannot arrive at full emancipation if woman herself is not free." Such a sweeping claim understates the important intellectual groundwork accomplished during the preceding three decades of "women's awakening" in Egypt. It also overestimates the degree to which Egyptian men were prepared to accept women as equal partners in social and political life. These caveats aside, 1919 *did* mark a watershed moment, when Egyptian women, particularly from the middle and upper classes, inserted themselves in the public life of their nation. There would be no turning back.[37]

Women's public display of patriotism in March 1919 had an immediate liberating effect on other women who witnessed the demonstration from the sidelines, read about it in the newspapers, or heard about it from friends. One such bystander, Fardous Tawfiq, the wife of a former military general, wrote a letter to the editor of *Al-Ahram*, the newspaper with the largest circulation in Egypt, expressing her admiration for the women who dared to act on their convictions. "You have performed your duty toward your beloved nation," she wrote, "and proven in the clearest terms the ardour of your dedication and devotion by taking your patriotism beyond word to the loftier deed." Tawfiq's letter was in its own way pathbreaking, not only because of its content—praising women's public activism—but also because of the fact that she signed the letter with her full name, the first such occurrence for a woman in the pages of *Al-Ahram*. Emboldened by the letter, other women began to write to the paper as well. *Al-Ahram* responded by creating a new, front-page column titled "The Voice of the Egyptian Woman," inviting others to express their views. One female reader wrote to celebrate the infectious nature of the protestors' enthusiasm. "The women marched as though they were in a wedding procession," she exulted, "the wedding of Egypt to freedom. They were delirious with joy." Female bystanders praised the protestors' patriotism and began asserting themselves in new, public ways.[38]

In 1919 female protestors embedded themselves in *national* politics at the highest level. With their actions, they also signaled the arrival of Egyptian women on the *international* diplomatic stage. Faced with British intransigence, Egyptian women deliberately directed their protests and their pleas to diplomatic representatives of the other Allied powers, and they followed up their actions with written petitions calling on the Western powers to live up to their own professed ideals of freedom. One petition, delivered to American diplomatic offices in Cairo on March 24 and written "in the name of the women of Egypt," called on Americans to come to Egypt's aid. "We believe in President Wilson and in his principles of liberty and human fraternity," the petitioners wrote. "We beg you to send our message to America and to President Wilson personally. Let them hear our call. We believe they will not suffer Liberty to be crushed in Egypt." Over one hundred women, including Shaarawi, Zaghlul, and many others from prominent families, signed the letter personally. With such appeals, Egyptian women added their voices to the growing cry of women around the world who pleaded with the peacemakers to listen to the voices of the "weaker sex" as well as the weaker nations as they laid the pillars of the new international order.[39]

"The Lighter Side of Things"

The importance that Egyptian women accorded to their public activism of 1919 stands in stark contrast to representations of the "ladies' protests" by the European colonizers who confronted them. Both in Western newspapers published in Egypt and in later memoirs, European men went out of their way to reassure readers (mostly men like themselves) that women's actions were no cause for alarm—laughable even, when seen in the appropriate light. By casting the women's demonstrations as a regrettable lapse in female propriety, and by stoking class divisions among the population of Cairo, British authorities sought to put Egyptian men and women back in their place and to reestablish the lines of deference that upheld imperial control.

Both English- and French-language daily newspapers kept foreigners in Egypt abreast of the unsettling events of 1919. The French-language *Journal du Caire* reported on the women's protest of March 16 the day after it occurred. The French, who had lost their opportunity to rule Egypt when Napoleon's army was kicked out of the country over a century earlier, had fewer stakes in the revolt than the British in 1919. Their interests in Egypt were primarily commercial, and French-language journalists watched nationalist protests unfold with some detachment and even a small dose of *schadenfreude* over Egyptians' rejection of British rule. Still, the *Journal du Caire* sought to reassure its readers that the women's demonstration posed no threat to paternalist colonial rule. The British, it falsely reported, "ordered the police not to intervene and to let the protestors pass." As for the demonstrators, "In automobiles and carriages, the indigenous Ladies paraded in the streets and before the Diplomatic Agencies and immediately returned to their homes, *without disturbing the public order for a single instant.*" Political demands, angry slogans, police repression: none of these appeared in the pages of the *Journal du Caire*, where the women's protests read more like a Sunday pleasure drive than a political revolt.[40]

The British daily, the *Egyptian Mail*, opted not to cover the protest, but it did publish a lengthy article about a follow-up demonstration scheduled four days later under the headline "The Procession That Never Came—Egyptian Women's March." At 10:00 A.M. on March 20, the paper recounted, "the southern streets of Cairo were packed by a *tarbooshed* throng who were awaiting the advent of the women." By referencing the *tarboosh*—a red fez worn by Muslim men—the reporter set a vivid scene for his readers and drew their attention to the men waiting on the sidelines. Soon enough, four hundred or more "dark-clad figures" arrived "attended by their maidservants," all obviously members of the "better class Egyptians." Having noted their dress, the British reporter lost all interest in the female protestors. His gaze was drawn instead to the men in the crowd, studying their response as British soldiers arrived to break up the demonstration. "The humour of the whole affair was apparent to the soldiery," he wrote, "whose smiling faces occasionally flashed satirical glances at the adjacent Egyptians who almost literally were hiding behind the women's skirts."

Amazingly, it was not women's transgression of gender norms that merited the notice of this British journalist; it was Egyptian men's purported failure to act as men—either by standing up for themselves and or by controlling their women—that drew his attention and derision. This failure of Egyptian manhood (a common theme in colonial writing about the Middle East) was presented in stark contrast to the gallantry of British soldiers, who, according to the article, displayed a "big-brotherly and tolerant attitude" and "endeavored to persuade the women that the procession was *mafeesh* [nonexistent]." The demonstration, the journalist wrote, thus ended before it began. The women "retired" to their homes. As for the men who came to watch, they were cheated of their spectacle and "gloomily dwindled away." From beginning to end, the article dripped with condescension. It also marginalized women at their own event. On the pages of the *Egyptian Mail*, the women's protest appeared as a showdown between tolerant British soldiers and cowardly Egyptian men.[41]

The arrogance and viewpoint of this journalist are easier to understand, if not to excuse, when we consider how the British chief of police perceived the affair. Thomas Russell Pasha (the title came with the job) had a long career in Egypt, much of it spent fighting the spread of illegal drugs. In 1919, however, he was the head of the Cairo city police charged with containing the popular uprising. For many Egyptians, he was the face of British colonial authority in the streets. The revolution of 1919 would take up two chapters in Russell's lengthy memoir. The second of these, titled "The Lighter Side of Things," begins, "During the many years of political struggle there were occasional episodes which started by being truly alarming, but which to everyone's relief finished on a note of comedy. The first of these was the Ladies' Demonstration of 1919." Russell continues, "The job that faced the London police when the suffragettes resorted to violence was unpleasant enough, but such a weapon in an Oriental country where women were still strictly harim [harem] was unheard of and the threat of attack by a mob of Muhammadan ladies made British brigadiers tremble." How would this frightening situation turn (in Russell's words) to comedy? By his own deft hand, the memoir explains, as Russell did everything in his power to keep the "ladies" in their place.[42]

Russell recalls that a delegation of women called on him to request permission to hold a march "to show their solidarity with the National Movement." He denied the request over the "shrill cries of defiance from the excited ladies." Actually, it was not the women he was particularly worried about. He saw in their request an "obvious trick" by which male students and "the mob" would mingle with the "ladies" and use "their presence as a shield against the police and troops." Again, a dismissive man brushed off women's indignation and opinions—their agency over their own lives—with the stroke of a pen.

In any case, Russell knew he had to prepare carefully for the protest to come, so he ordered a police cordon to be set up just out of sight of Saad Zaghlul's home, and there he waited with his British soldiers and a line of (Egyptian) conscript police who were instructed not to use violence "and, if necessary, (to) let their faces be scratched by irate finger-nails." Russell knew that local policemen might be reticent to restrain a demonstration of their own countrywomen, so he did his best to underline and exasperate class differences between them and the protestors. "Considerable licence," Russell writes, was given to the policemen "to practise their ready peasant wit on the smart ladies who confronted them." In other words, Russell instigated a deliberate policy of sexual harassment to intimidate the women and control his own men. The women, however, stood their ground and yelled back. According to Shaarawi, some of the Egyptian policemen, caught in the crosshairs, "were moved to the point of tears."[43]

Once the trap was sprung, Russell came out from behind the cordon to address the protestors himself. Claiming that he would have to consult his superiors before deciding if the demonstration could proceed, Russell disappeared, leaving the women for nearly three hours sweltering under a "pitiless sun" with "nowhere to sit except upon the hot curb-stones." "I found the poor dears in a sorry condition," Russell would recall, "their complexions ruined by the sun." Given the women were clad in cloaks and their faces covered by veils, Russell's observation seems both suspect and self-serving. His point, as he wraps up his tale, is to show off the craftiness of his maneuver. When he returned, Russell tells us, the women were only too grateful to retreat in their carriages, "leaving nothing on what might have been a field of battle except an occasional powder-puff or tiny handkerchief."[44]

By the end of the day, Russell concludes, a "threatened tragedy had turned into a perfect polite comedy," but, in fact, there was nothing amusing about the events of March 16 or those that followed. Russell's men were armed with guns, and protestors had already died in the standoff. Both his British colonial authority and his sex conferred on him status and power in the showdown with Egyptian nationalist women on Cairo streets in 1919. The primary reason that events did not end tragically was that Russell, as a British man, could not bring himself to take the "ladies" too seriously. Given time, he assumed, the women would tire of their adventure and return to their homes. He may also have hoped that their husbands would reestablish patriarchal authority and contain their wives, but if so, he was sadly mistaken. By the spring of 1919, Egyptian nationalist men and women were fully engaged in a common fight for national liberation.[45]

"The Entire Egyptian People"

As March edged toward April, the British retained the Wafd leaders in exile, and protests mounted. Women of the popular classes continued to fall to British bullets, including a young widow named Shafiqah bint Muhammad Ashmawi caught in the crossfire. "Egyptians of all classes followed her funeral procession," Shaarawi recalls, "It became the focus of intense national mourning." During these weeks of protest, she and other upper-class women visited the wounded, offered aid to their families, and carefully compiled lists of the dead.[46]

The fact that British authority figures were not used to thinking of women as political actors in Egyptian society worked to female militants' advantage in the spring of 1919, allowing some of them to transport clandestine pamphlets across the city and into the countryside undetected. Even after the British declared it a criminal offense to distribute nationalist literature, women willingly took on the risk, particularly schoolgirls and female schoolteachers. Shaarawi personally encouraged such forms of engagement, visiting the women's teachers' training college in Cairo on several occasions to praise the militancy of the pupils. Another well-connected nationalist woman named Hidiya Afifi (her father-in-law was a senator and a nephew of Zaghlul) stuffed pamphlets into her shopping baskets and took the train to Upper Egypt. At each train station, she would be met by a female schoolteacher who would take a basket and distribute its contents to local citizens. "The British soldiers who searched every train," writes a historian who interviewed Afifi years later, "never suspected that the diminutive gentlewoman, swathed in her veils, was distributing nationalist propaganda." Not all teachers sympathetic to the nationalist cause felt able to take part in the uprising, however. Nabawiya Musa, having received her baccalaureate certificate twelve years earlier, was now serving as the principal of a women's teacher training college in Alexandria, and she knew that if she angered the wrong people, the college could be shut down. "The English inspector was ready to destroy me if my school moved in any way," she later recalled.[47]

Eventually the British accepted the fact that the protestors were not going to disperse of their own accord. General Allenby—who secured his fame during World War I by capturing Palestine—was sent to Egypt as the new high commissioner to manage the uprising. Prepared to make concessions to secure domestic peace, on April 7, 1919, Allenby announced that the Wafd leaders would be released and granted permission to travel straight from Malta to Paris for the peace conference. The following day hundreds of thousands of Egyptians flooded into the streets to celebrate the news. In Cairo, women joined the celebratory procession headed by cabinet ministers and legislators, followed by students, lawyers, judges, and workers. Relegated to the rear of the parade, "upper-class women rode in carriages and women of the lower class rode in carts." Foreigners, watching from hotel balconies, cheered them on.[48]

Saad Zaghlul and the Wafd leaders hastened to Paris to make their case for Egyptian independence, but, unfortunately, the die had been cast before they arrived. Even as the Egyptian delegation was sailing from Malta, British officials were bombarding the American peace delegates with memos asserting that the Egyptian uprising represented (amazingly) both a communist attack on the international order and the opening bid of an Islamic holy war. On April 19, 1919, the day the Wafd leadership landed in Marseilles, President Woodrow Wilson told the British that America would officially recognize the Protectorate in Egypt. The Wafd leaders were dismayed, having truly believed that Wilson's support for national self-determination would lead to Egyptian independence. For weeks, Zaghlul endeavored to change Wilson's mind, seeking an audience with the president, but (unlike the entreaties of white, Western suffragists) his requests went unanswered. Having hit a brick wall with the peacemakers, Wafd leaders again switched tactics, appealing Egypt's case to the court of public opinion.[49]

Through publications and speeches, Wafd leaders sought to sketch a vivid portrait of Egypt as a modern nation prepared to take its place in the international order and unified behind the Wafd's mission. To underscore the latter point, nationalist men commonly pointed to women's participation in the uprising as evidence of the Egyptian people's unanimous support for independence. On August 2, 1919, for example, members of the Egyptian delegation invited some two hundred guests to a banquet in Paris. Over coffee and dessert, Wafd leaders told their guests about the movement that had gained the enthusiastic support of "the entire Egyptian people." Muslims and Christians, lawyers and peasants, men and women all were held up as evidence of this unanimity of spirit. "Ask any neutral witnesses to our recent demonstrations," the Wafd leaders challenged their guests. "They will describe to you moving scenes that made them spill tears of admiration. . . . One saw women carrying the national flag yelling out to the crowd, preaching their love of the Fatherland."[50]

French novelist Victor Margueritte (who would make waves several years later when he published a blockbuster novel featuring an emancipated Modern Woman as the central character) was among the sympathetic foreigners invited to the banquet. Margueritte was so disgusted by the injustice of Egypt's treatment at the peace conference that before year's end he would publish a sixty-eight-page book in defense of the Egyptian cause. His account features a lengthy description of the "high society ladies" who marched in the streets of Cairo and who acted as "passionate interpreters" of the popular will for independence. He even describes Shaarawi's defiant challenge to the British to shoot her and make her Egypt's Edith Cavell, asking his readers, "What scene could be more moving than this?" In vivid prose, Margueritte helped the Wafd leadership defend the popular uprising as a unified, national movement in defense of justice and freedom.[51]

Interestingly, in his account of Shaarawi's altercation with the British, Victor Margueritte claims Shaarawi was "brutalized" by the soldier who restrained her. This was a clear exaggeration of the actual confrontation but not a surprising one. Nationalist literature commonly referenced British attacks on Egyptian women to challenge the idea that Britain's colonial presence was civil. In one widely distributed account of British atrocities committed against civilians, Shaarawi's confrontation with the British appears alongside dozens of accounts of peasant women who were beaten, robbed, or raped by British soldiers. In such accounts, British men are shown to have compromised Egyptian women's honor and, by extension, that of the nation.[52]

Women were thus very much on the minds of Egyptian men as they pleaded for international recognition of their nation's independence in Paris in 1919. The same can be said for Wafd leaders back home who continued to press their case with the British. In a letter to General Allenby, Ali Shaarawi underscored the fact that the "most distinguished women in Egyptian society" had participated in the uprising. "The curtain that ordinarily separates our women of the upper classes from the outside world, did not prevent them from expressing their sentiments," he asserted. Wafd leaders brought up women's activism and victimhood often enough that one can almost overlook the fact that, as eager as they were to praise women's patriotism, male nationalists had much less to say about *women's rights* or women's political participation in an independent Egyptian state.[53]

Others back in Egypt were making that very connection. The newspaper *Al-Ahram*, for instance, lashed back at conservative writers who had been offended by men's willingness to cheer women's actions in defiance of harem customs. *Al-Ahram* dismissed such notions as nonsense, stating: "The only way to view the procession of women is as a step towards participating alongside men in the various walks and developments of public life. We pray to God for wisdom and guidance." Some women, too, began suggesting that the time was ripe to reconsider women's place in Egyptian society. On April 20, 1919, *Al-Ahram* published a letter from one newly constituted organization calling itself the Society for the New Woman. "We are," the secretary explained, "a group of women who decided to form a society to serve the nation by every means we deem correct and beneficial." The society's first objective was to collect donations for victims of British of oppression. "Following this," the letter continued, "we will work towards the advancement of the status of the Egyptian women." Huda Shaarawi donated money to the society and was named as honorary president.[54]

Another male author, this one publishing in the newspaper *Al-Minbar* (and republished in English in the *Egyptian Mail*), hailed the women's

Girls from of the Society for the New Woman demanding women's rights at the opening of the Egyptian Parliament in 1924. (From the personal collection of Margot Badran)

protests as the realization of Qasim Amin's dream articulated in *The Liberation of Women* twenty years earlier. Calling out to Amin beyond the grave, the article began, "We wish you were here now to see the tree you planted flourish and bear fruit. . . . We wish you were here to see the Egyptian woman." The women's demonstration, claimed this author, stood as "proof of the progress of this country." Whereas Amin called for enhancing women's education to make them better wives and mothers, this author praised women for beginning "to take part with man in national affairs." Frustratingly, he credits Amin for women's brave actions, but he also goes out of his way to praise women for speaking their minds. "If we are glad to see Egyptian woman in the arenas of public life," he concluded, "we are more glad to see her raise her voice to declare her feelings and demand the realization of her hopes." In 1919 women were speaking for themselves. What remained to be seen was whether men in power, British or Egyptian, would listen.[55]

"Half the Nation"

For the remainder of 1919, Wafd leaders continued to press their case for Egyptian independence in Europe. In June the British government finally relented and allowed the Egyptian delegation to travel to London, but the offer the British put on the table fell far short of independence, and negotiations fell apart. In Egypt, the mood remained tense. Near the end of the year, Saad Zaghlul returned home a popular hero, and the British government announced it was dispatching a commission to Egypt headed by Colonial Secretary Alfred Milner to investigate the uprising and seek possible remedies (while still protecting British interests). The Wafd leaders, who had no interest in haggling for concessions from their colonial oppressors, refused to cooperate. The Egyptian people greeted the Milner Commission with angry street protests and a nationwide boycott of British goods and services. Once again, women played a central role in organizing popular resistance, becoming more daring, vocal, and organized with each passing day.[56]

Women did not wait for Milner to arrive in Egypt before they began to rally against the British mission. From mid-November through early December, elite women took to their cars and carriages, driving through the streets of Cairo shouting "Down with the Milner Commission!" During one such demonstration, Shaarawi remembers, "British soldiers . . . jumped on the steps of our carriages taunting and hitting us."[57]

On December 12, 1919, female protestors convened a mass meeting at the Coptic Cathedral of Saint Mark—which effectively provided sanctuary from British repression—and issued a public statement in the name of the "Women of Egypt" denouncing the Milner Commission and calling for independence. The statement, sent to Western newspapers and signed by over four hundred women, including Shaarawi, was steeped in the diplomatic language of the day. The women chastised the Allied powers for failing to live up to Wilsonian principles. "Peoples," they wrote, "are not like old clothes that one passes off from one hand to another but in fact are the only ones qualified to determine their own destiny." The women spoke passionately of national self-determination as well as of individual freedom, writing, "It is not permissible for one nation to rob another nation of its rights just as it is not permissible for an individual to attack the freedom of another."[58]

Women helped lead the movement to boycott British goods, which began in late 1919 and went on for years. As household managers, women were well positioned to alter their families' consumption habits, while the most zealous among them sought to monitor the buying habits of their fellow countrymen and countrywomen. At one gathering in Alexandria, women delivered "several enthusiastic speeches" and then "declar[ed] their adherence to the boycott movement." Hidiya Afifi, the same woman who smuggled nationalist literature out of Cairo in shopping baskets earlier that year, was a zealous upholder of the boycott movement in the capital. On one occasion when Afifi was shopping, she happened to see two Egyptians walking into a British store across the street. Dropping everything, she ran out and berated the men "for breaking the nationalist boycott." Wafd leaders praised the women's boycott campaign, calling it "one of the most powerful and effective of the peaceful weapons in our legitimate struggle."[59]

As 1919 gave way to 1920, over a thousand women returned to Saint Mark's Cathedral and took another bold step down the path of political engagement, forming a Wafdist Women's Central Committee. Shaarawi was elected as the first president. The committee's stated goal was to assist the (male) Wafd leaders in obtaining full Egyptian independence. Saad Zaghlul cabled his congratulations to the women, writing, "The demonstration of your will to support the cause of independence fills our hearts with pride. With the creation of your committee you have shown to the civilized world that the mothers rearing the men who will assume control of the affairs of our nation in the future are most worthy of the lofty mission they have undertaken." In retrospect, his wording foreshadowed trouble. Zaghlul praised the *mothers rearing the men* who would govern the nation rather than the women of Egypt: individuals who may legitimately harbor political aspirations of their own.[60]

By the end of the year, men and women's divergent views about Egypt's future became more apparent. In December 1920 the British offered a proposal that would partially meet nationalists' demands but that still fell short of independence. Zaghlul sought input on the proposal from prominent male organizations, but he failed to ask the same of the Wafdist Women's Central Committee. Irate, Shaarawi lashed out. "What makes us . . . indignant," she wrote to Zaghlul, "is that by disregarding us the Wafd has caused foreigners to disparage the renaissance of women." Skeptical Westerners, she told him, had been claiming all along that Wafd leaders had been using women as "a ploy to dupe civilized nations into believing in the advancement of Egypt." But Egyptian women's involvement in the revolution was more than window dressing. "At this moment when the future of Egypt is about to be decided," Shaarawi declared, "it is unjust that the Wafd, which stands for the rights of Egypt and the struggles for its liberation, should deny half the nation its role in that liberation." Zaghlul, astutely, apologized.[61]

From 1920 to 1922, negotiations with the British proceeded in starts and stops, achieving little in the way of a tangible agreement. Wafd women kept up the pressure through boycotts and protests. Shaarawi welcomed female activists into her home on multiple occasions to organize, and the British were concerned enough to send in a spy and document the women's discussions. When the British again sent Zaghlul into exile in the spring of 1921, Shaarawi and other women helped ensure the continuity of the movement.[62]

In February 1922 two unrelated events changed the course of Shaarawi's life. First, her husband, Ali, passed away. Shaarawi buried her husband and returned to the movement, scarcely skipping a beat. She declared, "Let it never be said that there was a woman in Egypt who failed, for personal reasons, to perform her duty to the nation." Second, on February 28, 1922, Great Britain unilaterally proclaimed Egypt's independence, reserving control over communications, foreign defense, foreign commercial interests, and the Sudan. It was a far cry from the terms that the Wafd and the Egyptian people had demanded, but in time, most nationalists came to accept the British framework as a step toward achieving full independence. In March 1923 Zaghlul returned from exile, and in April a new constitution was adopted, establishing a mixed government, to be ruled by a hereditary monarch and governed by an elected legislature. "All Egyptians," the constitution proclaimed, "are equal before the law." In almost the same breath, however, a new electoral law established that only men would be allowed to vote in national elections. Women were deliberately excluded. In January 1924, when the Wafd assumed power and opened the new Parliament, not only were women denied a seat in its chamber, they were also barred from attending the inauguration ceremony (except as the wives of deputies or ministers). Belatedly, Egyptian women were forced to confront the patriarchal nature of Egyptian male nationalism. As women had been in so many other purported liberal democracies, Egyptian women found themselves excluded from the halls of power.[63]

The Egyptian Feminist Union

During the years separating the March uprising of 1919 and the adoption of the new constitution in 1923, Egyptian men and women fought together for their nation's freedom. For Egyptian women, the experience was transformative. Activism and leadership in the protest and boycott movements encouraged women to learn about political affairs, refine their organizational and speaking skills, and embrace the public limelight. Over the course of these years, they came to see themselves as individuals and citizens in addition to daughters, sisters, wives, and mothers. Wafd leaders openly celebrated women's political activism and even promised, albeit privately, to work toward women's liberation once independence had been achieved. Once in power, however, male Wafd leaders closed the gates behind them and tried to placate women with a limited package of reforms, clearly expecting them to acquiesce and retreat. Egyptian women refused to comply. Instead, the Wafd Women's Central Committee issued a communiqué protesting the government's failure to enfranchise women, while separately, another woman (Munir Thabat, who would go on to become a pioneering female journalist) denounced the Wafd for its shortsightedness in *Al-Ahram* and vowed that she and her sisters would fight "to liberate Egyptian women from all outdated restrictions and traditions until they achieve full equality with men."[64]

For Shaarawi, the Wafd's rebuff of women felt all too familiar. She had experienced the Egyptian Revolution of 1919 as a release from the gender constraints that had caused her so much unhappiness in her younger years: the limited access to education, the forced marriage to an older man with a family of his own, the expectation of a long life of seclusion. It led her to reflect back on lessons she had discussed in Eugénie Le Brun Rushdi's salon and in the female lectures she had helped to organize years earlier, particularly the Islamic reformist ideas forwarded by Sheikh Muhammad 'Abduh and reiterated by Qasim Amin: Egypt's independence depended on women's liberation. Shaarawi thought a lot about Qasim Amin during those tumultuous years, wondering what he would make of Egyptian women's passionate engagement in political life. "I hope," she reflected in

1920, "that Qasim's soul is content and happy with what Egypt and the Orient are now witnessing in regards to women's progress, women's keenness to be liberated, and the speed of their liberation." The Wafdists' arrival in power, however, threatened to throw the brakes on women's advancement. Shaarawi was not about to let this happen without a fight.[65]

On March 16, 1923, the fourth anniversary of the first women's demonstration in 1919, Shaarawi invited a dozen or more women who had been active in the nationalist uprising to her home. Together they founded a new organization, the Egyptian Feminist Union. After electing Shaarawi to serve as president, union members elaborated a sweeping program designed to enhance and protect women's rights in Egypt. The first goal was "to raise woman's intellectual and moral level so as to attain political and social equality with man in regard to customs and laws." The union demanded sexual equality in education, including building girls' secondary schools and opening the doors of higher education to women. It called on legislators to reform the laws regulating marriage (to raise the age of consent, to restrict polygamy, and to limit unilateral male divorce), and it called for gradual female suffrage. Over time, Egyptian feminists would add new demands to the list and adopt a more forceful and defiant tone. For the next three decades—until General Nasser led a new revolution in 1952 and overthrew the monarchy—the Egyptian Feminist Union remained the preeminent organization championing women's rights in Egypt and throughout the Arab world.[66]

Egyptian feminists remained profoundly cognizant of the society in which they lived. They challenged neither the legitimacy of religion nor the desirability of maintaining local customs. They insisted women's rights were in keeping with Islam and Pharaonic tradition. They did not speak unequivocally of gender equality in all aspects of public and private life. Instead they focused on social equality, particularly in terms of education. Initially this strategy paid off, and the Egyptian Feminist Union managed to extract notable concessions from male politicians, including raising the minimum marriage age for girls to sixteen, extending mothers' custody over their children in the case of divorce, and opening several girls' secondary schools, with the promise more would follow. In 1929 the Egyptian University in Cairo admitted women for the first time. For the upper- and middle-class Egyptian women who formed the core of the feminist movement, these victories were substantial. By the 1930s educational advances helped broaden women's horizons and allowed them to enter into new professions, particularly in medicine, law, and social work. Conservatives in Egypt fought these reforms, and even liberals balked at tackling many of feminists' most pressing demands. Men's power in the family remained entrenched, including the right to polygamy and the right to force the return of wives who left their homes without their husbands' permission. Appeals for women's suffrage went unanswered.[67]

From the outset, members of the Egyptian Feminist Union recognized that gender oppression transcended the boundaries of nation and religion, and that they stood to benefit from associating their struggle with the broader, international feminist movement. Carrie Chapman Catt, president of the International Woman Suffrage Alliance, and Dutch suffragist Aletta Jacobs had traveled to Egypt in 1911 as part of a world tour designed to stir up interest in feminist organizing outside the Western world. It is possible that Catt and Jacobs met Shaarawi on this visit. In 1923 one of the first decisions of the nascent Egyptian Feminist Union was to accept an invitation from Catt to send a delegation to the International Alliance's

Nabawiya Musa, Huda Shaarawi (*center*), and Saiza Nabarawi in Rome for the meeting of the International Woman Suffrage Alliance, 1923. (Carrie Chapman Catt Papers, Special Collections Department, Bryn Mawr College Library)

upcoming congress in Rome. Shaarawi headed a three-woman delegation, which also included girls' secondary school principal Nabawiya Musa and a young friend and close collaborator of Shaarawi's named Saiza Nabarawi.[68]

The trio set sail from Alexandria on May 4, 1923, in high spirits. Three days later they arrived in Rome, where members of the International Alliance extended them a warm welcome. In her presidential address, Catt singled out Shaarawi and her delegation for praise, saying, "In ancient days there were Egyptian queens and women military leaders of great renown; why not heroines today, bearing aloft the standard of civil and political equality for modern Egyptian woman? Bravo, women of Egypt!" For her part, Shaarawi told the congress of Egyptian women's aspirations for education, opportunity, and equality, tying their claims to the respect shown to women by ancient pharaohs and in early Islam. Challenging Westerners assumptions about mysterious "Oriental" customs, she insisted that that "in fact, nothing is more similar to an Oriental woman than a Western woman." Congress delegates and the press responded warmly. The Italian paper *Il Gironale d'Italia* saluted the "beautiful and cultivated" Shaarawi and congratulated the Egyptians for their "pre-eminent position" in the congress. It was, for Shaarawi and other delegates, an encouraging and exhilarating international debut.[69]

In the 1920s and 1930s Shaarawi would become a fixture in international feminist circles, serving on the executive board of the International Alliance, giving speeches to women's organizations across Europe and the United States (including a tour through southern France in 1934 in support of women's suffrage), and attending all seven of the Alliance congresses held during her tenure, including one in Istanbul, Turkey, in 1935. Shaarawi longed to host an Alliance congress in Cairo as well, but British authorities (who still retained control over foreign affairs) would not condone it. More fully than any other non-Western feminist in the interwar era, Shaarawi tirelessly sought common ground with women from Europe and North America. It was a decision that brought her rich rewards and no end of heartache, as she struggled to explain to Western feminists how impossible it was for Middle Eastern women to embrace *internationalism* when their own *national* self-determination was not fully secured, particularly in the French mandates of Syria and Lebanon and the British mandate of Palestine.[70]

By the 1930s, frustrated with Western-dominated women's organizations, Shaarawi and other Egyptian feminists began to network closer to home.

To such ends, Egyptian women participated in two "Eastern Women's Congresses," held in Damascus in 1930 and Tehran in 1932. These meetings brought Arab feminists together with women from as far away as Afghanistan, Japan, and China, to hammer out a "specifically Eastern basis" for women's rights claims. Committed to this regional feminist dialogue, by the late 1930s Shaarawi began focusing her attention more narrowly on pan-Arab solidarity in defense of Palestine, which was under intensive Zionist pressure due to the rapidly deteriorating situation for Jews in Europe. The Egyptian Feminist Union's decision to convene an Eastern Women's Conference for the Defense of Palestine in Cairo in October 1938 reflected this growing commitment to pan-Arab feminism. In 1944, under Shaarawi's leadership, women from the Middle East would found an Arab Feminist Union dedicated to realizing nationalist and feminist goals throughout the region.[71]

In the meantime, Shaarawi had become a source of inspiration to women of color and women from other colonized nations engaged in their own battles against racism and imperialism as well as sexism. Shaarawi's 1919 standoff with the British police on the streets of Cairo was featured on the pages of the African American civil rights newsletter the *Crisis*, halfway around the world. Women in Tunisia celebrated Shaarawi for demanding "the rights accorded [to women] by our religion but which men's selfishness and women's ignorance have denied them." In these small ways, Shaarawi helped prod international feminism beyond its white, Western, imperialist origins and helped feminists of color begin to redefine women's rights and emancipation in broader and more globally relevant terms.[72]

National Liberation and Individual Freedom

While at the Rome Congress in 1923, Huda Shaarawi and Saiza Nabarawi both dispensed with wearing the face veil (Nabawiya Musa had done so years earlier), finding it an obstacle to communicating with women from the rest of the world. In Europe, the women could easily justify such a change of clothing as a practical necessity, but it did raise the question of what they would do when they returned to Egypt. Nabarawi, who had been partially raised in Paris, had chafed at wearing the veil as a teenager. At the time, Shaarawi (who had been friends with Nabarawi's mother) encouraged the young woman to adapt to local norms, but she also promised her that when the time was ripe, they would both dispense with their face veils together. Had that time arrived?

A crowd of friends, well-wishers, and journalists was at the station in Cairo to greet Shaarawi and Nabarawi when they arrived home. As the train pulled into the station and let out its final burst of steam, the two women stepped onto the platform, their faces uncovered. Their gesture was met with a hushed silence and then with applause and the rustling of cloaks as many of the women who came to greet them reached up to remove their face veils as well. Smiling faces beamed up at Shaarawi and her codelegates.[73]

It was a historic act, played for all it was worth. It was also a lightning rod for political controversy and an act that foretold many of the struggles that would engulf feminism in the Middle East right up to the present day. To feminists' critics, the fact that Shaarawi and Nabarawi cast off their face veils upon returning from a women's conference in Europe only proved that feminism was a dangerous import designed to stir up unrest. Similarly, Shaarawi and other Egyptian feminists' willingness to address Western women as sisters engaged in a common fight at a time when European powers continued to exercise political control in large parts of the Middle East rendered it all too easy for critics to dismiss feminism as an offshoot of imperialism. For the remainder of the twentieth century and into the twenty-first, Middle Eastern feminists have often found themselves on the defensive, forced to rebut those critics who see local campaigns for women's rights as a Western tool designed to weaken local tradition and resistance to outside forces.

The story recounted here flies in the face of such accusations, which ignore the decades of work Egyptian women put into educating themselves about the source of their own oppression and defining their own interests and needs. They ignore women's unflagging defense of Egyptian sovereignty and their brave opposition to British occupation despite the risk to their reputations and their lives. And they ignore the degree to which the Egyptian battle for national liberation was fused, from the beginning, to the equally passionate battle for women's rights: a battle that spilled outward from Paris and breached the colonial divide in the watershed year of 1919.

CHAPTER IV

Springtime in Zurich

Former Enemies in Pursuit of Peace and Freedom

Arriving in Zurich, Switzerland, in early May 1919, American social activist Jane Addams felt as though she had stepped from darkness into the light. Just a week earlier she had been touring the former battlefields of northern France under leaden skies and pounding sleet. Here, the sun beamed down on valleys blanketed in flowers and crowned by glistening alpine peaks. To all the delegates to the International Congress of Women (convened by the soon-to-be-named Women's International League for Peace and Freedom), which opened in Zurich under Addams's leadership on May 12, 1919, Mother Nature's benevolent embrace felt symbolic. "During a whole week of unbroken splendor of sunshine and spring airs," reported one British delegate, "over and over again one heard the same simile used, that it was like getting out of a dark and stifling room into the light and air for women of all countries once more to meet for friendship and counsel."[1]

The warmth of human companionship was no small matter for fifty-eight-year-old Addams and the other delegates to the Zurich Congress, most of whom had embraced pacifism during World War I and had suffered social ostracism as a consequence. This was true even though few among them were absolutist pacifists who rejected war under any circumstances. From 1914 to 1918, in all the warring nations, pacifism was construed broadly. Merely questioning the inevitability of a fight to the finish could be deemed a pacifist act. On both sides of enemy lines, women who dared to call for a negotiated peace found themselves treated as outcasts, if not outright traitors.

For Jane Addams, social ostracism was a bitter pill to swallow. During the twenty-five years up to the outbreak of World War I, Addams had enjoyed near constant human companionship and had basked in the glow of the public limelight, largely due to the fame of Hull House, the settlement house she cofounded in Chicago in 1889. At Hull House, educated women and men lived embedded in a neighborhood of working-class, immigrant families, serving the needs of the community and bridging the social gap between rich and poor. Addams's microexperiment in social democracy was a resounding success, securing her status as a nationally and internationally recognized progressive reformer. Regional politicians and sitting presidents regularly sought her counsel. Some feminists whispered that Addams would make a strong candidate for president herself one day, as soon as American women won the right to vote.[2]

Addams's public actions during World War I brought much of that goodwill crashing down around her shoulders. In horrified response to the conflict in Europe, in January 1915 she helped found the American Women's Peace Party, which called on neutral parties—governments or private citizens—to mediate an end to the conflict. Three months later Addams traveled to Europe to preside over an international feminist, pacifist meeting in the Netherlands and to encourage the warring nations to pursue a negotiated peace. As war fever mounted in the United States, Addams's pacifist actions generated vociferous criticism. By 1916 her name, once hallowed, was equated with betrayal. "Jane Addams," decried one New York paper, "is a silly, vain, impertinent old maid . . . who is now meddling with matters far beyond her capacity." Crippled by recurrent illness and depression, Addams retreated from the public eye for the remainder of the war years. She suffered, she would later say, from the "destroying effect of 'aloneness.'"[3]

The end of World War I opened a new, international chapter in Addams's life, as she and other pacifist women prepared to meet again in Europe for the first time since 1915. Unlike the Western suffragists who participated in the Inter-Allied Women's Conference in Paris in 1919, the pacifist women in Addams's international circle insisted on meeting in a neutral state, where women from the Allied nations and Central Powers could sit down together to discuss the peace terms. Addams sent out a call for women to assemble in Zurich. "What a welcome [we] received from the Swiss people!" she would

Group of delegates to the Zurich Congress, enjoying the sunshine between meetings. (WILPF Papers, Special Collections and Archives, University of Colorado Boulder Libraries)

later write. "We had almost forgotten what it was like to be in a neutral country where it entailed no odium to be a pacifist." If the women's pacifism raised relatively few eyebrows in the Alpine nation, the same cannot be said for their feminism. "The women . . . must be practical," warned the Swiss *Journal de Genève,* "and let international political questions alone." Addams and the other delegates had other plans entirely.[4]

On May 12, 1919, at the same time that the International Congress of Women opened in Zurich, statesmen in Paris released the first public draft of the Versailles Treaty, the peace terms presented by the Allies to the defeated German state. In one of their first official acts, the female delegates in Zurich denounced the treaty as a victor's peace that exchanged justice for retribution. They demanded instead a peace settlement rooted in interdependence and cooperation between men and women as well as among the nations of the world. Firmly convinced that women were predisposed to serve as humanity's peacemakers and that women's voices were needed to tame men's base instincts, female delegates to the Zurich Congress asserted that global stability depended on women's full integration into national and international political life. Looking to the future, they called for a new diplomacy rooted in human compassion and mutual dependence.

Such arguments did not get women very far in 1919. By laying claim to a female propensity toward reconciliation, international-minded women only confirmed Western statesmen in the belief that women lacked the mettle for hard-nosed negotiating. In Paris, global leaders politely dismissed the women and shunted them to the margins of international diplomacy and politics, where they would remain throughout much of the twentieth century.

In response, the women in Zurich transformed what was initially conceived as a temporary, wartime assembly of pacifist-minded reformers into a permanent organization: the Women's International League for Peace and Freedom. For a century running, the WILPF has served as an organizational home for a broad cross-section of global feminists dedicated to an egalitarian and demilitarized world. From its headquarters in Geneva, it would work tirelessly throughout the interwar decades and beyond to carve out a place for women in the expanding world of international affairs. By forwarding Franco-German reconciliation, by campaigning for global disarmament, and by challenging the imperialist status quo, the WILPF sought to model the type of compassionate diplomacy that would be needed if the world was going to avoid another catastrophic war. In 1931 Jane Addams would be awarded the Nobel Peace Prize, the first of two WILPF leaders to be accorded that honor and a symbol of the importance of women's intervention in international affairs in a century overwhelmingly defined by mass violence and modern warfare. Though they often swam against the diplomatic tides, across the twentieth century and into the next, WILPF members have boldly asserted that international security rests on the willingness of global leaders to empower women as peacemakers, both in times of conflict *and* during the calm between the storms, when the fragile seeds of compassionate diplomacy can take root and blossom.[5]

Jane Addams's Initiation to Progressive Politics

Jane Addams, in her typically self-effacing manner, never sought personal glory for bringing feminist pacifists together during and after World War I. "Others have said I was the leader of this movement," she would write of the wartime gathering of pacifist women in 1915, "but in fact, the Europeans planned everything and just needed a woman from a neutral country as president." There is some truth to her claim. The impetus to build an international women's peace movement during World War I came from Europe, or, more specifically, from the Netherlands, where Dutch suffragist Dr. Aletta Jacobs bravely called women from warring and neutral nations together at The Hague. Still, Addams was not just any woman from any neutral country. She came to Europe with a long list of impressive credentials.[6]

Born in 1860 in rural Illinois, Addams was raised by her father, John, a successful flour mill owner and an Illinois state senator, and by her stepmother, Anna. (Jane's mother, Sarah Addams, went out on a frigid winter night to help deliver a neighbor's baby, slipped on the ice, and died from internal bleeding when Jane was two years old.) Addams's father was a member of Abraham Lincoln's new Republican Party. One of Addams's earliest childhood memories was returning home from playing with friends in April 1865 and finding two American flags, adorned in black ribbon, attached to the front gate of her home. Inside, her father wept as he told his young daughter that Lincoln had been shot. "The two flags, my father's tears, and his impressive statement that the greatest man in the world had died constituted my initiation," Addams writes, "into the thrilling and solemn interests of a world lying quite outside the two white gateposts."[7]

Deeply influenced by her evangelical Protestant upbringing but resistant to religious dogma, Addams aspired to become a doctor and work among the poor. As a teenager, she attended the Rockford Female Seminary, where she developed a reputation as a serious student and a talented orator. Addams seemed bound for a bright future, but shortly after she graduated her father died, and she found herself emotionally adrift. Seeking distraction, and following a pattern common to young American women of wealth in the late nineteenth century, Addams, now aged twenty-three, arranged to leave on a European tour.

Addams enjoyed Europe, ultimately making two separate extended trips to the continent. Unlike her travel companions, however, she was more drawn to the poor neighborhoods of Europe's large cities than she was to museums or monuments. There, in London's down-and-out East End, she was introduced to a novel institution: a settlement house called Toynbee Hall, where young Oxford graduates lived in an elegant building set among the poor tenements, offering free lectures, clubs, and classes to their working-class neighbors. Addams was inspired. She returned home to Illinois having found the sense of purpose that had eluded her since finishing college. Taking her cue from Toynbee Hall, she would confront poverty and pursue democratic fellowship by opening the first settlement house in the United States.[8]

On the west side of Chicago, in a neighborhood populated by recent immigrants, Addams found the perfect site for her grand social experiment: a spacious home built by real estate magnate Charles Hull. Addams threw much of her inheritance into renovating the home and preparing it to welcome its first residents. Hull House opened its doors in 1889 and quickly became a cherished institution, offering classes and clubs to men, women, and children in the surrounding neighborhood. Hull House was co-ed, but it particularly attracted ambitious female social reformers who appreciated the ability to "lead a life that was both independent *and* centered on community." In 1893 Chicago hosted the World's Fair, and international visitors flocked to Hull House to observe the institution for themselves. They in turn carried word of it—and its mild-mannered founder, Jane Addams—across the Atlantic.[9]

Living among radical settlement house residents and befriending poverty-stricken neighbors changed how Addams viewed social reform. Christian charity, she came to believe, could only go so far. Government intervention was necessary to right the wrongs of industrial capitalism. Addams soon found herself drawn into a variety of lobbying and organizational efforts. In the early twentieth century she fought exploitative sweatshops, battled child labor, championed unionization, and opposed racial segregation. In 1903 she became a founding member of the National Women's Trade Union League; in 1909 she joined the board of the newly minted National Association for the Advancement of Colored People. The experience of promoting all these causes convinced Addams that women needed to be able to vote and hold office, transforming her into an avid suffragist. The granting of honorary degrees by several prestigious universities and her selection by the *Ladies' Home Journal* as the "Foremost American Woman" all stood as testament to Jane Addams's towering status as an intellectual, activist, and social reformer on the eve of the First World War.[10]

Addams's Pacifism at Home and Abroad

The outbreak of World War I changed Addams's life forever. From August 1914 to April 1917 the war remained a distant European affair for most Americans; yet for Addams, who lived embedded in a community of recent immigrants, the animosities of the far-off conflict played out close to home. As her German neighbors distanced themselves from Russian and Italian friends, Addams revolted "not only against the cruelty and barbarity of war, but even more against the reversal of human relationships which war implied." Her heart broke at this rending of the social fabric, but what could she or others horrified by the war possibly do?[11]

Two European feminists from opposing enemy camps supplied an answer. In 1914 Emmeline Pethick-Lawrence from England and Rosika Schwimmer from Hungary had embarked on a joint speaking tour across the United States, insisting that women bore "no responsibility whatsoever" for the war's outbreak. The two women denounced the evils of "male statecraft" and demanded an immediate peace. After hearing them lecture, Addams agreed to call a mass women's meeting in Washington, D.C., to rally American women against the war.[12]

Three thousand women (and a few men) attended the peace meeting, held from January 9 to 11, 1915, where they heard powerful speeches decrying the carnage in Europe. In response, attendees formed a Women's Peace Party, which sought to carve out a bold new role for women in foreign policy making: "We demand that women ought to be given a share in deciding between war and peace in all the courts of high debate," the party platform read. Addams agreed to serve as chairwoman. From her headquarters in Chicago, she helped organize mass petition drives, antiwar theater productions, and letter-writing campaigns, all designed to promote a negotiated end to the war. Addams also met personally with President Woodrow Wilson on several occasions to try to persuade him to volunteer to mediate a settlement in Europe, to no avail.[13]

At the same time Addams was organizing American women to press for a negotiated peace, Dutch suffrage leader Aletta Jacobs was pursuing similar ends in blood-soaked Europe. Jacobs, the first female doctor in the Netherlands, was a long standing suffragist and social reformer. As war erupted in Europe, she despaired as feminists from warring nations— influenced by national propaganda campaigns demonizing the enemy— retreated into defensive nationalism. Unwilling to allow war to sever the bonds of sisterhood, Jacobs decided to act. In a letter to all members of the executive board of the International Woman Suffrage Alliance, she offered to host a meeting in her neutral nation, writing: "In these dreadful times, in which so much hate has been spread, we women have to show that we at least retain our solidarity . . . and mutual friendship."[14]

The responses she received were "hardly encouraging." The major French, German, and Belgian suffrage societies flatly refused to participate. English suffragists were divided, and the Alliance board refused to endorse the proposal. Jacobs proceeded anyway. Refusing to bow to wartime antagonisms, she issued a call for women from both warring and neutral nations to convene at The Hague on April 28, 1915, to issue a joint protest against the war and to strategize what women could do to bring about its rapid end.[15]

Seeking legitimacy as well as media attention, Jacobs astutely asked Addams if she would preside. "Even our opponents were impressed," Jacobs would later write, "with the news that the conference would be led by a woman of world repute, none other than Jane Addams, the founder of Hull House in Chicago, a well-known pacifist who would be accompanied by a large group of women." In total, forty-seven American women crossed the hostile waters of the Atlantic in 1915.[16]

Participation by women from the warring nations was mixed. The British government denied passports to the 180 British women who applied to travel to The Hague (although three British women, already out of the country, were able to participate). Germany was better represented with a delegation led by radical suffragists Lida Gustava Heymann and her life partner Dr. Anita Augspurg. Only a tiny handful of French feminists were willing to endorse the meeting. The Dutch planning committee reached out to one, a refugee from German-occupied northern France named Jeanne Mélin who had been vocal in her opposition to the war, even offering to pay Mélin's way to The Hague. In the end, neither she nor any other French woman was willing or able to attend, but in April 1915 over one hundred delegates from twelve warring and neutral nations came to The Hague, where they joined a thousand or more Dutch women to demand an immediate, negotiated peace.[17]

Addams opened The Hague Congress on April 28 with some degree of trepidation. Would women be able to transcend the bitter antagonisms produced by the war? And even if women could maintain their solidarity, would the Allied and neutral powers allow them to speak their minds? Dutch policemen flooded the meeting hall, expecting trouble. "I will confess that the first day we were a little cautious," Addams would later write. By declaring the question of war guilt off-limits, however, the delegates maintained an air of solidarity and the meeting proceeded without incident.[18]

Over the course of three days of deliberation, the delegates issued a formal protest against the "madness and the horror of war" and adopted a series of resolutions they hoped would serve as a roadmap out of the morass. They called on the belligerent powers to submit proposals for acceptable peace terms, and they asked neutral countries to serve as disinterested arbiters until agreement could be reached. They also demanded the vote for women, insisting that full female enfranchisement was a prerequisite to a just peace. Other resolutions advocated an end to secret treaties, the pursuit of general disarmament, and the creation of a permanent international court of arbitration. Determined to force the global powers to consider their proposals, the women voted to send envoys to each of the major belligerent and neutral countries to press for a negotiated peace. In the two months that followed, Addams, Jacobs, and Rosa Genoni from Italy visited prime ministers and foreign ministers in seven European countries (plus the Vatican), while a second group of women called on the governments of Scandinavia and Russia. The women were received respectfully, although their proposals were ignored, and the war continued its bloody march.[19]

All their work, Addams would later admit, had been in vain. Or had it? After returning from Europe, Addams presented the women's resolutions to one final head of state: Woodrow Wilson, who appeared "very much interested" in their proposals. When Addams met again with the president three months later, she saw that the pages she had given him were handled and worn. "You see I have studied these resolutions," Wilson told Addams. "I consider them by far the best formulation which up to the moment has been put out by anybody." As Addams and other women's peace activists would often point out, at least six of Wilson's famous Fourteen Points—including the call for all territorial transfers to be backed by popular consent, the rejection of secret treaties, and the plan for international mediation of disputes—closely resemble the resolutions formulated by women at The Hague in 1915. Although unable to end the war, pacifist women had made their own contribution toward shaping the peace to come.[20]

Addams returned home from Europe as the president of yet another organization, the newly constituted International Committee of Women for a Permanent Peace, charged with keeping communication channels open between feminists until they could reconvene at war's end. Her new title, unlike many that came before it, did little to endear Addams to her fellow Americans. By late 1915 war fever was already mounting in the United States. Addams got a taste of the shifting political climate soon after arriving home, when she addressed a peace rally at Carnegie Hall in New York. She told the crowd about conversations she had had with soldiers in

Europe, some of whom reported being given alcohol to steel their nerves before heading into battle. It was a mild claim, rooted in fact, but it was enough to infuriate war correspondent and antisuffragist Richard Harding Davis. In a letter to the editor of the *New York Times*, Davis berated Addams for insulting the courage of men in uniform, calling her a "complacent and self-satisfied woman." Theodore Roosevelt, who had formerly sought Addams's public endorsement when he was running for a second term as president, now denounced her and other female pacifists as "peace prattlers" who uttered "silly platitudes."[21]

Addams's fall from grace was swift and hard. For the remainder of the war, in public speeches, she was as likely to be greeted with boos and jeers as with applause. After America's declaration of war in 1917, many of her close friends threw their support behind the war effort, and Addams's sense of isolation deepened. Illness and depression hounded her. Working for Herbert Hoover and the U.S. Food Administration (which promoted food conservation at home to help supply hungry populations abroad) offered some relief, but without a doubt, the war years were the loneliest of her life. Only with the armistice of November 11, 1918, would Addams be able to look to the future again with hope.[22]

The 1919 Zurich Congress

As one of its final acts at The Hague in 1915, the International Committee of Women for a Permanent Peace vowed to reconvene in the same place and at the same time as the eventual peace conference to allow women to weigh in on the settlement. Long before the global conflict was over, in other words, pacifist women were already staking a claim for themselves as diplomatic actors in the postwar negotiations. Executing this plan once peace finally came, however, proved more difficult than they had imagined.

The announcement that the peace conference would be held in Paris proved the first obstacle. No woman from the defeated Central Powers would be able to secure permission to enter the French capital in 1919. Plans to convene a women's congress in Paris were thus quickly abandoned. Aletta Jacobs stepped into the breach and generously offered The Hague once again as a meeting site, but she also warned it would take some months to get everything arranged. Finally, in mid-March, with the negotiations advancing quickly in Paris, Swiss feminists offered their country as a neutral meeting ground. Unwilling to delay any longer, Addams wrote to prospective delegates, instructing them to finalize their travel plans and secure the necessary paperwork. The congress would convene in Zurich in early May 1919.[23]

Nearly 150 women from fifteen different nations made their way to Switzerland, a remarkable number given the difficulties of travel and the ongoing hostility of some governments to pacifist activism. In contrast to 1915, the British government did not try to block the British delegation's passage, as long as each of the women, twenty-six in all, agreed not to indulge in "Socialist propaganda" while abroad. Three Irish women also attended the Congress, although they refused to sit with the British delegation and promptly placed a resolution on the agenda in support of self-determination for Ireland. The three Australian delegates had the farthest to travel. It took them two months to reach Zurich by way of India, Egypt, and (after an unexpected detour) England.[24]

Other Allied governments made things difficult. France denied or delayed passports to prospective delegates (only three made it to Zurich, and not until the end of the congress). The Italian government was similarly uncooperative. Only Rosa Genoni managed to secure a visa, and even then, only when she swore the purpose of her trip was to study fashion. "This may seem like camouflage," reported Constance Drexel in the *Chicago Tribune*, "but, in fact, Signora Genoni is trying her best to keep her pledge as she is making a study between sessions of the attractive hats and blouses in the shop windows." Belgium sent no delegates at all. Its government threatened to "to expatriate any woman" who participated.[25]

The German delegates arrived from a defeated country wracked by strikes and, in some places, open revolution. Anita Augspurg and Lida Gustava Heymann sought to travel to Zurich from Bavaria, where German communists had set up a short-lived Soviet-style workers' republic. The two women supported the revolutionary government but suffered nonetheless when it refused to issue them passports (arguing that national boundaries and visas were a capitalist invention and thus unnecessary). By early May, however, the revolutionary government in Bavaria was overthrown, "passports were in vogue again," and Augspurg and Heymann were able to depart, two among twenty-five German delegates who would travel to Zurich for the Women's Congress.[26]

Railway strikes and labor shortages in Central Europe impeded Scandinavian and Dutch delegates' travel to the congress. The *New York Times*

Zurich Congress delegates Anita Augspurg (Germany), Charlotte Despard (Great Britain), Lida Gustava Heymann (Germany), Rosa Genoni (Italy), Leopoldine Kulka (Austria), and Alice Hamilton (United States). (WILPF Papers, Special Collections and Archives, University of Colorado Boulder Libraries)

covered their travails, describing how the northern European women were forced to cook meals "over their little spirit lamps on station platforms while waiting for trains that ran without schedules." Faced with repeated delays, the conductor of the train conveying Aletta Jacobs from Holland to Zurich simply gave up and turned around. "We were given the choice of either returning home or continuing at our own risk," Jacobs would recall. "Repeatedly we waited on cold platforms until a train materialized to take us a stage further."[27]

Jane Addams arrived in Zurich on schedule in early May, having traveled first to Paris with a coterie of well-respected women who composed the heart of the American delegation. Several were longtime Hull House friends who now held positions of authority and power. These included Florence Kelley, secretary general of the National Consumers League, and Dr. Alice Hamilton, a leading industrial toxicologist who had just become the first woman to be offered a faculty appointment at Harvard University. Jeanette Rankin also joined the delegation. Rankin was the first congresswoman in American history, elected to the House of Representatives by the people of Montana in 1916, four years before the passage of the Nineteenth

Amendment to the Constitution that would guarantee all American women the right to vote. Several months after taking office, Rankin would cast one of fifty votes against America's entry in the First World War. Finally, although the *New York Times* did not feel compelled to acknowledge her presence, civil rights activist Mary Church Terrell of Washington, D.C., was among the delegates traveling with Addams to Zurich.[28]

With generous monetary assistance from the Americans, Swiss feminists reserved the elegant Hotel Glockenhof for the meeting. As president of the congress, Addams sat on a raised platform at one end of the grand ballroom, along with an array of secretaries and interpreters who provided rapid translation between English, German, and French. The various national delegations sat at large tables decorated with flowers. Swiss girls acted as messengers, proudly displaying their official status with red and blue ribbons pinned to their dresses. Alice Hamilton found them natural and "delightful." "Their cheeks are crimson," she wrote home, "and I think there isn't as much face powder in use in the whole city to last an American typist one day." "Outside," another participant noted, "it was as though nature wanted to welcome the peace workers. The gardens, the shores of the lake, the green hillsides bloomed under the luminous sky of the first true days of spring."[29]

Zurich Congress in session, April 1919. (WILPF Papers, Special Collections and Archives, University of Colorado Boulder Libraries)

Addams's role was understated but pivotal. "She is not a leader who imposes her will," explained one of the Swiss organizers. "But even if she is not a general giving rigid orders, she has the rarer and more precious power of encouraging collaboration. . . . Everyone feels secure with her, as though they were sheltered by her wings." Under Addams's benevolent leadership, the Zurich Congress finally opened on May 12, 1919, and pacifist women prepared to do what male world leaders in Paris would not: sit down across the table from their former enemies and discuss what might constitute a just and lasting peace.[30]

The Allied Food Blockade

As Jane Addams prepared to call the Zurich Congress to order, she thought about the warnings she had repeatedly heard in Paris during her stay the weeks prior: too much lingering hostility divided former enemy camps for an international congress to succeed. "Inevitably we felt a certain restraint," she would later write, "when we considered seeing the 'alien enemy' face to face." Addams's first such encounter came the day she arrived in Zurich, when she bumped into Leopoldine Kulke, an Austrian woman who had attended the 1915 congress at The Hague. "She was so shrunken and changed that I had much difficulty in identifying her with the beautiful woman I had seen three years before," Addams wrote. "My first reaction was one of overwhelming pity and alarm as I suddenly discovered my friend standing at the very gate of death." Ashamed of her own comfort in the face of such obvious privation, Addams exchanged her room "in the best hotel in Zurich" for much "humbler" lodgings.[31]

The hunger and illness that followed the war were imprinted on the emaciated bodies of some of the German and Austrian delegates who attended the Zurich Congress. Food shortages had been a near constant in the latter years of the war on both sides of enemy lines, but in the spring of 1919, women from the vanquished states were suffering more than most. The Allied food blockade of the Central Powers, enforced by the British navy to considerable effect during World War I, remained largely in place after the armistice, as peace terms were being negotiated. The collapse of the German and Austro-Hungarian Empires interfered with food supply chains as well. War's end thus brought little immediate relief to the hungry populations of Central Europe, who, in some places, were facing near-famine conditions.[32]

For women who shouldered much of the burden of feeding their families, the ongoing blockade rendered postwar politics deeply personal. Just days after the armistice, the largest women's association in Germany sent an open letter to French, British, and American suffrage organizations (as well as to Woodrow Wilson's wife) imploring them to use their influence with their governments to lift the blockade. For the most part, the request was met with stony silence if not outright hostility. Allied suffragists asked why German women had not opposed their own government's wartime policies—including civilian requisitions in occupied France and Belgium—that had rendered their own families' lives precarious for so many years. In 1919 most Allied women, like men, had trouble evincing sympathy for the former enemy when their own suffering was still acute.[33]

Such a hardened attitude was more difficult to maintain when the "enemy" ceased to be an abstraction. In Zurich, the suffering fostered by the blockade was plain for all to see, as in the case of a German delegate who arrived at the congress one morning speechless and bereft, having just learned that her daughter had died of tuberculosis. "It was through hunger that the decline set in," one of the English delegates whispered quietly to another. For Alice Hamilton, stories of elderly victims of starvation were even more heartrending than those of children: "The Austrians say there is not food enough for children and for the old, the children must be saved, the old must die."[34]

For most of the attendees at the congress, Austrian delegate Leopoldine Kulke came to personify the politics of hunger. "I remember her four years ago at The Hague . . . clear-skinned and healthy," wrote another American delegate. "Here in Zurich I scarcely know her, hollow-eyed, mottled skin drawn over protruding bones, hands like birds' claws." On the first evening of the Congress, Kulke was invited to give a plenary address. In it, she described what it felt like to step from her war-torn country into the relative wealth of Switzerland. "You all know the fairy tale of the beggar who woke up . . . in the King's palace?" she opened. "I think this man must have felt about as I did on the first day after my arrival in Zurich. . . . I found coffee, rolls, eggs, milk, and sugar on the table for breakfast. . . . All of these articles we had not seen for a long, long while!" Hunger, she worried, was eating at the moral heart of her country, turning neighbor against neighbor in a bitter fight for survival. If the picture in Austria was bleak, however, Kulke's experience since arriving in Zurich offered hope. Here, she explained, "women who had crossed the Channel and the ocean shook hands with me and did not look at me with contempt but on the contrary, their eyes expressed the sincerest sympathy." Kulke could not survive on sympathy alone. She would die just three months after the Zurich Congress concluded its work.[35]

The day after Kulke's speech, by a unanimous vote the Zurich Congress adopted a resolution condemning the manmade famine in Central Europe as a "disgrace to civilization," demanding the Allied blockade be lifted immediately, and calling on the government leaders in Paris to develop international institutions to oversee a just distribution of the world's resources. The resolution was telegraphed to the peacemakers in Paris to drive home the urgency of the matter. Of the members of the Supreme Council, only President Wilson replied, telling the women their resolution "appeals both to my head and to my heart," but he had to admit, "The present outlook is extremely unpromising because of infinite practical difficulties." Although small shipments of food would begin to trickle in, the blockade would remain in place until the Central Powers agreed to the peace terms.[36]

The Versailles Treaty

The peace settlement with Germany was at the forefront of women's minds as they met together in Zurich. "It was a coincidence," reported the *New York Times*, "that the women's first sessions found the ink on the peace terms hardly dry." Although elements of the settlement had been released weeks earlier, only in mid-May could the global public take stock of the Allied peacemakers' proposed terms. By virtue of this chance timing, the International Congress of Women in Zurich became the first international body to weigh in on the merits or failings of the Versailles Treaty.[37]

Back in Paris, the Big Three—Woodrow Wilson, David Lloyd George, and Georges Clemenceau—had been locked in nonstop debate for months over what terms to impose on Germany as a consequence of its defeat in the First World War. Broad consensus among the statesmen over the need to punish Germany and extract payment for war damages gave way, over the course of the negotiations, to an acrimonious fight over the details. In the end, the Versailles Treaty required that Germany give up all its overseas colonies; cede part of its territory to France, Denmark, and Poland; decommission its air force as well as much of its navy; limit its standing army to 100,000 men; demilitarize the western border region of the Rhineland; and pay reparations in both a monetary sum and raw materials like coal and timber. Were the terms unprecedented in their severity? Certainly not. The Brest-Litovsk Treaty, which Germany had imposed on the defeated Russian Empire just a year earlier, was equally if not more onerous. The French had also lost territory and been saddled with hefty reparations bills after both the Napoleonic Wars and the Franco-Prussian War of 1870. But for the German people, who had anticipated a settlement in line with the principles of Wilson's Fourteen Points, official word of the treaty's terms came as a terrible blow.

For the women in Zurich, the Versailles Treaty spelled disaster. Permanent peace, they firmly believed, could be built only on a foundation of popular sovereignty, open diplomacy, mutual disarmament, and international governance. As proposed, the peace settlement elevated Allied territorial gains over the promise of national self-determination; it disarmed one side only—Germany—while leaving the Allies' armed forces intact; and it excluded Germany, at least temporarily, from the League of Nations. As for reparations, "the financial clauses will provoke suffering enough to cause anarchy and ruin for generations," warned Ethel Snowden, the outspoken British delegate charged with introducing a resolution on the Versailles Treaty to the assembled body. "Idealism never received such a blow as it has received from those well-meaning statesmen who have not had the courage to do the right thing."[38]

Not all the women at the Zurich Congress shared Snowden's socialist sympathies, but even moderate delegates found the peace terms troubling. By a unanimous vote, the delegates passed a resolution stating, "This International Congress of Women expresses its deep regret that the terms of peace proposed at Versailles should so seriously violate the principles upon which alone a just and lasting peace can be secured, and which the democracies of the world had come to expect." The women condemned the treaty for denying "the principles of self-determination," for recognizing "the right of the victors to the spoils of war," and for fostering "discords and animosities, which can only lead to future wars." Presciently, the women warned the Versailles Treaty would result in the "spread of hatred," and they implored the Allied leaders to "bring the peace into harmony with those principles first enumerated by President Wilson." This resolution— like the one condemning the blockade—was transmitted immediately to Paris. To this entreaty, even Woodrow Wilson could muster no reply. *Realpolitik*, not political idealism, had seized hold of Paris by May 1919. The peace terms with Germany would largely stand as is.[39]

For the pacifist feminists gathered at Zurich, the Versailles Treaty only drove home the point that they had been making since the outbreak of the war: men could no longer be trusted to manage global affairs. Constance Drexel laid out the women's critique on the pages of the *Chicago Tribune*: "The speakers declared in no mistakable terms that men seemed to have made such a great mess of things that woman had better get in and see what she could do as she certainly could not make matters any worse." Seventy-six-year-old Charlotte Despard, a veteran of the bitter suffrage wars in Britain, drew loud applause from the audience when she insisted it was high time for women to "enter into what the men consider the sacred precincts of their foreign affairs." Unable to alter the terms of the peace settlement in 1919, the International Congress of Women in Zurich looked to the future and sketched out an explicitly feminist and pacifist vision of the world order to come.[40]

The League of Nations

When it came to future peaceful relations, no section of the Versailles Treaty elicited more hope and controversy than that establishing the League of Nations. To Woodrow Wilson, "the League of Nations was the centerpiece of the peace negotiations": the guarantor of a new world order in which national power would be restrained by international interests and states would resolve their differences through arbitration rather than with arms. Much more than a universal tribunal, the League of Nations would be a standing world government, capable of acting in moments of crisis but also charged with developing peaceful relations to prevent crises from arising in the first place. As a sign of the importance accorded it by the peacemakers, the Covenant of the League of Nations was incorporated as the first section of all the treaties that marked the end of the First World War.[41]

The League Covenant, like every other document drawn up in Paris that spring, represented a compromise between competing interests. The democratic ideals that inspired the League were institutionalized with the creation of a General Assembly, in which member states would all have an equal voice. Practically speaking, however, power was concentrated in the hands of an Executive Council dominated by the Great Powers. Designed to prevent future wars, the covenant encouraged disarmament and arbitration of international disputes, but it required neither and lacked the ability to enforce its will. In lieu of allowing former German and Ottoman subjects to exercise the full right of self-determination, the League created a mandatory system, by which "advanced nations" (principally Great Britain and France) were charged with safeguarding the development of peoples deemed "not yet able to stand by themselves under the strenuous conditions of the modern world." Nominally a world government, the League, in its initial iteration, would exclude the defeated powers.[42]

The question of whether to endorse this League Covenant, imperfect as it was, proved one of the few real points of contention at the Zurich Congress in 1919. The issue at hand, according to Constance Drexel in the *Chicago Tribune*, was "whether the present League of Nations was a child worth cuddling and developing or such a misfit that it ought not to have been allowed to be born in the world." On the whole, the American, Scandinavian, Dutch and Swiss delegations were the strongest supporters of the League. They argued the covenant "was by far the best part of the treaty, and marked a great advance in international cooperation." In stark opposition, a more radical, British-led contingent complained that the League, as laid out in the Treaty of Versailles, was like a "boat with a hole in it." Ethel Snowden condemned the international body as a "League of conquerors against the conquered."[43]

The two factions met over several days to hammer out a compromise resolution that could capture pacifist feminists' appreciation of the League in concept while still expressing their criticisms of the League's proposed structure and mandate. In particular, they called for revising the covenant to allow for free and open membership to all nation-states (including the defeated powers) and to demand the simultaneous reduction of arms by all League members. They also insisted the League adhere to the principle of self-determination. While they did not question the legitimacy of the mandate system as a means of preparing colonized and subjugated peoples for self-governance, they did call on the League to guide all "backward races"—not just those formerly under German or Ottoman control—toward independence.[44]

Seemingly the only provision of the covenant that did not elicit some level of critique was article 7, which, thanks to the hard work of Marguerite de Witt Schlumberger and the Inter-Allied Women's Conference, opened all positions in the League to women and men on equal terms. As much as they applauded this provision, however, the Zurich delegates were under no illusion that it alone would significantly advance women's rights around the world. In their eyes, the League needed to go much further, and they voted to press the peacemakers to state explicitly that the international government was committed to the "establishment of full equal suffrage and full equality of women with men politically, socially and economically."[45]

Congress delegates also endorsed a "Women's Charter," which they wanted inserted in the final peace treaty, requiring all contracting parties to recognize that "the natural relation between men and women is that of interdependence and cooperation and that it is injurious to the community to restrict women to a position of dependence, to discourage their education or development, or to limit their opportunities." Specific provisions called for protecting women against slavery and sex trafficking, guaranteeing both sexes equality in marriage and in guardianship rights over their children, requiring the legal recognition of children born out of wedlock, acknowledging the independent citizenship status of married women, opening all educational and professional opportunities to men and women on an equal basis, guaranteeing equal pay for equal work, and providing some form of payment for the labor of motherhood. They also wanted international recognition of the principle that a mother should never be deprived of the ability to feed her children in times of war or conflict. "Without claiming that these principles are complete," the charter stated, "the Contracting Parties are of the opinion, that they are well fitted to guide the policy of the League of Nations, and that, if adopted by the communities which are Members of the League, they will confer lasting benefits upon the whole world."[46]

Much like the Inter-Allied Women's Conference that met in Paris several months earlier, the International Women's Congress in Zurich thus forwarded a sweeping social justice agenda, insisting that the League of Nations could hope to foster a peaceful world order only if it addressed the fundamental equality and security of all people, women as well as men. Racial equality was addressed too, thanks to the passionate speech and carefully worded resolution brought before the Zurich Congress by America's lone delegate of color, Mary Church Terrell (as we saw earlier). Overall, congress delegates called for altering the League Covenant to more clearly acknowledge the connection between individual rights and international peace. In other words (and in language that would become encoded in the Universal Declaration of Human Rights three decades in the future), they pushed for a League of Nations that would recognize "the inherent dignity and . . . the equal and inalienable rights of all members of the human family."[47]

With their resolutions and Women's Charter, feminists in Zurich demanded the right to enter the "sacred precincts" of international affairs. They did so, in part, to demand equality and justice for themselves and the members of their own sex, but they did so, as well, in the name of world peace. Global stability, they believed, depended on women's ability to temper men's warring instincts and rebuild international relations on a foundation of compassion, reciprocity, and trust. This meant, in the first instance, embracing former enemies as partners in the world order to come. The reconciliation of former enemies was a constant theme throughout the week of meetings in Zurich. On the last day of the congress, it took center stage.

"We Will Build a Bridge from Germany to France"

Although in her opening address Jane Addams encouraged the delegates to steer clear of "rancorous memories of willful misunderstanding or distrust of so-called enemies," the women who came to Zurich in 1919 were not blank slates. For the women from recently warring nations, the acrimony of the immediate past needed to be acknowledged before it could be overcome. From Monday through Friday, over simple meals in hotel restaurants, during long walks through Zurich's inviting gardens, and in chance encounters in the street, women from former enemy nations engaged in the emotionally difficult work of mending the frayed fabric of sisterhood. Such acts of microdiplomacy were critical to the overall success of the congress. By acknowledging one another's stories of adversity and by sharing similar tales of persecution due to pacifist beliefs, women from the Allied and Central Powers began rebuilding the bonds of trust that allowed for the Zurich Congress to proceed harmoniously and for international women's organizations to begin to heal and rebuild.[48]

This sense of unity was aided by the fact that among the Allied nations, only the Americans and the British sent sizable delegations to Zurich.

Russian women, whose nation was embroiled in a bloody civil war, and Belgian women, whose government opposed the meeting, were notably absent. France also had no delegates present for most of the congress. As a result, resolutions condemning the blockade and the Versailles Treaty were adopted without any input from women who had experienced the war years under German occupation. Constance Drexel found this absence notable, wondering aloud in the *Chicago Tribune* if the delegates would have mustered a unanimous vote condemning the Versailles Treaty had French women been present for the discussion.[49]

In fact, although none of the delegates would state so publicly, deliberations at the Zurich Congress were decidedly skewed in favor of the Central Powers. British delegate Mary Sheepshanks acknowledged as much years later writing, "there was a tendency in some of the speeches made at the Congress to 'lean over backwards' and, while condemning harshness to Germany, to forget Germany's brutality to France." American delegate Alice Hamilton made the same observation in a candid letter home to a friend. "To be quite honest," she wrote, "they are a bit difficult, these German women." Hamilton complained that the British and the Americans "were almost over-doing it" in their eagerness to demonstrate their solidarity with women from the Central Powers. "We sympathized and we pitied and we passionately declared that our governments were cruel (this British said) or culpably yielding (this we said). . . . We grew a bit tired of having all the repentance on our side." True reconciliation commanded an equality of grievances and reciprocal forgiveness. It required the conquered to find common ground with the conquerors.[50]

With the arrival in Zurich of Frenchwoman Jeanne Mélin on May 17, the final day of the congress, the women's ability to find common ground was finally put to the test. Significantly, Mélin came to Zurich directly from the Ardennes, a region that had been overrun by the Germans in the fall of 1914 and had remained under foreign occupation for the rest of the war. She was, in the eyes of the Zurich delegates, a living embodiment of the invaded region of northern France. If the work of reconciliation was to be grounded in forgiveness, Mélin had the moral authority to pardon. More than any other woman who came to Zurich that spring, she spoke for the displaced and terrified civilian victims of the First World War.[51]

Thirty-eight-year-old Jeanne Mélin and her parents, like most people living in northern France, had been ill prepared when war broke out in August 1914. Just three weeks into the fighting, German troops invaded

Jeanne Mélin (*far right*) with Jane Addams (*center*) at a WILPF meeting in 1922. (Fonds Jeanne Mélin, Bibliothèque historique de la Ville de Paris / fonds Bouglé)

Carignan, the town where her family lived and operated a successful brick-making factory. Rumors of German atrocities—some grounded in truth—added to the terror and chaos of those early days of occupation. Mélin and her mother fled Carignon with two cars and two horses while her father remained behind to guard their home and factory. Over the next eighteen days, mother and daughter crossed six departments, traveling some six hundred kilometers to the west. In the meantime, the Germans over took Carignan, pillaged the Mélins' home, and requisitioned their brick factory, dismantling the machinery and shipping it back to Germany. For the remainder of the war, Mélin lived the transient life of a refugee, made more lonely and difficult by her refusal to blame the Germans for her family's precarious state.[52]

Despite her privileged upbringing, Mélin's sympathies were decidedly on the left of the political spectrum. In the decade prior to World War I, Mélin had joined the French Socialist Party and participated actively in pacifist circles. Pacifism led her to feminism, and in 1912 she started a regional section of the French Union for Women's Suffrage (the same organization presided over by Marguerite de Witt Schlumberger in Paris). World War I did little to diminish her convictions. Writing a letter in 1915 from a cousin's home near Paris, Mélin asked, "When will women get to decide the destiny of men who up until now have had the crazed arrogance to lead the destinies of the world without our consent?" That same year, Aletta Jacobs issued her call for feminists to gather at The Hague, and Mélin broke with the French Union to support the effort (although personal circumstances prevented her from participating in the congress).[53]

Mélin lost touch with most of her international feminist friends during the turmoil of the war years, but in early 1919 Jane Addams reached out personally to invite her to Zurich, writing, "I particularly am hoping for your participation. We Americans strongly hope to see France well represented." Addams's request was not easy for Mélin to fulfill. She and her parents had returned to Carignon in 1918 to a home and factory laid waste by the German army. Neither Mélin's father, whose spirit was broken by the war (and who would die a year later), nor her brother, in poor health and suffering from nervous depression after returning from a German POW camp, could handle the demands of reconstruction. Mélin assumed responsibility for relaunching the family business even as she worked to establish a food cooperative and community center for returning refugees. Despite these weighty responsibilities, Mélin was moved by Addams's plea, and she was convinced (accurately, as it turns out) that she would have better luck securing permission to travel to Switzerland from a provincial backwater than others were having in Paris. On May 6, 1919, she wrote to the prefect of the Ardennes requesting a passport. Eleven days later, she arrived in Zurich.[54]

The unscripted drama that ensued became, for most of the women, the highlight of the Zurich Congress. With much of the difficult work already complete, on Saturday morning, the delegates were focused on practical matters: hammering out a constitution for their rebaptized permanent organization, the Women's International League for Peace and Freedom, and voting to establish a headquarters in Geneva. In the midst of this organizational business, Mélin arrived, "almost breathless," one delegate would write, "from the lately invaded territory of the Ardennes, to hail her comrades as the 'forces of tomorrow.' . . . It was an extraordinarily dramatic moment."[55]

Upon realizing the identity of the latecomer, Addams immediately offered Mélin the podium. Mélin stepped up and declared, "Me, a French woman from the invaded country, knowing all that we have suffered and will suffer still . . . I affirm that we women never wanted this war that was only possible because we were denied our political rights." Mélin, like most of the delegates in Zurich, firmly believed that women, once enfranchised, would never consent to another international cataclysm like the First World War. "Everywhere where women are in possession of their rights," Mélin concluded, "their influence will be felt in governmental decisions. . . . Everywhere they will ceaselessly reclaim their desire for Peace through Freedom and International Fraternity."[56]

The emotion in the room was palpable. Lida Gustava Heymann, seated on the dais, listened attentively to Mélin's speech, then took hold of a bouquet of roses decorating the table and placed them in Mélin's arms, saying: "A German woman gives her hand to a French woman and says in the name of the German Delegation that we hope that we women can build a bridge from Germany to France and from France to Germany, and that in the future we may be able to make good the wrongdoings of men." With clasped hands, the two women stood before the assembled body, many of whom had tears in their eyes. American delegate, Emily Balch, moved by the show of unity, rose spontaneously and vowed to do everything in her power to put an end to war. Unwilling to remain silent spectators any longer, the remaining assembly rose as well, raised their hands, and echoed the pledge in unison.[57]

Looking back at this moment a century on, it is hard to recapture the raw emotion—as well as the personal risk—that lay behind Mélin and Heymann's seemingly modest embrace. For most French and Germans, the work of cultural demobilization (forgiving "the enemy" in the interests of peace and reconciliation) lay months if not years in the future. Yet, as the Swiss *Gazette de Lausanne* explained at the time, "People cannot remain enemies forever. They will have to begin to live together again one day or another. Women have given us the first example of this and should be congratulated."[58]

Heymann was in a unique position to reach out to Mélin. She was among a small circle of radical German woman who had been opposed to the war from the outset and had suffered social ostracism, police harassment, and even imprisonment for their pacifist views during the conflict. In the first winter of the war, Heymann had published an open letter calling on women from all nations to demand an immediate, negotiated peace. Heymann's active participation in The Hague Congress of 1915 and her efforts to keep channels of communication open to Allied women set her apart from the vast majority of German feminists who, like their French counterparts, stood firmly behind their nation at war. In a plenary address at the Zurich Congress, Heymann described how she and other German feminist pacifists had demanded their government answer for its treatment of civilians under German occupation, even at a time when German victory seemed all but assured. She also acknowledged the disproportionate hardship born by the occupied nations during the war years. Heymann struck a similar theme at a meeting organized by German-speaking Swiss residents of Zurich to protest against the peace terms. Addressing the crowd, Heymann thundered, "Did you protest against the invasion of Belgium, the deportations from Lille (in northern France), or the Treaty of Brest-Litovsk? If not, you have no right now to protest against the peace terms." For Heymann, recognizing Allied women's suffering was a deliberate act of reciprocity, a verbal acknowledgment that the sorrow of one's enemy was as pressing as one's own.[59]

Such words and gestures mattered. Even for a radical like Jeanne Mélin, it was difficult to embrace a German woman while her home and her village lay in ruins. Heymann's willingness to assume moral responsibility for her government's actions opened a door to reconciliation that may have otherwise remained closed for a very long time. "For us French women," Mélin would later insist, "the most important declaration was [Heymann's] statement that she and many of her friends continually protested against the war, against the violation of Belgium [and] against the abominable deportations." The path of reconciliation was paved with stones of mutual remorse: from German women over their military's conduct in wartime and from Allied women over the suffering inflicted by the blockade and the peace terms. The almost total disenfranchisement of women from all the warring nations in 1914 facilitated this process. It allowed women to disassociate themselves from the disastrous decisions that had unleashed the global conflict. Still, forgiving "the enemy" just months after World War I ended was no easy feat. Mélin and Heymann's embrace represented a cultural breakthrough, and it would open the door for many similar exchanges to come.[60]

"Treasonable Utterances"

On the final evening of the Zurich Congress, the female delegates prepared to leave the warm cocoon they had spun for themselves at the Hotel

Glockenhof with much about the future international order still up in the air. Some of the topics that came up for discussion the last day of the congress pointed to vexing international problems, including both communism and Zionism, which would trouble world peace for decades to come. But a spirit of mutual understanding propelled the women forward. Determined to continue their work, the congress established itself as a new permanent organization aptly named the Women's International League for Peace and Freedom. By popular acclamation, Jane Addams was elected president. She and four other women agreed to depart immediately to bring the congress's recommendations directly to Paris. "It is creditable to the patience of the peace makers," Addams would write, "that they later received our delegation and allowed us to place the resolutions in their hands, but we inevitably encountered much bitter criticism from the Allied press." In fact, the polite response of the diplomats in Paris and the hostile response aired by journalists stemmed from a similar impulse. Both pointed to a determined effort to limit women's political influence to a narrowly defined set of gender-specific issues and to defend diplomacy and foreign relations as an exclusively masculine affair.[61]

Addams and her delegation arrived in Paris in late May 1919 armed with printed copies of the Zurich resolutions, which they sent to each of the peace delegations and which they presented personally to a few select statesmen. Meeting primarily with American, British, and French peace delegates, the women pushed for greater leniency with Germany in the Versailles Treaty, and they requested treaty language that would more clearly spell out an equal place for women in the new world order. Among the peacemakers, Foreign Minister Stephen Pichon of France "expressed the liveliest sympathy." Lord Robert Cecil of Great Britain also granted the women an extended interview. Finally, Addams and her codelegates engaged in "a long talk over the resolutions" with Georges Clemenceau's close collaborator André Tardieu. According to Addams, "They all received our resolutions politely and sometimes discussed them at length."[62]

The peacemakers, it must be acknowledged, had little to lose in expending an hour in polite conversation with the women. There is certainly reason to doubt, however, whether the statesmen took the women's proposals seriously. A sketch on the back of the Zurich Congress resolutions (filed among André Tardieu's papers in the French diplomatic archives) would indicate otherwise. There, a doodle of an archetypical French statesman of the Third Republic, with a high forehead, prominent nose, and tidy mustache, stares out from the page. This caricature of refined masculinity, no doubt drawn by one of the men entertaining Addams's delegation, seems at best to show a lack of serious consideration and at worst to outright mock the resolutions on the reverse side demanding women's equality as a precondition of global peace.[63]

The British diplomatic archives offer a different type of evidence, pointing less to indifference over women's demands and more to apprehension verging on alarm. Among the papers is a report from Lord Acton, the British consul general in Zurich, who was apparently assigned to spy on the Zurich delegates for the Foreign Office. "The general gist of the Congress," Lord Acton informed the foreign secretary, was "unanimous and bitter criticism of and opposition to the Peace Treaty of Versailles." Even more troubling were proclamations of British delegate Ethel Snowden outside the confines of the congress. "It may be said," Lord Acton reported, regarding a speech Snowden gave at a public protest against the peace terms, "that every sentence contained treasonable utterances and insertions."[64]

The idea that women's postwar peace efforts constituted treason also appeared outside the pages of confidential government reports. Back in America, where the wartime Espionage and Sedition Acts stoked fear and prejudice, Jane Addams withstood a barrage of similar accusations from hostile journalists and irate citizens. A fellow Chicagoan wrote to Addams in the name of all "REAL AMERICANS," saying, "You belong to the Socialists, Anarchists, and all other 'ISTS' that are against the Government. Your place is at Chicago, minding your own business, and not mixing with the ENEMY, or telling the Peace Commission how to run things." In asserting such claims, the anonymous author of this letter pointed to an editorial that had recently appeared in the *Chicago Evening Post* criticizing Addams for displaying "so great a love for the enemy that one wonders whether any love can be left for the enemy's victims." "Miss Addams is embittered," the *Seattle Times* chimed in, "because her country has refused to bow before the false gods she has worshiped with mistaken devotion for years."[65]

In addition to Addams, former congresswoman Jeanette Rankin attracted fiery vitriol in American newspapers. As far as the conservative press was concerned, Rankin's vote in opposition to the war in April 1917 and her participation in the 1919 Zurich Congress confirmed how ill-suited she (or any woman) was for political life. "It may be presumed," asserted the *Indianapolis Star*, "that Jeannette wept bitterly when she thought of the pitiful state of the German people in the act of making a partial reparation for the horrors inflicted on the world, just as she did when she refused to vote for war while in Congress." The *Cincinnati Enquirer* similarly referred to Rankin's emotional state in an article on May 19, 1919. "When, as a member of Congress, Jeannette Rankin of Montana, confronted with the decision voting for or against war in 1917 burst into tears and entered a negative, the people of the United States were disposed to excuse the action on account of her sex," the paper claimed, but now that Rankin was in Zurich pleading mercy for the "defeated and chained Huns," Americans' tolerance had worn thin.[66]

To women's critics, displays of emotion only proved that women could not behave as dispassionate political actors in the public sphere. The *Indianapolis Star* drove this point home bluntly in its final assessment of the Zurich Congress: "There is no telling what overly sentimental and weakly sympathetic folk will do even in a world crisis." The *Chicago Evening Post* claimed similarly, women's "sympathy lacks the direction of intelligent understanding." Women, these papers insinuated, were too emotional to be rational, too sympathetic to exact justice. In short, women were too peace loving to be trusted with peacemaking or to engage in the rough-and-tumble world of foreign diplomacy and international affairs.[67]

Such assertions encapsulate the Catch-22 in which many feminists found themselves trapped in the aftermath of the First World War. As they saw it, motherhood, or at least the potential for motherhood, rendered women naturally empathetic and pacific. The emotional qualities that made women good mothers were precisely the qualities that compelled them to demand a role for women in the new world order. Thus when Lida Gustava Heymann addressed the delegates in Zurich as "mothers of the world," her wording deliberately evoked women's life-giving capacity. As she and Anita Augspurg wrote in 1919: "Women, just because they are women, are against all forms of brutal force that seek to pointlessly destroy what has grown, what has become. They want to build up, to protect, to create anew." Jeanne Mélin drew a similar allusion when she insisted that women must demand political rights so that they would never again be forced to sacrifice their children to the "carnage." Significantly, neither of these women was a mother herself. The *idea* of motherhood mattered more than the experience of mothering. Pacifist feminists used maternalist rhetoric in order to legitimize women's political engagement, whether back home in their own countries or on the newly emerging international stage.[68]

To the male peacemakers, however, it was precisely because women were presumed to be more emotional and empathetic than men that they could not be trusted to take part in the peace negotiations. Allied statesmen, no less than conservative newspaper columnists, feared women would be too quick to sympathize with the suffering of their adversaries. Whether women were cast as dangerous, as in Lord Acton's Foreign Office report, or sentimental and weak, as in many American newspapers, the underlying message was consistent: women could not be trusted to engage in foreign affairs. Both in 1919 and in the decades that followed, statesmen did their best to contain women's political influence by delineating a limited number of social issues as the only appropriate venues for female expertise.

Although they were unable to alter the terms of the peace in 1919, and even though they were largely excluded from the "masculine" universe of diplomacy and international affairs in the interwar decades, members of the newly constituted Women's International League for Peace and Freedom did not give up. Instead, they pursued peace and global stability from outside the halls of power, modeling their vision of preemptive peace work, engaging in pragmatic acts of person-to-person diplomacy, and fostering reconciliation between former enemies. In the process, they played a vital role in carving out a niche for nonstate actors in the growing sphere of international politics and policy making.

Compassionate Diplomacy

In giving the WILPF a permanent home and structure in 1919, the delegates to the Zurich Congress staked a claim on the attentions of the international community going forward. With its transnational executive board and headquarters in Geneva, the WILPF would attract highly qualified pacifist and internationalist-minded women eager to work toward a more just and stable global order. The foundation it laid would be enduring. The Women's International League for Peace and Freedom, born in Zurich in 1919, remains the oldest women's peace organization in the world today.[69]

The challenge for the WILPF was in defining a plan of action for women who were, on the whole, excluded from institutions of political power. Not all nations extended the vote to women in the interwar decades, and where women were enfranchised, few governments were willing to grant them responsibility over foreign affairs, appoint them as diplomats, or send them as representatives to the League of Nations. WILPF members continued to challenge their exclusion from representative institutions and decision-making positions at the national and international levels, but on the whole, they tended to view the expansion of women's political rights as a cause "to be worked for but not to be waited for." Fostering a peaceful world order was their primary goal. In defiance of conventional gender stereotypes, WILPF leaders developed expertise on a wide range of international issues, and they pushed their agenda at the League of Nations.[70]

The ongoing blockade of Germany and the desperate cause of the hungry populations of Central Europe (as well as Russia and the Balkans) provided WILPF women with their first foray into postwar international politics. In her plenary address at the Zurich Congress, Jane Addams had defined the fight against hunger as the cornerstone of a "new internationalism," which would be simultaneously moral, humanitarian, and political in nature.[71]

Providing food to war-torn nations, Addams explained to the Zurich delegates, could serve as "a spiritual basis upon which the world may once again be restored to normal." She focused particularly on feeding starving children, the most innocent victims of men's follies. For her, confronting global hunger was a deliberately political act. Noting that some Swiss papers covering the congress had warned the women not to overstretch their "natural" domestic roles and to leave politics to men, Addams suggested that women could "well retort that the present situation of the world is not altogether to the credit of the men." By fighting hunger and famine, women could simultaneously create a more just, humane, and stable world order and demonstrate their capacity for international action. "The world had been brought to its knees by hunger," summarized one British woman in the audience, "and in this women must see their opportunity for developing their powers of cooperation in international life."[72]

Both Addams and the WILPF made food aid their first postwar priority. After the Zurich Congress, she and Alice Hamilton were able (with the help of American Herbert Hoover) to join a group of Quakers traveling to Germany to assess the population's needs. What they encountered, in Addams's words, was a "shipwreck of a nation." As Addams and Hamilton toured Germany, WILPF international secretary Emily Balch was in Geneva fielding requests for the nascent organization to aid with Europe's growing food crisis. Balch wrote to Addams in July 1919, relaying pleas from Hungarian WILPF members to allow milk shipments into their country to feed starving children. "How MONSTROUS it all is!" she wrote. "I am hoping that you may really be able to affect a stirring of the waters when you get home." She also received letters from the Save the Children Fund, a British philanthropic organization working to get food to Central Europe. British WILPF members collaborated with the Save the Children Fund. They also launched their own campaign to collect one million rubber teats for German milk bottles. Once back home, Jane Addams crisscrossed the United States raising money for Quaker relief efforts. "I am, of course, doing a lot speaking," she wrote to Balch in October 1919, "and we can only hope that in time the nationalistic lines will no longer hold where starving children are concerned."[73]

French members of the WILPF also raised funds for hungry populations in Central Europe, an act as important in its symbolism as in its economic effects. French children in northern France had endured years of privation under German occupation. When Addams met with French children in Lille in April 1919, she was shocked at the physical toll the war had taken, describing them as "a line of moving skeletons." It would have been easy for French women to view German and Austrian children's hunger as a just reward for such suffering, but WILPF members rebelled against such a reactionary response. In early 1919 French WILPF members sent a message to Woodrow Wilson saying, "We come to join our voices to those women of enemy countries who have asked for help for their children. We know what our own have suffered in the invaded regions and it is precisely for that reason that we appeal to you for theirs." Over the following year and a half, the French WILPF section raised 113,000 francs for hungry children in Central Europe, mostly in the form of small donations from families of modest means.[74]

At the same time that the French were raising money for famine victims in Central Europe, German WILPF members raised two thousand deutschmarks to aid children in northern France. German women also continued to press their government to set up a commission to research atrocities committed against French and Belgian women and girls during the war. Undertaking humanitarian aid was a means by which WILPF women from recently warring countries could acknowledge the common humanity of those recently labeled "the enemy" and work toward stabilizing foreign relations between *peoples* as well as nations.[75]

Antifamine work consumed a fair amount of the WILPF's attention in its first year, but the women in Zurich had not set out to found a humanitarian organization. British member Helena Swanwick explained why the WIL-PF's foray into relief work proved relatively brief: "There was only our one women's organization trying to do educative pacifist work," she explained. "If we abandoned that, we should indeed be surrendering to the age-old notion that women had no concern in public life except to wipe up the mess made by men. . . . I believed women should share responsibility for public policy with men." After the postwar crisis passed, the WILPF largely stepped back from direct humanitarian aid and focused its energies on shaping international policy, primarily by collecting evidence, disseminating data, educating the general public, and lobbying diplomats and members of the League of Nations. The WILPF, in effect, served as a nongovernmental organization before the term was invented, working as a private, transnational group of citizens to sway decision makers to enact policy in the interests of gender equality, social justice, and lasting peace.[76]

The WILPF drew on the expertise of its members, collaborated with friends in other international feminist organizations, and capitalized on women's ability to reach a broad international public in order to advance its agenda at the League of Nations. In one of the earliest of these efforts, the WILPF executive joined with leaders of other international women's organizations to pressure the League to assume responsibility for "trac[ing] and liberat[ing] deported Women and Children especially in Asia Minor." This request helped lead to the formation of the League of Nations Fifth Committee, which produced "one of the first and most comprehensive reckonings of the situation facing survivors of the Armenian Genocide." A decade later, as the League prepared to convene a World Disarmament Conference in Geneva, WILPF members collected six million signatures on petitions circulated all over the world to demand general disarmament as an antidote to mounting militarism in Europe and Asia.[77]

Colonial violence and oppression also spurred the WILPF to action in the interwar decades. In 1921 Egyptian women, who were by then two years into their national uprising against the British, sent a telegram to the organization imploring it to protest "against the merciless enforcement of the British government's reprisals" against Egyptian nationalists. Both the British WILPF section and the Geneva office sent telegrams of protest to the British foreign minister. In an expansion of WILPF activity into Latin America, in 1925 the American section sponsored a multiracial fact-finding mission to Haiti, which the American military had occupied a decade earlier. One of two African American women on the mission, Addie Waites

Hunton (who had spoken at the 1919 Pan-African Congress in Paris), helped draw up the final report demanding the immediate removal of American troops from the island nation. Finally, in 1927–1928, the WILPF sent a two-woman delegation to Indochina, China, and Japan to encourage "women of the two hemispheres" to get to know each other, confer together, and "unite to establish co-operation instead of conflict among the nations of the world." In southern China, Soumay Tcheng, the nation's first female lawyer, would serve as the WILPF delegates' guide (having first made her own dramatic mark on global diplomacy during the Paris Peace Conference of 1919, as we will see in the next chapter).[78]

Through these projects and others, in the interwar decades, WILPF members carved out a role for women in the expanding and democratizing international sphere. Deeply disappointed in the peace forged at Versailles, they refused to bow to pressures to confine their activism to "women's issues" and leave diplomacy to the men. In 1919, together with participants in the Inter-Allied Women's Conference in Paris, delegates to the International Women's Congress in Zurich unabashedly challenged men's hold over peacemaking and asserted that global stability hinged, to no small degree, on women's ability to help shape the terms of collective security both within and between nation-states. Along with female pan-Africanists and Egyptian nationalists, the WILPF also acknowledged that women's experience of oppression could not be separated from the racial and imperial power relations that worked to silence so many women across the world. After 1919 members would continue to pave new political ground, engaging in acts of compassionate diplomacy and working toward a more just and egalitarian international order. Through their words and their deeds, they defied all efforts to shelter foreign affairs from female influence, and they worked toward the day when men and women would be called on in equal measure to foster peace and freedom around the world.[79]

CHAPTER V

May Flowers in China

The Feminist Origins of Chinese Nationalism

rench journalist Andrée Viollis blinked once, then blinked again just to be sure. One of the latest peace delegates to arrive in Paris had just marched through her door. That fact, in and of itself, wasn't so surprising. Diplomats and statesmen were a dime a dozen in Paris that spring. But the delegate who politely shook Viollis's hand and sat down to be interviewed was no statesman, nor was she a man. This peace delegate was petite, young, and female. And she was from China.

As a cub reporter for the French *Le Petit Parisien* and a correspondent for the British *Daily Mail*, Viollis was still a relative novice to the world of high diplomacy and international relations when she was given the plum assignment of covering the Paris Peace Conference. It was a rare post for a female reporter, but as an intrepid New Woman and committed feminist, Viollis was firmly in favor of women's entry into masculine professions. Like most Western women of her generation, however, Viollis held a number of Orientalist beliefs about "the East," including the assumption that Asian women were submissive and unenlightened: objects of beauty to be admired rather than individuals endowed with intellect and authority. Such assumptions explain why Viollis, despite her cosmopolitan and militant background, was nothing short of floored when she sat down in April 1919 to talk with Soumay Tcheng (known also by her given name, Zheng Yuxiu, and later by her married name, Madame Wei Tao-ming).[1]

For her part, Soumay Tcheng was grateful for the interview. She had been knocking on doors, seeking to engage the interest of international reporters in China's diplomatic fate ever since her arrival in Paris several weeks earlier. It was, after all, what the Nationalist government in southern China had asked her to do when it appointed her as an official attaché to the Chinese delegation to the peace conference. Specifically, she was tasked with acting as a liaison between the Chinese plenipotentiaries and the press as well as with representing Chinese women at the negotiations. Tcheng's appointment was nothing short of extraordinary. In selecting her as a delegate, the Chinese government provided Soumay Tcheng with the credential denied to every other Allied woman in 1919: official diplomatic status.

Everything about Tcheng upended Viollis's expectations about Chinese women: her fashionable, Western-style clothing, her facility in English and French, her worldly knowledge and experience. Who was this woman? Viollis thought she knew quite a bit about China before meeting Tcheng. After all, her husband was the curator of a museum of Asian art in Paris. But in this case clearly, art did not reflect reality. Viollis crafted her amazement into the lead paragraph for her article for the *Daily Mail*: "Confess it," she began, "What do you know—what do most of us—know of China?" Poetry, light opera, polychrome figures on vases, she wrote, all evoke images of "ladies dressed in glowing silks with curved-up eyes, long pointed nails, and painfully small mutilated feet." Some are even prone to view China as "barbarous," but such old-fashioned thinking, Viollis warned, "is not only ridiculous; it may, it will, become a serious danger. And it will be hoped that our peace magnates will bear this in mind." The China of Soumay Tcheng deserved to be taken seriously.[2]

In retrospect, there are many questions that Andrée Viollis did not think to pose when she met Tcheng face-to-face in April 1919, much to her detriment. She might have asked, for example, about Tcheng's personal history. If so, she would have learned about Tcheng's career as a bomb-smuggler for Sun Yat-sen's Revolutionary Alliance (the underground political party that masterminded the downfall of the Qing dynasty in 1911 and the inauguration of the Chinese Republic in 1912) or as a would-be assassin of President Yuan Shikai's minister of finance in 1913. Viollis might also have followed the Chinese woman's comings and goings in Paris more closely that spring. Had she done so, she would have had quite the scoop. Just two months after their interview, Tcheng would mastermind an eleventh-hour confrontation with China's chief delegate to the peace conference that would play a critical role in determining whether China agreed to sign the Versailles Treaty.

This chapter follows the remarkable diplomatic career of Soumay Tcheng at the peace conference in 1919, placing her actions in the broader context of the wide-ranging cultural ferment of early-twentieth-century China known as the May Fourth Movement. This nationalist movement— named for the student protests that broke out in Beijing on May 4, 1919, against China's mistreatment at the peace conference—refers more broadly to an intellectual revolution that swept through China during and after the First World War. Led by a young generation imbued with the values of Western science and democracy, the May Fourth Movement stridently attacked traditional, Confucian values and institutions, ushering China into the twentieth century. Critical to Tcheng's personal story, the movement embraced women's emancipation as one of its core principles. Although Tcheng's actions in 1919 served fundamentally nationalist ends, her motivations were shaped by her determination to advance women's equality as much as they were to secure Chinese sovereignty. Her subsequent career as China's first female lawyer and judge, and her influence in drafting a new, republican civil code rooted in gender equality, further attest to the importance Tcheng attributed to improving women's social position throughout her life. Soumay Tcheng's diplomatic activism at the Paris Peace Conference, although long since forgotten, fundamentally reshaped China's relations with the Great Powers and advanced women's rights in the nascent Chinese Republic of the early twentieth century.

The Making of a Chinese Revolutionary

Soumay Tcheng was only twenty-seven years old when she was chosen to represent China at the Paris Peace Conference. During her preceding years of childhood and early adulthood, however, Tcheng packed in more personal growth and political adventure than most people experience in a lifetime. By 1919 her reputation as a child rebel, dedicated revolutionary, and budding advocate for women's rights set her apart from virtually all her peers. They also armed her with a rare set of credentials that made her an enticing choice as a peace delegate.

Tcheng was born in 1891 in the southern Chinese port city of Guangzhou, then commonly known in the West as Canton. The youngest of four children, Tcheng grew up in an extended, wealthy, traditional Mandarin family, ruled over with a stern eye by her paternal grandmother. During her younger years, her father lived far from the family in the capital city of Beijing, where he worked as an official in the finance ministry of the Man-chu court (which had ruled over China ever since establishing the Qing dynasty in 1644). It fell then to her mother and grandmother to decide how to handle Soumay, who at a young age was already chafing against the Confucian virtues of obedience and filial piety.[3]

A series of small acts of rebellion for a girl of her class background—standing up for a servant girl against one of her own cousins, making mud-pies with her brothers—transformed into full-blown revolt when the time came for Tcheng to have her feet bound. Footbinding was still widely prac-ticed by well-off families in China at the turn of the twentieth century. The process involved wrapping bandages tightly around a young girl's foot until her arch broke and her big toe curled around the others to form a point. The resulting foot, only a few inches long, was broadly seen as a sign of beauty and refinement. For the girls in question, the process was agonizing and resulted in a lifetime of limited mobility. Young Soumay wanted nothing of it. The first night her mother and grandmother came and wrapped her feet, she scarcely waited until they left the room before tearing off the bandages. A few days later she threw a screaming tantrum until her grandmother finally relented. "Very well then," her grandmother said in exasperation, "take the bandages off. Her feet will grow the size of an elephant's. No one will ever marry her, but so be it. I wash my hands of the whole business." Not for the last time, young Soumay got her way.[4]

Where did Soumay Tcheng's rebellious spirit come from? Undoubtedly endowed with a heavy dose of natural spunk and courage, Tcheng could not have followed the life path she did without the moral support of her family, beginning with her mother. When she was a child, Tcheng recalls, "I hardly ever left my mother's side. . . . We were the closest possible friends." As she grew older, Tcheng came to love, admire, and pity her mother in equal measure. The twenty-five years separating the two women may well have been centuries for the vast differences that defined their lives. Tcheng's mother resented the social customs that so severely limited her horizons—her lack of formal education, her limited mobility due to bound feet, her inability to choose her own husband—but she felt powerless to challenge them. In her mother's generation, women often saw suicide as their only means of escape, and Tcheng's mother seriously considered taking her own life when she learned that her husband was keeping a second home with a concubine. Only the desperate pleas of Tcheng and her brother put a stop to the tragedy.[5]

Unable to alter her own destiny, Tcheng's mother encouraged her daughter to fight the battles she could not, telling her: "Soumay, you must strike out for yourself. . . . There have been many women in our history who have done great things for their country." Tcheng's earliest and fondest memories were of curling up in her mother's lap to listen to the tale of the most famous of these Chinese heroines: Hua Mulan, the legendary woman warrior who disguised herself as a man to replace her father on the battlefield, winning glory for her nation and honor for her family. "I never grew tired of hearing about her," Tcheng would later recall, "and begged for the story over and over again." The legend of Mulan was much more than an adventurous tale. As an adult, Tcheng would later recognize it as "a projection of the dreams [my mother held] originally for herself and later gave to me."[6]

Though closest to her mother, Tcheng bore the stamp of her father's influence as well. Tcheng's father indulged his high-spirited daughter, whom he belatedly got to know around the age of ten, when she moved with her mother and siblings to live with him in Beijing. A member of the literati (the Mandarin class of scholar-bureaucrats long tapped by the emperors of China to run the affairs of state), Tcheng's father loyally served the ruling Manchu family. Despite his conservative breeding and instincts, Tcheng's father was among those within the government who believed that some degree of reform was needed to check court corruption, which had plagued the Manchus in the later years of their rule. His position at court would also have exposed him to some of the more progressive ideas regarding women's social position circulating in China's major cities. These included the demands of the earliest antifootbinding associations, which petitioned the emperor to put an end to the practice at the end of the nineteenth century.[7]

Upon first introduction, Soumay's father found his daughter's "insatiable mind and exuberance" to be something of a shock. Nevertheless, "before a week had passed a relationship extremely unusual between a Chinese girl and her father had been established." Most important, her father supported her desire to acquire a formal education. Having already learned the fundamentals of Confucian philosophy from a tutor who came to the family home (a privilege available to daughters of the literati class, similar to the education provided to some secluded upper-class girls in Egypt), Tcheng's father allowed her to enroll in a girl's school shortly after arriving in Beijing. Her father also took her with him on his daily rounds for government business, treating her, she says, "as he would a favorite son." As she learned more about her country and its place in the world, Soumay began to dream of continuing her studies abroad.[8]

Such dreams were abruptly cut short at age fourteen when her grandmother announced that she had found Soumay a husband. The engagement was celebrated with great ceremony, but the more the young woman learned about the man to whom she was betrothed, the more she began to despair. In particular, Soumay heard from her brother that her fiancé was something of a playboy and her future father-in-law did not approve of "modern, educated women." That was all she needed to know. Bucking convention, Soumay wrote a letter to her intended husband, stating in effect: "Why don't you marry someone more to your taste? I intend to go to America or Europe to finish my studies and this does not seem to fit into your picture of marriage." Scandal erupted. Only her mother took her side. Everyone agreed that to save the family honor, Soumay had to leave Beijing. Europe seemed too far away, so they settled on an American missionary school for girls in Tianjin, just far enough away to satisfy the jilted family and to allow Tcheng to begin to develop her independence. Tcheng gave up her loose fitting blouses and trousers for American-style dresses and a much-cherished hat—"one of those high, flaring plates loaded with assorted trimmings"—and applied herself diligently to learning English and "acquiring some knowledge of the modern world."[9]

By the time she was fifteen, Tcheng's instinctive rebelliousness had blossomed into full-blown revolutionary consciousness. Both her father's quiet frustration with the ineptitude of the Manchu regime he served and the undercurrent of cultural and political dissent circulating in Beijing and Tianjin eventually led Tcheng to hear about the Revolutionary Alliance of Sun Yat-sen. For over a decade, both in China and abroad, Sun had been raising funds and building an underground movement capable of overthrowing the now weak and ineffective Manchu government. Despite the Manchu regime's early successes securing control over a vast and prosperous empire, by the nineteenth century it was suffering under internal rebellion and external threats from both Europeans and the Japanese. Beginning with the disastrous Opium Wars of the mid-1800s, Great Britain and other foreign powers forced the Manchu rulers to sign away important trading rights and territorial concessions in order to retain their throne. Internal efforts to reform the monarchy ultimately collapsed, and by the twentieth century revolutionaries like Sun were arguing convincingly that to turn China into a modern nation capable of defending its sovereignty, the Qing dynasty had to go. Having learned that many of Sun's followers were plotting revolution from nearby Japan, Tcheng persuaded her family to allow her to travel to Kobe to continue her education. Once in Japan, she made contact with members of the Revolutionary Alliance and began attending secret meetings.

Sun Yat-sen and his allies quickly recognized the benefit of bringing into their fold a young woman of unquestionable pedigree who could help provide valuable political cover as they built the resistance. On their orders, Tcheng returned to Beijing and, with the aid of one of her brothers (but without the knowledge of her parents) established her family home as a revolutionary headquarters. Events progressed rapidly. By the end of 1911 Tcheng and her coconspirators heard that southern China was in open revolt. Revolutionary uprisings snowballed, as one province after another declared its independence from the Qing dynasty. On January 1, 1912, Sun Yat-sen became president of a new Chinese Republic. All that remained was to capture the northern provinces and force the Manchu rulers to abdicate.

Tcheng's revolutionary cell in Beijing, the "Dare to Die" unit, was told to prepare to eliminate government officials viewed as obstructionist to the revolutionary cause: a difficult proposition as they had no bombs to carry out an attack. The material would need to be smuggled into the capital from the coastal city of Tianjin. "I volunteered to be the carrier," Tcheng would later recall. "Being a girl, I would raise less suspicion than a man." For a period of three months, two times a week, Tcheng traveled to Tianjin by train, where she was given two suitcases—one holding the explosives; the other, material for the bombs—to transport back to Beijing. A friend with diplomatic privileges arranged to meet her at the train station and help her pass through customs. The plan was put into motion, and all transpired without a hitch, until the final trip when the suitcase filled with explosives at her feet began making a "series of hissing and spluttering noises." Frozen with fear and certain that her suitcase was about to detonate, Tcheng thought her time was up. Somewhat given to romanticism, she began imagining her martyrdom and the moving tribute that Sun Yat-sen would make to "Soumay Tcheng, Girl Patriot of Peking."

The noise, it turned out, was from a leaking radiator. Tcheng delivered her cargo as planned and then passed out in a dead faint. In the end, the threat of violence proved enough to bring down the Qing dynasty. In mid-February 1912 the dowager empress formally abdicated. At the same time, in order to consolidate national support behind a new government, Sun Yat-sen stepped aside to allow the current Chinese premier, General Yuan Shikai (who claimed to be the only person capable of defeating the republic's enemies), to become the provisional president of the new Republic of China.[10]

Soumay Tcheng's role in facilitating the revolution was certainly unusual for a young woman barely out of her teens, but it was not entirely unique. In fact, many girls and women participated actively in the overthrow of the Qing dynasty. One of China's most legendary female warriors, Qiu Jin—who wrote passionately about women's right to determine their own fate—helped plot the assassination of various Manchu government officials and was beheaded for her revolutionary activity in 1907. Others followed in her footsteps. Somewhere between one hundred and two hundred women joined the Revolutionary Alliance. Hundreds of others formed "women's armies" and fought in the later stages of the revolution. Chinese revolutionary women were willing to risk their lives out of love of country and out of the belief that their military actions would prove that women were deserving of full citizenship in an eventual republic.[11]

It did not take long for Yuan Shikai's government to quash their hopes. One of the first acts of his provisional government was to disband all women's armies. Female members of the Revolutionary Alliance, recognizing they would need to act quickly if they were not to be sidelined, organized themselves in regional and national suffrage societies. Some styled themselves after England's militant suffragettes. In one notable instance, they forced their way into the hall of the National Assembly in Nanjing to demand recognition of women's rights in the constitution. When legislators refused to comply, the women smashed out windowpanes and held up debate until troops were called in to protect the Assembly.[12]

In August 1912 the provisional government decisively denied women the right to vote or hold political office in the emerging republic, and it took steps to quell the feminist unrest. Many female revolutionary militants no longer felt safe, including Soumay Tcheng, who received a warning from a sympathetic police officer that Yuan Shikai had ordered her assassination. Her family's house was ransacked in the government's quest for incriminating evidence, much to the shame of her father, who felt the family honor had been compromised. Humiliated and convinced that Tcheng would not be safe in China for the foreseeable future, her family finally agreed to her longstanding request to travel to France to further her education. Tcheng began to pack her bags.[13]

The threats against Tcheng were part of a broader crackdown on Chinese radicals orchestrated by Yuan Shikai. Though appointed president of a nascent republic, Yuan was already dreaming of installing himself as a new emperor. Eliminating the leaders of the Revolutionary Alliance was essential to his plans. In March 1913 one of Tcheng's friends and fellow revolutionaries fell to an assassin's bullet. Tcheng was so enraged that she postponed her plans to leave for France and volunteered to personally carry out a retaliatory attack. The chosen target was the minister of finance, who was raising a foreign loan to keep Yuan's government afloat. When the day came, Tcheng's coconspirators strapped dynamite beneath her clothes, handed her a bomb disguised as a suitcase, and put her on a train to Beijing.[14]

Prepared to die for the cause, Tcheng's plans were derailed when she realized a secret service agent was shadowing her on the train. As she reached the capital, she knew her plans would have to be aborted. With the help of her coconspirators as well as a sympathetic hotel "boy" and a rickshaw driver who set a new speed record tearing across the city, Tcheng managed to unload her incriminating baggage and slip into the Foreign Legation Quarter (the part of Beijing inhabited by members of the European diplomatic corps, where Chinese law held little sway). There, dressed in a quickly procured evening gown, she lost herself among the well-heeled Chinese and foreign dignitaries arriving for dinner at the ultra-elite Hotel des Wagons-Lits. When a government agent tracked her down in the restaurant and demanded to know what she was up to, she waved a small decorative fan "languidly back and forth" and replied with "refined indignation," "Do I *really* look like the kind of person who would carry bombs?" The aborted assassination attempt was the last straw. With the blessing of her entire family, including her horrified grandmother, Tcheng set off for France.[15]

A Chinese Woman in Paris

On the surface, France may seem a haphazard destination for a young Chinese woman looking to pursue her studies at the end of the Qing dynasty.

In fact, the sea route from Hong Kong to Marseille was well traveled by Chinese students in the first decades of the twentieth century. Much of this international exchange was due to the efforts of the son of an open-minded Qing court official named Li Shizeng, who traveled to France in 1902 and was seduced by French utopian socialist and anarchist ideas. A bit of a Chinese Renaissance man, Li simultaneously opened a bean curd factory (undertaking the Herculean challenge of convincing the French to give up cheese for tofu) and, in 1912, founded the Association for Frugal Study to help arrange for young Chinese men and women to study in France. Returning foreign exchange students shared their stories and fed the dreams of Chinese youth, including Soumay Tcheng. "Before I even touched foot on shore," she recalls, "I was a most ardent Francophile. To me, France was the mother and progenitor of everything I believed in: the words Liberté, Egalité, Fraternité, were wonderful living ideas, not just cold letters engraved in stone over a classic doorway; and I felt an emotional kinship with the French whose grandfathers had given their lives in the cause of freedom." Tcheng met Li through her revolutionary contacts in China, and it was he who arranged for her to go to Paris.[16]

Despite her admiration for France's revolutionary past, the young Chinese woman must have experienced tremendous culture shock upon arriving in Paris. Tcheng recorded a bit of her feelings at the time: "In spite of the absorbing effort to learn French, of which I did not know one word," she would later confess, "I was very lonely and sad." Tcheng's sense of isolation came not only from her difficulty in communicating in a foreign tongue but also from her quick realization that the French people "considered [her] rather [more] as a savage than as equal." This statement, made in passing in the 1926 edition of her memoir, is the only instance in any of Tcheng's speeches or writing where she hints at France's imperial status and worldview. In Asia, France claimed the entire Indochinese peninsula as a colonial holding, while within China, it enjoyed a sizable territorial concession in Shanghai. Although Tcheng would soon emerge as a vocal critic of the unequal treaties that granted foreigners extraterritorial rights on Chinese soil, she was notably silent on France's colonial past and its self-appointed mission to civilize the "savage" peoples of Africa and Asia. This silence can be explained by Tcheng's diplomatic instincts, which kicked in from the moment she left Chinese soil. Emphasizing the affinity of France and China as sister Republics, she believed, served her country's interests far more than criticizing the French for their sense of cultural superiority.

In any case, Tcheng's unconquerable spirit soon began to work its magic on the French. Within three months she began to pick up the rudiments of the language and settle into her new home.[17]

Tcheng could hardly have chosen a less propitious moment to arrive in France. Just as she began to feel comfortable in her new surroundings, Europe gave in to the nationalist follies of the First World War. Tcheng would remember going to the Montparnasse train station where tearful wives and mothers bid their husbands and sons goodbye as they headed to rejoin their regiments: "I think that this shock to civilization was more of a shock to me than to most Europeans," she would write, "because I, fresh from revolution, had so long thought of the West as a stabilized society, and as I came to it with such eagerness out of the violence of revolution and defeat, the tragedy of the war struck me with double force." Despite the obvious difficulties the war presented, Tcheng chose to remain in Paris and pursue her studies. She watched the famous "taxicab army" ferry soldiers from the French capital to the battlefront at the Marne. She grew accustomed to the flow of refugees through the capital, and in 1915 she was accepted at the University of Paris, the Sorbonne, to study law.[18]

Having watched World War I unfold from the French home front, Tcheng became an ardent supporter of the Allied cause. She also began establishing herself as an unofficial spokeswoman for her nation abroad. At several times in 1917, she addressed public meetings in Paris advocating that China join France, Britain, and the United States in the fight against the Central Powers. When China eventually did so in August 1917, the Sorbonne hosted a mass meeting, attended by the French minister of war. Tcheng was asked "to give a Chinese woman's point of view," and she remembers the surprise of the French crowd as she walked up on stage: "I am certain that it was the first time a great many of them had ever seen a Chinese woman, and they undoubtedly expected something right out of a silk painting—a small, delicate, and shy lady with tiny feet, dressed in long exotic robes. Instead of which, I marched out. . . . There was certainly nothing shy nor tiny about either me or my feet." In her speech, she expressed her pride in seeing China array itself "against the enemies of democracy and freedom." Soon after that meeting, Tcheng interrupted her studies to return home and help recruit Chinese laborers to come to France's aid. Ultimately, some 140,000 Chinese men would heed the call.[19]

Tcheng was in China, still actively engaged in war recruitment, when the news arrived of the November 11 armistice that ended the First World

War. The Chinese people were elated. Having helped the Allies secure this historic victory, China would now have a seat at the peace negotiations and, it hoped, finally achieve the Great Power status it had lost under the Manchu regime. Most specifically, it hoped to recover Shandong, a graceful and wealthy coastal province to the southeast of Beijing, where the Yellow River empties into the sea. The Germans had claimed Shandong as a territorial concession in the late nineteenth century (establishing, among other interests, the Tsingtao Brewery), but, with no small amount of intimidation, the Japanese had seized control of the peninsula during World War I.

China's desire to recapture Shandong at the peace conference was complicated by the bewildering state of political affairs at home. Yuan Shikai had died of natural causes in 1916. Since then, China had broken into a series of competing warlord states, with two main centers of power. In Beijing, the northern government headed by Premier Duan Qirui claimed to be the only legitimate ruling body in the country and was recognized as such by most foreign powers. In the meantime, Sun Yat-sen's Nationalist Party (also known as the Guomindang, the successor to the Revolutionary Alliance) had declared its opposition to Duan and established a competing government in the southern city of Guangzhou.

To foster the appearance of national unity, the two governments agreed to both nominate delegates to represent China at the peace conference. Foreign Minister Lu Zhengxiang, appointed by the government in Beijing, would serve as the chief delegate. He and four other Chinese plenipotentiaries were joined by some sixty individuals, all appointed as official attachés and charged with helping the delegation achieve its goals in Paris. Soumay Tcheng was in Guangzhou as the Nationalist Party was naming its delegates. Her active involvement in the 1911 Revolution, her French and English language skills, her familiarity with the host city of Paris, and her ability to speak for her sex all helped her win a spot on this elite list. Apparently with little controversy, Tcheng was appointed as China's sole female representative to its national delegation and prepared immediately to return to France.[20]

To Paris, Via the United States

In haste, Soumay Tcheng prepared to leave Shanghai, although Paris was not her immediate destination. Instead, she took a steamer to the United

States. Tcheng justified the circuitous path as offering her an opportunity to explain the aims of the Nationalist Party and the political situation in China "to people who were sympathetic to our cause." Tcheng's assumption that Americans would be supportive of China's position was not unusual in 1919. On the whole, educated Chinese saw the Americans as less invested in imperialist interests and more committed to Chinese republicanism than were the other major powers. This idea of American friendship stretched back to the mid-nineteenth-century Opium Wars, at the end of which China had been forced to open its markets and port cities on terms vastly favorable to the West. Although the United States was among the countries to benefit from "most-favored-nation status" in this era, by the late nineteenth century, as European and Japanese governments scrambled to acquire more expansive Chinese territorial concessions, it largely stood to the side. America's "Open Door" policy in China was not particularly rooted in altruism. The country's imperial ambitions were merely tied up elsewhere, most notably in Cuba and the Philippines following the Spanish-American War. But motivations mattered little to the Chinese, who saw the Americans as less greedy and more sympathetic than the Europeans.[21]

Sino-American relations only strengthened after the fall of the Qing dynasty. In 1912 the United States became the first foreign state to recognize the Republic of China as a legitimate government. When America entered World War I in 1917, it encouraged China to do the same, suggesting the move would help China improve its international standing at war's end. Woodrow Wilson's wartime proclamations in favor of democracy and national self-determination provided the Chinese with further evidence of the Americans' high-minded vision of the peace to come and fueled expectations that the eventual peace treaty would restore to China its territorial sovereignty by canceling all the unequal treaties, phasing out extraterritorial jurisdiction (by which foreigners were exempt from Chinese law), and returning all foreign concessions to Chinese hands. Translated copies of Wilson's Fourteen Points speech flew off of Chinese newsstands. When word of the armistice reached China, students in Beijing stood outside the American Legation chanting, "Long live President Wilson!" For his part, Wilson invited Wellington Koo, the Chinese ambassador to the United States and one of China's five plenipotentiaries, to travel with the American delegation across the Atlantic. With the opening of the peace negotiations in Paris, Chinese delegates—including Soumay Tcheng—looked quite naturally to the Americans as their allies and anticipated seeing them fulfill their wartime pledges.[22]

Tcheng arrived in North America on March 5, 1919, landing first in Victoria, British Columbia, and then heading south and east. She cut her teeth as a government press agent in interviews with American journalists, explaining the Chinese delegation's aims in Paris. "I enjoyed myself thoroughly," she would later recall. The *New York Times* took delight in reporting on its conversation with the "young Chinese woman" who had "much the vivacity of a Frenchwoman in her manners and gestures." In the interview, Tcheng rehearsed some of the rhetorical strategies that she would employ with the press once she arrived in Europe, describing the former Manchu regime as an occupying power that had kept the Chinese people in a state of semislavery, denied them access to scientific or material progress, and interrupted China's natural evolution as a philosophical, peace-loving state. "Now we wish to have the liberty restored that we lost through the Manchu government," she explained. She also began to think about how she might use her own personal story to advance China's interests, in this case, describing her time in an American missionary school to emphasize her affinity with the United States. Encouraged by her "pleasant experience with the American press," Tcheng boarded a ship in New York and crossed the Atlantic, prepared to fulfill her mandate as the sole female member of China's peace delegation.[23]

When Tcheng finally arrived in Paris on April 6, 1919, the peace negotiations were already well under way. French journalists greeted her at the train station, eager to welcome her back to her adopted country and hear about her plans for the weeks ahead. One headline described her as a "Chinese Feminist and Sincere Francophile." Insisting (with perhaps a little exaggeration) that she spoke French as purely as her native language, journalists noted her "joy at finding herself again in France, and most of all, in Paris." The newspaper *Excelsior* guessed that she had come to collaborate with the Inter-Allied Women's Conference. For its part, *Le Petit Parisien* suggested that, in addition to "following" the work of the peace conference, Tcheng would be joining forces with a "feminist peace group," most likely referring to the nascent Women's International League for Peace and Freedom, which was preparing to meet in Zurich in a few weeks' time. Too tired from her extensive travels to elaborate on her intentions, Tcheng simply expressed her "strong desire to see feminists' demands satisfied by the peace conference" and headed off to catch some much-needed sleep.[24]

Peace delegate Soumay Tcheng arriving in Paris, reported in *Excelsior*, April 7, 1919. (Bibliothèque national de France)

The May Fourth Incident, from Paris to Beijing and Back Again

Tcheng would not be able to rest for long, nor would she be able to devote much time that spring to addressing the feminist questions "uppermost in her mind." Tcheng told the San Diego *Evening Tribune* later in 1919 that she "gave up all idea of doing anything for the women of China as soon as the [Shandong] award was made to Japan." Indeed, no sooner had Tcheng unpacked her bags in Paris than the news began to leak that the Supreme Council of the peace conference planned to award Shandong Province to Japan.[25]

Despite the strong sympathies that the Americans had with the Chinese, the Japanese had their own claim on Shandong. When Japan entered World

War I in 1914, one of its first moves had been to seize Shandong from the Germans. The Japanese then proceeded to strong-arm Yuan Shikai's government into signing a treaty known as the "Twenty-One Demands," by which Beijing recognized the legitimacy of the Japanese occupation. Later in the war Japan signed a series of secret agreements with the Russian, British, and French governments, further solidifying its territorial claims.

Against this inconvenient political reality, the Chinese delegation turned to Woodrow Wilson, who had consistently argued that the old diplomacy of secret treaties could not serve as the basis of a new, just world order. In the early weeks of the peace conference, the Americans had seemed impressed by Chinese arguments that their government had only signed away rights to Shandong under duress. They listened attentively as Wellington Koo eloquently defended the province as the "cradle of Chinese civilization," the birthplace of the national sage, Confucius. Also seemingly working in China's favor was the fact that Wilson distrusted the Japanese. His feelings were in part a reflection of American anti-Japanese prejudice, but they also derived from concern about Japan's imperial ambitions in Asia.[26]

The Japanese, however, held one strong point of leverage over the American president: Wilson had rejected the "racial equality clause" that the Japanese delegation had submitted for inclusion in the League of Nations Covenant (much to the displeasure of Mary Church Terrell and other African Americans in Paris). The Allies' refusal to adopt the racial equality clause cast the Shandong question in a new light. Wilson feared antagonizing the Japanese further and potentially pushing them to walk out of the negotiations. In light of these concerns, he began to soften to Japanese territorial demands. Soumay Tcheng arrived in Paris just as Wilson's wavering on Shandong was becoming public and as the Chinese delegation began stepping up its pressure on Wilson to fulfill his pledge to national self-determination. Inside the halls of power, things did not look good. "Outside," Tcheng would later recall, "the voices of the people, who had fought the war to save democracy and to have a just peace, were entirely too quiet for my tastes." On April 30 the Big Three (France, Britain, and the United States) made a final decision to recognize Japanese rights to Shandong.[27]

The Chinese were incensed. Back home, university and secondary school students reacted with particular furor. Two decades of educational reform and greater academic freedom had given rise to a young and engaged generation of students who avidly followed political affairs. At war's end, in 1918, large numbers of these students had joined in victory parades celebrating the triumph of democracy. Now, a mere six months later, they again took to the streets, this time to register their anger.[28]

News of the Allies' betrayal of China at the peace conference hit the students in Beijing like a bombshell. While some blamed their own leaders for complying with Japanese territorial demands, others turned their wrath on the West, and particularly on Woodrow Wilson, in whom they had placed so much hope. On the morning of May 4, 1919, in Beijing, about three thousand students gathered before the stately Gate of Heavenly Peace (in Chinese, Tian'anmen, the exact site where, in 1989, student protesters would unleash a mass movement for democratic reform). After firing off speeches denouncing the Allies' treachery in Paris, the students marched through the city and demanded that China reject the peace terms. The May Fourth Incident, as the protests would collectively be called, spread to other Chinese cities and to Chinese abroad, where intellectuals and workers joined with students in expressing their dismay and publicly demanding that the Chinese delegation refuse to sign the peace treaty. American philosopher and education reformer John Dewey, who had arrived in China just days before the demonstrations, wrote home of his astonishment at seeing such young men and women leading the movement: "To think of kids in our country from fourteen on, taking the lead in starting a big cleanup reform politics movement and shaming merchants and professional men into joining them," he said. "This is sure some country."[29]

It was not just the young age of the May Fourth leaders that stood out to contemporary observers. One of the remarkable features of the budding movement, noted the *North-China Herald*, was "the large part now taken by the women of China. They are as keen as their brothers in the desire for the betterment of their country's welfare." In southern China, Shandong "has become a cry which rallies even women and schoolboys," reported the *Shanghai Times*. Students from boys' and girls' schools joined together to form new student unions to coordinate the protests, the first such coeducational collaboration in Chinese history. And while the most visible leaders of the May Fourth protests were generally men, female students, some of them scarcely in their teens, did not hesitate to take to the streets or to seize the bullhorn.[30]

Who were these May Fourth girls and women, and what were they hoping for when they joined in protests and cried for justice? In the 1990s historian Wang Zheng tracked down some of these activists—by then elderly women in their eighties and nineties—to pose this very question. The women she interviewed recalled their experiences in 1919 in vivid detail. For example, a woman named Lu Lihua (who, as an adult, would establish the first women's basketball team in China) was finishing a program at a girls' physical education school in Shanghai when the protests broke out. "The year I graduated was the same year that the May Fourth movement happened," she would recall. "I was like a fish in water. I joined all kinds of activities and made speeches. . . . People said I was brave." May Fourth, she remembered, developed quickly into a mass movement in Shanghai, "and many young people joined. Quite a lot of them were female students." Cheng Yongsheng, also a physical education student in 1919, was among the protestors. "I made speeches and petitions, burned Japanese goods, and participated in other activities," she said. For Huang Dinghui, who was barely twelve years old and a student at the Zhounan Girls' School in 1919, May Fourth was a life-changing experience. Elected by her class to provide updates on the protests, Huang immersed herself in the turmoil: "Although my participation in the May Fourth movement lasted only a few months," she would later explain, "the people's unity, high spirits, and righteous indignation were extremely exciting, enormously encouraging and profoundly educational." The May Fourth protests in China set many young women like Lu, Cheng, and Huang down a path of political activism.[31]

In the meantime, in Paris, the news that Shandong would be granted to the Japanese mobilized China's female delegate to action as well. On May 4, at the same time that students were gathering at Tian'anmen in Beijing, Soumay Tcheng was meeting with overseas Chinese students and workers in Paris. Under the banner of the "Chinese Society for International Peace," the group decided to approach the leaders of the major powers, including President Wilson, to demand China be treated fairly in the peace negotiations. On May 9 the same group, along with members of the Chinese delegation, staged a large public protest in Paris, attended by over five hundred people. At the meeting, "Miss Tcheng, a well-known feminist," was one of the speakers who "severely criticized" the decision on Shandong and insisted that China could not sign a peace that offered only a "dark future for our people." Wilson, who had been invited to the meeting, was notably absent, sending his regrets "that his engagements prevented him from attending."[32]

The question of whether to endorse the Versailles Treaty consumed the Chinese delegation right up until the signing ceremony on June 28. The May Fourth protests in China and abroad clearly demonstrated public opposition to signing the humiliating accord. The Nationalist Government in Guangzhou was also adamantly opposed to signing. Most of China's delegates to the peace conference were coming to the same conclusion. Chief plenipotentiary Lu Zhengxiang was under tremendous pressure, but he also feared the international repercussions of boycotting the treaty and refused to commit to a course of action without official authorization from home. The weak and faction-ridden government in Beijing, however, refused to send clear instructions, leaving the ultimate decision whether to sign to him. Lu was torn, and on June 27, on the eve of the signing ceremony, he disappeared from Paris entirely. China's fate seemed to be in his hands.[33]

The Rosebush Gun

Soumay Tcheng's description of the events that ensued after Lu left Paris reads like a chapter torn from a spy novel. When the organized group of Chinese students and workers in Paris got word of Lu's disappearance, they feared the chief delegate had slipped out of the capital to travel to the signing ceremony unimpeded by angry protestors. Their concerns were only amplified when Tcheng learned from a fellow delegate's wife that Lu had taken up temporary residence in St. Cloud, a stylish western suburb of Paris on the route to the palace at Versailles (the home of the absolutist kings of France and the scheduled location for the treaty-signing ceremony the following day). With no time to waste, Tcheng and other student leaders sent word to their comrades to rendezvous in the Tuilleries Garden later that afternoon; from there, the group would proceed to St. Cloud to confront Lu. As the sun began to set, however, the others were slow to arrive. Impatient and worried, Tcheng and a friend took a taxi directly to St. Cloud, leaving instructions for the others to follow as quickly as possible.[34]

They found the address without a problem, but neither Tcheng nor the others who arrived later that evening could convince Lu to open the door. By nightfall up to three hundred students and workers were milling around the garden outside the residence when an automobile drove up carrying the secretary to the Chinese delegation. The man dashed from the car to the house with a "bulging brief-case under his arm." Sensing trouble, Tcheng and the others agreed that they needed to get their hands on the documents in the portfolio. The secretary who possessed them, Tcheng noted, "was an older man—an official of an earlier regime in China, and a conservative timid character of the type which would be intimidated by any violent demonstration, and terrified by such young people as ourselves, who thought nothing of taking matters into our own hands." Thinking on her feet, and no doubt drawing on her earlier revolutionary experience, Tcheng snapped off a small branch from a rosebush and rubbed it in the dirt to make it look like a gun. When the secretary emerged later from the house, two of Tcheng's comrades tried to talk him into surrendering the briefcase. When he refused, remembers Tcheng, "I stepped out of the shadows in front of him and pointed my rosebush gun right at him." The secretary dropped the briefcase in terror and took flight.[35]

Tcheng and her coconspirators now had the documents, but Lu still refused to see them, and so the group stood vigil in the garden through an unseasonably cold night (taking turns bribing an enterprising concierge, who, for a fee, allowed the students to warm themselves briefly in his office before shooing them back outside). Finally, around 10:00 the next morning, Lu agreed to hear the protestors out. "We stated our case," writes Tcheng, "and as usual, I fear I did a good deal of the talking." One last time, the group of Chinese students and workers hammered home the case for boycotting the treaty. As the hour of the signing ceremony drew near, Tcheng recalls, "Mr. (Lu) still sat—a crumpled and sulky figure in a chair, with us firing verbal ammunition at him from all sides. . . . The hour came and went. Mr. (Lu) did not go to Versailles." On June 28, 1919, the chairs set out for the Chinese delegation in the Versailles Palace's glistening Hall of Mirrors remained empty. China became the only Allied country to refuse to sign the Versailles Treaty, due in part to the efforts of its female peace delegate.[36]

Tcheng played a critical role in compelling China's rejection of the peace settlement. Why, then, is her name seldom mentioned in historical accounts of the Paris Peace Conference? Historians are most comfortable describing events that can be validated by primary sources, produced by participants in or witnesses to the events in question. In this case, primary source evidence is scant. The students themselves, who were acting secretly and on the fly, left behind no telling documentation. Most of the ambitious journalists in Paris on June 27, including Andrée Viollis, were focused on the German delegation, forced to come to Versailles to sign (as they saw it) an unjust and humiliating peace. No one had his or her eyes on China until its plenipotentiaries failed to appear in the Hall of Mirrors the following day.[37]

Fortunately, corroborating evidence does exist to validate Tcheng's account. Plenipotentiary Wellington Koo was also at St. Cloud meeting with Lu Zhengxiang and the Chinese delegation secretary on the evening of June 27, 1919. Koo remembers the secretary's alarming experience as he attempted to leave the house and return to Paris: "Two or three minutes after he left he rushed back in looking pale," Koo would later recall in an oral interview recorded at Columbia University. "He told the Foreign Minister that he had been attacked in the garden. . . . The crowd closed in on him . . . they threatened to kill him, and one of the members, a girl student actually pointed a pistol at him through her overcoat pocket." Further in the memoir, Koo identifies the girl in question as Soumay Tcheng. In addition, in a front-page article published in the French newspaper *L'Instransigent* just a year after the events in question, a journalist who knew Tcheng in 1919 also described her as the mastermind behind the plot to prevent Lu from signing the treaty. Tcheng, for her part, would discuss her 1919 actions over the years, for example, telling the *Washington Post* in 1942 that in organizing the "student barricade" of Lu's St. Cloud residence on June 27, 1919, she had acted on direct orders from Sun Yat-sen.[38]

Tcheng clearly understood the historic importance of the diplomatic events that she helped to orchestrate, even bringing home her own personal souvenir. Once the peace conference was over, she took the rosebush branch back to her family home in Shanghai, where it remained until the Japanese invaded southern China in the opening years of the Second World War. Later she would write, "I speculate at times what was the reaction of the Japanese when they looted my home in Shanghai in 1937, as they came across an old stick carefully wrapped in paper in a drawer." Had China's subsequent history unfolded differently, Tcheng's "rosebush gun" might be prominently displayed in a museum somewhere. It—and the woman who wielded it—helped seal the Chinese rejection of the Versailles Treaty.[39]

This rejection had lasting consequences. Although the Americans would pressure the Japanese into temporarily returning Shandong to China just a few years after the Paris Peace Conference, Japanese imperialistic ambitions had been stoked. Japan invaded Manchuria in 1931. The following year it unleashed its bombs on Shanghai. In 1937 it opened an outright assault on China, announcing in Asia the outbreak of the Second World War.

Equally notable, the spurning of Chinese diplomats in Paris in 1919 emboldened May Fourth era reformers (whether Nationalists or, as was increasingly the case, Communists) to hasten their drive for modernization as a step toward restoring Chinese national dignity and reclaiming territorial sovereignty. As Chinese political elites debated the surest means of achieving national unity and independence, the question of women's proper role in a modernizing state took on newfound urgency. In 1919 Soumay Tcheng was already helping shape the conversation.

Modern Women and Women Warriors

As an official delegate to the peace conference, Tcheng rose up in a spirited defense of China's right to national self-determination, but what about the feminist issues that she hoped to champion when she first stepped off the train in Paris in April 1919? Tcheng's government appointed her, in part, to represent the women of China. Pressing political concerns drew her attention away from the various women's rights conferences that she might have contributed to in Europe that spring. It would be wrong, however, to see her activism on behalf of *national* self-determination as somehow divorced from the question of *individual* self-determination for the women of China. In 1919 Soumay Tcheng, much like Huda Shaarawi and the Egyptian women who took to the streets in Cairo, saw the struggle for national and female liberation as one and the same. In both direct and indirect ways, Tcheng's unconventional diplomacy of 1919 helped advance Chinese women's rights in the years ahead.

The Nationalist government specifically charged Tcheng with two seemingly distinct responsibilities at the peace conference: serving as a media liaison and representing Chinese women. In fact, Tcheng combined the two roles by using her own image to cement the idea—both at home and abroad—that emancipated womanhood was central to China's emergence as a modern power. As an appointed representative of her nation, Tcheng very quickly came to recognize the fascination that she evoked among a Western population culturally conditioned to see Chinese women as submissive and subjugated: one sign, among many, they thought, of the politically immature state of "the Orient." Tcheng sought to undo such stereotypes and, in the process, to link China's political maturity to women's liberation.

The effectiveness of this strategy is strikingly apparent in the interview that Tcheng conducted with Andrée Viollis in April 1919. Viollis, we will recall, thought she knew what to expect when she arranged the interview with the Chinese delegate: a shy, delicate woman on hobbled feet. Instead, Soumay Tcheng appeared. By the time the two women had finished their conversation, Viollis had revised not only her mental picture of the "typical" Chinese lady but also her image of the country of China writ large. "Yesterday," she wrote, "while Mlle. Cheng, wearing a dainty Parisian dress, her dark lustrous eyes glowing with sincerity in her delicate ivory face, was talking to me, now in French and now in English, about her mission to Paris and all the peace problems, young China stood suddenly revealed to me with its great possibilities, its aims, its ideals."

The article proceeded to describe Tcheng's hopes for the restitution of China's economic and political sovereignty at the peace conference. Viollis gave sympathetic voice to these claims, but her article featured the bearer of the ideas as much as, if not more than, the ideas themselves. "All I know," Viollis wrote in the conclusion of her article, "is that your Government has found in you a very able ambassador as well as a charming one. When I think that most of us imagine Chinese women shut up in harems with just the mentality and knowledge of slaves! What a change!" During the years she spent in Europe and in the United States, Tcheng artfully fashioned her dress, mannerisms, and linguistic skills to embody Chinese modernity for a Western audience; she promoted herself as the personification of a modern, liberated nation that was ready to emerge as Great Power in the international arena.[40]

Tcheng's style was anything but accidental: it reflected a conscious desire to emulate the free-spirited look that was just coming into fashion in postwar Europe and to shape a new image of womanhood back home. Knee-length skirts, transparent stockings, bare arms, and short bobbed hair were the unofficial uniform of the Modern Woman. Tcheng wore them all well. The deep pocketbook of the Tcheng family fortune helped in this respect, but Tcheng's fashion choices were never merely decorative. To a Western audience, they spoke to the underlying values of the woman who wore them and the nation she represented.

Nearly every article that appeared in Western newspapers about Tcheng—and there were many in both France and the United States stretching from 1917 through the 1940s—commented on her clothing and hairstyles. In December 1919, when she again passed through the United

Soumay Tcheng in New York on her way back to China, *New York Times*, December 14, 1919. (Library of Congress)

States on her way back to China, the *New York Times* published a head-to-toe photograph of her looking every bit the American flapper. That same month, the *Los Angeles Evening Herald* interviewed Tcheng, recording her opinions about the injustice of the Paris Peace Conference and the unfortunate segregation of Chinese Americans in Chinatowns, but not before describing her "modern European garb" including a "fur coat and jewels."[41]

To be fair, newspapers often commented on women's clothing in the early twentieth century regardless of the bearer's ethnicity or country of origin. Much less frequent, however, was the assumption that the political evolution of an entire nation could be read in a woman's fashion choices, which is how the Western media described Soumay Tcheng. Beginning with Andrée Viollis and throughout the 1920s, newspaper articles repeatedly equated Tcheng with "Young China." The *Los Angeles Evening Herald*, for example, described her as "representing the young Chinese movement." So often did Western journalists comment on Tcheng's youth, stylishness, and modernity that by 1919 she seems to have begun fudging her age to help this story along. Although the *Evening Herald* article correctly identified her in 1919 as twenty-seven, that same year Parisian papers were shaving a full four years off her age. (By 1943 Tcheng had lost yet another year, claiming she was born in 1896 rather than 1891, but by then she had married her charming Sorbonne classmate, Wei Tao-ming, a man eight years her junior, a scandalous age discrepancy for the time.) Lying about her age was not a matter of vanity: Tcheng's effectiveness as an envoy of her nation depended on her ability to personify "young China" for the Western audience she hoped to woo.[42]

Tcheng's clothing and hairstyles carried meaning back home in China as well. The Modern Woman, historians have noted, emerged in China as a product of the May Fourth Movement. The first articles introducing the concept of Western New Womanhood appeared in China in 1918. Tcheng and a handful of other women of her generation served as the prototypes, but by the 1920s urban, educated, and often politically engaged young Chinese women readily adopted modern Western styles. Bobbed hair became a symbol of political as well as cultural emancipation, a positive association during the radical May Fourth era but potentially lethal after 1927, when the Nationalists turned on the leftist wing of their party, and Guomindang leaders began associating Modern Womanhood with communism. In the 1930s, as Western-influenced fashion, hairstyles, and cosmetics further shaped Chinese popular culture, Modern Women became more visible in China's major cities, but they also risked being branded as self-indulgent consumerists who threatened the moral fabric of the nation. Tcheng was attuned to the shifting political winds. By the time she moved to Washington, D.C., in 1943 as the wife of Wei Tao-ming (who had been appointed Chinese ambassador to the United States in the middle of World War II), American papers noted that she had given up her bobbed hair and short skirts "and returned to the graceful Chinese gowns worn by Madame Chiang [Kai-shek]."[43]

All these shifting fashion choices may well lead us to ask how much Tcheng's look reflected her own personal preferences and identity or how much she dressed to strike a particular image for those watching and judging her, whether in the West or back home in China. Tcheng purchased her first Western-style outfit as a teenager to attend the American missionary school for girls in Tianjin. Christian missions represented the epitome of Western cultural imperialism in Asia, yet Tcheng did not find the clothing an imposition. On the contrary, as a young woman, she embraced the "Occidental style" as an outward symbol of liberation. "My clothes were probably terrible," she would later admit, her hairstyle "an unattractive cross between a pompadour and a bun at the nape of the neck" and her hat a gaudy contraption overloaded with feathers. But she loved that hat: "I was so fascinated with it," she says, "that I could hardly be persuaded to take it off indoors." Despite the fashion's Western origins, Tcheng embraced the new style because for her, it came part and parcel with an agenda she heartily embraced: "training young women to do more in the world of affairs than in the past." Once she arrived in Europe, the same hairstyles and clothing that marked her as a liberated woman also served the purpose of associating China with emancipation and modernity, an association that promised to advance China's position as a Great Power. Tcheng played up her look for all it was worth. As the French newspaper *Le Figaro* proclaimed in 1920, Tcheng "incarnates the modern soul of her country." Throughout her many years in the West, her fashion was always an extension of her diplomacy.[44]

If Tcheng emphasized her adoption of European culture to demonstrate her country's evolution, in another equally important way she drew on distinctly Chinese tradition in representing her country in 1919. In the process she again drew tight links between her nationalist and feminist goals and helped to legitimize female activism in service of the nation back at home. Specifically, in writing and interviews, Tcheng cast herself as a modern-day Hua Mulan. Granted, the legendary Mulan had not always been a feminist icon—after all, she had to transform herself into a man to engage in heroic feats—but among educated Chinese women of Tcheng's generation, Mulan became a role model of female public engagement. From her youngest years, listening to the tale of Mulan on her mother's lap, Tcheng had idolized the woman warrior. As an adult, she consciously sought to live up to her role model.[45]

Tcheng narrated her own life in the mold of Mulan. She emphasized details like the fact that when her father took her with him on government business when she was young, he dressed her in boys' clothing so that she could accompany him in public without raising eyebrows. As she grew, the story of Mulan remained a guidepost for her unconventional life. Tcheng would recall, for example, that in 1913, as she traveled to Beijing to carry out the aborted assassination attempt on Yuan Shi-kai's finance minister, "The beautiful story of Mulan, that my mother had told me in my childhood, came back to me. All the details seemed singularly vivid." In Tcheng's hands, the Mulan story shifted from a moral lesson in filial piety to an object lesson in women's militant potential. With the rosebush gun incident in 1919, Tcheng embodied Chinese female martial tradition as much as Western New Womanhood, a history she alluded to directly in her *Daily Mail* interview with Viollis. In response to the journalist's exclamation, "What a change!" Tcheng handily replied, "It is not a change, it is just a return to tradition. In old days Chinese women could become generals, Ministers." "Then let me hope," responded Viollis, "that some day I may call you '*Mademoiselle le Ministre.*'" In both her words and her deeds, Tcheng melded European Modern Womanhood with Chinese legendary female heroism to legitimize women's activism in the public sphere.[46]

May Fourth Feminism

The legend of the female general Hua Mulan motivated a generation of Chinese women—including Soumay Tcheng—to seek a place as men's equals in the heroic struggle for Chinese independence and unity. As inspirational as Mulan's story was, however, it alone cannot explain the widespread political activism of young Chinese women in 1919, whether in Beijing, Shanghai, or, as in Tcheng's case, overseas. All their actions can be read as a concrete response to the intense debate surrounding the Woman Question (as it was phrased at the time), which had begun a couple of years prior to the Paris Peace Conference and exploded into a full blown national obsession after the protests of May Fourth.

The term "May Fourth Movement" serves as a catchphrase in Chinese history for a broader period of intellectual and social ferment, which lasted roughly a decade, from 1915 to 1925. While Communists in China celebrate this era as the founding moment of the Chinese Communist Party, there was nothing doctrinaire about the debates that raged in those years. On the contrary, the period between the fall of the Qing dynasty and the unification of the country under the Guomindang saw some of the most wide-ranging debate of any in Chinese history. The term May Fourth Movement encompasses new cultural ideas popularized by young Chinese intellectuals as well as student activism during and after 1919, both of which blossomed in this stimulating intellectual environment.[47]

The question of women's rights sat at the very center of both cultural and social developments of the May Fourth era. After the fall of the Qing dynasty, educational reforms helped spawn a new generation of intellectuals who broadly embraced Western liberal concepts of freedom and individualism as the key to Chinese modernization and independence. These New Culturalists, as they were sometimes called, founded periodicals like *New Youth* and *New Tide*, which proclaimed their modernity in their very titles. In article after article, these journals attacked the Confucian ideals of hierarchy and social order, including the cardinal principle that husbands hold sway over their wives and parents have the right to determine their children's marital fortunes. As a result, New Culturalists went on the offensive against a host of longstanding institutions that reinforced women's subordinate status in the family and in society: footbinding, concubinage, and arranged marriage among them. They argued that women's entrenched subservience was preventing China from evolving into a modern society.[48]

May Fourth intellectuals saw women's emancipation as fundamental to their cultural and political goals; yet, up until 1919, most of the writers promoting the development of feminist consciousness in China were men. For this reason, New Culturalists began to look for ways to encourage women's "enlightenment." Male radicals translated Western texts in order to stimulate discussion around the Woman Question. In 1918 Cornell University graduate Hu Shi (who would later precede Soumay Tcheng's husband as the Chinese ambassador to the United States) helped to translate and publish Henrik Ibsen's scandalous play *A Doll's House* in *New Youth*, setting off a broad discussion about whether the protagonist, Nora, was justified in walking out on her husband. In March 1919 Hu Shi published his own one-act play entitled *The Greatest Event in Life*, a simplified and altered version of Ibsen's play, which features two young Chinese students who fall in love while studying overseas. Their parents disapprove of their marriage, but the young people run away together in the end.[49]

The May Fourth Incident of 1919 fed the sense of urgency surrounding the Woman Question in China, and texts advocating women's rights multiplied and gained broad circulation. In the aftermath of the May protests, student societies staged productions of *The Greatest Event in Life* across the country. At the same time, a recent graduate of the Normal School in Hunan Province named Mao Zedong—the future leader of the People's Republic of China—published a series of articles about a young Hunanese woman named Zhao Wuzhen who committed suicide on the way to her wedding in order to escape an arranged marriage she abhorred. Mao portrayed Miss Zhao as a victim of "perverse customs" that denied women happiness and subjected them "to many kinds of inhuman mistreatment."[50]

Hu Shi's and Mao Zedong's plays and articles of 1919, as well as many others, helped give shape to a new language of women's emancipation that was very important to the female students who came of age in the May Fourth era. At the same time, there were telling limitations to men's May Fourth feminism. Hu Shi's and Mao Zedong's writing, although focused on the social oppression of women, tended to draw emphasis away from the ways that women might actively collaborate in their own emancipation. Highlighting women as victims more than as agents of history, and emphasizing the need to liberate women for the good of country rather than out of concern for women's individual rights, May Fourth male intellectuals could carry women only so far.[51]

After 1919, however, men were no longer alone in decrying women's oppression. Female students, awakened to gender discrimination by New Culturalists' writing and empowered by the experience of public protest following the May Fourth Incident, began taking matters into their own hands. Before the end of 1919 the first United Women's Associations were formed in southern China. Lu Lihua, the future girls' basketball coach referred to above, was among those who joined. "The Feminist Movement Association was formed after the May Fourth students' movement," she recalled. "At the time there were over ten women's organizations in Shanghai, and I joined them all." Lu was not alone. The 1920s marked the high point of feminist influence on political life in China.[52]

Soumay Tcheng was both a beneficiary and a shaper of May Fourth feminism in China. By refusing to bow to the will of the Western powers, the Chinese delegation in Paris—including Tcheng—helped embolden the May Fourth generation to demand a new Chinese political and social order rebuilt on broadly democratic lines. The development of a vibrant women's movement was one of the immediate results. Tcheng witnessed the effects of this cultural tsunami when she returned home to China for a visit in 1920, and, in typical fashion, she plunged head first into the storm.

A Warrior for Women's Rights

When Tcheng arrived back in China in 1920, in the midst of the nationalist ferment that followed the May Fourth Incident, the germination of female enlightenment was readily apparent. Tcheng cheered these developments and sought out opportunities to help young women develop their intellect and independence. She did not have to wait for long for an opportunity to arise.

Shortly after Tcheng returned to China, the governor of Sichuan Province, an old revolutionary friend, invited her to come to the capital city, Chongqing, to speak about her experiences in Paris. "Their invitation itself was a departure from tradition," Tcheng would later note, "for a woman's place was in the home and not on the lecture platform." In 1920 paved roads did not yet stretch as far as the mountainous, inland town of Chongqing. Instead, Tcheng voyaged by steamer through the gorges of the Yangzi River, marveling at the sheer cliffs rising from the riverbanks and at the "torrents of water [as they] rushed by in a mad whirl." For Tcheng, who had spent most of her life in the bustling cities of Guangzhou, Beijing, and Paris, Chongqing seemed a "quiet, sleepy city" where the "traditions of social life were observed as strictly as in the olden times." Within city walls, sedan chairs remained the primary mode of transportation. Despite Chongqing's relative isolation and traditionalism, Tcheng found the people "anxious to keep abreast of the developments in world affairs."[53]

Before her public lecture, Tcheng was invited to meet with a group of students at a local girls' school, whom she cordially invited to come to her talk later that day. The students responded sadly that their (male) principal was "opposed to the emancipation of women" and had forbidden them to attend. Tcheng found the principal's attitude "ridiculous," and she encouraged the girls to "strike out for themselves." To her pleasure, many of the young women managed to come. "I made a long speech," Tcheng recalls, "in which I dwelt on the Peace Conference, the part that the new China must play in world affairs, and emphasizing the important role of women, who must have every opportunity for education if they were to exercise their rights." In a nod to the female students who "were listening intently," Tcheng proceeded to champion "the cause of freedom and equality of the sexes." Her words hit home. After her address, the young women refused to return to their classes until the principal was fired (which he was the very next day, after Tcheng intervened with her friend the governor). Tcheng also arranged for six of the students, including the governor's sister and niece, to return to Paris with her so that they might pursue advanced studies.[54]

The story did not end there. As her boat began to pull back from the banks of the Yangzi to return to Shanghai, Tcheng was drawn out of her reverie by the sound of "excited giggles in the shadows around [her]."

Twenty—not six—young women stepped into the light. Tcheng was dumb-founded. "Fourteen additional students of that school had been so aroused by my ideas," she would recall, "that they had braved all possible conse-quences and had determined to run away with me to Europe." Tcheng cheered the girls' courage but panicked at the responsibility they were asking her to take on. Her first impulse was to send them all home. But then she thought back on her own rebellious past and (as journalists in France would later report), "a wave of conspiratorial sympathy came over her." Ultimately, Tcheng convinced the families to allow their daughters to go. In February 1921 Paris newspapers reported on Tcheng's return to the French capital, noting that she was accompanied by a group of twenty-some young Chinese women anxious to acquire a modern education and to help rebuild their country. Many of them would later return home to build illustrious careers as doctors, judges, and heads of industry.[55]

The young women remained under Tcheng's wing over the next four years as she worked toward finishing her own legal education at the Sor-bonne. Tcheng's successful completion of her doctoral degree in June 1925 was a momentous occasion. As the first Chinese woman to graduate with a law degree from a European university, Tcheng was given the royal treat-ment. The largest hall at the Sorbonne, adorned in Gobelin tapestries, was reserved for the occasion. The examiners appeared in their traditional red gowns, trimmed in ermine fur. Tcheng, for her part, says she "dressed for the occasion as carefully as I would have for any wedding." Knowing her appearance would be a matter of media attention, she adorned herself in a careful blend of East and West: a blue crepe-de-chine dress, "cut in the latest Shanghai fashion," decorated with jade earrings and a brooch. Her hair was fashionably bobbed: "quite in the style of her Western sisters," remarked the *Los Angeles Times*. "The scene was historic," enthused the American magazine *Good Housekeeping*, which ran a feature story on Tch-eng later that year. It marked "a date when a woman of the East came as a winning equal into the arena of Occidental learning." Tcheng's degree and subsequent legal career were considered newsworthy in as far-flung cor-ners of the world as French Indochina and Egypt, where Huda Shaarawi would dedicate a special feature to Tcheng in her feminist journal *L'Egyptienne*.[56]

Tcheng's doctoral thesis on "The Constitutional Movement in China" traced the evolution of constitutional ideas since the fall of the Qing dynasty, comparing the nascent republic's development with its Western precedents.

Soumay Tcheng dressed for her 1925 doctoral defense at the Sorbonne, featured in the Egyptian feminist periodical *L'Egyptienne*, October 1927. (Bibliothèque nationale de France)

The work is erudite and technical, yet it reveals little of the feminist pre-occupations that would define much of Tcheng's future law practice and professional life. Only the dedication page provides a glimpse of the feminist viewpoint of the author.[57]

Tcheng dedicated her thesis to two women: her mother and Madame Hugues Le Roux. She describes the latter as "her sister," but New York expatriate Bessie Hugues Le Roux and Soumay Tcheng were related neither by blood nor by nationality. They were sisters in spirit. Widowed of her first husband at a relatively young age, Bessie first came to France with her sister-in-law in the early 1900s. The two made a living for themselves as "gentlewomen" writers, publishing both novels and a muckraking journalistic account of the lives of women workers in America. Somewhere along the way, Bessie met law student Soumay Tcheng, and the two for-eign women became close friends. Later, Bessie would marry Frenchman Hugues le Roux, a journalist, writer, and senator (who, ironically, pub-lished a number of books decrying the decline of marriage and the rise of the Modern Woman). Despite her choice of a husband, Bessie devoted countless hours to promoting Soumay Tcheng as the archetype of young, emancipated China. As the coauthor of Tcheng's memoirs, Bessie turned the Chinese woman's story into an engaging narrative that could capture the imagination of both French- and English-speaking audiences. She did so not only out of friendship but also out of the belief that Tcheng's life story would inspire and edify. As she wrote in a foreword to the 1926 English-language edition: "A nation, to be sure, is no greater than its women, but whatever drawbacks to progress the Chinese women's education may have hitherto presented, Soumay Tcheng's example illustrates the future way."[58]

Tcheng's decision to dedicate her doctoral dissertation to her mother also speaks to the value she placed on personal relationships with the women who most shaped her budding feminist consciousness. Tcheng's mother encouraged her daughter to embrace a life of freedom and opportunity. In Tcheng's childhood, she imbued her with the spirit of Hua Mulan. Later she offered her daughter moral support in her scandalous rejection of an arranged marriage. As Tcheng grew older and as her mother gradually learned of her revolutionary activism, she fought back her maternal impulse to put a halt to her daughter's dangerous exploits. Instead she told Sou-may: "Act. Come to the aid of Chinese women. Men and their families treat them like toys. They don't stop with preventing them from educat-ing themselves: they deny that they are even capable of learning. Show what a woman of this country is capable of doing. You will help all women." By dedicating her doctoral thesis to her mother, Tcheng was, in effect, acknowledging and making good on this admonition.[59]

Armed with a law degree, Tcheng returned to China in 1926. Two years later, Chiang Kai-shek's armies unified the country under Nationalist rule (often lashing out ruthlessly against their Communist opponents in the pro-cess). In the interim, Tcheng set up a law practice in Shanghai with her friend from Paris, Wei Tao-ming. Some of their earliest clients were women seeking to divorce their husbands. Although Tcheng and Wei agreed to encourage wives and husbands to make amends, they willingly took on cases of couples whose differences were irreconcilable. "I was rather pleased," remembers Tcheng, "because I felt that it was an opportunity to start helping the many unhappy Chinese women in their struggle for freedom." Not all her clients were obscure housewives. Most notably, Tcheng agreed to handle a high-profile divorce case between two of the most famous Peking Opera stars of the era: Meng Xiaodong and his third wife Mei Lanfang. In winning Mei a lucrative settlement, Tcheng saw her legal fortunes soar.[60]

Ironically, working in divorce law seems to have finally convinced Tcheng, at the advanced age of thirty-six, to contemplate marriage herself. When the Nationalists took Shanghai in late 1927, Tcheng and Wei dissolved their legal partnership, admitted their feelings for each other, and tied the knot. Marriage, however, did not slow either partner's budding political career. Wei joined the new Ministry of Justice. Tcheng too was in high demand. Though she accepted a judgeship at the International Court of Shanghai (making her the first female judge in Chinese history), Tcheng soon resigned to work directly for the new Nationalist government. She also renewed contacts with Western feminists, most notably by helping arrange for a visiting delegation from the Women's International League and Peace and Freedom to meet with Chinese feminist and political leaders in early 1928.[61]

Shortly thereafter she returned briefly to France as a government emissary, sent abroad to reassure the West of the liberal and democratic intentions of the new Nationalist regime. The French press welcomed her home, even as some male reporters struggled with what to make of the female envoy. One wrote (after, *bien sûr*, commenting on her clothing and her short, "Joan of Arc" hairdo) that he was ready to believe anything that came from the mouth of such a "charming diplomat." Another, simultaneously more radical and more sarcastic, wrote that if he were a French woman, he would be outraged at the attention being showered on the "ultramodern Madame Soumé-Tcheng" even as women in France remained stymied in their own quest for political rights. "If you won't do anything for us," the journalist imagined French women saying, "at least hide from us the spectacle of women's triumph among the less civilized people of the world." In sending Tcheng to represent the government abroad, the Chinese Nationalist Party demonstrated the degree to which it had come to see open support for women's emancipation as critical to gaining international recognition and respect.[62]

The Nationalists' victory did not exactly guarantee women's triumph in the years that followed, but Chinese women gained substantial new rights during the years of Nationalist rule. Once again, Soumay Tcheng

played a critical role. In 1928 she was appointed as a member of the Legislative Yuan, which acted as China's provisional parliament until the ratification of a new constitution. Only two women were trusted with this
responsibility: Tcheng and Madame Chiang Kai-shek, the president's wife.
Owing to her legal training, Tcheng was also appointed to serve on the
five-member commission established to write a new Chinese Civil Code.
"It was a position I had particularly hoped for," Tcheng would later write,
"because, although the principle of absolute equality for women was recognized, it was still a great undertaking to embody it in law." Tcheng was
not the lone feminist on the commission: many of the male commission-
ers were equally committed to the principles of individual rights and gender equality. Nonetheless, the republican Civil Code represented, in many
respects, the culmination of Tcheng's personal, lifelong battle to undo the
Confucian family order that she saw as the cause of her own mother's misery and that she had rebelled against continually in her personal life.[63]

The code, which was promulgated between 1929 and 1931, was nothing short of revolutionary. It recognized equal inheritance rights between
sisters and brothers. It granted young men and women freedom of choice
in their marriage partners and guaranteed equality in divorce to husbands
and wives. It endowed unmarried women with full legal capacity (to make
contracts or to own property, for example). It guaranteed married women
the right to keep their family names if they so chose (although, by default,
it had women prefix the husband's family name to their own), and it provided the possibility for married women to retain their own separate property after marriage. From Chinese feminists' perspective, the code still
had shortcomings. Concubinage was not yet declared illegal, but the Civil
Code did provide any wife whose husband took a concubine with a number of remedies, including divorce or judicial separation. The Civil Code
represented a fundamental improvement in women's status in the family
and society at the same time that the constitution promised them full political rights.[64]

Civil rights crucial to Chinese women's equality and happiness thus
became entrenched in the Nationalist period and have been sustained ever
since, regardless of whether the Nationalists or the Communists were in
power. At the same time, women's political rights, like men's, have remained
largely theoretical. In the 1930s the Nationalists delayed holding democratic elections and placed renewed emphasis on tradition in an effort to
promote social stability. The Japanese invasion of China in 1937 suspended

democratic institutions indefinitely, as the nation's energies were turned to fighting the occupying army and as women were enjoined to mother the nation at war. Civil war between the Nationalists and the Communists followed almost immediately on the heels of the Second World War, resulting in the establishment of the People's Republic of China in 1949. In power, the postwar Chinese Communist Party (CCP) solidified male political control, even as it continued to battle gender oppression in the family and in the economy. The CCP's longstanding commitment to women's "enlightenment" and emancipation, dating back to the May Fourth Movement, contributed to the myth that the Communist Party singlehandedly liberated Chinese women from centuries of oppression and subjugation. Stories of the heroic women who made this transition possible fit uncomfortably in this narrative, and many faded from memory.

China's political development since World War II helps explain why Soumay Tcheng—the lone female delegate to the Paris Peace Conference of 1919—has largely been written out of the history books. Tcheng was decidedly not a Communist. Throughout the interwar and World War II decades, her loyalties were firmly with the Nationalist Guomindang. Never once in her 1943 memoir does Tcheng mention the Communist Party or the attraction that it held for many Chinese radicals, including radical feminists, in the 1920s to 1940s. After the 1949 Revolution brought the CCP to power, Tcheng and her husband opted to leave mainland China permanently for Taiwan and the United States, a decision that likely saved them from imprisonment but also helped secure Tcheng's historical erasure.

Of course, remaining in China after 1949 did not garner most female activists of the May Fourth era particular honor; quite the contrary. There was little room in the Maoist version of history for the thousands of young women, radicalized by the May Fourth Movement, who formed Chinese feminist organizations and actively campaigned for their own emancipation in the years that followed. After 1949 many were ostracized and silenced. Although the Maoist-era CCP was committed to expanding women's educational and career opportunities, it did so by telling the Chinese people that only the communist state could represent women's interests. Women whose lives or words suggested otherwise—including Soumay Tcheng's—had no place in this narrative.[65]

Only now, a hundred years later, is Soumay Tcheng's story beginning to be rediscovered in her homeland. The first Chinese-language biography of Tcheng appeared in 2003; her memoir was translated into Chinese a decade later. In 2018 Tcheng was featured in a Chinese television documentary on famous female lawyers. Who knows? Her rosebush gun may yet resurface and find its way onto a museum shelf, restoring China's woman warrior of 1919 to her rightful place in history. Tcheng played a central role in engineering the Chinese delegation's rejection of the Versailles Treaty; her diplomatic efforts on behalf of republican China firmly associated China's international image with modern womanhood, and her subsequent legal and political career helped advance women's civil equality in her homeland. In Soumay Tcheng, Hua Mulan found a worthy successor indeed.[66]

CHAPTER VI

Autumn on the Potomac

Women Workers and the Quest for Social Justice

W hether they hailed from the old empires of Europe, the ris- ing powerhouse of North America, or the subjugated colo- nies and pseudo-colonies of Asia and the Middle East, most of the women drawn into the international political fray in 1919 belonged to the social elite. Marguerite de Witt Schlumberger, Mary Church Ter- rell, Ida Gibbs Hunt, Huda Shaarawi, Jane Addams, and Soumay Tcheng all benefited from education and resources unimaginable to the vast major- ity of women around the world. Their money allowed them to traverse oceans and continents in pursuit of their principles, while their social sta- tus secured them access to powerful statesmen. Wealth conferred privilege in 1919, as it does today, and it largely—but not entirely—determined which women's voices would cut through the diplomatic cacophony of the peace negotiations.

In the bourgeois and upper-class universe of the Paris Peace Confer- ence, Rose Schneiderman and Jeanne Bouvier were exceptions to the rule. Both women grew up in abject poverty. Bouvier, the older of the two, was born in 1865 to a rural French artisan family of modest means. When the Great Wine Blight struck southeastern France in the 1870s, her father's income as a wine barrel maker dissolved overnight. Forced to sell every- thing, Bouvier's family moved to a silk-weaving mill town outside Lyon in search of work. Seventeen years Bouvier's junior, Rose Schneiderman was born in 1882 in a shtetl on the Polish frontier of the Russian Empire.

Her father, like many poor Russian Jews, scraped together a living as a tailor, while her mother took in occasional sewing from neighbors to make ends meet. When Rose was eight years old, the family fled to the United States in search of a better life. Tragically, Rose's father died a year after the family arrived, leaving her mother to raise three fatherless children in New York's Lower East Side.

Desperate family circumstances drove both Bouvier and Schneiderman into the wage labor force by age thirteen. As was so often the case for poor girls in the late nineteenth century, both eventually landed jobs in the garment industry, working long hours at the needle for meager pay. Less typical for the era, each sought to improve her miserable circumstances by joining a labor union. Both rose through union ranks, building relationships with male labor leaders and well-off female social reformers along the way. This activist trajectory eventually led both women to the doorstep of the peace conference.

Under normal circumstances, working-class women like Schneiderman and Bouvier would have had little reason to pay much attention to peace negotiations such as those transpiring in Paris. Matters of high diplomacy seldom worked their way down to the factory floor. The year 1919 was different. Workers' contributions to the Allied victory had been substantial, and they earned trade unionists considerable goodwill among sympathetic allies. As for more recalcitrant statesmen, the Russian Revolution and widespread labor unrest at war's end worked a different kind of magic. Even skeptical industrialists began to see labor reform as an effective means of staving off a global revolt.

In response to these pressures, in January 1919 the peacemakers announced they were forming a Commission for International Labor Legislation (often referred to simply as the Labor Commission) to advise them on how best to address workers' concerns. Part 13 of the Versailles Treaty was the product of the commission's labors. Declaring that universal peace "can be established only if it is based upon social justice," the treaty established a new body—the International Labor Organization (ILO)—to serve as the branch of the League of Nations responsible for formulating international labor standards. It also specified that the first International Labor Conference, the body of the ILO responsible for setting policy, would be held in Washington, D.C., in October 1919. Five key concerns were placed on the agenda: limitations on work hours, provision for unemployment, regulation of women's employment (focused on childbirth and hazardous work conditions), restrictions on child labor, and prohibitions on night work for women and youth. The focus on female workers in two of the five agenda items escaped no one's attention, least of all labor women (a term encompassing both female trade unionists and well-off allies who supported their unionization efforts).[1]

For Jeanne Bouvier and Rose Schneiderman, the labor deliberations in Paris and Washington justified, even demanded, working women's active participation in the broader peace process. Before the year was over, each would cross the Atlantic, in opposite directions, in pursuit of international social justice for working women. Schneiderman would journey first to Paris, in March 1919, as a representative of the National Women's Trade Union League of America (NWTULA) to the Labor Commission. The following October it would be Bouvier's turn to board a steamer, this one headed toward Washington, D.C., for the inaugural International Labor Conference and the First International Congress of Working Women, convened at Schneiderman's prompting by the NWTULA.

Both in the French capital and on the banks of the Potomac, labor women insisted that a new world order would be neither stable nor peaceful if female workers were forever condemned to lives of squalor. Standing up to politicians, employers, and male union leaders—who more often saw women as their wards than as their peers—female wage earners boldly insisted that the kind of social justice promised in the Versailles Treaty depended on tackling gender inequality in the working world. Thanks to a herculean, months-long, international effort, Schneiderman, Bouvier, and their female collaborators wrung important concessions from the peacemakers and the ILO, including, most notably, recognition of women's right to help shape labor policy and groundbreaking international maternity leave standards, which have since been expanded and adopted throughout the developed world (the United States standing as a lone exception).[2]

The international network that labor women established through their collaborative work in Paris and Washington bore fruit in the interwar decades and beyond, as a core group of female activists in 1919 advanced to positions of influence and power. Formal international ties and informal friendships provided this pioneering generation of female labor reformers with the shared knowledge and collective strength necessary to press for progressive social policies at the national and international levels. Schneiderman, for her part, would become a trusted advisor of Eleanor and Franklin Delano Roosevelt on labor policy. In the 1930s she would serve on Roosevelt's National Recovery Administration Labor Advisory Board before moving on to become secretary of labor for the State of New York. Schneiderman's career path was unusual but not unique. Other American and European delegates to the 1919 Women's Congress would rise to similarly prominent government positions and exercise ongoing influence at the ILO. Jeanne Bouvier, unfortunately, did not enjoy the same level of success. An unpleasant incident with a French male labor leader on the sea voyage home from America in 1919 prompted Bouvier's expulsion from the ranks of union leadership. In hindsight, we can see in her fall from grace the potent mix of masculinity, sex, and power that rendered women's battle for social justice so long and difficult and that continues to impede women's professional development in many parts of the world today.

Rose Schneiderman, from Old World to New

In the industrializing world of the early twentieth century, millions of women worked in wage labor, mostly in the poorest paid and most exploitative economic sectors, namely, agriculture, domestic service, textiles, and clothing. From 1914 to 1918 the demands of the war economy allowed hundreds of thousands of such female workers to move into better-paying "men's" jobs in metalworking, engineering, and chemicals, although most were summarily dismissed when peace returned. Up through World War I (and for a long time after) only a minority of these working-class women ever joined a labor union, and only a tiny fraction among them achieved the kind of notoriety that could open international diplomatic and policy-making doors. Those few women who did make the leap from tenements and sweatshops to the staterooms of Paris were tenacious fighters with remarkable life stories, as Rose Schneiderman's journey from a poor Russian village to the Paris Peace Conference amply illustrates.[3]

Schneiderman's politics were forged in adversity and struggle, beginning from her youngest years growing up in an impoverished but close-knit family in the Polish Pale of Settlement, the western edge of the Russian Empire where Jews were permitted to settle. There she lived in a one-room, dirt-floored home with her mother, father, and younger brother Harry. Work as a tailor kept her father away from home from dawn to well past dusk, but he was always there on the Sabbath, when her mother would grace the table with a sweet sponge cake or a golden loaf of challah.[4]

When Rose was six, the family moved in with relatives in a nearby city, where her father was able to secure work sewing army uniforms and where Rose could attend a Russian-language school. All seemed well until one day, without warning, her father disappeared. A week later he wrote the family that he was on his way to America and would send money for their passage as soon he was able. In the summer of 1890 Rose, her mother, and her now two younger brothers followed. Sneaking across the border into Germany, where a ship waited to transport them to America, was a terrifying experience, but the family had little choice. They could not afford the passport fees. "Fortunately," Schneiderman would later reflect, "in those days there was no red tape at the end of the journey, no quotas, no visas, no affidavits." For the Schneidermans in the late nineteenth century, the danger was in leaving the Old World, not in seeking entry to the New.[5]

After a difficult ocean crossing (Rose and her mother were horribly seasick and Harry contracted measles), the family was finally reunited and settled into a single-bedroom, fourth-floor apartment in a tenement on New York's Lower East Side. Rose started school and began to learn English. Before long her family celebrated its first Passover in America. "There was an abundance of food," Schneiderman would recall, "but, more important, there was a sense of safety and hope that we had never felt in Poland." As with so many immigrants, America was the Schneidermans' Promised Land, but the sense of safety they felt that Passover would not last for long. The following year Rose's father died of a sudden illness. With three children to support and another on the way, Rose's mother fought a losing battle to keep the family together. One after another, Rose and her brothers were sent to live in a Jewish orphanage, where at least they would be fed and be able to attend school.

When Rose was thirteen her mother brought her home. "Mother thought I was old enough to look for work," she would later write, "and I agreed with her." For several years Rose worked as an errand girl in a department store, but while the work was respectable, it paid next to nothing. Fed up, she applied for factory work, eventually securing a job sewing linings into men's caps. As was standard in such sweatshops, Rose had to supply her own machine, needle, and thread. This and many other injustices led her and several other young women from the shop to found the first all-female local of the United Cloth Hat and Cap Makers Union. Barely out of her teens and standing no more than four and a half feet in height, the fiery redhead had found her calling. Rose Schneiderman's evenings were soon filled with union meetings among militant friends.[6]

In 1905 Schneiderman helped lead an industry-wide cap makers strike that brought her in touch with the National Women's Trade Union League of America. Formed two years earlier by a handful of wealthy women eager to help female workers organize to achieve better wages and work conditions, the NWTULA would soon become the driving force in Schneiderman's life. Early leaders included working-class trade union activists like Irish American seamstress Leonora O'Reilly and wealthy social reformers like Jane Addams and Margaret Dreier (Robins) of New York, the latter of whom would soon become the organization's longtime national president. With their help, Schneiderman was able to quit her factory job and become a full-time organizer, overseeing a hard-fought strike by thousands of immigrant female shirtwaist makers in the bitter New York winter of 1909 to 1910. One of the few firms that refused to come to terms with the strikers was the Triangle Shirtwaist Factory, where 146 workers—most of

Rose Schneiderman (*center, leaning forward*) campaigning for women's suffrage in the 1910s. (Rose Schneiderman Papers, Photos 010, Box 1, Folder 2, Tamiment Library/Robert F. Wagner Labor Archives, New York University)

them young, immigrant women and all of them locked in by the management—would perish in a tragic building fire in 1911.[7]

During the years of the First World War, Schneiderman divided her time between union organizing and campaigning for women's suffrage, having come to believe that working women needed the vote to push for labor reform. In March 1918 she was elected president of the New York branch of the NWTULA. It was in this capacity that league president Margaret Dreier Robins would later invite Schneiderman to travel to Paris, along with Swedish American former shoemaker and union organizer Mary Anderson, to represent American working women before the Labor Commission at the peace conference. There was no question in Schneiderman's mind whether she would accept. "I want you to know how proud and grateful I am for being given this wonderful opportunity," Schneiderman wrote to Robins. "I feel the great responsibility that goes with the mission, and hope I may be given the wisdom and foresight necessary to discharge my duties in a way which will truly be representative of the working women of America." Ironically, a shipping strike delayed Schneiderman and Anderson's departure until mid-March 1919, jeopardizing their mission as the negotiations advanced in France. Fortunately, many other labor feminists were already hard at work in Paris lobbying on working women's behalf. Prominent among them was French seamstress and union leader Jeanne Bouvier.[8]

Jeanne Bouvier, Silk Weaver, Dressmaker, and Union Militant

"Petite and lively with curly grey hair and youthful eyes that light up a smiling, expressive, and kindly face: in short, this is Jeanne Bouvier. Always on scene when it comes to defending the rights of workers, and especially women; a worker of the highest professional capacity, and a militant trade unionist." With these words, published in June 1919, the French socialist feminist paper *La Vague* introduced its readers to one of their own, a woman who had risen from desperate poverty to represent the working classes at the Paris Peace Conference.[9]

Whereas Rose Schneiderman's earliest memories took her back to her family's Sabbath table in Poland, Bouvier's harkened back to the day of her brother's baptism in rural southeastern France. Left at home with her godmother on the big day, young Jeanne snuck out the door—unwashed and barefooted—and ran all the way to the church to catch a peek at the beautiful baby in his christening robes. The incident was completely in character for the free-spirited girl, who seems to have spent a large portion of her youngest years climbing trees and getting into trouble.[10]

At the age of ten, Jeanne was sent to a nearby Catholic school to prepare for her first communion, but her education ended abruptly the following year when the root-killing phylloxera blight overtook local grape vines, devastating the wine industry. Her family, dependent on her father's income as a cooper (a wine barrel maker), was forced to sell everything and move to a nearby silk-weaving town in search of work. Broken emotionally, her father more or less abandoned the family, and at age eleven, Jeanne became the principal breadwinner, accepting a factory job working thirteen hours a day for fifty centimes: miserly wages that she supplemented by crocheting piecework at home when her factory day ended.[11]

Poverty hounded Jeanne Bouvier for years to follow, as she moved back and forth between factory jobs and domestic service, eventually settling in Paris. After years of such grueling work, she finally was able to rent a place of her own: a seventh-story walk-up without a stove or chimney. It took weeks of skimping on meals for Bouvier to purchase her first bed. Over time, her financial situation improved as she secured an entry-level job in a dressmaking workshop. Dressmaking was among the best-paid sewing work available to women in the late nineteenth century, and it allowed Bouvier to earn extra income sewing made-to-order dresses for wealthy private clients after work hours. Laboring almost around the clock, she was able to meet her basic needs and eventually rent a room with a fireplace in a building with running water on each floor.

Bouvier might have settled into this "comfortable" existence indefinitely but for one of her private clients, an "ardent feminist," who badgered her into joining a trade union. The client in question was an avid reader of *La Fronde*, France's first all-female-run newspaper, which had lately been publishing a series of articles about labor organizing among Parisian seamstresses and laundresses. "I am astonished," the client told Bouvier one afternoon, "that an intelligent woman like you has not enrolled in a union." Caving to the pressure, Bouvier joined the Federation of Clothing Workers and began attending meetings. Although initially at sea among the fiery discussions of expropriation and revolution, Bouvier could soon sing the "Internationale" with the best of them. "My life," she writes, "was henceforth intimately linked to unions." Bouvier was a quick study, and union leaders began to seek her out for paid and unpaid union positions, including on the administrative committees of the French General Confederation of Labor and the Paris Labor Exchange (Bourse du travail), where she held regular office hours and advised women workers about their rights.[12]

As was the case with Schneiderman, union work eventually brought Bouvier in close touch with well-to-do female social reformers and suffragists. "I knew nothing about the laws that governed us," she would later write, explaining her reticence to sign on to the suffrage cause. "I didn't know if they were good or bad. In the face of such ignorance, why vote?" A moment of personal crisis in 1899 changed her mind. That year, a lengthy illness landed her in the hospital. Temporarily unable to collect wages, Bouvier found herself broke at the end of the month when rent came due. Fortunately, she had invested a small sum in securities, hoping the money would serve her in retirement. Bouvier decided to borrow against this savings to raise the needed cash. Much to her surprise, however, the credit agency she approached turned down her initial request. In 1899, as Bouvier learned the hard way, French law deprived married women of the right to freely dispose of their own income. Although Bouvier was single, she could not legally take out a loan unless and until her concierge wrote a letter certifying to that effect. "I was indignant!" Bouvier would later write. "To be in such a state of social inferiority because one is a woman. It is inadmissible!" From that day forward, Bouvier counted herself a suffragist and a feminist, despite the hostility of most male union leaders to the purportedly "bourgeois" women's movement.

Among the "bourgeois" women who took an avid interest in the plight of female wage earners was the tireless feminist and pacifist Gabrielle Duchêne, who would soon become Bouvier's closest collaborator in forwarding working women's rights in France and at the peace conference. Born in 1870 into a family of comfortable means, Duchêne dedicated much of her early adult life to aiding poor working-class women, first by establishing a mutual aid cooperative for Parisian laundresses and later by supporting women's unionization. In 1913 she agreed to head the labor section of the moderate feminist National Council of French Women, where she focused on the plight of the 1.5 million French women engaged in exploitative industrial piecework at home. By the eve of World War I, she and Bouvier had joined forces to draw attention to the plight of industrial homeworkers, particularly in the garment industry. Together, the two women lobbied successfully for the passage of the wartime law of July 10, 1915, which established a minimum wage for home workers (a symbolic milestone, although weak enforcement minimized its effect).[13]

In addition to supporting female unionization and labor reform, Duchêne was also a pacifist, and in 1915 she endorsed Dutch suffragist Aletta Jacobs's International Women's Conference at The Hague—which controversially united suffragists across enemy lines—driving a wedge between her and many of her feminist friends who opposed any such action as long as enemy troops occupied French soil. Not so for Jeanne Bouvier. The two women continued to collaborate throughout the war, pushing the French government to enforce the 1915 minimum wage law and working to establish a new French Office for Women's Interests. Both women were horrified by the carnage of the conflict engulfing Europe, but they also hoped desperately that the war would pave the way for a more just and equitable social order when it was finally over. To such ends, in early 1919 Duchêne and Bouvier drafted a women's charter and sent it to France's delegates to the peace conference. The charter called for a peace settlement that would recognize the legal equality of men and women in marriage, work, and politics. Years before the international community would deploy such language, Duchêne and Bouvier defined sexual equality as a matter of "fundamental human rights."[14]

Through Duchêne, Bouvier came in contact with many of France's most prominent feminists and social reformers, some of whom began actively organizing in early 1919 to demand a voice for women at the peace conference. From the beginning, these women repeatedly turned to Bouvier (along with a younger associate named Georgette Bouillot) to represent working-class women in their diplomatic efforts. Magazine editor and feminist Valentine Thomson established the precedent, inviting Bouvier to join with other "delegates of female labor" who paid a call on Woodrow Wilson on January 25, 1919, to deliver a personal message of gratitude on behalf of French women to the American president.

Several weeks later French suffragist Marguerite de Witt Schlumberger extended a similar invitation, asking Bouvier to join forces with the Inter-Allied Women's Conference, which was gearing up to demand representation for women in the peace negotiations. Along with Gabrielle Duchêne, Bouvier agreed to head up a labor subcommittee to the Inter-Allied Women's Conference and to prepare a list of resolutions that working

Delegation of French women, including Jeanne Bouvier (*second from right*) and Georgette Bouillot (*next to Bouvier, holding bouquet of flowers*), heading to meet to Woodrow Wilson on January 25, 1919, in *La Vie Féminine*, February 15, 1919. (Collections Bibliothèque Marguerite Durand—Ville de Paris)

women hoped to see inserted in the eventual peace treaty. Such a plan was not mere fantasy. With the announcement in late January 1919 that a Labor Commission to the peace conference had been established, feminists understood that global leaders would be discussing matters like work hours, wages, and conditions that could lead to international labor standards applicable across the industrialized world. Seizing the initiative, the labor subcommittee of the Inter-Allied Women's Conference became the de facto body representing female wage earners at the peace negotiations. Determined and persistent, Bouvier, Duchêne, and their collaborators helped open a new era in women's international labor activism.[15]

Lobbying the Labor Commission at the Paris Peace Conference

Members of the Inter-Allied women's labor subcommittee met regularly on Sundays from late February through the end of March 1919. Jeanne

Bouvier and Gabrielle Duchêne anchored the committee along with three other French labor activists and feminists. Several dozen other European women (and a few sympathetic men) attended the weekly meetings, including representatives from labor, suffrage, and social democratic organizations from France, Denmark, Sweden, Romania, Poland, Belgium, and Great Britain. Committee members studied whatever relevant documentation they could get their hands on: existing international labor conventions, resolutions regarding women's work from recent international congresses, and working documents from the Labor Commission itself. Their goal was to determine the "minimal indispensable guarantees necessary to create less unjust and more humane work conditions" worldwide. Shorter work hours, a minimum wage, and paid maternity leave were all on their agenda. So too was the central issue of representation. Women demanded unequivocally that they be given a voice in elaborating the international labor standards that could forever alter the lives of working women around the world.[16]

Several Americans participated on Bouvier and Duchêne's labor subcommittee as well, but as with the Inter-Allied Women's Conference more generally, most were upper-class volunteers with organizations like the Red Cross: women who came to Europe during the war and were still there when the peace negotiations began. Across the Atlantic, the National Women's Trade Union League president Margaret Dreier Robins worried deeply that the American participants were "not equipped to speak with any authority on behalf of working women." For the past two years, the NWTULA had been actively preparing for eventual peace negotiations and had drafted a "working women's charter" laying out the economic and political rights that American labor women expected to be included in the peace settlement. Time was of the essence, and Robins immediately contacted Rose Schneiderman and Mary Anderson—both of whom were leaders in the league and of working-class background—and told them to pack their bags. At her own expense, Robins announced, she was sending the two trade unionists to Paris to represent the NWTULA. Schneiderman and Anderson departed in mid-March, shivering their way from New York to Europe (their ship having been stripped of its heating apparatuses during the war), eager to join Duchêne, Bouvier, and the others in pushing for international recognition of the rights of working women.[17]

The Labor Commission, which held women's fate in its hands, was unlike any other body established at the peace conference that spring because it was composed of private citizens as well as government-appointed diplomats. American Federation of Labor president Samuel Gompers chaired the commission, which also included the head of the French General Confederation of Labor, Léon Jouhaux, and British labor leader George Barnes. The announcement that workers' representatives would have a say in the elaboration of postwar policy heartened labor women considerably. The peacemakers' subsequent announcement that not a single woman would be invited to sit on the commission, however, left them deeply concerned.

From the outset, feminists and female labor activists in Europe registered their alarm over women's exclusion from the commission. Julie Siegfried, the president of the National Council of French Women, wrote immediately to her prime minister, Georges Clemenceau, informing him that women fully expected "to take part in or be heard by the Labor Commission." British union activist Mary Macarthur, who had served as a labor advisor to Prime Minister David Lloyd George's wartime government, similarly fired off an indignant telegram in late January 1919 warning: "Omission to consult representative women on international labour policy subject of much comment here / organized women workers have instructed me to respectfully request an explanation from government." The official response—that union men on the Labor Commission would more than adequately represent working women's interests—did little to appease Macarthur or any of the Allied women converging on Paris in 1919.[18]

In mid-March the peacemakers finally resolved to answer Inter-Allied women's persistent demands for representation at the peace conference by inviting them "state their case" before the commissions deemed most relevant to their interests: Labor and the League of Nations. Several days later the women received an invitation to appear before the Labor Commission on March 18. Duchêne and Bouvier's subcommittee kicked into high gear in preparation. Sadly, the rapid speed of these developments caught Americans Schneiderman and Anderson literally at sea; they would arrive in Paris too late to join the women's delegation to the Labor Commission.[19]

A dozen women from Great Britain, the United States, Belgium, Italy, and France gathered in the vestibule of the Ministry of Labor on the morning of March 18. Among them were Bouvier and Duchêne as well as Inter-Allied Women's Conference delegate Margery Corbett Ashby. Julie Siegfried and Ghénia Avril de Sainte-Croix joined as representatives of the International Council of Women. Commission president Samuel Gompers—a man "about as attractive as a baboon," in Corbett Ashby's uncharitable assessment—greeted the women and ushered them into the room. Speaking in turn, the women laid out their principal demands: a unified labor code for men and women; equal pay for equal work; stronger limits on child labor; an eight-hour workday and forty-four-hour work-week; a universal ban on night work for men and women; protections for industrial homeworkers; and an official role for women in the formulation of national and international labor policy. Duchêne spoke in defense of a living wage. Bouvier discussed the importance of social insurance, and Corbett Ashby called for paid maternity leave. Corbett Ashby also ended up serving as an impromptu interpreter when the man hired for the job, "a perfectly charming British officer who had shell shock and not the remotest acquaintance with any labour problem," so badly muddled the assignment that Gompers pleaded with her to take over.[20]

It is difficult to say how much the women accomplished. The Labor Charter, adopted in whole by the peacemakers and incorporated into the Versailles Treaty, created a new permanent body, the International Labor Organization, charged with elaborating international labor standards on everything from work hours and wages to labor conditions and social insurance. In a nod to some of women's concerns, the Labor Charter endorsed the principle of equal pay for equal work, called for the hiring of female as well as male industrial inspectors, and placed the question of maternity leave on the agenda of the first International Labor Conference.[21]

On the central issue of whether women would be able to help shape future policy decisions at the ILO, however, the Labor Commission made only tepid recommendations. At annual International Labor Conferences (the policy-making branch of the ILO), ILO member states were each to be allowed four delegates: two representing government and one each representing employers and workers. Feminists wanted a guarantee that women would be assured a place among these representatives. The Labor Charter, instead, settled for encouraging member states to appoint "at least one woman" as a nonvoting "advisor" to their delegations, but only "when questions specifically affecting women are to be considered." The end result, in 1919, is that not one of the forty states that participated in the inaugural ILO Conference in Washington, D.C., chose to appoint a woman to serve as a voting delegate. The commission also suggested that a "certain number" of women be hired as staff members at the ILO office in

Geneva (the administrative branch of the organization), but what that number might be, and whether these women were to serve as clerks and typists or powerful section chiefs, was left to the discretion of future directors.[22]

These terms did not satisfy labor women. Rose Schneiderman and Mary Anderson, who finally arrived in Paris just after the Labor Commission had completed its work, were flatly disappointed. As far as they could tell, the commission had utterly failed to provide "for the representation of working women in any place of real authority." This was the message they relayed to President Woodrow Wilson when they managed to secure an appointment with him a few weeks later. "He was most gracious and kind," Schneiderman would recall, somewhat charitably. In fact, Wilson proved generally uninterested in the women's concerns, turning the conversation as soon as he could to his own woes in the peace negotiations. When Schneiderman and Anderson asked him if he would consider appointing a woman as one the American government's two voting delegates to the upcoming International Labor Conference in Washington, he claimed he would give the request "careful consideration." No such appointment ever materialized.[23]

Schneiderman and Anderson also pressed their case with the British representative on the Labor Commission, George Barnes (known to be sympathetic to women's cause), as did other female activists in Paris that spring. Among them was a delegation from the newly formed Women's International League for Peace and Freedom, headed by Jane Addams. The WILPF delegation, just off the train from Zurich, rushed to meet Barnes to request that he amend the Labor Charter to require one of the two government representatives from each country to be a woman. Barnes responded that the Labor Commission had already granted "pretty well all the things that the women had suggested," and there was nothing more to discuss. The doors to negotiation in Paris were closed. If labor women wanted their voices to be heard, they would have to find a way to assert them at the ILO Conference in Washington the following October.[24]

How to make that happen became a central preoccupation for Schneiderman and Anderson. The two women spent almost a month in France networking with their European counterparts. Gabrielle Duchêne acted as the women's unofficial host and translator. "We could not have gotten along without her," Anderson would later recall. "I think we went to her house every day." Duchêne also appears to have invited the two American women to participate in one of the final meetings of the labor subcommittee of the Inter-Allied Women's Conference. Having completed its mandate at the peace negotiations, the subcommittee drew up an ambitious international labor charter to guide women's activism going forward. The charter called for mandatory female representation at the ILO and recommended that labor women meet on an annual basis to develop their own international policy recommendations.[25]

With such ideas in mind, Anderson and Schneiderman decided to make a trip to London to confer with British labor feminists before heading home. Prior to the Americans' departure, French labor leaders threw them a farewell banquet, complete with toasts to the future of women's international collaboration. Jeanne Bouvier was among those to raise her glass. "Dear American comrades," she said in salute, "today women demand to be represented" and to help develop the "international statutes" that will "serve as the base for a new world." French labor leader Léon Jouhaux offered a toast as well, although his was directed not to Schneiderman and Anderson but to several other American guests: a banker and businessman who had falsely represented themselves as friends of labor. His was a rousing toast to the health of the Bolsheviks and the Russian Revolution. Both amused and slightly scandalized, Schneiderman and Anderson prepared to cross the English Channel.[26]

Conferring with Labor Feminists in London

Upon arriving in London, Schneiderman and Anderson immediately sought out two women widely recognized as up-and-coming leaders in the British labor movement. The first was Mary Macarthur, the woman who earlier in 1919 had sent the scathing telegram to David Lloyd George to protest women's exclusion from the Labor Commission. Thirty-nine-year-old, Scottish-born Mary Macarthur had been drawn into union activism back in 1901, when her shopkeeper father sent her to spy on the local branch of the Shop Assistants Union. Horrified by what she saw, Macarthur defied her father, joined the union, and became an active speaker and organizer. Within several years, Macarthur moved to London, accepted the position of secretary general of the British Women's Trade Union League, and helped found a National Union of Women Workers.[27]

Along with Macarthur, the two Americans met with a second British woman, Margaret Bondfield, to discuss "the establishment of the International Labor Organization, what it would mean to labor, and how to get our program across to them." Forty-six-year-old Bondfield, one of the most distinguished British labor women of her era, had also come out of the shopworkers movement, having served as a poorly paid, live-in shop assistant for a number of years. Bondfield was drawn to union activism after happening to read about the National Shop Assistants Union in a piece of newspaper wrapped around her fish and chips. By World War I Bondfield had risen high in British union ranks. She collaborated with Macarthur at the British Women's Trade Union League, and she edited a monthly newspaper for female trade unionists called the *Woman Worker*. Bondfield informed the two visiting Americans that both she and Macarthur had every intention of traveling to Washington, D.C., for the inaugural ILO Conference in the fall. "Why not," Schneiderman said in response, "have our National Women's Trade Union League sponsor an international conference of working women, trade-union women, at the same time?" Bondfield thought it an excellent idea.[28]

Back in the United States the following June, Schneiderman and Anderson reported on their trip to Europe at the convention of the National Women's Trade Union League of America. There they formalized the suggestion: "Our experience in Paris and in London convinced us," they said, that "the time had come for labor women everywhere to get together and work together." Macarthur and Bondfield, who attended the meeting as guest delegates from abroad, wholeheartedly endorsed the idea, and league president Margaret Dreier Robins reached deep into her own pocketbook to fund the endeavor. On August 5 a call went out to labor women from forty-four nations inviting them to join in "fellowship and conference" in Washington the following October. It is time, the call said, for working women "to assume responsibilities in the affairs of the world."[29]

The First International Congress of Working Women

Thanks to the groundwork laid by American, French, and British labor feminists and their collaborators in Paris, two separate and equally historic conferences would convene in Washington, D.C., in the fall of 1919. The first was the inaugural Conference of the International Labor Organization (meeting from October 29 to November 29 and referred to here as the ILO Conference). The ILO Conference was mandated by the Versailles Treaty and charged with drawing up the world's first international labor standards. The second was the First International Congress of Working Women (meeting from October 28 to November 6 and referred to here as the Women's Congress). The Women's Congress, which convened under the auspices of the National Women's Trade Union League of America, allowed labor feminists to confer, network, and organize together so as to more effectively press their demands on behalf of working women at the ILO Conference down the road. At the Women's Congress, Rose Schneiderman and Jeanne Bouvier would join with over two hundred other labor feminists from across Europe, North America, South America, and Asia to demand stringent regulations on matters such as work hours and maternity leave, which were of vital importance to women workers worldwide.

The NWTULA had less than three months to organize the Women's Congress, and its members carried off this mighty task with considerable aplomb and skill. League president Margaret Dreier Robins recognized that

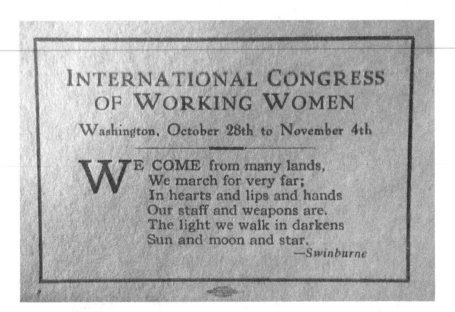

Welcome card presented to delegates to the First International Congress of Working Women in Washington, D.C., October 1919. (Fonds Jeanne Bouvier, Box 22, Bibliothèque historique de la Ville de Paris / fonds Bouglé)

the voyage to America would be a rare luxury for many delegates, and she worked hard to make sure the meeting would be enjoyable as well as productive for foreign guests. Delegates were asked to pay only their travel expenses; the Americans covered the rest. Rooms were secured at the elegant Burlington Hotel in central Washington, D.C. Various women's organizations volunteered to sponsor social events, while Washington's unionized taxi drivers agreed to shuttle the women around the capital for free. Margaret Bondfield, who represented Great Britain along with Mary Macarthur, had nothing but praise for the "magnificent way" in which the Americans arranged the Congress. "The American women simply radiated good will," she would write, "not only those connected directly with the Labour movement, but all sections of the women in Washington vied with each other to offer hospitality to the working women of the different countries."[30]

Of the two-hundred-some women who attended in the First International Congress of Working Women, twenty-eight participated as voting delegates, including women from Argentina, Belgium, Britain, Canada, Czechoslovakia, France, India, Italy, Norway, Poland, Sweden, and the United States. The remaining nonvoting delegates (who had not been credentialed by an internationally recognized trade union) hailed from Cuba, Denmark, Japan, the Netherlands, Serbia, Spain, and Switzerland. While broadly international, the congress did have notable geographic gaps. The American organizers were unable to secure timely permission to invite women from the defeated Central Powers of Germany and Austria. They also hit diplomatic roadblocks when it came to China, which had declined to sign the Versailles Treaty, and Soviet Russia, with which the United States did not have diplomatic relations. No women came from Africa or the Middle East. The congress did attract some prominent observers, including Eleanor Roosevelt, the wife of the future president of the United States, who would join the NWTULA shortly thereafter.[31]

Unsurprisingly, the United States had the largest number of participants. First-generation immigrants were well represented by Schneiderman, Anderson, and others, but one large block of American wage earners was conspicuously missing: African Americans. Ten black female community leaders—including civil rights and women's activist Mary Church Terrell—drew attention to this absence by issuing a protest to the NWTULA stating, "Negro women, as you well know, are very little organized in unions or other organizations. They have, therefore, very limited means of making their wishes known." Their point was well taken. Black female wage earners were concentrated in poorly paid, nonunionized sectors of the American economy like agriculture and domestic service. In general, African American workers were not a priority for the early American labor movement. In their protest, Terrell and her cosigners challenged this bias and "respectfully" asked the League to organize black female workers so "that they may have a share in bringing about industrial democracy and social order in the world." Although no African American women would participate in the Congress, their protest was read aloud during the meeting and printed in the official proceedings: a small step toward acknowledging a problem that would fester for a long time to come.[32]

Like Bondfield and Macarthur, Jeanne Bouvier made the journey from Europe to participate in the Women's Congress. Departing the port at Le Havre on October 11, she felt a shiver of trepidation as her ship was swallowed by the maritime night. It was her first ocean crossing, and thankfully it was a calm one, or at least it was until her ship arrived off the coast of New York. Then the skies opened up, and a violent storm tossed the ship from one cresting wave to the next. "I thought my final hour had arrived," Bouvier would later write. The next day, however, the storm had passed and the ship was able to coast slowly into New York harbor, with all the passengers gawking at the towering skyscrapers. "Soon enough," Bouvier recalled, "we saw Lady Liberty illuminating the World."[33]

Greeted by labor feminists in New York, Bouvier spent several days touring the city's famous museums and visiting some of its venerable institutions, including Columbia University. She was also taken to the New York headquarters of the NWTULA, where she learned about the league's training programs for female union leaders. For Bouvier, who had been forced to invent her own militant career from scratch, such programs inspired no small degree of envy. "I thought my American sisters were very lucky," she would write. "I felt like the poor relative in the great family of female unionism."[34]

Several days later, Bouvier and the other foreign delegates to the Women's Congress converged on Washington, where local schoolteachers had planned a special outing: a boat trip on the Potomac to visit George Washington's stately home at Mount Vernon. The women set out on an unseasonably warm day, the trees along the riverbanks dressed in brilliant autumn colors of red and gold. As the chief representative of America's "sister republic," Bouvier was given a place of honor in the proceedings. To her fell the privilege of placing a bouquet of flowers on Washington's tomb. As they toured the former president's home, one of the Americans drew her attention to a display containing the key to the Bastille, which General Lafayette had presented to Washington after the French Revolution. "I was deeply moved by all these relics of the friendship between two men who fought for freedom, in this country which so warmly welcomed women workers," Bouvier would later write. Although equally pleased with the outing, British delegate Margaret Bondfield filtered the day through a different historical lens: "Of course, you know George Washington defeated the armies of King George," she would remind readers of the *Woman Worker* back home. Bondfield also noticed that despite the reverence shown the first American president and the fine words spoken in defense of democracy

International Congress of Working Women, daytrip to Mount Vernon, November 3, 1919. Participants included Margaret Bondfield, Mary Anderson, and Rose Schneiderman (*first row, third, fourth, and sixth from left*), and Jeanne Bouvier, Tanaka Taka, and Margaret Dreier Robins (*second row, fifth, eighth, and ninth from left*). (Rose Schneiderman Papers, Photos 010, Box 1, Folder 4, Tamiment Library/Robert F. Wagner Labor Archives, New York University)

and liberty, "at the back of the little group . . . there stood an old white-haired negro," a man who now worked at the historical site but who had begun his life on the plantation as a slave.[35]

The women paused for a group photograph, then returned to the capital. "On the journey back," Bondfield would write, "we had an impromptu concert: songs of every nationality, including the sweet, soft Japanese murmur in quarter tones, which our western ears are too dull to hear. We also had speeches, and tea, such a tea! It, like the songs and speeches, struck an international note." Friendships took root onboard the boat and deepened in the days ahead. On such outings, as much as in formal meetings, delegates to the First International Congress of Working Women forged bonds of solidarity and fashioned a sense of collective strength that would serve them well in battles to come.

The Maternity Protection Convention of 1919

On October 28 delegates to the International Congress of Working Women got down to business. " "I never forgot my feelings when the meeting opened," Mary Anderson would write, "and I saw all those splendid women, from all over the world, come together to make plans for working women everywhere." In addition to Bondfield and Macarthur from Britain, Anderson particularly noted the presence of two impressive Scandinavian delegates, both factory inspectors: Kerstin Hesselgren of Sweden and Betzy Kjelsberg of Norway. Jeanne Bouvier stood out as well: "She was small and a great talker," Anderson would recall, "which rather complicated our proceedings because she spoke in French, which had to be interpreted." The last woman to make a strong impression on Anderson was, in some respects, the most remarkable of all: Tanaka Taka of Japan, who would (not unlike Chinese delegate Soumay Tcheng at the Paris Peace Conference) disrupt Western women's stereotypes about the submissive East by powerfully insisting on Asian women's right to defend their interests.[36]

Bouvier set a defiant tone from the very first day of the Women's Congress, by placing on the table a resolution to demand equal representation between men and women in all future ILO Conferences. Specifically, she proposed amending the ILO constitution to allow every member state six delegates—two each from government, employers, and labor—but with the provision that one delegate from each of the represented groups be a woman. The Women's Congress enthusiastically concurred, passing the resolution and sending it down the road to the ILO for consideration. The all-male ILO delegates ignored the request completely. Political parity was an idea well ahead of its time.[37]

At the ILO Conference, then, it fell entirely to nonvoting female advisors to bring "women's concerns" to the attention of the all-male voting body. In total, twenty-three women were appointed to serve in an advisory capacity to the ILO Conference. Many of these women also participated as delegates to the Women's Congress, including Bouvier, Bondfield, Macarthur, and Tanaka, who shuttled back-and-forth between the two meetings throughout the first week of November. Rose Schneiderman was not among those serving double duty at the ILO Conference; the American Senate's refusal to ratify the Versailles Treaty precluded American men and women alike from playing a direct part in the historic ILO Conference. Limited to speaking when voting delegates ceded the floor, female advisors to the ILO Conference worked hard to exercise power behind the scenes. Their influence was felt most strongly on the Commission on Women's Employment, where "women's issues" were given central stage. The first question brought before this commission was maternity leave, one of the five major agenda items set for the ILO in the Versailles Treaty and a matter of passionate interest among labor women in Washington in 1919.[38]

If there was one point on which men and women, workers and employers, Western and non-Western nations could all agree, it was that wage labor should not compromise women's ability to give birth and raise their young children. Female labor leaders uniformly praised women's role as mothers, and they often couched their rhetoric in maternal terms. In her opening address to the 1919 Women's Congress, for example, Margaret Dreier Robins asserted: "Women are builders of the race. To us is entrusted the protection of life. The social and industrial order must meet this challenge." Everyone, it seems, extolled motherhood; yet when it came to the details of how to accommodate the needs of working mothers, consensus quickly evaporated. Should pregnant women receive time off from work? Should such leave come before or after childbirth (or both)? Should maternity leave be paid or unpaid? Should working mothers be allowed to breastfeed their babies at work? All these questions were aired in Washington in 1919.[39]

Preexisting national maternity laws informed the discussions at both the Women's Congress and the ILO Conference. In the quarter century prior to the First World War, many European countries had adopted laws mandating three or four weeks of maternity leave, but in almost all cases, such leave was strictly *unpaid* and applicable only *after* childbirth. Both France and the United States fell outside this norm, at opposite extremes. In the United States, maternity leave legislation was all but nonexistent. France, by contrast, had passed an expansive law in 1913, which mandated *paid* maternity leave for working women, including two weeks before and four weeks after childbirth. During World War I the desperate need for female war workers had led the French to also adopt a law requiring factories to grant nursing breaks to mothers so that they could breastfeed their infant children. In all cases, legislation was designed primarily to protect the state's interest in healthy children (as future workers and soldiers) rather than in the economic or social needs of working mothers.[40]

In 1919 labor women championed an entirely different type of maternity policy: one rooted in up-to-date medical research regarding the health needs of mothers as well as infants, and one specifically designed to help women effectively combine motherhood and wage labor. On this issue, Jeanne Bouvier took the lead, having been greatly influenced by two female doctors—Clotilde Mulon and Lasthénie Thuillier-Landry—who had taken part in the meetings of the Inter-Allied Women's Conference labor subcommittee in Paris the previous spring. Working mothers, Mulon and Thuillier-Landry insisted, needed a minimum of six weeks rest *before and after* childbirth. On Bouvier's prompting, the Women's Congress endorsed this twelve-week standard, further elaborating that maternity leave must be *paid*, and that mothers as well as infants should be entitled to free medical care.[41]

Having won the support of the Women's Congress, Bouvier took this proposal down the road to the ILO, where she sat as an advisor on the Commission on Women's Employment. There she met strong resistance from (male) employers' delegates, who balked at the amount of leave time demanded and who insisted employers not be held responsible for the expense. Bouvier, supported by the other women on the commission, refused to back down. "To my great joy," she would later write, "my proposal was adopted." When maternity leave came up before the plenary ILO Conference, British delegate Mary Macarthur offered a passionate defense of the commission recommendations, taking the conference "like a storm." In the end, the Maternity Protection Convention of 1919 called on ILO member states to adopt legislation providing working mothers with twelve

Jeanne Bouvier in Washington, D.C., 1919. (Fonds Jeanne Bouvier, Box 22, Bibliothèque historique de la Ville de Paris / fonds Bouglé)

weeks paid maternity leave, with medical support for mothers and infants
and two paid daily breaks for nursing mothers upon return to work. It was
a singular victory.[42]

Unanimity of opinion among labor women helped Bouvier and her colleagues champion a generous maternity leave policy at the ILO, but on the
question of *who* should qualify for maternity allowances, consensus dissolved. A majority of delegates to the Women's Congress—including the
French, British, and Americans—argued that *all* women should receive
social support for motherhood regardless of whether or not they were
employed. It was a radical proposal, in essence calling on the international community to recognize that motherhood was in fact *work*, of value

to society and deserving of remuneration, rather than a natural or God-given responsibility to be borne at the mother's expense. Male delegates to the ILO were not ready to go that far. Maternity benefits remained tied to wage labor, although at the last minute, Bouvier convinced France's labor delegate, Léon Jouhaux, to insert language into the Maternity Protection Convention to cover shop assistants and other commercial workers as well as industrial laborers.[43]

Overall, the Maternity Protection Convention adopted in Washington in 1919 represented a radical departure from past practice and a major step toward achieving "social justice" for working women. In mandating twelve weeks paid maternity leave, the ILO challenged member states to facilitate the combination of motherhood and wage labor, in essence recognizing that many women did not have the luxury of leaving the workforce once they got pregnant (and opening the possibility that women might, in fact, choose both work *and* family, if they were fortunate enough to be able to make that choice). In debating the possibility of motherhood allowances for *all* women, moreover, the Women's Congress advanced the idea that reproductive labor was in fact *labor*, worthy not only of society's reverence but also of its support. Although few nations were willing to adopt the Maternity Protection Convention immediately, in the decades that followed, the convention would be expanded and adopted throughout nearly all the developed world. The First International Congress of Working Women thus permanently shifted the terms of the international debate around women, work, and motherhood and helped shape a discussion that continues in earnest in many corners of the world today.[44]

An International Ban on Women's Night Work

Besides maternity leave, the other major issue on the ILO Conference agenda in 1919 that was of specific concern to women was the question of whether the ILO should endorse an international ban on women's night work. Female activists were of many minds on the question, as they were on the broader matter of protective labor legislation for female wage earners. While women (and most men) widely supported special protections for pregnant women and working mothers, the idea that whole categories of work should be closed off to women based on their sex evoked no such consensus. On the whole, the debate pitted American and British women, who supported a ban on women's night work, against the French and Scandinavians, who adamantly opposed it. Much to everyone's surprise, however, the most powerful defender of the night-work ban at the ILO Conference proved to be Tanaka Taka of Japan, who shocked both Western women and male delegates by vehemently defending the interests of the young Japanese textile workers whom she vowed to represent.

An international push to ban women's night work began in earnest in the last quarter of the nineteenth century. It arose in response to the exploitative conditions in early industrial factories, including long work hours that kept women tethered to their jobs well into the night. To critics, such practices put women's families and fertility at risk. In 1877 Switzerland became the first country in the world to ban women's night work. Other European countries followed suit, and in time the momentum led to the precedent-setting Berne Convention of 1906, a multinational treaty prohibiting women's night work in factories with ten or more employees. Nearly a dozen European nations signed on.[45]

Similar developments paved the way for the adoption of protective legislation for women workers in the United States. The Supreme Court decision *Muller v. Oregon* (1908) upheld the principle that female workers' freedom could be restricted in ways that men's could not because the public held an interest in a women's reproductive health. Between 1908 and 1920, amid concerns about "weary, tousled . . . half dressed" female workers "trying to snatch an hour of sleep after [a] long night of work at the mill," sixteen American states passed laws banning women's night work.[46]

Many American and European feminists were fervently opposed to this trend of treating women workers as a class apart. They argued that protective labor legislation hurt working women by placing them at a competitive disadvantage with men in the job market. Emphasizing that the best means of combatting exploitation was higher wages and better work conditions for everyone, men and women, international feminist congresses routinely called for lifting bans on female night work. They also pointed out that laws limiting women's work hours in the factory forced the unskilled to accept the poverty wages of industrial home work even as they drove skilled women workers out of some high-paying jobs, like typesetting, that had to be done at night. Jeanne Bouvier, Gabrielle Duchêne and the other women who testified before the Labor Commission at the Paris Peace Conference advanced all these arguments asking "that protective measures only be taken in order to support maternity." Despite such concerns, the Labor

Commission placed the "extension and application" of the Berne Convention on the agenda for the ILO Conference in Washington.[47]

Seeking to formulate a united position on the issue before it came up at the ILO Conference, the Women's Congress took up the question of the night work ban in early November 1919. Initially, in Washington as in Paris, women's feeling seemed to run against special protections for women, except where maternity was concerned. A Swedish delegate to the Women's Congress, Dr. Alma Sundquist, argued that a ban on women's night work effectively barred women "from many suitable and remunerative occupations," and she called on the Women's Congress to champion "the rights of women as citizens and individuals." A Czech delegate echoed these concerns. What women needed most, she said, was a "free choice of occupation" and "equal pay for equal work." Most of the British and American delegates listened to these arguments with dismay. Rose Schneiderman captured the essence of their objections, declaring "the equality of women to kill themselves by night work is no equality to us." In the end, the Women's Congress adopted a compromise position, endorsing the 1906 Berne Convention prohibiting women's night work, but urging that such a ban be expanded to include men's work as well.[48]

Several days later, the ILO Commission on Women's Employment took up the question of women's night work. Here, American and British proponents of protective legislation, like Schneiderman, found they had an unexpected ally: Tanaka Taka, the sole female member of the Japanese delegation to the ILO Conference. Tanaka had come to Washington as the official advisor to Japanese government delegate Kamada Eikichi. Armed with flawless English-language skills, a deep academic knowledge of industrial issues, and degrees from both Stanford and the University of Chicago, Tanaka was well suited to the task. In the ILO Commission on Women's Employment, she did much more than advise. She powerfully opposed both Kamada and the Japanese employers' representative, Mutō Sanji, by demanding the international community acknowledge the vulnerability of female workers in Japan.[49]

The showdown came at a commission meeting on November 8, 1919. Speaking first for employers, Mutō warned that a prohibition on women's night work in Japan would raise the price of cotton, hurting both Japanese home weavers and international consumers of cotton cloth. As the managing director of the Kanegafuchi Spinning Company, Mutō was well placed to know. The textile industry in Japan relied on a large number of female workers, many of them girls aged ten to sixteen, who were expected to work long shifts well into the night. Mutō saw employers' role as a paternalistic one, looking out for workers' welfare, but he (or at least the company he directed) was skeptical of women's ability to define those interests for themselves. In a 1919 promotional brochure, the Kanegafuchi Spinning Company explained that it was opposed to raising women's wages, for example, because (it claimed), "the recipient is often tempted to spend more on luxuries than necessities."[50]

Japanese government delegate Kamada Eikichi was equally concerned about the effects of a ban on women's night work on his country's industries, and he prepared a statement for the commission asking that Japan be granted a delay in implementation of any international night work standards. Far from conversant in English, Kamada asked his female advisor, Tanaka, to present this statement for him. Tanaka began to execute the request, but then, to the shock of all present, she stopped reading Kamada's statement midstream, pulled out her own carefully concealed notes, and proceeded to demand an immediate ban on Japanese women's night work. Tanaka decried the "very bad conditions for working women . . . in Japan, particularly in the textile industry." In a direct challenge to both Mutō and Kamada, she insisted that female textile workers in her country were maltreated "physically and mentally," and that a night work ban was necessary to "rescue" them from their "present state of horror."[51]

Mayhem erupted as the Japanese delegates processed what Tanaka had said. Mutō leapt to his feet and insisted that Tanaka be silenced. Failing to convince the chairwoman of the commission to do so, Mutō turned to his male colleagues and demanded they strip Tanaka of her advisory status, claiming she was "deranged from . . . being in the family way." Tanaka was in fact pregnant, but she was not deranged; she was merely well informed. To prepare for her trip to Washington, she had toured Japan's textile mills and spoken with countless women workers about their concerns. She had also, on her own initiative, brought with her to Washington a young woman named Ogata Setsu, who had formerly been employed by the Kanegafuchi Spinning Company and could speak to working conditions there from direct experience. At the Women's Congress, Tanaka and Ogata "were always together."[52]

In response to Mutō's complaints, the Japanese did strip Tanaka of her advisory status, but bravely, she refused to back down. Instead, she approached Americans Mary Anderson and Margaret Dreier Robins, whom

THE JAPANESE DELEGATES

The picture shows Madame Tanaka and Miss Ogata, the mill worker, standing on the steps of the Conference Hall.

Tanaka Taka and Ogata Setsu in Washington, D.C., 1919, *Woman Worker*, February 1920. (Women's Library Collection, London School of Economics Library, Periodicals D2833)

she had gotten to know at the Women's Congress, and asked them to help her plead her case. In the meantime, the Japanese press began to publish news of the scandal, firmly coming down on Tanaka's side. In a matter of days, Tanaka was reinstated, and Mutō and Kamada agreed to support a gradual ban on women's night work in Japan. In exchange, some kind of deal was apparently reached to save the men's honor by wiping all discussion of the conflict from official ILO Conference records.[53]

In the end, the ILO Conference adopted the Night-Work (Women) Convention of 1919, prohibiting female laborers from working between

10:00 P.M. and 5:00 A.M. Women's split opinions on the issue made it easier for male ILO delegates to perpetuate the principle that women needed special protections in the workplace, even if those protections abridged women's right to work. To many Western feminists, most Scandinavian social democrats, and some European labor women, the extension of the international night-work ban was a decided blow, but in the economically tumultuous years of the 1920s and 1930s, many labor women—particularly in the United States—remained grateful for any workplace protections that worked to shield them from exploitation.

In joining in the debate, Tanaka Taka helped build support for the night work ban. She also registered an important victory for international feminism, even if some Western women might have found it an unsettling one. By challenging her male colleagues, and by winning support for her forthright defense of female textile workers in the Japanese media, Tanaka chipped away at the presumption that men could capably define women's interests without their input, even in corners of the world that many Westerners persisted in viewing as "backward." Thus, even as Tanaka stood up *for* women, she also stood up *to* the West, or at least to those Western women and men prone to believe that women from Asia were too oppressed or submissive to defend their own interests. Asian women, Tanaka implied, were eager to collaborate with European and American women to improve global labor conditions, but female solidarity would need to be built on terms of mutual understanding and respect. The International Congress of Working Women of 1919 helped international labor feminists take a small step down that road.

International Labor Feminism After 1919

The ILO Conference adjourned on November 29, 1919. In total, the delegates would adopt six International Labor Conventions, which they hoped would serve as the building blocks for a more just global economic order. In addition to maternity protections and the prohibition on night work for women, the conventions dealt with hours of work, unemployment, child labor, and night work for youth. The central premise, articulated in the Versailles Treaty, that "the well-being, physical, moral and intellectual, of industrial wage-earners is of supreme international importance" was thus enshrined in concrete international standards. The establishment of the

International Labor Office in Geneva placed this new economic regime on a firm organizational footing. Despite all the upheaval of the twentieth century, the ILO has functioned continuously ever since 1919. In 1969, upon its fiftieth anniversary, the ILO would be awarded the Nobel Peace Prize for its promotion of peaceful relations among social classes as well as the nations of the world.[54]

Several days after the 1919 ILO Conference wrapped up its business, Jeanne Bouvier returned to New York with the other members of the French delegation to catch a steamer home. A coal miner's strike delayed the ship's departure and then forced it to make an unscheduled stop in the Azores to refuel. Bouvier would thus celebrate Christmas on a tropical island in the middle of the Atlantic, amid blooming hydrangea and orange trees laden with fruit. On December 31, 1919, her ship finally arrived in port, and Bouvier caught the first train back to Paris. Glancing up as she disembarked at the Saint-Lazare train station, the French woman happened to read the hands on the clock: ten minutes to midnight. By the time she laid her head on her pillow later that night, 1919 had come to a close and a new year had begun.[55]

Against all odds, in 1919 Bouvier and a remarkable group of female dressmakers and cap liners, shoemakers, shop assistants, cotton spinners, and their allies briefly commanded the global stage. There they defended female wage earners' right to define the terms of "social justice" for themselves. By sheer force of will, they forced powerful statesmen, wealthy businessmen, and influential trade unionists to pay heed, and they left their mark on the first international labor standards, designed to mitigate the "injustice, hardship, and privation" that sowed misery and threatened global "peace and harmony" the world over. The Maternity Protection Convention adopted by the ILO in 1919 was largely of their making.[56]

The women who participated in the International Congress of Working Women of 1919 were well aware of the historic nature of their undertaking, and they worked hard to build on their success. Before disbanding, they voted to create an International Federation of Working Women to champion labor feminism—which is to say gender *and* industrial justice—across the globe. The new federation widely disseminated the resolutions adopted by the Women's Congress; it promoted women's lobbying and legislative efforts through a regular newsletter, and it organized two further international conferences, one in Geneva in 1921 and another in Vienna in 1923. Although dominated by women from Western industrial nations, the federation's masthead in 1920 listed "corresponding members" in Japan (Tanaka Taka) and India as well as in Argentina. Federation members, moreover, openly discussed how they might expand their membership in Asia and Latin America. The federation's global aspirations were foreshortened, however, when a majority of members voted in 1923 to join the European-based International Federation of Trade Unions, the largest mixed-sex trade union organization in the world.[57]

Both Rose Schneiderman and Jeanne Bouvier, who played such vital roles in championing working women's interests in Paris and in Washington in 1919, remained actively involved in the International Federation of Working Women throughout its years of existence. Schneiderman would return to Europe with Margaret Dreier Robins in 1923 as a delegate to the Third International Congress of Working Women. Bouvier would serve as a vice president on the federation's executive board, representing workers' interests in European feminist circles.

The need for such representation arose almost immediately, when the International Woman Suffrage Alliance—headed by Carrie Chapman Catt—announced it would hold its first postwar congress in Geneva in 1920. Rumor had it that Dutch and British feminists were planning to challenge the international ban on women's night work, and the federation asked Bouvier to attend the congress and speak on behalf of labor women. Although the issue had divided delegates to the Women's Congress in 1919, the federation took the position that, at least for the time being, economically vulnerable women were better served by embracing special protections—such as those limiting women's work hours—than they would be in supporting abstract appeals to gender equality. Equally important to Bouvier's mission, the federation sought recognition of the principle that middle-class feminists had no right to speak *for* female wage earners without consulting *with* them. Bouvier fulfilled her mandate to the letter. "I stated," she would later report, "that if the delegates of the Suffragist Congress continued to protest against the decisions at the International Labor Conference in Washington they would create lasting antagonism between suffrage women and working women."[58]

For the wealthy, white feminists who made up the bulk of the Alliance's membership, Bouvier's speech was a wake-up call, not unlike the one issued by Mary Church Terrell to the Women's International League for Peace in Freedom in Zurich the year prior. Class, like race, informed the many forms of gender oppression that women faced around the world. Global feminists would need to find ways to acknowledge those differences if they wanted to forge an inclusive movement. The question of protective labor legislation for women continued to divide feminists—sometimes bitterly—in the interwar decades, but in the face of consistent pressure from labor women, all three of the major international feminist organizations (the Alliance, the Women's International League for Peace and Freedom, and the International Council of Women) backed away from an inflexible equal rights agenda, conceding that working women had as much right to "self-determination" as anyone else.[59]

If labor feminists' class status continued to set them apart in international feminist circles, in trade union organizations, it was their status as women that proved most challenging. Although situations varied from country to country and from industry to industry, in much of the industrialized West, male-dominated trade unions remained ambivalent about—if not outright hostile to—female wage earners in the interwar decades. "Time in the trenches changed nothing in the spirit of French male workers," Bouvier would complain bitterly. "They displayed the same hostility toward unionized women as before they left." Immediately after World War I tens of thousands of European women were summarily fired from their jobs as soldiers returned from battle. Sometimes they were given a token of severance pay or social insurance. Sometimes they received nothing at all. Those women who managed to retain their employment often found themselves accused of stealing "men's" jobs out from under them. By the early 1930s, widespread economic insecurity brought on by the Great Depression induced new fears. In the face of mass unemployment, male union leaders backed away from programs designed to organize women workers. In their eyes, economic justice was better served by defending good-paying jobs for male heads-of-household, even if a breadwinner wage remained well out of reach for many working families and threatened countless single women with destitution.[60]

Against this backdrop, many labor feminists came to see government regulation and robust international labor standards as their surest path to economic security. In this quest, transnational ties, forged in 1919, served labor women exceptionally well. Rose Schneiderman remained in close contact with Margaret Bondfield of Great Britain as she took over the presidency of the National Women's Trade Union League of America in 1926 and then, a few years later, when she served on President Franklin Delano Roosevelt's National Recovery Administration Labor Advisory Board, where she would help oversee policies designed to increase women's wages. "Imagine," she would write to Bondfield, "setting standards for millions of women and girls. The codes are the Magna Carta of the working woman."[61]

Bondfield did not need to imagine what it felt like to shape laws and policies that would improve the lives of working women; she made a career of it. In 1923 Bondfield would be elected to the House of Commons. In 1929 she would become minister of labor (and the first female cabinet member in the history of Great Britain). Bondfield remained a force to be reckoned with at the ILO as well, serving as a voting delegate alongside other European alumni of the 1919 Women's Congress, including Betzy Kjelsberg of Norway and Kerstin Hesselgren of Sweden. Hesselgren, who became Sweden's first female member of Parliament, was a particularly effective advocate for women in Geneva. In 1937 she would be appointed to chair the League of Nations Committee on the Status of Women, a precedent-setting body that helped pave the way for the United Nations Commission on the Status of Women after World War II.[62]

Rose Schneiderman's codelegate in Paris in 1919, Mary Anderson, enjoyed an equally illustrious government career and also remained in close touch with Bondfield, Kjelsberg, and Hesselgren. From 1920 to 1944 Anderson would head the Women's Bureau of the U.S. Labor Department. At the ILO (which America finally joined in 1934) she would draw on the transnational networks she had fostered since 1919 to promote women's economic rights. Anderson was joined in this effort by American ILO delegate Grace Abbott, who had served as secretary to the ILO Conference in 1919. In 1937 Abbott would cosponsor a resolution requesting that ILO member states study the relationship between women's status and their political and economic rights. This resolution guided the ILO away from special protective legislation and toward the pursuit of equal economic opportunities for working women and men in the decades following World War II.[63]

Frenchwoman Jeanne Bouvier returned home from Washington at the end of 1919 intent on following a similar activist path as her international friends, and for a brief period the dream seemed within reach. Serving again as an advisor to the French delegation at the third ILO Conference in Geneva in 1921, Bouvier renewed her contacts with American, European, and Japanese labor feminists: foreign friends with whom she would stay in touch for many years thereafter. By 1923, however, her relationship with French male trade unionists, and particularly with labor leader Léon Jouhaux, had completely soured. Before long, France's longest-serving female union militant would be hounded out of the organized labor movement. What did Bouvier do to warrant such treatment?[64]

The original sin that precipitated Bouvier's ignominious downfall apparently took place on the steamer trip back to France from America in 1919. The ship departed around noontime, and soon after the vessel pulled back from the harbor, passengers made their way to the dining room. There the Spanish delegates—representing government, employers, and labor— gathered around a single table for lunch while the French delegation carefully split, seating themselves at three separate tables scattered around the room. "It seemed strange," Bouvier would write, "that the delegates of a monarchist country sat together where the delegates of a republican and democratic state divided themselves in three factions." Only later did she learn the reason for this odd behavior. French labor delegate Léon Jouhaux had insisted on bringing his mistress with him to America and on seating her next to him at the dining table onboard ship. Such behavior offended the government and employers' representatives, who refused to sit with the workers. Bouvier felt "deeply humiliated." To her, Jouhaux's actions were an affront to all French trade unionists who entrusted him with the responsibility of representing them abroad. In Bouvier's mind, Jouhuax treated the return trip like a "private pleasure cruise" and dishonored the entire French working class in the process.[65]

After returning to France, Bouvier might have allowed the incident to drop had Jouhaux and other male union leaders supported women workers in their organizing efforts. They did not. The French unions, Bouvier complained, continued to behave like old feudal institutions "where men are the lords and the women serve them. . . . As for women's social or professional interests, they are completely neglected." As far as Bouvier was concerned, on virtually every policy of import to women—maternity leave, industrial homework, social education—Jouhaux and the French General Confederation of Labor let women down. Bouvier repeatedly challenged Jouhaux and other male union leaders over these policies, and she continued to criticize their sexual improprieties as well (Jouhaux was apparently not alone in parading his mistress in public). Such forthrightness won her few friends and many enemies. Before long, Bouvier lost her position on the executive committee of the General Confederation of Labor as well as at the Paris Labor Exchange. Class solidarity demanded that women know their place and hold their tongues. Bouvier refused and paid the price.[66]

The tragic end to Bouvier's long union career is a reminder of how difficult it was for working women to pierce the overwhelmingly male world of trade unionism and labor politics in the century after the ILO was founded. Labor women had to fight to get a hearing in Paris and Washington in 1919, and they remained very much in the minority at ILO Conferences for decades. At ILO headquarters in the interwar era, women were hired as secretaries and translators but rarely in positions of authority. Despite these liabilities, women spoke out and left their stamp on early international labor policy. Transnational alliances—many of them forged in 1919—helped this pioneering generation of labor feminists build an international network that would grow as the years passed. On its website today, the ILO proclaims gender equality to be key to achieving "conditions of freedom, equity, security, and human dignity" for working people across the world: a testament to the far-reaching legacy of labor women's intrepid defense of social justice after the First World War.[67]

Epilogue

Rome, 1923

D espite all the hopes invested in it, the Paris Peace Conference of 1919 did not usher in an era of peace and prosperity. The early 1920s were difficult and even violent years in many parts of the world. The Turks fought a war of independence to shed the vestiges of Ottoman rule and stave off the colonial ambitions of the West. The Egyptians remained in open revolt against their British colonizers. In China, troops under the command of the Nationalist Party fought entrenched warlords to unify the country. In Russia, the Bolsheviks finally vanquished their internal enemies only to face a disastrous famine threatening millions with starvation. The Communist victory in Russia set off a Red Scare in the United States, already seething with racial violence, and stirred workers in Europe to revolt in the face of soaring inflation and high unemployment. New ultranationalist movements fed on postwar economic turmoil. These included Benito Mussolini's National Fascist Party, which bullied its way into power in Italy in late October 1922.

Altogether, these global events provided an ominous backdrop to the Ninth Congress of the International Woman Suffrage Alliance, which convened in Rome on May 12, 1923. It was the largest suffrage congress ever held, reported America's *Time* magazine, drawing well over one thousand delegates, including women "from all lands." In 1923 the Alliance declared prosaically, "for the suffragists of the world, all roads led to Rome." It was an exaggeration, but an understandable one. The Ninth Congress was decidedly more global than any that came before it. Participants hailed from over forty nations and every inhabited continent: Brazil and Bulgaria, Czechoslovakia and China, Egypt and India, Ukraine and Uruguay were all represented. Among the dominant personalities at the gathering were a dozen or more women who had fought their way onto the political stage in 1919. In Rome, nearly four years later, these veteran female activists came together with eager newcomers to take stock of their achievements, reflect on their disappointments, and build momentum for the battles to come.[1]

Reunited in Rome

For American suffrage leader and Alliance president Carrie Chapman Catt, the congress in 1923 marked a bittersweet end to a long, international career. Catt had served at the helm of the Alliance since its founding in 1904. The time had come, she felt, to pass the gavel. The final battle to win ratification of the Nineteenth Amendment—establishing women's constitutional right to vote in the United States—had consumed much of Catt's energy in 1919 and 1920, leaving European Alliance leaders to take the lead at the Paris Peace Conference. Now, two of the European suffragists who made a name for themselves at the time of the negotiations—Marguerite de Witt Schlumberger and Margery Corbett Ashby—faced off in a bid to replace Catt as Alliance president.

Schlumberger, now sixty-six years old and a vice president of the Alliance for nearly a decade, was a natural choice. In addition to her years on the Alliance board, she had also won considerable respect for seizing the initiative and convening the Inter-Allied Women's Conference of 1919. Despite her high standing in international women's circles, however, Schlumberger was a problematic nominee. The French woman had made no effort to disguise her patriotic devotion to her nation's cause during and after World War I. Alliance members worried that a Schlumberger presidency would drive German women out of the organization altogether. "Impossible, TOO OLD, TOO SLOW, TOO FRENCH," grumbled Dutch suffragist Rosa Manus to a friend.[2]

In the end, the relatively youthful, forty-one-year-old Margery Corbett Ashby of Great Britain received the most votes. A longtime suffragist at home, Corbett Ashby emerged as a major figure in international feminist circles in 1919 when she replaced Millicent Garrett Fawcett as Britain's foremost delegate to the Inter-Allied Women's Conference. Corbett Ashby's diplomatic successes in Paris—speaking before the Labor and League of Nations Commissions, lobbying Britain's peace delegates, and working with women from other Allied nations—burnished her reputation and gave her a passion for international feminist work. Elected in 1923, Corbett Ashby would serve as Alliance president for over two decades, until her retirement in 1946.[3]

On the whole, the slate of officers elected in 1923 reflected the ongoing predominance of Western women in the Alliance in the interwar period, but there were hints of change to come. Avra Theodoropoulou, who founded the Greek League for Women's Rights after World War I, joined the Executive Board that year, a position she would retain for over a decade. With strong ties throughout the Balkans, Theodoropoulou would serve as one link between women in the West and the Middle East in the interwar decades.[4]

A second newcomer to the board in 1923, Dr. Paulina Luisi of Uruguay, also signaled the Alliance's expanding geographic reach. Because most of Latin America (with the exception of Brazil) had sat out the fighting in World War I, the Paris Peace Conference did not catalyze female activism south of the United States border in the same way it did in many other parts of the world. Nevertheless, by 1919 Latin American women were coming into their own. That year, Luisi—Uruguay's first female bachelor's degree holder and physician—founded a Uruguayan Alliance for Women's Suffrage and began calling for the creation of a Pan-American Association of Women to build regional support for women's rights. Although Luisi would soon become disillusioned with Carrie Chapman Catt (whom she found patronizing and dismissive), she would go on to become one of the truly exceptional international female figures of the interwar decades, representing her country at the League of Nations Disarmament Conference and at the International Labor Organization as well as on multiple committees of the Alliance and the International Council of Women and helping inspire a wave of Latin American feminist activism.[5]

The participation of women from the Middle East and Asia as well as South America at the Rome Congress of 1923 spurred Alliance leaders to speak in soaring terms about a global feminist movement in the making. "Let us then in this Congress of 1923 plan a worldwide campaign for the emancipation of women," proclaimed Catt in her presidential address. "Let us organize the campaign well, and carry it to the remotest quarters of the globe; carry it with such energy and spirit that there will be no pause until the women of the entire civilized world have been raised to the dignity of adult, sane, intelligent citizens." Emboldened by women's suffrage gains in northern Europe and North America, and encouraged by the visible emergence of women's activism in the Global South, Alliance members looked hopefully to a future when all women of the world could come together to achieve universal gender equality.[6]

The final public meeting of the Rome Congress made a dramatic visual display of the Alliance's global aspirations. The evening, dedicated to "Women of all the Continents," featured speakers from new Alliance affiliates from the Middle East, Latin American, and East Asia. It was, in the eyes of one French delegate, the "most successful" of all the congress events. Huda Shaarawi—the dynamic organizer of the women's protests against the British Protectorate in 1919 and president of the newly formed Egyptian Feminist Union—garnered much praise for her speech that evening. So, too, did Dorothy Jinarajadasa of India, Eusca Ohashi of Japan, and Bertha Lutz of Brazil. Lutz's affiliation with global feminists' goals was particularly consequential. Just over two decades later, in the aftermath of the Second World War, Lutz would anchor the battle to delineate women's rights in the United Nations Charter and to create a standing Commission on the Status of Women at the nascent United Nations.[7]

Chinese women, although not yet affiliated with the Alliance, also were given a spot on the program. The woman who spoke was a relatively unknown figure, Evelyn Waung Tcheu of the Chinese Legation in Rome, but according to the official Congress Report, a second Chinese woman attended the meeting as well: "Mlle. Tscheng" of Paris. Was Soumay Tcheng in Rome in 1923? It is quite possible. Tcheng was living in Paris at the time, working steadily toward her law degree. She had also begun collaborating with Western suffragists. According to one French newspaper, Tcheng had planned to attend the Geneva Congress in 1920, but unspecified circumstances had forced her to alter her plans at the last minute (most likely, she was waylaid by the group of young female runaways begging to accompany her back to Paris). In November 1922 Tcheng had also participated in a "feminist demonstration" at the Sorbonne alongside Marguerite de Witt Schlumberger, Ghénia Avril de Sainte-Croix, and Suzanne Grinberg of France as well as Paulina Luisi of Uruguay. The purpose of the Sorbonne demonstration was to rally votes for an (ill-fated) female suffrage bill before the French Senate. Tcheng spoke in favor of the bill in support of her French friends, but she also used the occasion to remind

Westerners once again that Chinese women had long ago served as "ministers" and "generals" and that they, no less than Western women, were eager to help bring "concord and peace" to the world.[8]

If it is quite possible that Soumay Tcheng was at the Rome Congress, it is certain that Mary Church Terrell and Ida Gibbs Hunt were not, nor, it appears, was any woman from sub-Saharan Africa or the African diaspora. This constituted a troubling absence at a congress that pledged "to promote the conception of human solidarity as superior to national and race solidarity." Fine intentions were one thing; working toward their realization was another. For all their earnest global aspirations, white feminists often seem to have perpetuated racial and imperial hierarchies within international feminist organizations, at times without even fully realizing it. When Catt spoke, for example, about emancipating women of the "civilized" world, she assimilated concepts rooted in Western notions of progress into her feminist worldview, effectively excluding millions of women from "uncivilized" colonies of Africa and Asia. Given such assumptions, it is unsurprising that at the time of the Rome Congress, Ida Gibbs Hunt chose to devote her attentions elsewhere: to planning the third Pan-African Congress, soon to convene in London and Lisbon. Mary Church Terrell, for her part, was wrapped up launching a new organization designed to unite women of color around the world: the International Council of Women of the Darker Races. Hunt and Terrell remained committed to forwarding gender equality alongside white women as well, but after 1919 they, like many prominent African American women, gravitated to the Women's International League for Peace and Freedom (WILPF), which put more resources into challenging imperialism and organizing across racial lines than did the Alliance.[9]

As was customary, other major international women's organizations, including the WILPF, were invited to send a nonvoting delegation to the congress as a show of sisterly solidarity. Emily Balch, the WILPF's first international secretary in Geneva, came to Rome along with Austrian member Yella Hertzka. Both women had participated in the Zurich Congress of 1919 and would work diligently for the feminist peace organization throughout the interwar decades. Balch, like her friend and collaborator Jane Addams, would be awarded a Nobel Peace Prize (in 1946) for her tireless leadership.

The International Federation of Working Women was also represented at the Rome Congress by a local woman named Laura Casartelli Cabrini, who had participated as an advisor to the Italian delegation at the 1919 International Labor Conference in Washington, D.C. A trip to Rome in 1923 was out of the question for most American trade union leaders, including Rose Schneiderman, who were saving their money to travel to the federation's third international conference in Vienna later that year. French labor feminist Jeanne Bouvier, who had given such a spirited defense of working women's right to self-determination at the Alliance's Geneva Congress in 1920, did not make the trek to Rome either, but the lessons she had doled out three years earlier had not been forgotten. On the question of whether to support protective labor legislation for women, Rome delegates continued to express such "acute differences of opinion" that the only resolution they could agree on "was principally identical with the Geneva one, stating that the restrictions, if any, should be agreed to by the women concerned." Labor feminists' consistent demand that working women have a voice in the laws and international standards guiding their lives thus prevailed in 1923 and lived on into the interwar era.[10]

The Rome Congress marked an important moment of transition for an organization founded principally to promote women's political enfranchisement around the world. For the first time in the Alliance's history, over half the delegates—including women from countries in northern Europe and North America as well as from Australia, New Zealand, and several states in India—possessed national voting rights equivalent to men in their home countries. Six delegates to the congress were, in fact, elected members of Parliament (one each from Denmark and Finland and a remarkable four from the German Reichstag). The new world government was also represented at the Rome Congress, in this case, by Dame Rachel Crowdy, chief of the Social Services Section of the League of Nations. Enfranchised women devoted an entire day to lively discussions about how female voters might best exercise their newly acquired power of the ballot to forward gender equality. The following day the conversation turned to how to keep up the momentum so that women from "unenfranchised" nations—from East Asia, the Middle East, South America, and southern Europe—might follow in in their footsteps.

Newly emerging hierarchies within global feminism were put on bold display on the final day of the congress, when the delegates went to pay a call on the Italian Ministry of Interior. The women chose to make their way to the meeting on foot, marching in a grand procession through the streets of Rome. Officers of the Alliance led the parade, followed by female parliamentary representatives and then by the mass of women endowed by their governments with the right to vote. Unenfranchised women brought up the rear. "I leave you to imagine our delegation's place in the lineup," grumbled one French woman who participated. "We were not terribly proud."[11]

French senators' stubborn resistance to female suffrage meant that throughout the interwar decades, French women would frequently find themselves at the metaphorical back of the line. Already in 1923 they were forced to march jealously behind Indian delegates Dorothy Jinarajadasa, Herabai and Mithan Tata, and several others who had pushed the British parliament to include national women's suffrage in the Government of India Act of 1919, and who now benefited from its adoption in Madras (Tamil Nadu), Bombay (Mumbai), and several princely states. When the Turkish government adopted female suffrage in 1934, French women would be forced to watch with envy as women from the Islamic world began to pass them by. Women from Ecuador and Brazil, who were enfranchised in 1929 and 1932, respectively, would similarly leapfrog ahead of the French, who would not gain the right to vote until 1944.[12]

Italian women also marched in the rear of the processional in Rome in 1923, which was precisely the point. The parade was deliberate political

Benito Mussolini (*lower left*) addresses the International Woman Suffrage Alliance in Rome, Italy, 1923. (Library of Congress)

theater, staged for members of the Italian public and for their new leader, Benito Mussolini. "We dare to hope," Carrie Chapman Catt said to the prime minister on behalf of the Alliance, "that it will be your Government, most honored, most excellent Signor Mussolini, that will lead this land of ancient renown into the modern majority." With over a thousand women's eyes on him, Mussolini told the congress, "I do not believe that enfranchising women will have catastrophic consequences," and he pledged his government to grant the vote "to several categories" of Italian women in the near future. In 1923 such a promise still seemed plausible. Fascism was a young and variable ideology, disdainful of liberal institutions but also deliberately modern in its outlook. Within three short years, Mussolini (by then styling himself *Il Duce*, the omnipotent leader) would cancel all elections, transform Italy into a single-party dictatorship, and enact new laws designed to reassert male dominance and return women to hearth and home. It was an ominous portent of things to come. Italian women would not gain the right to vote until 1945, after Mussolini's defeat and execution.[13]

Legacies of 1919

In 1919 global statesmen gathered in Paris to end a war and remake the world. They came together having issued bold proclamations to the people at home that their sacrifices had not been in vain. Democratic governance, national self-determination, international cooperation, and social justice: these, they said, were the principles on which the new world order would be grounded. Among themselves, the peacemakers argued about how to translate vague promises into practical policies and embed them in complex institutions. Time and again, high ideals gave way to competing interests, lingering distrust, and entrenched prejudice. The settlement they produced had its merits, but the foundation of lasting peace was not among them.

If within the halls of power, fine rhetoric was often drowned out by political realism, outside, statesmen's words took on a life of their own. To the weak and the oppressed, lofty wartime proclamations seemed to herald the dawn of a new age. Representatives of these peoples—ethnic minorities, colonial nationalists, trade unionists, and pan-Africanists, among others—made their way to Paris to seek a hearing before the peacemakers. Countless articles, books, and documentaries have memorialized their efforts. Not so for women. Though they came to Paris in droves; though they organized congresses, drafted charters, and staged protests; though they attracted the interest of contemporary journalists and captured the ear of the peacemakers themselves; though they spoke in the name of "more than half of humanity," the women of 1919 and their remarkable battle for women's rights at the time of the Paris Peace Conference have been all but forgotten.

Marguerite de Witt Schlumberger, Mary Church Terrell, Ida Gibbs Hunt, Huda Shaarawi, Jane Addams, Soumay Tcheng, Rose Schneiderman, and Jeanne Bouvier: these women and their collaborators—who came from different countries, ethnicities, religions, and social classes—all, in their separate ways, sought to hold the peacemakers to their word. They were idealistic, but they were not naïve. They knew the diplomatic universe of the peace conference belonged to men and men alone. They knew that to influence the peace negotiations, they were going to have to defy convention and demand to be heard. The resulting explosion of international female activism was unprecedented in scale and scope. Despite these women's extraordinary eloquence and determination, the peacemakers failed to address the vast majority of their concerns. The world has suffered for this shortsightedness ever since.

According to recent United Nations data, women's subordination remains a major impediment to global peace and security. The ability to help shape national and international law was women's central demand in 1919; yet women today make up less than one quarter of elected legislators worldwide. Despite women's ardent pleas in 1919 for equal pay for equal work, on average today women around the world earn roughly two-thirds that of men. In 1919 women insisted that gender equality must begin in the family. Still today a shocking 750 million girls are married before reaching adulthood. In 1919 women were denied a seat at the negotiating table. Even today less than 10 percent of signatories to peace agreements are women despite the fact that the United Nations has found that when women do participate in postconflict negotiations, the agreements reached are quantifiably more successful and enduring. "Progress is achieved through women," Bernard Kouchner, founder of Doctors without Borders, would proclaim bluntly in the first decade of the twenty-first century. It was precisely this message that women delivered to global leaders nearly one hundred years earlier at the time of the Paris Peace Conference, as the groundwork for the modern international order was being laid.[14]

Women's demands in 1919 were not a sideshow. They spoke to the issues at the heart of the negotiations: peace, stability, and democracy. Although they did not all speak in the same voice, female activists of 1919 variously rejected the Versailles settlement as a treaty of retribution, demanded an end to imperialism and racial inequality, insisted on economic justice for all workers irrespective of sex, and reclaimed the right of all people to elect their representatives. Adopting the language of the most powerful statesmen of the day, women collectively demanded a new world order rooted not only in *national* self-determination but also *individual* self-determination: the right of all people, regardless of their sex, to help shape the laws, policies, and customs that structure their lives. They proclaimed gender equality to be integral to social justice, and they claimed democracy as the birthright of all citizens. They were relentless in pursuit of their ideals, and they forced powerful statesmen to take notice.

Women achieved tangible results even against extraordinary odds. The Covenant of the League of Nations specifically delineated that all positions in the new world government would be open to men and women on equal terms. The founding Charter of the International Labor Organization was less exacting but nonetheless called for the appointment of female "advisors" to national delegations. This opening allowed women to leave their mark on the first international labor standards, adopted by the ILO in 1919, calling for expansive paid maternity leave laws that have since been adopted and expanded throughout most of the developed world (the United States standing as a notable exception). As a result of women's efforts, international governmental bodies would slowly open their doors to female diplomats and policy experts in the interwar decades.

Despite such notable victories, on the whole, the peacemakers disappointed women far more than they advanced their cause. Contrary to the pleas of female activists, the peacemakers of 1919 declined to make any principled stance on behalf of global female enfranchisement, validating the assumption that a democratic and just world order could be built in women's absence. The men who crafted the peace of 1919 brushed aside women's (as well as men's) calls for racial equality and popular sovereignty in Asia and Africa. They were also careful to recognize women's political legitimacy only insofar as it had a direct bearing on women's and children's specific interests. By failing to empower women in the negotiations or to endorse democratic governance in the settlement, the peacemakers declared the issue of women's rights to be peripheral to the central goal of establishing a lasting peace. Women disagreed, and history has borne out their concerns.

The female activists of 1919 demanded the right to participate in national and international governance for a reason: they saw it as the surest means of combating the discrimination and insecurity that had long defined their lives in their homes, in the economy, and in society. On these issues, even women from widely varying national, ethnic, and economic backgrounds were in fundamental agreement: a "people's peace" (to borrow Woodrow Wilson's term) could be realized only if it secured the fundamental rights of *people*, not just nations. In issuing such concerns, the women who spoke out in 1919 anticipated the United Nations' Declaration of Human Rights of 1948 and the assertion often repeated by century's end: "Women's Rights Are Human Rights."[15]

The peacemakers' refusal to address the vast majority of women's concerns in 1919 set the world down a precarious path; yet global leaders' short-sightedness failed to shatter women's hopes or silence their voices. Women's empowerment in the international spotlight coupled with their disillusionment with the outcome of the 1919 peace negotiations transformed women's rights into a global cause. Because the Paris Peace Conference raised questions regarding national borders, political sovereignty, racial justice, and economic rights simultaneously in so many parts of the world, the hopes it raised were equally global in scope. Wartime calls for a new world order rooted in democratic governance and national self-determination provided a new legitimizing framework for women's demands in many far-reaching corners of the world.

The women who congregated in meeting halls, drafted petitions, and seized the podium in 1919 represented a broad cross-section of the global population. Overlapping interests spurred cross-pollination, encouraging women to build new movements and seek out new forms of collaboration, while the diversity of their experiences rendered global feminism intersectional from its moment of inception. Women who did not know one another in 1919 would build alliances in years that followed. Chinese feminist Soumay Tcheng would campaign for French women's right to vote in the 1920s. Egyptian feminist Huda Shaarawi would do the same a decade later. The Women's International League for Peace and Freedom would send a delegation of European women to China, Japan, and Indochina in the late 1920s to foster stronger cooperation between Western and Asian feminists. Alliance president Margery Corbett Ashby would travel to Cairo in 1935 to support Egyptian women's quest for the vote. Print media helped solidify international bonds even when travel was impractical. African

American civil rights activists would publish news of the 1919 Egyptian women's protests in their newsletter the *Crisis*. In 1927 Egyptian women would devote an entire page of their feminist periodical *L'Egyptienne* to Soumay Tcheng, who had recently been appointed as a judge in China and whom they upheld as a model of emancipated womanhood.[16]

Such alliances did not coalesce into a single, global feminist movement. Instead many feminisms and many movements blossomed. The Women's International League for Peace and Freedom, the International Federation of Working Women, and the International Council of Women of the Darker Races all arose directly out of the ferment of 1919. The Little Entente of Women (founded by women in the Balkans in 1923), the Pan-Pacific Women's Association (founded in 1930), and the Arab Feminist Union (founded in 1945) formed in its aftermath. Simultaneously, in the interwar decades, "Eastern" women would convene conferences in Damascus (1930) and Tehran (1932), while Indian women would organize an All-Asian Women's Conference in Lahore (1931). Pan-American women, for their part, began to gather at regional meetings in Baltimore (1922) and then in Santiago (1923); in Havana in 1928 they would found a standing Inter-American Commission of Women, which would champion both Pan-American and international women's rights in the interwar decades. The multiplication of regional women's organizations reflected the difficulties—both practical and ideological—of uniting women across cultures and continents, but the determination with which women pursued such international collaborations also points to the powerfully unifying force of gender oppression and discrimination around the world.[17]

World War I and the peace conference that followed spurred feminists to expand their vision and alter their strategies. In 1919 global statesmen in Paris called for a sweeping international settlement and the establishment of the world's first standing government. Women immediately recognized the promise of this newly interconnected international system and used it to press their interests. By seeking representation in the peace negotiations, by demanding recognition of women's rights and interests in the Versailles Treaty, and by securing female participation in the new institutions of global governance, female activists of 1919 set a critical precedent. They demonstrated that international treaties and bodies could be powerful tools in pressing recalcitrant nations to alter the laws and practices restricting women's choices and freedoms. Male and female feminists have drawn from this playbook ever since. Their efforts are reflected in the adoption of the multilateral Equal Nationality and Equal Rights Treaties of 1933, in the establishment of the UN Commission on the Status of Women in 1946, in the sweeping agenda of the UN Decade for Women from 1975 to 1985, and, most recently, in the development of the "Equality in Law for Women and Girls by 2030" initiative, adopted by multiple international organizations and agencies in January 2019, exactly one hundred years after global female activists placed women's rights on the international agenda at the Paris Peace Conference after the First World War.[18]

Today, fueled by the communication and transportation revolution of the twenty-first century and the globalizing power of social and traditional media, dozens of international organizations have arisen, all of which seek to empower women in their homes, in the economy, and in political life. International global agencies—like UN Women—exist to aid them in this quest, and female political activists in far corners of the world continue to brave violence and imprisonment to join in the fight. Since the beginning of the twenty-first century, seven women—hailing from Iran, Kenya, Liberia, Yemen, Pakistan, and Iraq—have been awarded the Nobel Peace Prize: all for their work empowering women and combatting sexual violence around the world. These brave activists, and countless others, unknowingly travel a path paved by pioneering women a century ago: women who ignored tradition and overcame prejudice to insist on gender equality as a precondition to a just, stable, and peaceful world. Through their conferences and speeches, marches and charters, the courageous female activists of 1919 transformed women's rights into the global rallying cry that continues to echo around the world today.[19]

Acknowledgments

*P*eace on Our Terms is a work of global history, undertaken with tremendous humility. From the outset, I knew this story would force me to reach outside my academic comfort zone and into historical terrain well removed from my fields of expertise. Fortunately, in this endeavor I have been upheld by a truly exceptional group of colleagues, archivists, librarians, granting agencies, editors, students, friends, and family members, who have asked me probing questions, shared their knowledge, pointed out relevant sources, translated foreign documents, and reassured me that no matter how overambitious in scope, *Peace on Our Terms* is a story worth telling. This book's shortcomings are entirely my own; it owes its strengths to a far-flung band of individuals whom it is truly a pleasure to acknowledge here.

Writing about the global past means traveling to distant places in search of sources: in this case, fifteen archives in four different countries. Such research requires time and money, and I was fortunate to have both thanks to the support of the National Endowment for the Humanities. The NEH awarded me two separate fellowships between 2016 and 2018: the first allowed me to undertake research in Europe; the second provided a year of uninterrupted time to write. Throughout the years that I worked on this project, the NEH was under near constant attack, suffering the disruption of government shutdowns and repeatedly threatened with defunding. I hope this book will serve as evidence of the benefits that flow from investing in the humanities. I offer my warm appreciation to the staff members at the NEH who have continued to work under such trying circumstances.

My home institution, California State University, Sacramento, has also generously funded this project, and I wholeheartedly thank the College of Arts and Letters, the Research and Creative Activities Subcommittee, and University Enterprises for their support. Jill Shannon in Research Development skillfully coached me on how to convey my project's importance to nonspecialists. My department chair, Jeffrey Wilson, expressed nothing but happiness when I told him of my grants, even though my leave from teaching caused him considerable additional work. College of Arts and Letters Dean Sheree Meyer and Associate Dean Christina Bellon have offered similarly unwavering encouragement.

I first began to conceptualize this project in 2015, with no real sense of its viability. That spring I summoned all the courage I possessed and presented my ideas to the incomparable feminist historian Karen Offen, hoping against hope that she wouldn't laugh or send me packing. Instead, she offered her unflagging support. Karen has served as midwife to this project from day one. Through countless discussions, email exchanges, and conference panels, she helped me identify the most pertinent scholarship and pressed me to broaden my vision and sharpen my analysis. She read every page of the manuscript, often more than once. Since that first meeting, I have asked her for many favors. Never once has she turned me down. I cannot possibly find terms effusive enough with which to express my appreciation. I only hope that someday I will be able to make half the mark on the field of women's history that Karen has over the course of her career.

This project may have had just one midwife, but it has had many doulas. Louise Edwards and I met at a conference in Minnesota just as I was beginning to explore interconnections between Western and Chinese feminism. Louise made the mistake of offering me words of encouragement as I waded into Chinese history. I clamped onto her and never let go. I owe Louise a profound debt of gratitude for helping me bring Soumay Tcheng's story to light and for serving as a consistent champion of this project as a whole. Dorothy Sue Cobble has similarly counseled me on the intricacies of international labor feminism. Her own work on the First International Conference of Working Women is nothing short of brilliant. I have benefited immeasurably from her guidance, and I am proud to serve as her partner-in-crime in advocating for American women to finally benefit from century-old international standards for paid parental leave. I approached Margot Badran for help with trepidation, after immersing myself in her path-breaking books and articles, but I knew that no one would be better qualified to help me frame the story of Egyptian feminism responsibly. Margot is a superb scholar with a foot in two continents, but despite her many personal commitments, she did not hesitate to proffer assistance when I asked. For her sage advice, and for her willingness to share photographs from her personal collection (some gifted to her by the Egyptian women who lived through the history told here), I am profoundly grateful.

Many other historians have inspired me and guided me along this path. I thank Anne-Marie Pois for sparking my interest in women's peace history so long ago; Harriet Alonso for her important work on feminist pacifism and for helping me seek funding for this project; Adele Logan Alexander for answering emails from a stranger and helping me locate materials on Ida Gibbs Hunt; Carl Bouchard for his unmatched diplomatic history expertise and for sharing the letters he found from French feminists to Woodrow Wilson; and Brandy Thomas Wells for her insight into African American women's internationalism. I am grateful as well to Emmanuelle Cronier, who offered timely advice about French trains, to François Dremeux, who helped me acquire a Chinese-language biography in Hong Kong, and to my former advisor and friend Laird Boswell, who supplied sources from Wisconsin's databases in a moment of need. I thank my colleagues Jeffrey Dym, Brendan Lindsay, and Patrick Ettinger for helping me to date a tricky source, Michael Vann for pushing me to tackle a world history topic in the first place, and Richard Cooper for feeding me a steady diet of diplomatic history material, some of which helped shape the prologue. Finally, I am deeply grateful to Marwa Helmy, who translated a key document for this book from the original Arabic.

I cannot possibly thank all the dedicated archivists and librarians who helped me access the thousands of primary sources that I consulted in preparing this book. Several, however, made an extra effort to help my research go smoothly. A special thanks goes out to Annie Metz, Bibliothèque Marguerite Durand; Marie-Françoise Garion, Bibliothèque historique de la Ville de Paris; France Chabod, Centre des archives du féminisme; Els Flour, Centre d'archives et de recherches pour l'histoire des femmes; and David

Hays, Special Collections and Archives, University of Colorado Boulder. Several other individuals went out of their way to help me acquire the photos that enrich this book. Thanks in particular to Jennifer Sanchez, Special Collections and Archives, University of Colorado Boulder; Anna Towlson, Women's Library, London School of Economics; Marianne Hansen, Bryn Mawr College Special Collections; Kelly Dyson and Chamisa Redmond, Library of Congress; Meaghan Alston, Moorland-Spingarn Research Center, Howard University, and Danielle Nista, Tamiment Library, New York University. Thanks also to the Association of African American Life and History for permission to use the photograph of Ida Gibbs Hunt in Madagascar and to Rahul Bhatia of the Wilson Center for helping scan Margot Badran's photo collection.

In writing this book, I have been incredibly fortunate to have at arm's reach four amazing scholars, knowledgeable about women's historical experience in different parts of the world and willing to provide ongoing and rapid feedback as I churned out chapters. I call this group my "brain trust," and I happily count these women as my colleagues and my friends. Serpil Atamaz, Paula Austin, Becky Kluchin, and Katerina Lagos shaped this project profoundly, saved me from making countless errors, and helped me write a book that speaks to the diversity of female experience. I am indebted to all of them. To Becky I add special thanks for the lunches, walks, soccer matches, baseball games, and everything else that has helped keep me sane and grounded while finishing this book.

From the day I first conceived it, I knew that I wanted to write a book that could appeal to the general public as well as to fellow historians. If I have come even remotely close to accomplishing this goal, it is due to the help of a group of friends who provided feedback on my manuscript and whom I came to think of as my "public trust." Tracy Wahl, Naomi Williams, Lori Ann Joseph, and Stacy Garfinkel brought to this project their collective experience as radio producers, novelists, lawyers, consultants, and, most of all, avid readers. They made sure that I worked hard not only to produce good history but also to craft a good story. I owe them all a debt of gratitude, most of all to Stacy, who read every chapter and has served as my sounding board from beginning to end. Finally, a special thank you to my friend Josephine Zhou, who not only translated Chinese sources for this book but also told me of her own feminist awakening as a young woman in China, inspired by her natal country's long history of strong, female warriors.

Back when I was in graduate school, my first advisor (whose son was a foreign correspondent for the *New York Times*) told me that when I was ready to publish a book, I should get a literary agent. "Academics are lousy at championing their own work," he insisted. He was right, and while it took me awhile to listen, I am glad I eventually did. A deep thank you to Sandy Dijkstra for believing in this project and most especially to Elise Capron for representing me so ably through thick and thin. I am happy the book has found its home at Columbia University Press, which is committed to publishing global histories that illuminate the pressing problems of our contemporary world, including those stemming from gender inequality. As an editor, Caelyn Cobb lent to this project wide-ranging knowledge of international history and women's studies, and I am very grateful for her critical eye. The students in my spring 2019 history graduate seminar were the first audience in the world to read the whole manuscript in order from beginning to end. It is my pleasure to thank Alexander Adiego, Kelly Cullity, Alex Dilley, Pete Eden, John Fedorko, Corinne Lethco, Terry Spring, and Mikaela Springer for their sage suggestions.

No one has been more supportive of this project and more willing to make sacrifices to see it through to its end than my family. With love and appreciation, it is my pleasure to acknowledge my parents and parents-in-law who didn't blink when I asked if they would be willing to provide me feedback on the manuscript and help me to write a book their friends might someday want to read. Bob and Myrna Siegel and Ron and Betty Ingram were my "family trust": usually the first readers to get back to me as I sent chapters out for feedback and always generous in their comments. It has been such a pleasure to include them in this project, and I hope they take pride in having shaped the book it has become.

I'm pretty sure that when Steven Ingram promised to love and cherish me two decades ago, he did not simultaneously promise to edit all my written work, but he may as well have for all that I have asked of him since. There is nobody whose opinion I value more than his. Our relationship continues to be a meeting of the minds as well as of the hearts. This book, like everything else in my life, is richer, wiser, funnier, and more human thanks to him. A final thanks goes to my children, Braeden and Amelie Ingram. During the time it took me to research and write this book, Braeden and Amelie both became young adults with probing, critical voices and imaginative literary styles of their own. To Braeden, who once offered to read a chapter that was causing me grief with an adolescent's discerning eye ("If you can get a teenager to care about your book, anyone will want to read it"), and to Amelie, who similarly volunteered her own suggestion when I was struggling with how to conclude chapter 3 ("The Egyptian women fought back and they were awesome. . . . mic drop"): this book is for you.

Abbreviations

ACW	Mary Church Terrell, *A Colored Woman in a White World*
BSH	Strachey Family Papers, Women's Library, London School of Economics, London
CCP	Carrie Chapman Catt Papers, Library of Congress, Washington, D.C., microfilm
FCB	Fonds Cécile Brunschvicg, Centre des archives du féminisme, Université d'Angers, Angers
FA	First Accession
FJB	Fonds Jeanne Bouvier, Bibliothèque historique de la Ville de Paris / fonds Bouglé, Paris
FJM	Fonds Jeanne Mélin, Bibliothèque historique de la Ville de Paris / fonds Bouglé, Paris
FO	Foreign Office Papers, National Archives of the United Kingdom, Kew
FRUS	U.S. Department of State, *Papers Relating to the Foreign Relations of the United States*, University of Wisconsin-Madison Digital Collections
HY	Huda Shaarawi, *Harem Years: The Memoirs of an Egyptian Feminist*
ICWP	International Council of Women Papers, Archive and Research Center for Women's History, Brussels
ILO	International Labor Organization

IWSA	International Woman Suffrage Alliance (1913–1920) Papers, Women's Suffrage Movement Archives, University of Manchester
KBFP	Kendrick-Brooks Family Papers, Library of Congress, Washington, D.C.
LOC	Library of Congress, Washington, D.C.
MCA	Margery Corbett Ashby Papers, Women's Library, London School of Economics, London
MCT/LOC	Mary Church Terrell Papers, Library of Congress, microfilm
MCT/MSRC	Mary Church Terrell Papers, Moorland-Spingarn Research Center, Howard University, Washington, D.C.
MGF	Millicent Garrett Fawcett Papers, Women's Library, London School of Economics, London
MM	Jeanne Bouvier, *Mes mémoires ou 59 années d'activité industrielle, sociale et intellectuelle d'une ouvrière, 1876–1935*
MRY	Wei Tao-ming, *My Revolutionary Years: The Autobiography of Madame Wei Tao Ming*
MSH	Mary Sheepshanks Papers, Women's Library, London School of Economics, London
NAACP	National Association for the Advancement of Colored People
NACW	National Association of Colored Women
NAWSA	National American Woman Suffrage Association
NWTULA	National Women's Trade Union League of America
PAT	Papiers André Tardieu, Ministère des Affaires Étrangères, Centre des archives diplomatiques, la Courneuve
RICW	*Report of the International Congress of Women, Zurich, May 12 to 17, 1919*
RSP	Rose Schneiderman Papers, Tamiment Library, New York University, microfilm
SA	Swarthmore Accession
WEBDB	W.E.B. Du Bois Papers, Special Collections and University Archives, University of Massachusetts Amherst Libraries, http://credo.library.umass.edu/view/collection/mums312
WHH	William Henry Hunt Papers, Moorland-Spingarn Research Center, Howard University, Washington, D.C.
WILPF	Women's International League for Peace and Freedom Records, Special Collections, University of Colorado Boulder Libraries

WSC	Women's Suffrage Collection, Manchester Central Library, Part 2, Papers of Millicent Garret Fawcett, Manchester, microfilm
WW	Mary Anderson, *Woman at Work: The Autobiography of Mary Anderson as Told to Mary N. Winslow*
WWP	Woodrow Wilson Papers, Library of Congress, Washington, D.C.

Notes

Prologue: The Closing Days of the First World War

1. Jacqueline Van Voris, *Carrie Chapman Catt: A Public Life* (New York: Feminist Press at the City University of New York, 1987), 150–52.
2. "Combined services": Catt to Fawcett, October 24, 1918. See also Catt to Fawcett, November 22, 1918; Fawcett to Catt, November 23, 1918; and "Minutes of the Headquarters Committee," December 14, 1918, all in Women's Suffrage Collection, Manchester Central Library, Part 2, Papers of Millicent Garret Fawcett, Manchester (hereafter WSC), M50/2/22, Reel 18. "Never": "Women at Peace Table," *New York Times*, November 19, 1918. See also "Women and the Peace Conference," *Common Cause*, December 20, 1918.
3. H. M. Swanwick, *I Have Been Young* (London: Victor Gollancz, 1935), 323.
4. I use the term *gender equality* throughout this book as a catchall phrase to encapsulate the varied demands for "sex equality," "women's rights," "women's awakening," "women's emancipation," and other such formulations that animated national and international women's movements of the early twentieth century. In its contemporary sense, gender equality refers to a state of being in which women and men are endowed with full legal personhood and enjoy equal rights and opportunities across all sectors of social, economic, cultural, and political life.
5. On the Wilsonian vision of peace, see Arthur Walworth, *Wilson and His Peacemakers: American Diplomacy at the Paris Peace Conference, 1919* (New York: Norton 1986); Erez Manela, *The Wilsonian Moment: Self-Determination and the*

International Origins of Colonial Nationalism (Oxford: Oxford University Press, 2007); and Carl Bouchard, *Cher Monsieur le Président: Quand les Français écrivait à Woodrow Wilson (1918–1919)* (Ceyzérieu: Champ Vallon, 2015). On the war's unleashing of new political vocabularies and moral expectations, see William Mulligan, *The Great War for Peace* (New Haven: Yale University Press, 2014).

6. Carrie Chapman Catt, "Woman Suffrage as a War Measure" (1918), unpublished speech, Carrie Chapman Catt Papers, Library of Congress, Washington, D.C. (hereafter CCP), Reel 7.

7. "Strong and beautiful words": Union française pour le suffrage des femmes to President Woodrow Wilson, February 1, 1919, Fonds Cécile Brunschwicg, Centre des archives du féminisme, Université d'Angers, Angers (hereafter FCB), 1AF163. On Wilson's response, see "Wilson Spurs Fight for Women's Vote," *New York Times*, June 14, 1918. For Schlumberger's letter to Wilson after the war ended, see Witt-Schlumberger to Wilson, January 18, 1919, FCB 1AF164; and Woodrow Wilson Papers, Library of Congress, Washington, D.C. (hereafter WWP), Reel 390.

8. "Two Million Cheer Wilson," *New York Times*, December 15, 1918; and "The Arrival in Paris. Wonderful Welcome from the People," *Manchester Guardian*, December 15, 1918.

9. André Beaufre, *1940: The Fall of France* (New York: Knopf, 1968), 10–11.

10. Flora Annie Steel, "Woman Makes a New World," *Daily Mail*, November 12, 1918.

11. On India, see Sumita Mukherjee, *Indian Suffragettes: Female Identities and Transnational Networks* (New Delhi: Oxford University Press, 2018), 26–76. On Korea, see Insook Kwon, "'The New Women's Movement' in 1920s Korea: Rethinking the Relationship Between Imperialism and Women," in *Feminisms and Internationalisms*, ed. Mrinalini Sinha, Donna Guy, and Angela Woollacott (Oxford: Blackwell, 1999), 37–61; and Inyoung Kang, "Overlooked No More: Yu Gwan-sun, a Korean Independence Activist Who Defied Japanese Rule," *New York Times*, March 28, 2018, https://www.nytimes.com/2018/03/28 /obituaries/overlooked-yu-gwan-sun.html. On Syria, see Ellen L. Fleischmann, "The Other 'Awakening': The Emergence of Women's Movements in the Modern Middle East, 1900–1940," in *Globalizing Feminisms, 1789–1945*, ed. Karen Offen (New York: Routledge, 2010), 170–92. On Japan, see Barbara Maloney, "Women's Rights, Feminism, and Suffragism in Japan, 1870–1925," in *Globalizing Feminisms, 1789–1945*, ed. Karen Offen (New York: Routledge, 2010), 51–62.

12. UN Women, "Women, Peace, and Security Experts Look Ahead to 2020," March 18, 2019, http://www.unwomen.org/en/news/stories/2019/3/news -women-peace-and-security-experts-look-ahead-to-2020. See also J. Ann Tickner and Jacqui True, "A Century of International Relations Feminism:

From World War I Women's Peace Pragmatism to the Women, Peace and Security Age," *International Studies Quarterly* 62 (2018): 221–33; and Swanee Hunt and Cristina Posa, "Women Waging Peace," *Foreign Policy*, no. 124 (May–June 2001): 38–47. UN Security Council Resolution 1325, adopted in October 2000, specifically calls for members states in the United Nations and the UN secretary-general to expand the role of women in peace negotiations and conflict resolution and to incorporate gender perspectives into peacekeeping operations. See https://www.un.org/womenwatch/osagi/wps/#resolution.

13. While I use the term *global feminism* in the singular to describe the common struggle for female emancipation around the globe, I deliberately frame the manifestations of this struggle in the plural, in recognition of the multiple and conflicting priorities that national, international, and transnational feminist movements have developed in pursuit of this shared goal. While a predominantly Euro-American international feminist movement had already taken hold decades earlier, and while a small number of women from other parts of the world had begun to organize and to demonstrate in the decade leading up to World War I, only after 1919 would international and transnational women's rights campaigns truly become global. The terms *feminism* and *feminist*, which I use to describe many women and movements, were already widely used in France by the 1890s and increasingly used in England and the United States by the 1910s. Equivalent terms (*nisa'ilyah* in Egypt, *nüquan yundong* in China, *feminismo* in Latin America) began to appear more frequently in other languages and cultures between 1919 and the mid-1920s. On the early origins of international feminist organizations, see Leila J. Rupp, *Worlds of Women: The Making of an International Women's Movement* (Princeton, N.J.: Princeton University Press, 1997). On early socialist-inspired feminist organization, see Ellen Carol Dubois, "Woman Suffrage around the World: Three Phases of Suffragist Internationalism," in *Suffrage and Beyond: International Feminist Perspectives*, ed. Caroline Daley and Melanie Nolan (New York: New York University Press, 1994), 252–76; and Richard J. Evans, *Comrades and Sisters: Feminism, Socialism, and Pacifism in Europe, 1870–1945* (New York: St. Martin's Press, 1987). On Indian, Chinese, and Latin American feminism and suffragism between 1910 and 1919, see Mukherjee, *Indian Suffragettes*, 28–51; Louise Edwards, *Gender, Politics, and Democracy: Women's Suffrage in China* (Stanford, Calif.: Stanford University Press, 2008), 65–102; and Katherine M. Marino, *Feminism for the Americas: The Making of an International Human Rights Movement* (Chapel Hill: University of North Carolina Press, 2019), 14–19. On the adoption of the terms feminist and feminism across the world, see Karen Offen, "On the French Origin of the Words 'Feminism' and 'Feminist,'" *Feminist Issues* 8, no. 2 (Fall 1988): 45–51; Karen Offen, "Defining Feminism: A Comparative Historical Approach," *Signs: Journal of Women in Culture and Society*, 14, no. 1 (Autumn 1988): 119–57;

Nancy F. Cott, *The Grounding of Modern Feminism* (New Haven, Conn.: Yale University Press, 1987), 13–16; Margot Badran, *Feminists, Islam, and Nation: Gender and the Making of Modern Egypt* (Princeton, N.J.: Princeton University Press, 1995), 19; Christina Kelley Gilmartin, *Engendering the Chinese Revolution: Radical Women, Communist Politics, and Mass Movements in the 1920s* (Berkeley: University of California Press, 1995), 7–8; and Marino, *Feminism for the Americas*, 4.

14. On Paris's unique role as a breeding ground for dissident ideologies after World War I, see Jennifer Anne Boittin, *Colonial Metropolis: The Urban Grounds of Anti-Imperialism and Feminism in Interwar Paris* (Lincoln: University of Nebraska Press, 2010); and Michael Goebel, *Anti-Imperial Metropolis: Interwar Paris and the Seeds of Third World Nationalism* (Cambridge: Cambridge University Press, 2015).

1. A New Year in Paris: Women's Rights at the Peace Conference of 1919

1. All quotes from this letter are drawn from Marguerite de Witt Schlumberger to the Honorable Woodrow Wilson, January 18, 1919, Woodrow Wilson Papers, Library of Congress, Washington, D.C. (hereafter WWP), Series 5, Sub-Series B, Reel 390. My thanks to Carl Bouchard for sharing this and other letters from this collection.

2. On French letters to Wilson, see Carl Bouchard, *Cher Monsieur le Président: Quand les Français écrivaient à Woodrow Wilson (1918–1919)* (Ceyzérieu: Champ Vallon, 2015), 156–201.

3. Schlumberger to Wilson, July 13, 1918, Fonds Cécile Brunschvicg, Centre des archives du féminisme, Université d'Angers, Angers (hereafter FCB), 1AF163; and Gilbert F. Close, confidential secretary to the president, to Madame Schlumberger, January 24, 1919, FCB, 1AF164.

4. *En mémoire de Madame de Witt-Schlumberger* (n.p., [1925]); and "Who's Who," *Congresso internazionale femminile*, Rome, May 16–23, 1914, 50–51.

5. Quoted by Cécile Brunschvicg in *En mémoire de Madame de Witt-Schlumberger*, 25–26.

6. Leila J. Rupp, *Worlds of Women: The Making of an International Women's Movement* (Princeton, N.J.: Princeton University Press, 1997), 16; and David Rubinstein, *A Different World for Women: The Life of Millicent Garrett Fawcett* (New York: Harvester Wheatsheaf, 1991).

7. On suffragettes in Great Britain, see Susan Kingsley Kent, *Sex and Suffrage in Britain, 1860–1914* (Princeton, N.J.: Princeton University Press, 1987), 184–219. On suffragettes in America, see Jean H. Baker, *Sisters: The Lives of America's*

Suffragists (New York: Hill and Wang, 2005), 183–223; and Nancy F. Cott, *The Grounding of Modern Feminism* (New Haven, Conn.: Yale University Press, 1987), 51–81.

8. Laurence Klejman and Florence Rochefort, *L'égalité en marche: Le féminisme sous la Troisième République* (Paris: Presses de la Fondation nationale des sciences politiques, 1989), 286.

9. Marguerite de Witt Schlumberger, "French Suffragists and the War," *Jus Suffragii*, September 1914, 161. On French women during World War I, see Françoise Thébaud, *La femme au temps de la guerre de 14* (Paris: Stock/Laurence Pernaud, 1986); and Susan R. Grayzel, *Women's Identities at War: Gender, Motherhood, and Politics in Britain and France During the First World War* (Chapel Hill: University of North Carolina Press, 1999).

10. On Schlumberger's pronatalism, see Christine Bard, *Les filles de Marianne: Histoire des féminismes 1914–1940* (Paris: Fayard, 1995), 65.

11. On feminism and maternalism, see Karen Offen, *European Feminisms, 1700–1950: A Political History* (Stanford, Calif.: Stanford University Press, 2000), 20–26; and Rupp, *Worlds of Women*, 85. On the use of the term "feminism" in the United States, see Cott, *The Grounding of Modern Feminism*, 13–50.

12. Eleanor Flexnor and Ellen Fitzpatrick, *Century of Struggle: The Woman's Rights Movement in the United States* (Cambridge, Mass.: Harvard University Press, 1975), 269–85.

13. "President Puts Suffrage to Fore," *New York Times*, October 26, 1917.

14. Union française du suffrage des femmes and Allied Women to President Wilson, February 1, 1918, FCB, 1AF163. British suffragists advised Schlumberger on the wording of this letter.

15. "Greatest of crimes": Ana de Castro Osorio to Schlumberger, December 5, 1917, FCB, 1AF163. On Schlumberger's appeal to Wilson, see Mona Siegel, "Courtiser Woodrow Wilson: l'appel des féministes françaises pour le suffrage des femmes, 1917–1918," *Matériaux pour l'histoire de notre temps*, special no. 129–130, "Les peuples font la paix 1918-1923" (2018): 10–15.

16. "I have read": Woodrow Wilson to Carrie Chapman Catt, June 7, 1918, FCB, 1AF163. "All the papers": Schlumberger to Catt, July 12, 1918, FCB, 1AF163. See also "Wilson Spurs Fight for Women's Vote," *New York Times*, June 14, 1918.

17. "The President and the People," *Common Cause*, December 20, 1918, 1.

18. On Drexel's advice, see Constance Drexel, "French Suffragists Seek Out Wilson Just As They Do at Home," *Chicago Tribune*, Paris ed., January 21, 1919, clipping in FCB, 1AF163. On Brougham's advice, see Schlumberger to Fawcett, January 11, 1919, Millicent Garrett Fawcett Papers, Women's Library, London School of Economics, London (hereafter MGF), 7MGF/A/1/177; and H. Bruce Brougham to Fawcett, January 14, 1919, FCB, 1AF164.

19. Stri Mitra [Valentine Thomson], "Le Président Wilson et les femmes françaises," *La Vie Féminine*, February 15, 1919, 1283. Quotes that follow are drawn from this source. On Thomson, see Bard, *Les filles de Marianne*, 72. On Avril de Saint Croix, see Karen Offen, "'La plus grande féministe de France': Pourquoi a-t-on oublié l'inoubliable féministe internationale française Ghénia Avril de Sainte-Croix?," in *Les Féministes de la première vague*, ed. Christine Bard (Rennes: Presses universitaires de Rennes, 2015), 181–94.

20. In addition to the long report in *La Vie Féminine*, see "Les délégués du travail féminine chez le Président Wilson," *Le Petite Parisien*, January 26, 1919; and "Les femmes françaises chez le Président Wilson," *Le Temps*, January 27, 1919.

21. On the language of supplication in letters to Wilson, see Bouchard, *Cher Monsieur le Président*, 168–74.

22. Woodrow Wilson, "Remarks to the Delegation of Working Women of France in Paris," January 25, 1919. See Gerhard Peters and John T. Woolley, *The American Presidency Project*, https://www.presidency.ucsb.edu/documents/remarks-the-delegation-working-women-france-paris.

23. Minutes, Inter-Allied Planning Committee, January 22, 1919, FCB, 1/AF/165.

24. Woodrow Wilson: "Remarks to the Delegation of Working Women of France in Paris," January 25, 1919. Wilson had also described the war as a "people's war" in his September 30, 1918, speech before the Senate in support of the woman suffrage amendment. After the war he began to speak of "a people's peace," including remarks to American soldiers on Christmas Day 1918. See Gerhard Peters and John T. Woolley, *The American Presidency Project*, https://www.presidency.ucsb.edu/documents/remarks-united-states-soldiers-humes-france.

25. Schlumberger's statement to Woodrow Wilson, January 27, 1919, WWP, Series 5, Sub-Series B, Reel 391. See also "Union française pour le suffrage des femmes: Réception d'une délégation par le Président Wilson," *La Française*, February 8, 1919.

26. Alice La Mazière, "Les femmes siègeront-elles à la conférence de la paix," *La Vie Féminine*, March 1, 1919, 1304; and typescript travel instructions, UFSF, n.d., FCB, 1/AF/164.

27. Delegates to the Inter-Allied Women's Conference were as follows: Marguerite de Witt Schumberger (France), Cécile Brunschvicg (France), Marguerite Pichon-Landry (France), Katharine Bement Davis (United States), Florence Jaffray Harriman (United States), Juliette Barrett Rublee (United States), Millicent Garrett Fawcett (Britain), Ray Strachey (Britain), Rosamond Smith (Britain), Margharita Ancona (Italy), Jane Brigode, (Belgium), Louise Van den Plas (Belgium), Marie Parent (Belgium), Miss Atkinson (New Zealand), and Nina Boyle (fraternal delegate representing South Africa). All the original

British delegates returned home at the end of February. In March they were replaced by Margery Corbett Ashby and Margery Fry. In the same month Lady Aberdeen of Scotland, president of the International Council of Women, affiliated her organization with the effort and joined in the lobbying. From France, in addition to the three official delegates, Suzanne Grinberg served as conference secretary and Louise Compain and Valentine Thomson participated as editor and translator. Ghénia Avril de Saint-Croix, head of the National Council of French Women, collaborated throughout. Many other prominent French feminists, including Maria Vérone, Gabrielle Duchêne, and Jeanne Bouvier, participated in some of the meetings and served on delegations to the peace conference commissions.

28. Fry to Mrs. Hubback, March 29, 1919, 7MGF/A/1/193.

29. Corbett Ashby to Fawcett, April 4, 1919, 7MGF/A/1/194. On the first-wave international women's movement, see Rupp, *Worlds of Women*, 51–81.

30. Catt to Fawcett, October 24, 1918, Women's Suffrage Collection, Manchester Central Library, Part 2, Papers of Millicent Garret Fawcett, Manchester (hereafter WSC), M50/2/22, Reel 18; "Message des suffragistes françaises, italiennes et belges à Mrs. Chapman Catt," February 15, 1919; and Schlumberger to Catt, February 1919, FCB, 1/AF/144.

31. Ray Strachey, "Paris," unpublished typescript [1919], Strachey Family Papers, Women's Library, London School of Economics, London (hereafter BSH), 7BSH/5/1/1/20.

32. On the description of the salon, see Suzanne Grinberg, "Les femmes et la conférence de la paix," *La Renaissance Politique, Littéraire, Economique*, March 29, 1919, 20. "February 10, 1919": La Mazière, "Les femmes siègeront-elles?," 1305.

33. Grinberg, "Les femmes et la conférence de la paix," 21; and La Mazière, "Les femmes siègeront-elles?," 1304–5.

34. Grinberg, "Les femmes et la conférence de la paix," 21.

35. Grinberg, "Les femmes et la conférence de la paix," 21. "The arbiter": Saint-Réal, "Les femmes à la conférence de la paix," *Le Gaulois*, February 11, 1919.

36. "La conférence des femmes suffragistes alliées," *La Française*, February 22, 1919, 1. "Delighted": Saint-Réal, "Les femmes à la conférence de la paix."

37. Grinberg, "Les femmes et la conférence de la paix," 22.

38. "Greek guardsman": "Women and the Peace Conference," *Manchester Guardian*, February 18, 1919. On the description of the meeting, see Grinberg, "La conférence des femmes suffragistes alliées," *La Française*, February 22, 1919, 1.

39. "Almost inevitably": "Visit to a Japanese Statesman," *Common Cause*, March 21, 1919, 599. "Young and cheerful": Grinberg, "Les femmes et la conférence de la paix," 22. For a full list of the statesmen who met with an Inter-Allied women's delegation, see "Inter-Allied Suffrage Conference," *Jus Suffragii*, April 1919, 89.

40. Grinberg, "Les femmes et la conférence de la paix," 21–22

41. "Approved fully": Manuscript letter, undated, signed "La Présidente de la délégation française," FCB, 1AF167. "People's Peace": "Conférence des femmes alliées, *La Française*, March 8, 1919, 1.

42. "Certain aspects": "The Permanent Commission," *Common Cause*, March 21, 1919, 1. On the question of atrocities, see John Horne and Alan Kramer, *German Atrocities, 1914: A History of Denial* (New Haven, Conn.: Yale University Press, 2002).

43. Various spellings of her name appear in contemporary and historical documents. In French her last name is generally rendered as Essayan.

44. Armenian International Women's Association, "Zabel Yessayan Project," http://aiwainternational.org/content.aspx?page_id=22&club_id=616355 &module_id=251966; and Arzu Öztürkmen, "The Women's Movement Under Ottoman and Republican Rule," *Journal of Women's History* 25, no. 4 (2013): 258. On the Armenians during World War I, see Michael A Reynolds, *Shattering Empires: The Clash and Collapse of the Ottoman and Russian Empires, 1908–1918* (Cambridge: Cambridge University Press, 2011), 142–65; and Donald E. Miller and Lourna Touryan Miller, *Survivors: An Oral History of the Armenian Genocide* (Berkeley: University of California Press, 1999).

45. Mrs. Zahel Essayan, "La libération des femmes et des infants non-Musulmans en Turquie," typed report, 8 pp., FCB, 1/AF/166.

46. The full name of the commission to which they appealed was the Commission on the Responsibility of the Authors of the War and on Enforcement of Penalties. For the petition, see "Conseil international des femmes, résolution adopté avec la Conférence des femmes suffragistes des pays alliés et des Etats-Unis," n.d., Papiers André Tardieu, Ministère des Affaires Étrangères, Centre des archives diplomatiques, la Courneuve (hereafter PAT), 166PAAP/462. On the refusal of the commission to act, see Grinberg, "Les femmes et la conférence de la paix (deuxième article)," 10. "Distress and suffering": Suzanne Grinberg, "La Conférence et les femmes suffragistes alliées," *La Française*, February 22, 1919, 1. "When he heard": Grinberg, "Women at the Peace Conference," *Jus Suffragii*, March 1919, 72. On Camdon's advice, see Fawcett, handwritten diary, February 15, 1919, 7MGF/A/1/175d.

47. On women's letters to the British delegation, see Foreign Office Papers, National Archives of the United Kingdom, Kew (hereafter FO) 608/181/6, FO 608/239/12, and FO 608/149/9. On women's letters to the French delegation, see PAT, 166PAP/462. On Lady Aberdeen's request and the Foreign Office response, see Lady Aberdeen to the British Secretariat, January 28, 1919, FO 608/149/9. On Lady Aberdeen, see Eliane Gubin et al. *Women Changing the World: A History of the International Council of Women 1888–1988*, trans. Tony Langham and Plym Peeters (Brussels: Éditions Racine, 2005).

48. U.S. Department of State, *Papers Relating to the Foreign Relations of the United States* (hereafter FRUS), *The Paris Peace Conference, 1919*, vol. 3 (Washington, D.C.: U.S. Government Printing Office, 1919), Council of Ten Minutes of Meetings January 12 to February 14, 1919, 1022–23, http://digital.library.wisc .edu/1711.dl/FRUS.FRUS1919Parisv03.

49. "Entirely sympathetic": Wilson to Fawcett, February 14, 1919, Autograph Letter Collection, Women's Library, GB 106 9/01/1161A–1161B, microform 6.1, box 2. On peace delegates' statements, see FRUS, *The Paris Peace Conference, 1919*, vol. 3, 1022–23.

50. "Offered the delegation" and "competing zealously": La Mazière, "Les femmes siègeront-elles," 1305. "Went one better": Fawcett to Catt, February 19, 1919, 7MGF/A/1/175e, box 1; "Clemenceau Supports Women's Suffrage," *Common Cause*, February 21, 1919, 539.

51. Notes recorded March 12, 1919, FO 608/149/9. See also FRUS, *The Paris Peace Conference, 1919*, vol. 4, Council of Ten: Minutes of Meetings February 15 to June 17, 326, http://digital.library.wsic.edu/1711.dl/FRUS.FRUS1919Parisv04; and Dutasta to Witt-Schlumberger, March 12, 1919, FCB 1AF167.

52. Grinberg, "Les femmes et la conférence de la paix (deuxième article)," 10.

53. "Women's hour": Constance Drexel, "Women Gain Victory at Paris Conference," *Los Angeles Times*, March 15, 1919. "Great feminist victory": "Les Démarches de la Conférence suffragiste interalliée," *La Française*, March 29, 1919, 1. "Statesmen from East and West": Mary Sheepshanks, "Features of the Month," *Jus Suffragii*, April 1919, 86.

54. On Gompers, see Maria Vérone, "Notre reception," *Le Droit des Femmes*, April 1919, 53–55; Andrée Viollis, "Conference Women," *Daily Mail*, March 19, 1919.

55. On Fawcett's optimism, see Fawcett to Catt, February 19, 1919, MGF/A/1/175e. "Tremendously glad": Corbett Ashby to her father, n.d. [March 1919], 7MCA/A/031, Box FL 477. "As to Paris": A. B. Ashby to Margery Corbett Ashby, March 11, 1919, 7MCA/A/030, Box FL 476. "*Agents de police*": Corbett Ashby to her mother, March 21, 1919, 7MCA/A/031. Margery Fry also represented Great Britain during the final weeks of the conference.

56. "Access to big folk": Corbett Ashby to her mother, March 21, 1919, 7MCA/A/031, Box FL 477. On her access, see "President's Report for Quinquennial Period, 1914–1920," *International Council of Women: Report on the Quinquennial Meeting, Kristiania, 1920* (Aberdeen, Scotland: Rosemont Press, [1920], 70, International Council of Women Papers, Archive and Research Center for Women's History, Brussels (hereafter ICWP). "Bossing the show": Fry to Hubback, March 29, 1919, 7MGF/A/1/193.

57. "Volunteered to propose": "President's Report for Quinquennial Period, 1914–1920," 70–71. "Accepted enthusiastically": Corbett Ashby to her mother, March 29, 1919, 7MCA/A/031. On the approval of Cecil's proposal, see Michel

Marbeau, "Les femmes et la Société des nations (1919–1945): Genève, la clé de l'équalité?," in *Femmes et relations internationales au XXe siècle*, ed. Jean-Marc Delaunay and Yves Denéchère (Paris: Presses Sorbonne nouvelle, 2006), 167.

58. "Strewn everywhere": Grinberg, "Les femmes et la conférence de la paix (deuxième article)," 11. "Curious scene" and "profoundly embarrassed": Corbett Ashby to Fawcett, April 13, 1919, 7MGF/A/1/197.

59. Corbett Ashby to Fawcett, April 13, 1919, 7MGF/1/1/197. The statesman was most likely Paul Hymans of Belgium. On Girard-Mangin, see Elisabeth Shipton, *Female Tommies: The Frontline Women of the First World War* (Stroud, Gloucestershire: History Press, 2017), 98–101.

60. "Speeches of the Members of the Women's Delegation to the League of Nations Commission," *Jus Suffragii*, May 1919, 105. "Offend plenipotentiaries": Grinberg, "Les femmes et la conférence de la paix (deuxième article)," 11.

61. M.-L. Puech, "Le Conseil international des femmes et la Conférence des femmes suffragistes reçues à la commission de la Société des nations," *La Française*, April 26, 1919, 1–2.

62. "France: The Inter-Allied Conference in Paris," *Jus Suffragii*, May 1919, 104–5. For further analysis of the Inter-Allied women's intervention in Paris, see Karen Offen, *Debating the Woman Question in the French Third Republic* (Cambridge: Cambridge University Press, 2018), 596–601.

63. Puech, "Le Conseil international des femmes," 1–2. "Don't you wish": Corbett Ashby to Fawcett, April 13, 1919, 7MGF/1/1/197.

64. Constance Drexel, "Women's Views Given League," *Los Angeles Times*, April 12, 1919; and "Women's Petitions to League Framers," *New York Times*, April 13, 1919.

65. "It is a step": "Inter-Allied Women's Conference in Paris," *Sydney Morning Herald*, May 23, 1919. "It is splendid": "Suffragists Hail News from Paris," *New York Times*, March 28, 1919. "February 10": Grinberg, "Les femmes et la conférence de la paix (deuxième article)," 12.

66. On women's demands for representation at the San Francisco Conference in 1945 following World War II, see Glenda Sluga, "'Spectacular Feminism': The International History of Feminism, World Citizenship, and Human Rights," in *Women's Activism: Global Perspectives from the 1890s to the Present*, ed. Francesca de Haan et al. (New York: Routledge, 2013), 44–58. On Latin American women's leadership in San Francisco in 1945, see Katherine M. Marino, *Feminism for the Americas: The Making of an International Human Rights Movement* (Chapel Hill: University of North Carolina Press, 2019), 198–224. On recent international relations theory calling for revisiting World War I feminist activism, see J. Ann Tickner and Jacqui True. "A Century of International Relations Feminism: From World War I Women's Peace Pragmatism to the Women, Peace and Security Age," *International Studies Quarterly* 62 (2018): 221–33.

67. On pan-American feminists' advocacy of an international Equal Rights Treaty, see Marino, *Feminism for the Americas.*

68. Maria Vérone, "Les femmes et la Ligue des nations," *Le Droit des Femmes,* May 1919, 71. On Crowdy's appointment, see Madeleine Herren, "Gender and International Relations Through the Lens of the League of Nations (1919–1945)," in *Women, Diplomacy, and International Politics Since 1500,* ed. Carolyn James and Glenda Sluga (London: Routledge, 2016), 182–201; and Susan Pedersen, *The Guardians: The League of Nations and the Crisis of Empire* (Oxford: Oxford University Press, 2015), 48. On Avril de Sainte-Croix, see Offen, "'La plus grande féministe de France,'" 190; and Gubin et al. *Women Changing the World,* 156–59. Uruguayan feminist Paulina Luisi would also play a role in the Advisory Committee on sex trafficking; see Marino, *Feminism for the Americas,* 39.

69. On Kollontai and female delegates, see Michael Marbeau, "Les femmes et la SDN (1919–1945): Genève, la clé de l'égalité?," in *Femmes et relations internationales au xxe siècle,* ed. Jean-Marc Delaunay and Yves Denéchère (Paris: Presses Sorbonne nouvelle, 2006), 163–86. On married women's citizenship, see Catherine Jacques, "Des lobbys féministes à la SDN: L'exemple des débats sur la nationalité de la femme mariée (1930–1935)," in *Femmes et relations internationales,* 267–77. On women's push for representation on the Mandate Commission, see Rupp, *Worlds of Women,* 151. On links between women's social activism at the League of Nations and human rights after 1945, see Laura Beers, "Advocating for a Feminist Internationalism between the Wars," in *Women, Diplomacy, and International Politics since 1500,* ed. Carolyn James and Glenda Sluga (London: Routledge, 2016), 214.

70. "Women and the League of Nations," *Common Cause,* May 2, 1919, 1.

71. Jane Brigode and Louise Van den Plas, "Belgium," *Jus Suffragii,* May 1919, 103. On Mussolini and suffrage, see Victoria De Grazia, *How Fascism Ruled Women: Italy, 1922–1945* (Berkeley: University of California Press, 1992), 36–37.

72. "Fierce hostility": Maria Vérone, "Le mouvement suffragiste au Sénat," *Le Droit des Femmes,* April 1919, 59–60. On French interwar suffrage campaigns, see Sian Reynolds, *France Between the Wars: Gender and Politics* (New York: Routledge, 1996), 204–21.

2. Winter of Our Discontent: Racial Justice in a New World Order

1. An organization called the International Committee of Women for Permanent Peace, created on a temporary basis during World War I, convened the Zurich Women's Congress in 1919. Delegates voted to establish this organization on a

permanent basis and to rename it the Women's International League for Peace and Freedom, as discussed in chapter 4. For clarity, in this chapter I refer to the organization solely by its permanent name, WILPF.

2. Alice Hamilton cited in Katherine Joslin, introduction to Jane Addams, *Peace and Bread in Time of War* (Urbana: University of Illinois Press, 2002), xxiii.

3. Mary Church Terrell, *A Colored Woman in a White World* (New York: Humanity Books, 2005) (hereafter *ACW*), 383. Whether to capitalize "black" and "white" is fraught with historical and sociological significance. I have chosen to render both terms as lowercase so as not to reify the categories that the women whose actions I am highlighting here were seeking to challenge.

4. Imanuel Geiss, *The Pan-African Movement: A History of Pan-Africanism in America, Europe, and Africa* (New York: Africana, 1974), 237.

5. W.E.B. Du Bois, "The Talented Tenth (1903)," in *Du Bois: Writings* (New York: Library of America, 1986), 842–61.

6. Terrell, *ACW*, 41.

7. Terrell, *ACW*, 49–80, 93; and Beverly Washington Jones, *Quest for Equality: The Life and Writings of Mary Eliza Church Terrell, 1863–1954* (New York: Carlson, 1990), 3–16.

8. Adele Logan Alexander, *Parallel Worlds: The Remarkable Gibbs-Hunts and the Enduring (In)Significance of Melanin* (Charlottesville: University of Virginia Press, 2010), 19–50. I am much indebted to Alexander's careful biographical work on Ida Gibbs Hunt.

9. Alexander, *Parallel Worlds*, 50–53.

10. Alexander, *Parallel Worlds*, 64.

11. "Should an Amendment to the Constitution Allowing Women to the Ballot Be Adopted?," handwritten manuscript [1879], Mary Church Terrell Papers, Library of Congress (hereafter MCT/LOC), Reel 20. In *ACW*, 180, Terrell says she wrote the essay as a freshman.

12. Terrell, *ACW*, 93.

13. Kevin K. Gaines, *Uplifting the Race: Black Leadership, Politics, and Culture in the Twentieth Century* (Chapel Hill: University of North Carolina Press, 1996).

14. Terrell, *ACW*, 127, 132; and Alison M. Parker, "What Was the Relationship Between Mary Church Terrell's International Experience and Her Work Against Racism in the United States?," *Women and Social Movements in the United States, 1600–2000* 16, no. 1 (March 2012).

15. Terrell, *ACW*, 195–227, 261–77.

16. Terrell, *ACW*, 180.

17. Eleanor Flexner and Ellen Fitzpatrick, *Century of Struggle: The Woman's Rights Movement in the United States* (Cambridge, Mass.: Harvard University Press, 1975), 70; Rosalyn Terborg-Penn, *African American Women in the Struggle for the Vote, 1850–1920* (Bloomington: Indiana University Press, 1998), 96, 108; and

David Levering Lewis, *W.E.B. Du Bois: Biography of a Race, 1858–1919* (New York: Henry Holt, 1993), 419.

18. Terrell, *ACW*, 243–44; and Brittany Cooper, *Beyond Respectability: The Intellectual Thought of Race Women* (Urbana: University of Illinois Press, 2017), 72–75.

19. Terrell, *ACW*, 190; and Gaines, *Uplifting the Race*, 25.

20. Alexander, *Parallel Worlds*, 81, 127.

21. Alexander, *Parallel Worlds*, 70.

22. Alexander, *Parallel Worlds*, 127–28.

23. Cited in Jacqueline Anne Rouse, "Out of the Shadows of Tuskegee: Margaret Murray Washington, Social Activism, and Race Vindication," *Journal of Negro History* 81, no. 1/4 (1996): 40.

24. Ida Gibbs Hunt, "Peace and Civilization: The Other Side of the Shield," undated manuscript [1907], William Henry Hunt Papers, Moorland-Spingarn Research Center, Howard University, Washington, D.C. (hereafter WHH), Box 4, Folder 76. Hunt's biographer, Adele Logan Alexander, dates this essay to 1919 owing to its reference to a "Peace Conference." Other elements of the essay suggest an earlier date, including references to the segregation of Japanese children in American schools in 1906–1907 and a specific reference to "The Hague Conference" at one point in the notes. On the 1907 Hague Conference, see Maartje Abbenhuis, *The Hague Conferences and International Politics, 1898–1915* (London: Bloomsbury Academic, 2019).

25. Ida Gibbs Hunt, "The Price of Peace," *Journal of Negro History* 23, no. 1 (January 1918): 81.

26. Alexander, *Parallel Worlds*, 138–52.

27. Alexander, *Parallel Worlds*, 150–51; and Lewis, *W.E.B. Du Bois*, 568.

28. Several pamphlets from the Union française pour le suffrage des femmes (UFSF) from 1911 to 1914, including the one with Hunt's handwritten notes, can be found in WHH, Box 3, Folder 60.

29. Hunt to Terrell, April 20, 1915, MCT/LOC, Reel 4; and La Croix-rouge française to Hunt, October 12, 1914, WHH, Box 3, Folder 60.

30. Hunt, "To Belgium" [1914], Kendrick-Brooks Family Papers, Library of Congress, Washington, D.C. (hereafter KBFP), Box 13, Folder 8; and Hunt to Terrell, April 20, 1915, MCT/LOC, Reel 4.

31. Richard S. Fogarty, *Race and War in France: Colonial Subjects in the French Army, 1914–1918* (Baltimore: Johns Hopkins University Press, 2008), 8, 25.

32. Bill Harris, *The Hellfighters of Harlem: African-American Soldiers Who Fought for the Right to Fight for Their Country* (New York: Carroll & Graf, 2002), 11–43.

33. Mark Whalan, *The Great War and the Culture of the New Negro* (Gainesville: University Press of Florida, 2008), 6, 17, 110; and Alexander, *Parallel Worlds*, 169–71.

34. Lewis, *W.E.B. Du Bois*, 424; Gaines, *Uplifting the Race*, 215; and Terrell, *ACW*, 291.

35. Terrell, *ACW*, 291–300, 357–67.

36. Alice Post to Terrell, December 10, 1918, MCT/LOC, Reel 4.

37. Terrell, *ACW*, 369; and Leila J. Rupp, *Worlds of Women: The Making of an International Women's Movement* (Princeton, N.J.: Princeton University Press, 1997), 26–29.

38. Alice Post to Terrell, December 10, 1918; and unsigned letter to Jane Addams, April 3, 1919, MCT/LOC, Reel 4.

39. Alice Post to Terrell, March 25, 1919, MCT/LOC Reel 4; and Terrell passport issued 1919, MCT/LOC, Box 51.

40. "Editorial—Close Ranks," *Crisis*, July 1918, 111; Hunt to Du Bois, July 12, 1918, and Terrell to Du Bois, November 23, 1918, W.E.B. Du Bois Papers, Special Collections and University Archives, University of Massachusetts Amherst Libraries (hereafter WEBDB); and Lewis, *W.E.B. Du Bois*, 544.

41. Alexander, *Parallel Worlds*, 178.

42. Du Bois letter from Paris, December 1, 1918, *Crisis*, February 1919, 164; W.E.B. Du Bois, "French and Spanish," *Crisis*, April 1919, 269; Alexander, *Parallel Worlds*, 177; and Lewis, *W.E.B. Du Bois*, 565.

43. "The Denial of Passports," *Crisis*, March 1919, 237; and W.E.B. Du Bois, "Dusk of Dawn," in *Du Bois: Writings* (New York: Library of America, 1986), 745–46.

44. On Du Bois's descriptions of Diagne's help, see W.E.B. Du Bois, "My Mission," *Crisis*, May 1919, 8; and "Dusk of Dawn," 745. On Billy Hunt's friendship with Diagne, see Alexander, *Parallel Worlds*, 117. On Ida Gibbs Hunt's mediation between Diagne and Du Bois, see Hunt to Du Bois, August 28, 1921, WEBDB.

45. "Memorandum to M. Diagne and Others on a Pan-African Congress to Be Held in Paris in February, 1919," *Crisis*, March 1919, 224–25; "Dusk of Dawn," 746; Lewis, *W.E.B. Du Bois*, 568–69; and Alexander, *Parallel Worlds*, 178.

46. W.E.B. Du Bois, "The Pan African Congress," *Crisis*, April 1919, 271–74; Geiss, *The Pan-African Movement*, 234–40; and Clarence G. Contee, "Du Bois, the NAACP, and the Pan-African Congress of 1919," *Journal of Negro History* 57, no. 1 (1972): 13–28.

47. Addie W. Hunton and Kathryn M. Johnson, *Two Colored Women with the American Expeditionary Forces*, intro. Adele Logan Alexander (New York: Hall, 1997), xv–xxix, 8. On women's participation, see Du Bois, "The Pan African Congress," 273; "A Session of the Pan-African Congress, Paris, February 19–22, 1919," *Crisis*, May 1919, 32; and Alexander, *Parallel Worlds*, 183. Sixteen additional African American women were eventually recruited to come to France in 1918, but they arrived after the war had ended.

48. On Siegfried, see Du Bois, "The Pan African Congress," 273.

49. Du Bois to Hunt, April 17, 1919, WEBDB.

50. Terrell, *ACW*, 249, 379; W.E.B. Du Bois, "French and Spanish," *Crisis*, April 1919, 269; and Tyler Edward Stovall, *Paris Noir: African Americans in the City of Light* (Boston: Houghton Mifflin, 1996).

51. Terrell, *ACW*, 378–79.

52. Fogarty, *Race and War*, 270–74; and Alice L. Conklin. *A Mission to Civilize: The Republican Idea of Empire in France and West Africa, 1895–1930* (Stanford, Calif.: Stanford University Press, 1997), 142–73.

53. "To remove prejudice" cited in Reginald Kearney, "Japan: Ally in the Struggle Against Racism, 1919–1927," *Contributions in Black Studies* 12, no. 1, art. 14 (1994): 117, https://scholarworks.umass.edu/cibs/vol12/iss1/14. Thanks to Laurence Badel for bringing this essay to my attention. On Terrell's meeting Trotter in Paris, see Terrell, *ACW*, 381.

54. Terrell, *ACW*, 380. On the Australian prime minister, see Margaret MacMillan, *Paris 1919: Six Months That Changed the World* (New York: Random House, 2002), 319–20. It is not clear from Terrell's memoir if she met with Makino before or after the Zurich Congress.

55. Terrell, *ACW*, 384–85; and Addams, *Peace and Bread*, 88–89.

56. Terrell, *ACW*, 371.

57. Terrell, *ACW*, 371–72. Although Terrell was the only nonwhite delegate at the Zurich Congress, at least two other women of color, African American YMCA workers Addie Waites Hunton and Mary Talbert, also attended as observers. See Brandy Thomas Wells, "1919: The National Association of Colored Women, Mary B. Talbert, & France," paper presented to Annual Meeting of the American Historical Association, Chicago, January 6, 2019.

58. Terrell, *ACW*, 373.

59. "Resolution A VII.— Race Equality," *Report of the International Congress of Women, Zurich, May 12 to 17, 1919* (Geneva: Women's International League for Peace and Freedom, 1919), 110; and Terrell, *ACW*, 374.

60. Terrell, *ACW*, 374; and "Mary Church Terrell (U.S.A.)," *Report of the International Congress of Women, Zurich, May 12 to 17, 1919* (Geneva: Women's International League for Peace and Freedom, 1919), 212. On Terrell's rhetorical strategies, see Cooper, *Beyond Respectability*, 72–75.

61. "Mary Church Terrell (U.S.A.)," 212–17.

62. "Mary Church Terrell (U.S.A.)," 217; and Terrell, *ACW*, 376. On the controversy with Balch, see Terrell to Emily Balch, February 1, 1929, Mary Church Terrell Papers, Moorland Spingarn Research Center, Howard University, Washington, D.C. (hereafter MCT/MSRC), Box 1, Folder 22.

63. Terrell, *ACW*, 394–95.

64. Terrell, *ACW*, 386–87; Terrell to General Parker, May 25, 1919, MCT/LOC, Reel 4.

65. On the 1919 Pan-African resolutions, see Geiss, *The Pan African Movement*, 239. On article 22, see "Treaty of Peace with Germany (Treaty of Versailles)," Library of Congress, Washington, D.C. (hereafter LOC), https://www.loc.gov /law/help/us-treaties/bevans/m-ust000002-0043.pdf. "Great questions": "The Pan Africa Congress," *West Africa,* November 10, 1923, 1367.
66. Joan Quigley, *Just Another Southern Town: Mary Church Terrell and the Struggle for Racial Justice in the Nation's Capital* (Oxford: Oxford University Press, 2016), 87–88; Stovall, *Paris Noir,* 27–28; David F. Krugler, *1919, the Year of Racial Violence: How African Americans Fought Back* (Cambridge: Cambridge University Press, 2015); and Michael Schaeffer, "Lost Riot," *Washington City Paper,* April 3, 1998, http://www.washingtoncitypaper.com/news/article/13015176/lost-riot.
67. Terrell, "Black People and Arguments by Democrats in Favor of the League of Nations," Providence, R.I., October 26, 1920, MCT/LOC, Reel 21, included in Parker, "What Was the Relationship Between Mary Church Terrell's International Experience and Her Work Against Racism in the United States?."
68. Geiss, *The Pan-African Movement*, 258–62, 279–82.
69. Hunt to Du Bois, June 7, 1921, WEBDB.
70. Béton to Hunt, September 18, 1923, WEBDB.
71. On Terrell, see Quigley, *Just Another Southern Town*, 72. On Baker, see Barbara Ransby, *Ella Baker & the Black Freedom Movement: A Radical Democratic Vision* (Chapel Hill: University of North Carolina Press, 2003), 176.
72. "If I am to be ignored": Hunt to Du Bois, September 11, 1923; "I've worked hard": Hunt to Addie Waites Hunton, September 1927, both WEBDB.
73. Hunt, "New Sphere of Women" [1920], KBFP, Box 13, Folder 8; and Alexander, *Parallel Worlds*, 195.
74. On the WILPF's interracial organizing, see Melinda Plastas, *A Band of Noble Women: Racial Politics in the Women's Peace Movement* (Syracuse, N.Y.: Syracuse University Press, 2011), 34–83; and Joyce Blackwell, *No Peace Without Freedom: Race and the Women's International League for Peace and Freedom, 1915–1975* (Carbondale: Southern Illinois University Press, 2004), 7, 67. On the WILPF's anti-imperial activism, see Mona Siegel, "The Dangers of Feminism in Colonial Indochina," *French Historical Studies* 38, no. 4 (October 2015): 661–89.
75. "Coloured Troops in Europe," published by the Women's International League (May 1920), 6, 12, WILPF Swarthmore Accession, Box 33, Folder 10.
76. Terrell to Addams, March 18, 1921, MCT/LOC, Reel 5. On the "Black Horror" campaign, see Sally Marks, "Black Watch on the Rhine: A Study in Propaganda, Prejudice and Prurience," *European Studies Review* 13 (1983): 297–333; and Erika A. Kuhlman, *Reconstructing Patriarchy After the Great War: Women, Gender, and Postwar Reconciliation Between Nations* (New York: Palgrave Macmillan, 2008), 42–67.

77. "The papers over here": Hunt to Terrell, August 18, 1919, MCT/LOC, Reel 4. On her friend's lynching and her husband's reappointment, see Terrell, *ACW*, 140, 303. On the myth of the black rapist, see Elizabeth Gilmore, *Gender and Jim Crow: Women and the Politics of White Supremacy in North Carolina, 1896–1920* (Chapel Hill: University of North Carolina Press, 1996), 96.

78. Addams to Terrell, March 29, 1921, MCT/LOC, Reel 5. "Whose feelings have been wounded": "The WILPF Vienna Congress Resolution on Colonial Troops," in *Social Justice Feminists in the United States and Germany: A Dialogue in Documents, 1885–1933*, ed. Kathryn Kish Sklar, Anja Schüler, and Susan Strasser (Ithaca, N.Y.: Cornell University Press, 1998), 284–86.

79. Geiss, *The Pan-African Movement*, 282–93; and Lisa Materson, "African American Women's Global Journeys and the Construction of Cross-Ethnic Racial Identity," *Women's Studies International Forum* 32, no. 1 (January–February 2009): 35–42.

3. March(ing) in Cairo: Women's Awakening and the Egyptian Revolution of 1919

1. Afaf Lutfi al-Sayyid Marsot, "The Revolutionary Gentlewomen in Egypt," in *Women in the Muslim World*, ed. Lois Beck and Nikki Keddie (Cambridge, Mass.: Harvard University Press, 1978), 261–76. "Edith Cavell": Huda Shaarawi, *Harem Years: The Memoirs of an Egyptian Feminist, 1879–1924* (hereafter *HY*), trans. Margot Badran (London: Virago Press, 1986), 113. For the transliteration of Arabic names in this chapter, I have generally followed the conventions used in my English language sources.

2. Erez Manela, *The Wilsonian Moment: Self-Determination and the International Origins of Colonial Nationalism* (Oxford: Oxford University Press, 2007), 63–75.

3. On budding Ottoman Turkish feminist consciousness, see Serpil Atamaz-Hazar, "Reconstructing the History of the Constitutional Era in Ottoman Turkey Through Women's Periodicals," *Aspasia* 5 (2011): 92–111; and Serpil Atamaz, "Call to the Rescue: World War I Through the Eyes of Women," in *War and Collapse: World War I and the Ottoman State*, ed. Feroz Ahmad and Hakan Yavuz (Salt Lake City: University of Utah Press, 2016), 405–526.

4. Shaarawi, *HY*, 37.

5. Leila Ahmed, *Women and Gender in Islam: Historical Roots of a Modern Debate* (New Haven, Conn.: Yale University Press, 1992), 133–38; and Margot Badran, *Feminism in Islam* (Oxford: Oneworld, 2009), 19.

6. Shaarawi, *HY*, 39–42.

7. Shaarawi, *HY,* 52, 55.

8. Shaarawi, *HY,* 58. On the Khedival proposal, see Sania Sharawi Lanfranchi and John Keith King, *Casting Off the Veil: The Life of Huda Shaarawi, Egypt's First Feminist* (London: I. B. Tauris, 2012), 14–15.

9. Shaarawi, *HY,* 60.

10. Shaarawi, *HY,* 68–69; and Beth Baron, "Unveiling in Early Twentieth Century Egypt: Practical and Symbolic Considerations," *Middle Eastern Studies* 25, no. 3 (1989): 370–86.

11. Shaarawi, *HY,* 76–82; and Margot Badran, *Feminists, Islam, and Nation: Gender and the Making of Modern Egypt* (Princeton, N.J.: Princeton University Press, 1995), 37.

12. Beth Baron, *The Women's Awakening in Egypt: Culture, Society, and the Press* (New Haven, Conn.: Yale University Press, 1994), 13–37, 91–93.

13. Baron, *The Women's Awakening,* 103–67.

14. Qasim Amin, *The Liberation of Women and the New Woman: Two Documents in the History of Egyptian Feminism,* trans. Samiha Sidhom Peterson (Cairo: American University in Cairo Press, 2000), 8. On Amin's two texts, see Ahmed, *Women and Gender,* 138–40; and Badran, *Feminism in Islam,* 55–64.

15. Amin, *The Liberation of Women,* 72.

16. Amin, *The Liberation of Women,* 15, 35–61. See also Badran, *Feminism in Islam,* 21.

17. Qasim Amin, *Kitāb Taḥrīr Al-Marʾaï, Huṭbaï Bi-Qalam Hudá Šaʿrāwī* (Al-Qāhiraï Al-maktabaï al-šarqiyyaï, 1920), 193–96. Warm thanks to Marwa Helmy for translating Shaarawi's afterword from the Arabic. On the controversy surrounding Amin, see Ahmed, *Women and Gender,* 155–63; Thomas Philipp, "Feminism and Nationalist Politics in Egypt," in *Women in the Muslim World,* ed. Lois Beck and Nikki Keddie (Cambridge, Mass.: Harvard University Press, 1978), 278–80; Nadia Sonneveld, "From the Liberation of Women to the Liberation of Men? A Century of Family Law Reform in Egypt," *Gender & Religion* 7, no. 1 (2017): 88–104; and Sara Al-Qaiwani, "Nationalism, Revolution and Feminism: Women in Egypt and Iran from 1880–1980" (Doctoral thesis, London School of Economics, 2015), 76–77.

18. Badran, *Feminists, Islam, and Nation,* 52–53.

19. Bahithat al-Badiya, "A Lecture in the Club of the Umma Party (1909)," in *Opening the Gates: An Anthology of Arab Feminist Writing,* ed. Margot Badran and Miriam Cooke (Bloomington: Indiana University Press, 2004), 227–38. "Laden with": Bahithat al-Badiya cited in Ahmed, *Women and Gender,* 180. On Nasif, see also Badran, *Feminists, Islam, and Nation,* 54–55; and Hoda Yousef, "Malak Hifni Nasif: Negotiations of a Feminist Agenda Between the European and the Colonial," *Journal of Middle East Women's Studies* 7, no. 1 (2011): 70–89.

20. Badran, *Feminists, Islam, and Nation*, 55.
21. Lanfranchi, *Casting Off the Veil*, 29–39; and Shaarawi, *HY*, 83–84.
22. Shaarawi, *HY*, 84.
23. Shaarawi, *HY*, 101–2.
24. Shaarawi, *HY*, 102–6.
25. Shaarawi, *HY*, 107.
26. Lanfranchi, *Casting Off the Veil*, 53–57.
27. Shaarawi, *HY*, 111.
28. Cited in Manela, *The Wilsonian Moment*, 65–66.
29. *Les revendications nationales égyptiennes: Mémoire présenté à la conférence de la paix par la delegation égyptienne chargée de défendre la cause de l'indépendance de l'Égypte* (Paris: Impr. Lux. [1919]), 39–40), Afaf Lutfi al-Sayyid Marsot, *Egypt's Liberal Experiment, 1922–1936* (Berkeley: University of California Press, 1977), 45–50; and Manela, *The Wilsonian Moment*, 68–71.
30. Shaarawi, *HY*, 116.
31. Badran, *Feminists, Islam, and Nation*, 75.
32. Badran, *Feminists, Islam, and Nation*, 75. See also al-Sayyid Marsot, *Egypt's Liberal Experiment*, 51.
33. Nabila Ramdani, "Women and the 1919 Egyptian Revolution: From Feminist Awakening to Nationalist Political Activism," *Journal of International Women's Studies* 14, no. 2, (May 2013): 47. "In spite": Bahiga Arafa, *The Social Activities of the Egyptian Feminist Union* (Cairo: Elias Modern Press, 1954), 3.
34. "On the morning": Shaarawi, *HY*, 113. On Safiya Zaghlul, see Ramdani, "Women and the 1919 Egyptian Revolution," 47; and Al-Qaiwani, "Nationalism, Revolution, and Feminism," 125–29. "Crowds": cited in Yunan Labib Rizk, "Al-Ahram: A Diwan of Contemporary Life (275)," *Al-Ahram Weekly*, no. 420 (March 11–17, 1999), http://weekly.ahram.org.eg/Archive/1999/420/chrncls.htm.
35. Shaarawi, *HY*, 114–15.
36. Shaarawi, *HY*, 114–15.
37. "Discours pronounce par Madame Charoui Pacha au Club du Woman Party," *L'Egyptienne*, December 1925, 341.
38. Quotes cited in Rizk, "Al-Ahram (275)."
39. "To the United States Diplomatic Agent in Egypt, March 24, 1919," Records of the Department of State Relating to Internal Affairs of Egypt, 1910–1919, Reel 2, 883.00/135.
40. "Les incidents du Caire—La manifestation des dames indigènes," *Le Journal du Caire*, March 17, 1919. Emphasis added.
41. "The Procession That Never Came—Egyptian Women's March," *Egyptian Mail*, March 21, 1919.

42. Thomas Russell Pasha, *Egyptian Service, 1902–1946* (London: John Murray, 1949), 207–9. The account that follows is taken from this work.

43. Shaarawi, *HY*, 115.

44. Russell, *Egyptian Service*, 207–9.

45. Russell, *Egyptian Service*, 209.

46. Shaarawi, *HY*, 118; and Badran, *Feminists, Islam, and Nation*, 77.

47. "The British soldiers": al-Sayyid Marsot, "Revolutionary Gentlewomen," 271. On Shaarawi, schoolgirls, and Musa, see Badran, *Feminists, Islam, and Nation*, 77–78.

48. Shaarawi, *HY*, 118.

49. Manela, *The Wilsonian Moment*, 145–52.

50. *Discours prononcés au déjeuner offert par la délégation égyptienne le 2 août 1919* (Paris: Impr. de Becquet, [1919]), 10.

51. Victor Margueritte, *La Voix d'Egypte* (Paris: Plon-Nourrit, 1919), 13.

52. *Rapport présenté à la conférence de la paix sur la répression par les troupes britanniques du mouvement national égyptien au mois de mars 1919* (Paris: Impr. H. Richard, 1919), 11, 23, 26, 27, et al.

53. Ali Shaarawi's letter quoted in Jessie Fauset, "Nationalism and Egypt," *Crisis*, April 1920, 313.

54. Rizk, "Al-Ahram (275)." See also Badran, *Feminists, Islam, and Nation*, 51.

55. "The Egyptian Woman. Eulogy by Native Press," *Egyptian Mail*, March 21, 1919.

56. al-Sayyid Marsot, *Egypt's Liberal Experiment*, 52, 55; and Manela, *The Wilsonian Moment*, 156.

57. "Elite women": cited in Yunan Labib Rizk, "Al-Ahram: A Diwan of Contemporary Life (331)—the Women Take the Cudgels," *Al-Ahram Weekly Online*, no. 475 (March 30–April 5, 2000), http://weekly.ahram.org.eg/Archive/2000/475/chrncls.htm. "Jumped on": Shaarawi, *HY*, 120; and Badran, *Feminists, Islam, and Nation*, 77–78.

58. See "L'Égypte et la Commission Milner," *Le Journal du Caire*, December 13, 1919; and "Les dames égyptiennes et la Commission Milner," *Le Journal du Caire*, December 17, 1919.

59. "Enthusiastic speeches": "Egyptian Ladies and the Boycott," *Egyptian Gazette*, December 19, 1919. "Breaking the nationalist boycott": al-Sayyid Marsot, "Revolutionary Gentlewomen," 271–72. "Powerful and effective": cited in Badran, *Feminists, Islam, and Nation*, 84.

60. Rizk, "Al-Ahram (331)"; and Shaarawi, *HY*, 120.

61. Shaarawi, *HY*, 122.

62. Shaarawi, *HY*, 125–27.

63. Shaarawi, *HY*, 129–30. See also Margot Badran, "Dual-Liberation: Feminism and Nationalism in Egypt, 1870s–1926," *Feminist Issues* 8, no. 1 (1988): 31.

64. Wafd Women's Central Committee communiqué and Thabet cited in Rizk, "Al-Ahram (331)." See also Badran, *Feminists, Islam, and Nation*, 86.

65. Amin, *Kitāb taḥrīr al-marʾaï, ḫuṭbaï bi-qalam Hudá Šaʿrāwī*, 193–96.

66. Céza Nabaraouy (Saiza Nabarawi), "L'évolution du féminisme en Égypt," *L'Égyptienne*, March 1925, 45; and Badran, *Feminists, Islam, and Nation*, 66, 91–108.

67. Badran, *Feminists, Islam, and Nation*, 128, 133, 143–52.

68. On the 1911 visit to Egypt, see Aletta H. Jacobs, *Memories: My Life as an International Leader in Health, Suffrage, and Peace*, ed. Harriet Feinberg, trans. Annie Wright (New York: City University of New York, 1996), 158; and Rupp, *Worlds of Women*, 76.

69. "In ancient days": "Address of the President, Carrie Chapman Catt, to the Ninth Congress of the International Woman Suffrage Alliance," *Report of the Ninth Congress, Rome, Italy, May 12th to 19th, 1923* (Dresden: B. G. Teubner, [1923]), 31. "Nothing" and quotes from *Il Girornale*: cited in Margot Badran and Lucia Sorbera, "In No Need of Protection," *Al-Ahram Weekly Online*, no. 648 (July 24–30, 2003), http://weekly.ahram.org.eg/Archive/2003/648/cu4 .htm. On the Egyptian delegation to the Rome Congress, see Yunan Labib Rizk, "A Diwan of Contemporary Life (337)—Egyptian Women Make Their Mark," *Al-Ahram Weekly Online*, no. 481 (May 11–17, 2000), http://weekly .ahram.org.eg/Archive/2000/481/chrncls.htm; and Lanfranchi, *Casting Off the Veil*, 95–97.

70. Badran, *Feminists, Islam, and Nation*, 108–10, 210.

71. "Specifically Eastern basis": cited in Charlotte Weber, "Nationalism and Feminism: The Eastern Women's Congresses of 1930 and 1932," *Journal of Middle East Women's Studies* 4, no 1, Special Issue: Early Twentieth-Century Middle Eastern Feminisms, Nationalisms, and Transnationalisms (Winter 2008): 83– 106. See also Badran, *Feminists, Islam, and Nation*, 236–46; Margot Badran, "Rosa Manus in Cairo, 1935, and Copenhagen, 1939: Encounters with Egyptians," in *Rosa Manus (1881–1942): The International Life and Legacy of a Jewish Dutch Feminism*, ed. Myriam Everard and Francisca de Haan (Boston: Brill, 2017), 184–206; and Charlotte Weber, "Unveiling Scheherazade: Feminist Orientalism in the International Alliance of Women, 1911–1950," *Feminist Studies* 27, no. 1 (Spring 2001), 125–57.

72. Fauset, "Nationalism and Egypt," 313; and Mademoiselle G. Charoni, "L'Évolution du féminisme en Egypte," *La Petite Tunisie*, February 10–15, 1935. See also Leila J. Rupp, "Challenging Imperialism in International Women's Organizations," *NWSA Journal* 8, no. 1 (1996): 8–27.

73. Lanfranchi, *Casting Off the Veil*, 98; Rizk, "Al-Ahram (337)"; and Shaarawi, *HY*, 7, 129. For a recent critique of Shaarawi's act of unveiling, see Ahmed, *Women and Gender*, 178.

4. Springtime in Zurich: Former Enemies in Pursuit of Peace and Freedom

1. "The Women's Congress at Zurich—Some Impressions (by a Delegate)," *Observer*, May 25, 1919, clipping in Fonds Jeanne Mélin, Bibliothèque historique de la Ville de Paris / fonds Bouglé, Paris (hereafter FJM), Box 32, Folder 2.

2. Louise W. Knight, *Jane Addams: Spirit in Action* (New York: Norton, 2010), 172.

3. "Jane Addams" cited in Knight, *Jane Addams*, 204. "Destroying": Jane Addams, *Peace and Bread in Time of War* (Urbana: University of Illinois Press, 2002), 80. See also Harriet Hyman Alonso, *Peace as a Women's Issue: A History of the U.S. Movement for World Peace and Women's Rights* (Syracuse, N.Y.: Syracuse University Press, 1993), 60–70.

4. "What a welcome": Addams, *Peace and Bread*, 91. "The women": cited in "'Women as Permanent Peacemakers: An Account by One of Them of the International Gathering in Switzerland Which Denounced the Allies' Treaty Terms," *New York Times*, June 22, 1919.

5. Laura Beers, "Advocating for a Feminist Internationalism between the Wars," in *Women, Diplomacy, and International Politics Since 1500*, ed. Carolyn James and Glenda Sluga (London: Routledge, 2016), 202–21; and Erika Kuhlman, "The 'Women's International League for Peace and Freedom' and Reconciliation after the Great War," in *The Women's Movement in Wartime: International Perspectives, 1914–1919*, ed. Alison S. Fell and Ingrid Sharp (New York: Palgrave Macmillan, 2007), 227–43.

6. Anne Wiltsher, *Most Dangerous Women: Feminist Peace Campaigners of the Great War* (London: Pandora Press, 1985), 48.

7. Jane Addams, *Twenty Years at Hull House* (New York: Bedford St. Martins, 1999), 18.

8. Knight, *Jane Addams*, 35–64.

9. Knight, *Jane Addams*, 82–83.

10. Knight, *Jane Addams*, 159–60.

11. Addams, *Peace and Bread*, 4–5.

12. "No responsibility" cited in Michael Kazin, *War Against War: The American Fight for Peace, 1914–1918* (New York: Simon & Schuster, 2017), 40.

13. "We demand" cited in Knight, *Jane Addams*, 196. See also Kazin, *War Against War*, 40–48; Alonso, *Peace as a Women's Issue*, 63–66; and David S. Patterson, *The Search for Negotiated Peace: Women's Activism and Citizen Diplomacy in World War I* (New York: Routledge, 2008), 45–48.

14. "Jacobs to Presidents and Officers of the Alliance, November 24, 1914," *Jus Suffragii*, December 1914, 200.

15. Aletta H. Jacobs, *Memories: My Life as an International Leader in Health, Suffrage, and Peace*, ed. Harriet Feinberg, trans. Annie Wright (New York: City University of New York, 1996), 83.

16. "Jacobs, *Memories*, 84. On the American delegation, see Alonso, *Peace as a Women's Issue*, 67–68.

17. Alice Boissevin to Mélin, March 18, 1915, FJM, Box 39, Folder 2. Delegate counts were as follows: Sweden (12), Norway (12), Italy (1), Hungary (9), Germany (28), Denmark (6), Canada (2), Belgium (5), Austria (6), Great Britain (3), United States (47), and Netherlands (1,000). On the French reaction to The Hague Congress, see Karen Offen, *Debating the Woman Question in the French Third Republic* (Cambridge: Cambridge University Press, 2018), 559–60.

18. *Jane Addams' Account of Her Interviews with the Foreign Ministers of Europe, Reprint of report, published in 'The Survey,' July 17, 1915* (London: Women's International League, [1915]), 6, Women's International League for Peace and Freedom Records, Special Collections, University of Colorado Boulder Libraries (hereafter WILPF), Swarthmore Accession (hereafter SA), IV-33-9. See also Addams, *Peace and Bread*, 10–11.

19. Gertrude Bussey and Margaret Tims, *Pioneers for Peace: Women's International League for Peace and Freedom, 1915–1965* (London: WILPF British Section, 1980), 19–22.

20. "Resolutions Adopted at the Congress at The Hague 1915" and "Evening Meetings—Jane Addams (U.S.A.)," *Report of the International Congress of Women, Zurich, May 12 to 17, 1919* (hereafter *RICW*) (Geneva: Women's International League for Peace and Freedom, [1919]), 196, 280–85; and Addams, *Peace and Bread*, 35. Many of the women's resolutions had been adapted from the union program of the British League for Democratic Control. See also Knight, *Jane Addams*, 222.

21. Richard Harding Davis, "An Insult to War," *New York Times*, July 13, 1915. "Peace prattlers" and "silly" cited in Knight, *Jane Addams*, 204.

22. Knight, *Jane Addams*, 218.

23. Jacobs, who was still arranging for a meeting at The Hague as late as March 25, 1919, was clearly frustrated at Addams's executive decision. See telegrams and letters in WILPF, First Accession (hereafter FA), I-1-4 and II-1-7.

24. "Women as 'Permanent Peacemakers,'" *New York Times*, June 22, 1919.

25. "This may seem": Constance Drexel, "Women Propose to Unscramble Eggs of Peace," *Chicago Tribune*, Paris ed., May 17, 1919, in WILPF/FA 1-14-16. "To expatriate": "Women as 'Permanent Peacemakers,'" *New York Times*, June 22, 1919.

26. "Women as 'Permanent Peacemakers,'" *New York Times*, June 22, 1919.

27. "Delegates": "Women as 'Permanent Peacemakers,'" *New York Times*, June 22, 1919. "We were given": Jacobs, *Memories*, 94. Official delegate counts in Zurich

were as follows: Australia (3), Austria (4), Denmark (6), Great Britain (26), France (4, but only 3 listed by name), Germany (25), Netherlands (5), Hungary (2), Ireland (3), Italy (1), Norway (6), Romania (1), Sweden (12), Switzerland (23), United States (27). See WILPF, News-Sheet, no. 1, Zurich, May 26, 1919, 1, in WILPF/SA III-16-3.

28. "Women Go Abroad to World Congress," *New York Times*, April 10, 1919. On the vote to declare war in 1916, see Kazin, *War Against War*, 183.

29. "Delightful": Alice Hamilton to Jessie Hamilton, May 15, 1919, in Barbara Sicherman, *Alice Hamilton: A Life in Letters* (Urbana: University of Illinois Press, 2003), 225. "Outside": Union mondiale de la femme, Compte rendu de la Conférence internationale des femmes à Zurich, [1919], WILPF/FA 1-13-7.

30. Marguerite Gobat, "Jane Addams," *Aujourd'hui*, June–July 1919, 80, in FJM, Box 24, Folder 1.

31. Addams, *Peace and Bread*, 90–91. "Best hotel": Constance Drexel, "Europe's Unrest Unbalances the Women Leaders," *Enquirer* (Buffalo, N.Y.), May 20, 1919, clipping in WILPF/SA III-16-1.

32. Bruno Cabanes, *The Great War and the Origins of Humanitarianism, 1918–1924* (Cambridge: Cambridge University Press, 2014), 189–247; and Maureen Healy, *Vienna and the Fall of the Habsburg Empire: Total War and Everyday Life in World War I* (Cambridge: Cambridge University Press, 2007).

33. "German Women's Appeal," *The Times*, November 16, 1919; "German Women's Guilt: Rebuke by Women of France," *The Times*, November 23, 1918; Millicent Garrett Fawcett, "The Blockade—To the editor of the Times," *The Times*, December 2, 1919, all in International Woman Suffrage Alliance (1913–1920) Papers, Women's Suffrage Movement Archives, University of Manchester (hereafter IWSA), 3/106. On the food blockade in Germany, see Belinda Davis, *Home Fires Burning: Food, Politics, and Everyday Life in World War I Berlin* (Chapel Hill: University of North Carolina Press, 2000).

34. "It was through hunger": Wiltsher, *Most Dangerous Women*, 209. "The Austrians say": Sicherman, *Alice Hamilton*, 227.

35. "I remember": Mary Chamberlain, "Close-Up of the German Delegates at Zurich," *New York Tribune*, June 22, 1919, clipping in WILPF/FA 1-14-4. The text of Leopoldine Kulke's speech, published in German in the official report of the Zurich Congress, can be found in English translation in WILPF/FA 1-13-8. Addams's comments on Kulke's death are in *Peace and Bread*, 91.

36. *RICW*, 63–66, 162, 241–42. On the blockade in the spring of 1919, see Margaret MacMillan, *Paris 1919: Six Months That Changed the World* (New York: Random House, 2002), 159–60.

37. "Women as 'Permanent Peacemakers,'" *New York Times*, June 22, 1919.

38. *RICW*, 61–62.

39. *RICW*, 62.

40. "The speakers" and "sacred precincts": Constance Drexel, "Blockade Cause of Famine Aver Women in Zurich, *Chicago Tribune*, Paris ed., May 14, 1919, clipping in WILPF/FA I-14-6.

41. MacMillan, *Paris 1919*, 85.

42. For the full text of the covenant and analysis of the League of Nations Commission's decisions, see Alan Sharp, *The Versailles Settlement: Peacemaking After the First World War, 1919–1923* (New York: Palgrave Macmillan, 2008), 42–80.

43. Constance Drexel, "Women Propose to Unscramble Eggs of Peace," *Chicago Tribune*, Paris, May 17, 1919, clipping in WILPF/FA I-14-16. "Best part": *RICW*, 54. "Boat": *Towards Peace and Freedom: The Women's International Congress, Zürich, May 12th to 17th, 1919*, August 1919, 8, WILPF/SA III-16-5.

44. *RICW*, 243–46.

45. *RICW*, 246–48.

46. *RICW*, 246–48.

47. "Universal Declaration of Human Rights," United Nations, illustrated ed., 2015, http://www.un.org/en/udhrbook/pdf/udhr_booklet_en_web.pdf.

48. *RICW*, 3.

49. Constance Drexel, "Here Is Place Where Germans Get Sympathy," *Chicago Tribune*, Paris, May 15, 1919, clipping n WILPF/FA I-14-6.

50. "There was a tendency": typescript memoir, "The Long Day Ended," 61, Mary Sheepshanks Papers, Women's Library, London School of Economics, London (hereafter MSH) 7MSH (FL 642). "To be quite honest": Sicherman, *Alice Hamilton*, 230

51. Two other French women, Andrée Jouve and Blanche Reverchon, arrived the day before, the former from near Grenoble and the latter from Paris.

52. Isabelle Vahé, "Jeanne Mélin (1877–1964): Un parcours singulier dans la mouvance féministe et pacifiste en France au xxe siècle" (Ph.D. thesis: Université de Paris, 2004), 223–28.

53. Mélin to "Very Dear Friend," August 11, 1915, FJM, Box 39, Folder 2.

54. "I particularly": Addams to Mélin, April 25, 1919; and Mélin to the Prefect of the Ardennes, May 6, 1919, both in FJM, Box 40, Folder 1. See also Vahé, "Jeanne Mélin," 319–20.

55. "The Women's Congress at Zurich. Some Impressions (by a Delegate)," *Observer*, May 25, 1919, clipping in FJM, Box 32, Folder 2.

56. "Me, a Frenchwoman": "Compte rendu de la conférence internationale des femmes à Zurich," WILPF/FA, I-13-7. "Everywhere": *RICW*, 155.

57. "A German woman": *RICW*, 154–55.

58. "Congrès international féministe," *Gazette de Lausanne*, May 27, 1919, clipping in WILPF/FA I-14-7. John Horne, "Démobolisations culturelles après la Grande guerre," *14–18 Aujourd'hui* (2002): 49–53.

59. "Did you protest": "The Women's Conference at Zurich: Reports of the Delegates," *Manchester Guardian*, May 27, 1919. See also Union mondiale de la femme, Compte rendu de la Conférence international des femmes à Zurich, [1919], 4–5, WILPF/FA 1-13-7; and "German Radical Women Organize for Peace," *Social Justice Feminists in the United States and Germany: A Dialogue in Documents, 1885–1933*, ed. Kathryn Kish Sklar, Anja Schüler, and Susan Strasser (Ithaca, N.Y.: Cornell University Press, 1998), 189–96; Anne-Marie Saint-Gille, "Les féministes allemandes actrices du pacifisme pendant la Première guerre mondiale," in *Le premier féminisme allemand (1848–1933): Un mouvement social de dimension internationale*, ed. Patrick Farges and Anne-Marie Saint-Gille (Villeneuve d'Ascq, France: Presses Universitaires du Septentrion, 2013), 63–76; and Regina Braker, "Bertha Von Suttner's Spiritual Daughters: The Feminist Pacifism of Anita Augspurg, Lida Gustava Heymann, and Helene Stöcker at the International Congress of Women at the Hague, 1915," *Women's Studies International Forum* 18, no. 2 (1995): 103–11.

60. Mélin to Mme. Brunschwicg, May 22, 1919, reprinted in *Women's International League Monthly News Sheet*, August 1919, 3, clipping in WILPF/SA VI-42-4.

61. Addams, *Peace and Bread*, 93. On the French WILPF, see Norman Ingram, *The Politics of Dissent: Pacifism in France, 1919–1939* (Oxford; Clarendon, 1991).

62. "Liveliest sympathy": *Towards Peace and Freedom*, 17, WILPF/SA III-16-5. "A long talk": "Deputation to Paris," *Women's International League Monthly News Sheet*, July 1919, 2. "They all received": Addams, *Peace and Bread*, 50.

63. Caricature on the back of the typescript report, "Congrés international de femmes, Zurich, 12–17 mai 1919," Papiers André Tardieu, Ministère des Affaires Étrangères, Centre des archives diplomatiques, la Courneuve (hereafter PAT), 166PAP/462. It seems likely the caricature is of Tardieu. The unknown artist could be peace delegate Léon Bourgeois, who was known for drawing caricatures of his colleagues in meetings.

64. "Women's Congress at Zurich," Lord Acton to Lord Curzon, May 27, 1919, Foreign Office Papers, National Archives of the United Kingdom, Kew (hereafter FO) 608/150/14.

65. Unsigned, typed letter and unsigned editorial, "The Women at Zurich," *Chicago Evening Post*, May 20, 1919, clipping in WILPF/FA 11-1-12. "Most Unjust Criticism," *Seattle Times*, May 22, 1919, clipping in WILPF/SA III-16-1.

66. "It may be presumed": "Lady Pacifists at Work," *Indianapolis Star*, May 21, 1919. "When, as a member": *Cincinnati Enquirer*, May 1919, 6. Both in WILPF/SA III-16-1.

67. "Lady Pacifists at Work," *Indianapolis Star*, May 21, 1919; and "The Women at Zurich," *Chicago Evening Post*, May 20, 1919. Both in WILPF/SA III-16-1.

68. "Mothers of the world" and "carnage": *RICW*, 155, 204. "Women are": Ingrid Sharp, "Blaming the Women: Women's 'Responsibility' for the First World

War," in *The Women's Movement in Wartime: International Perspectives, 1914–1919*, ed. Alison S. Fell and Ingrid Sharp (New York: Palgrave Macmillan, 2007), 76. On the Catch-22 of gendered rhetoric, see Erika A. Kuhlman, *Reconstructing Patriarchy After the Great War: Women, Gender, and Postwar Reconciliation Between Nations* (New York: Palgrave Macmillan, 2008).

69. Leila J. Rupp, *Worlds of Women: The Making of an International Women's Movement* (Princeton, N.J.: Princeton University Press, 1997), 29–33.

70. Jo Vellacott, "Feminism as If All People Mattered: Working to Remove the Causes of War, 1919–1929," *Contemporary European History* 10, no. 3 (November 2001): 382.

71. *RICW*, 195–97.

72. For Addams's speech, see *RICW*, 195–97. "The world": "Evening Meetings," *Towards Peace and Freedom*, 8, WILPF/SA III-16-5.

73. "Shipwreck": Addams, *Peace and Bread*, 95. "How monstrous": Balch to Addams, July 7, 1919, WILPF/FA II-1-12. On the rubber milk teats, see H. M. Swanwick, *I Have Been Young* (London: Victor Gollancz, 1935), 315. "I am, of course": Addams to Balch, WILPF/FA II-1-12. On Addams's postwar tour, see Knight, *Jane Addams*, 233. On the Save the Children Fund, see Cabanes, *The Great War*, 248–99.

74. "Moving skeletons": Addams, *Peace and Bread*, 96. "Join our voices": printed statement, "Addressed to President Wilson by a French Section of the Permanent International Committee of Women," WILPF/SA IV-31-11. On the 113,000 francs, see WILPF, "Report: Zurich 1919-Vienna 1921," 26, FJM, Box 23, Folder 2.

75. Völkerversöhnende Frauenarbeit, II. Teil, November 1918/December 1920, 20, WILPF/SA IV-32-6.

76. "There was only": Swanwick, *I Have Been Young*, 316. On the WILPF's policy work in the interwar decades, see Vellacott, "Feminism as If All People Mattered," 386–92; and Beers, "Advocating for a Feminist Internationalism Between the Wars," 202–21.

77. "Tracing and liberating": Joint Resolution of the International Council of Women, the International Woman Suffrage Alliance, and the Women's International League for Peace and Freedom, [1920], International Council of Women Papers, Archive and Research Center for Women's History, Brussels, file 938. "First and most comprehensive": Keith David Watenpaugh, "The League of Nations' Rescue of Armenian Genocide Survivors and the Making of Modern Humanitarianism, 1920–1927," *American Historical Review* 115, no. 5 (2010): 1323. On the WILPF disarmament campaign, see Bussey and Tims, *Pioneers for Peace*, 101–2; and Marie-Michèle Doucet, "Prise de parole au féminin: La paix et les relations internationales dans les revendications du mouvement de femmes pour la paix en France (1919–1934)" (Ph.D. diss., Université de Montréal, 2015), 204–25.

78. "Merciless": Press release, "Protest of Egyptian women against the merciless enforcement of British reprisals" [1921]; telegram to Jane Addams "on appeal of Egyptian women"; and "Le différend anglo-égyptien," *La Suisse*, December 12, 1921, all in WILPF/FA III-7-2. On *Occupied Haiti*, see Alonso, *Peace as a Women's Issue*, 114. On the 1927–1928 WILPF mission to Asia, see Mona Siegel, "The Dangers of Feminism in Colonial Indochina," *French Historical Studies* 38, no. 4 (October 2015): 661–89; Siegel, "Feminism, Pacifism and Political Violence in Europe and China in the Era of the World Wars," *Gender & History* 28, no. 3 (November 2016): 641–59; and Marie Sandell, *The Rise of Women's Transnational Activism: Identity and Sisterhood Between the World Wars* (London: I. B. Tauris, 2015), 151–60.

79. For a recent call to return to the WILPF's World War I peacemaking principles, see J. Ann Tickner and Jacqui True, "A Century of International Relations Feminism: From World War I Women's Peace Pragmatism to the Women, Peace and Security Age," *International Studies Quarterly* 62 (2018): 221–33.

5. May Flowers in China: The Feminist Origins of Chinese Nationalism

1. In the 1920s and 1930s Viollis would travel from Moscow to Tunis to Saigon, establishing herself as a pathbreaking war correspondent and investigative journalist. On her journalistic career, see Mary Lynn Stewart, *Gender, Generation, and Journalism in France* (Montreal: McGill-Queen's University Press, 2018), 97–120; and Alice-Anne Jeandel, *Andrée Viollis: Une femme grand reporter, une écriture de l'événement, 1927–1939* (Paris: L'Harmattan, 2006). Most of the Chinese proper names in this chapter are rendered using the modern pinyin system. I have made exceptions for spellings of names familiar to nonspecialists (such as Chiang Kai-shek). After she was married, Soumay Tcheng published under her married name Madame Wei Tao-ming (rendered in pinyin as Wei Daoming).

2. Andrée Viollis, "Miss Cheng of China, What Her Country Wants, a Vicious Advocate," *Daily Mail*, April 16, 1919. On Viollis's husband, see Anne Renoult, *Andrée Viollis: Une femme journaliste* (Angers: Presses de l'université d'Angers, 2004) 53.

3. "Cheng Yu-Hsiu," in *Biographical Dictionary of Republican China*, ed. Howard L. Boorman et al. (New York: Columbia University Press, 1967), 278; Tang Dongmei, *Chuan yue shi ji cang mang: Zheng Yuxiu zhuan* (Beijing: Zhongguo she hui chu ban she, 2003), 4 (many thanks to Josephine Zhou for assistance translating and interpreting this biography); and Wei Tao-ming, *My Revolutionary Years: The Autobiography of Madame Wei Tao Ming* (hereafter *MRY*) (New York:

Scribner's, 1943), 5. Tcheng published two earlier versions of her memoir: one in French and one in English, respectively, Soumé Tcheng and B. Van Vorst, *Souvenirs d'enfance et de révolution* (Paris: Payot, 1920); and B. Van Vorst, *A Girl from China (Soumay Tcheng)* (New York: Frederick A. Stokes, 1926). While I rely most heavily on the 1943 edition, as it provides the most detail on the period of 1919, I cross-reference all three in this chapter.

4. Wei, *MRY*, 10–11.

5. Van Vorst, *A Girl from China*, 6, 53–56.

6. Van Vorst, *A Girl from China*, 10; and Wei, *MRY*, 1–5.

7. On antifootbinding societies, see Wang Zheng, *Women in the Chinese Enlightenment: Oral and Textual Histories* (Berkeley: University of California Press, 1999), 37–38.

8. Wei, *MRY*, 15–20.

9. Wei, *MRY*, 23–29.

10. Wei, *MRY*, 55–62.

11. Louise Edwards, *Gender, Politics, and Democracy: Women's Suffrage in China* (Stanford, Calif: Stanford University Press, 2008), 31–64; Louise Edwards, *Women Warriors and Wartime Spies of China* (Cambridge: Cambridge University Press, 2016), 40–64; and Elisabeth Croll, *Feminism and Socialism in China* (New York: Schocken Books, 1980), 64.

12. Edwards, *Gender, Politics, and Democracy*, 84; Croll, *Feminism and Socialism*, 71; and Wang, *Women in the Chinese Enlightenment*, 180–81.

13. Wei, *MRY*, 78–82.

14. In the 1920 and 1926 versions of her memoir, Tcheng names Yuan Shikai as the intended victim of the attack rather than his minister of finance. Tcheng's "Dare-to-Die Unit" did plot a failed attack on Yuan Shikai a year earlier. It is possible that Bessie Van Vorst, who helped Tcheng write her life story in both French and English, confused the two events in the earlier versions of the memoir. Compare Tcheng and Van Vorst, *Souvenirs d'enfance*, 202–3; Van Vorst, *A Girl from China*, 187; and Wei, *MRY*, 85.

15. Wei, *MRY*, 97.

16. Tcheng refers to Li by his given name, Li Yuying. Wei, *MRY*, 103–4. On the Association for Frugal Study, see Paul Bailey, "The Chinese Work-Study Movement in France," *China Quarterly* 115 (1988): 1–19.

17. Van Vorst, *A Girl from China*, 229–30.

18. Wei, *MRY*, 104–6.

19. Wei, *MRY*, 108–9. On Chinese laborers, see Xu Guoqi, *China and the Great War: China's Pursuit of a New National Identity and Internationalization* (Cambridge: Cambridge University Press, 2005), 130.

20. According to Tcheng, Sun Yat-sen's close ally Lin Sen recommended appointing her to the delegation. Wei, *MRY*, 114. On the Chinese delegation, see

Immanuel C. Y. Hsü, *The Rise of Modern China*, 5th ed. (Oxford: Oxford University Press, 1995), 482–86; and Xu, *China and the Great War*, 244–47.

21. Wei, *MRY*, 115.

22. Xu, *China and the Great War*, 156–60, 245; Arthur Walworth, *Wilson and His Peacemakers: American Diplomacy at the Paris Peace Conference, 1919* (New York: Norton 1986), 359; Margaret MacMillan, *Paris 1919: Six Months That Changed the World* (New York: Random House, 2002), 331; and Erez Manela, *The Wilsonian Moment: Self-Determination and the International Origins of Colonial Nationalism* (Oxford: Oxford University Press, 2007), 99–103.

23. On Tcheng's arrival in North America, see "Woman Lawyer Arrives," *Evening Tribune* (San Diego), March 5, 1919; and "Chinese Woman at Peace Meeting for Associated Press," *Sacramento Union*, March 6, 1919. "I enjoyed myself": Wei, *MRY*, 115. "Vivacity of a Frenchwoman": "A Chinese Portia," *New York Times*, June 1, 1919; and Wei, *MRY*, 116.

24. "Mlle. E. Tcheng, féministe chinoise et francophile sincère est arrivé à Paris," *Excelsior*, April 7, 1919; and "Une jeune révolutionnaire chinoise à la Conférence de la paix," *Le Petit Parisien*, April 7, 1919.

25. Uppermost in her mind": "Chinese Woman in U.S. to Aid Countrymen," *Los Angeles Evening Herald,* December 3, 1919. "Gave up all idea": "Chinese Portia Indignant at Award," *Evening Tribune*, November 18, 1919.

26. Manela, *The Wilsonian Moment*, 178.

27. "Outside the voices of the people": Wei, *MRY*, 116. On Wilson and Shandong, see Manela, *The Wilsonian Moment*, 183; and MacMillan, *Paris 1919*, 319–20.

28. Chow Tse-tsung, *The May Fourth Movement: Intellectual Revolution in Modern China* (Cambridge, Mass.: Harvard University Press, 1960), 85; and Rana Mitter, *A Bitter Revolution: China's Struggle with the Modern World* (Oxford: Oxford University Press, 2005), 46–47.

29. Dewey cited in Chow, *The May Fourth Movement*, 102. On the May Fourth Incident, see Manela, *The Wilsonian Moment*, 187.

30. "Chinese Women Students," *North-China Herald*, June 7, 1919; "China and Kiaochau. Telegram to Paris," *Shanghai Times*, May 12, 1919; and Chow, *The May Fourth Movement*, 123, 258.

31. Wang, *Women in the Chinese Enlightenment*, 150–51, 266, 292–93.

32. "A well-known feminist": "Chinese to Appeal to American Senate," *New York Times*, May 11, 1919; and "Chinese to Ask America for Aid," *Los Angeles Times*, May 11, 1919. "Dark future": Tang, *Chuan yue shi ji cang mang*, 202.

33. Manela, *The Wilsonian Moment*, 193; and Ministères des affaires étrangères et la guerre, "La Chine et la traité de la paix," *Bulletin périodique de la presse chinoise du 15 mai au 15 juillet 1919*, no. 5 (September 3, 1919), 1.

34. Wei, *MRY*, 120.

35. Wei, *MRY*, 123. The incident is also described in Tang, *Chuan yue shi ji cang mang*, 203–4.

36. Wei, *MRY*, 124–25. On China's absence at Versailles, see Manela, *The Wilsonian Moment*, 193; and Xu, *China and the Great War*, 264.

37. Renoult, *Andrée Viollis*, 77.

38. "The Eve of June 28," in *The Wellington Koo Memoir* (Chinese Oral History Project Microfilm Publication, Columbia University), Reel 1; Shamrock, "Soumé Tcheng," *L'Instransigent*, July 23, 1920; and "New Chatelaine—Madame Wei, Wife of Envoy, Is Personality in Her Own Right," *Washington Post*, October 9, 1942.

39. Wei, *MRY*, 125.

40. Viollis, "Miss Cheng of China."

41. "Miss Soumy [*sic*] Tcheng," *New York Times*, December 14, 1919, photo section; and "Chinese Woman in U.S. to Aid Countrymen," *Los Angeles Evening Herald*, December 3, 1919.

42. "Representing": "Chinese Woman in U.S. to Aid Countrymen," *Los Angeles Evening Herald*, December 3, 1919. On Parisian papers, see "Une jeune révolutionnaire chinoise à la Conférence de la paix," *Le Petit Parisien*, April 7, 1919. On birth in 1896, see Wei, *MRY*, 3.

43. "Returned to the graceful gowns": "Diplomat's Wife: Modern Style," *Washington Post*, October 25, 1942. On Chinese modern women, see Louise Edwards, "Policing the Modern Woman in Republican China," *Modern China* 26, no. 2 (April 2000): 115–47; and Madeleine Y. Dong, "Who Is Afraid of the Chinese Modern Girl," in *The Modern Girl Around the World: Consumption, Modernity, and Globalization*, ed. Alys Eve Weinbaum et al. (Durham, N.C.: Duke University Press, 2008), 194–219.

44. "My clothes": Wei, *MRY*, 28–31. "Incarnates": "Souvenirs d'enfance et de révolution par Soumé Tcheng," *Le Figaro. Supplément littéraire du dimanche*, August 29, 1920; and Wei, *MRY*, 28–31.

45. On Mulan as role model, see Wang, *Women in the Chinese Enlightenment*, 20–21, 179, 225, 291, 347–51; and Edwards, *Women Warriors and Wartime Spies*, 27–28.

46. "Beautiful story": Tcheng and Van Vorst, *Souvenirs d'enfance*, 58, 207. "It is not a change": Viollis, "Miss Cheng of China."

47. Chinese historians disagree about how to periodize this movement. I adopt Wang Zheng's chronology here. Wang, *Women and the Chinese Enlightenment*, 9. Chow Tse-tsung's classic study argues for a narrower chronology of 1917 to 1921. Chow, *The May Fourth Movement*, 6.

48. Wang, *Women and the Chinese Enlightenment*, 10–13.

49. Jerome B. Grieder, *Hu Shih and the Chinese Renaissance; Liberalism in the Chinese Revolution, 1917–1937* (Cambridge, Mass.: Harvard University Press, 1970),

91; Yang Lianfen, "The Absence of Gender in May Fourth Narratives of Women's Emancipation: A Case Study on Hu Shi's *The Greatest Event in Life*," *New Zealand Journal of Asian Studies* 12, no. 1 (June 2010): 6–13.

50. Mao Zedong, "Concerning the Incident of Miss Zhao's Suicide," *Public Interest*, November 21, 1919, republished in *Women in Republican China: A Sourcebook*, ed. Hua R. Lan and Vanessa L. Fong (Armonk, N.Y.: M. E. Sharpe, 1999), 81.

51. Christina Kelley Gilmartin, *Engendering the Chinese Revolution: Radical Women, Communist Politics, and Mass Movements in the 1920s* (Berkeley: University of California Press, 1995), 27.

52. Wang, *Women in Chinese Enlightenment*, 160, 168. On United Women's Associations, see Edwards, *Gender, Politics, and Democracy*, 110–14.

53. Wei, *MRY*, 128–29.

54. Wei, *MRY*, 130.

55. "Une visite aux étudiantes chinoises à Paris," *Le Petit Parisien*, February 1, 1921; and Wei, *MRY*, 129–35.

56. "Dressed for the occasion": Wei, *MRY*, 139. "Cut in the latest": "Literary Gossip," *Los Angeles Times*, September 26, 1926. "The scene was historic": "A Girl from China," *Good Housekeeping*, November 1925, 14. On the reception in Indochina, see "La carrier de Mlle. Soume Tcheng," *L'Echo Annamite*, May 5, 1927; and "Le féminisme en Indochine," *L'Echo Annamite*, June 2, 1927. On Egyptian reaction, see "Mlle. Soumé Tcheng," *L'Egyptienne*, October 1927, hors-texte.

57. Soumé Tcheng, "Le mouvement constitutionnel en Chine. Étude de droit comparé" (Doctoral thesis, Faculté de droit de l'Université de Paris, 1925).

58. Van Vorst, *A Girl from China*, xi. On women workers in America, see Bessie Van Vorst and Marie Van Vorst, *The Woman Who Toils, Being the Experiences of Two Gentlewomen as Factory Girls* (Toronto: Morang, 1903). On Hugues le Roux, see Edward Berenson, *The Trial of Madame Caillaux* (Berkeley: University of California Press, 1992), 116–17.

59. Tcheng and Van Vorst, *Souvenirs d'enfance*, 61–65, 146.

60. Wei, *MRY*, 139, 147.

61. Mona Siegel, "Feminism, Pacifism, and Political Violence in Europe and China in the Era of the World Wars," *Gender & History* 28, no. 3 (November 2016): 641–59.

62. "Charming diplomat": Jacques Lefebvre, "La guerre du Chantoung," *L'Ouest-Éclair*, May 10, 1928; "Ultramodern": Le Petit Grégoire, "Sourires," *L'Ouest-Éclair*, January 31, 1928. On the Nationalist Party, see Edwards, *Gender, Politics, and Democracy*, 174.

63. Wei, *MRY*, 168.

64. Wei, *MRY*, 168–70; Edwards, *Gender, Politics, and Democracy*, 182–85; and Margaret Kuo, *Intolerable Cruelty: Marriage, Law, and Society in Early Twentieth-Century China* (Lanham, Md.: Rowman & Littlefield, 2012), esp. 12, 68, 145–46.

65. Cheng Yu-Hsiu," in *Biographical Dictionary of Republican China*, 278–80; and Wang, *Women and the Chinese Enlightenment,* 166, 186, 236–37, 328.

66. For Tcheng's biography, see Tang, *Chuan yue shi ji cang mang;* for her memoir, see Soumay Tcheng, *Mei gui yu qiang: Zheng Yuxiu zhu,* trans. Lai Tingting (Taibei shi: Ying shu Gaiman qun dao shang wang lu yu shu gu fen you xian gong si Taiwan fen gong si, 2013). The television documentary is "Jiànzhèng" 20180119 mínguó dà lǜshī (liù) chuánqí nǚ lǜshī—zhèngyùxiù | CCTV fǎzhi, https://youtu.be/uSFd-yP100g.

6. Autumn on the Potomac: Women Workers and the Quest for Social Justice

1. I borrow this use of the term "labor women" from Dorothy Sue Cobble, "'The Other ILO Founders': 1919 and Its Legacies," in *Women's ILO: Transnational Networks, Global Labour Standards, and Gender Equity, 1919 to Present,* ed. Eileen Boris, Dorothea Hoehtker, and Susan Zimmermann (Boston: Brill, 2018), 27. I am deeply indebted in this chapter to Cobble's careful research on the 1919 International Congress of Working Women.

2. On global parental leave standards in 2018, see Amy Raub et al., "Paid Parental Leave: A Detailed Look at Approaches Across OECD Countries," World Policy Analysis Center, 2018, https://www.worldpolicycenter.org/sites/default /files/WORLD%20Report%20-%20Parental%20Leave%20OECD%20 Country%20Approaches_0.pdf.

3. On female war work, see Laura Lee Downs, *Manufacturing Inequality: Gender Division in the French and British Metalworking Industries, 1914–1939* (Ithaca, N.Y.: Cornell University Press, 1995); Lynn Dumenil, *The Second Line of Defense: American Women and World War I* (Chapel Hill: University of North Carolina Press, 2017), chap. 4; and Susan R. Grayzel, *Women's Identities at War: Gender, Motherhood, and Politics in Britain and France During the First World War* (Chapel Hill: University of North Carolina Press, 1999), chap. 3.

4. Rose Schneiderman with Lucy Goldthwaite, *All for One* (New York: Paul S. Eriksson, 1967), 11–14.

5. Schneiderman, *All for One,* 20.

6. "Mother thought": Schneiderman, *All for One,* 34. On Schneiderman's union activism, see Alice Kessler-Harris, "Rose Schneiderman and the Limits of Women's Trade Unionism," in *Gendering Labor History* (Urbana: University of Illinois Press, 2007), 71–92.

7. Elizabeth Ann Payne, *Reform, Labor, and Feminism: Margaret Dreier Robins and the Women's Trade Union League* (Urbana: University of Illinois Press, 1988).

8. "I want you to know": Rose Schneiderman to Mrs. Raymond Robins, March 10, 1919, Rose Schneiderman Papers, Tamiment Library, New York University (hereafter RSP), Reel 113.

9. "Mademoiselle Bouvier—Ouvrière de l'aiguille, militante de la Bourse du Travail de Paris," *La Vague*, June 5, 1919.

10. Jeanne Bouvier, *Mes mémoires ou 59 années d'activité industrielle, sociale et intellectuelle d'une ouvrière, 1876–1935* (hereafter *MM*), ed. Daniel Armogathe (Paris: La Découverte/Maspero, 1983), 35–36.

11. Bouvier, *MM*, 52–57.

12. Bouvier, *MM*, 101, 111. On *La Fronde*, see Mary Louise Roberts, *Disruptive Acts: The New Woman in Fin-de-Siècle France* (Chicago: University of Chicago Press, 2002), 73–106.

13. On Duchêne, see Emmanuelle Carle, "Gabrielle Duchêne et la recherche d'une autre route," *Archives du féminisme* 7 (2004): 29–32; Emmanuelle Carle, "Women, Anti-Fascism and Peace in Interwar France: Gabrielle Duchêne's Itinerary," *French History* 18, no. 3 (September 2004): 291–314; Karen Offen, *Debating the Woman Question in the French Third Republic* (Cambridge: Cambridge University Press, 2018), 443–52; and Christine Bard, *Les filles de Marianne: Histoire des féminismes 1914–1940* (Paris: Fayard, 1995), 71–79.

14. Office français des intérêts féminins, "Charte Internationale de la Femme" [early 1919], Papiers André Tardieu, Ministère des Affaires Étrangères, Centre des archives diplomatiques, la Courneuve (hereafter PAT), 166PAP/462. In addition to Duchêne and Bouvier, Suzanne Duchêne and Valentine Thomson were signatories.

15. On the first delegation to Wilson, see Stri Mitra [Valentine Thomson], "Le Président Wilson et les femmes françaises," *La Vie Féminine*, February 15, 1919. A list of all the participants in the Inter-Allied Women's Conference labor subcommittee can be found in Comité féminin française du travail, *Charte internationale du travail* (Paris: Secrétariat du C.F.F.T, 1919), 3–4, https://archive.org/stream/charteinternatiooocomi#page/n1/mode/2up. For minutes from one of the committee's meetings, see "Compte rendu de la séance du 18 février," Fonds Cécile Brunschvicg, Centre des archives du féminisme, Université d'Angers, Angers (hereafter FCB), 1AF165.

16. Comité féminin française du travail, *Charte internationale du travail*, 7.

17. "Not equipped": Mary Anderson, *Woman at Work: The Autobiography of Mary Anderson as Told to Mary N. Winslow* (hereafter *WW*) (Minneapolis: University of Minnesota Press, 1951), 117. On the league's "working women's charter," see Dorothy Sue Cobble, "A 'Higher Standard of Life for the World': U.S. Labor Women's Reform, Internationalism, and the Legacies of 1919," *Journal of American History* (March 2014): 1059–60. On the lack of heat on the ship, see Anderson, *WW*, 118.

18. "Take part": Julie Siegfried to the President of the International Peace Conference, February 8, 1919, PAT, 166PAP/462. "Omission": telegram from Mary Macarthur to David Lloyd Georges, January 30, 1919, Foreign Office Papers, National Archives of the United Kingdom, Kew (hereafter FO) 608/239/12.

19. "State their case": U.S. Department of State, *Papers Relating to the Foreign Relations of the United States*, University of Wisconsin-Madison Digital Collections (hereafter FRUS), *The Paris Peace Conference, 1919*, vol. 4, The Council of Ten: Minutes of Meetings February 15 to June 17, 326. For the invitation, see Arthur Franklin to Marguerite de Witt Schlumberger, March 14, 1919, FCB 1AF172.

20. "About as attractive" and "perfectly charming": Margery Corbett Ashby to her father, [March 18, 1919], Margery Corbett Ashby Papers, Women's Library, London School of Economics, London (hereafter MCA), 7MCA/A/031, Box FL 477. Andrée Viollis, "Conference Women—No Night Work for Anyone," *Daily Mail*, March 19, 1919.

21. "Les femmes et la conférence de la paix," Union française pour le suffrage des femmes, *Bulletin annuel de la Fédération affilée à l'Alliance international* (Imprimerie A. Chiron, 1919), 14.

22. Cobble, "The Other ILO Founders," 33. At the International Labor Office, few women were hired above the secretarial level in the interwar decades. See Françoise Thébaud, "Les femmes au BIT: l'exemple de Marguerite Thibert," in *Femmes et relations internationales au XXe siècle*, ed. Jean-Marc Delaunay and Yves Denéchère (Paris: Presses Sorbonne nouvelle, 2006), 177–87.

23. "For the representation" cited in Cobble, "A 'Higher Standard," 1062. "Careful consideration": Anderson, *WW*, 121.

24. "Deputation to Paris," *Women's International League Monthly News Sheet*, July 1919, 2. See also "Women and the General Labour Conference," *Report of the International Congress of Women, Zurich, May 12 to 17, 1919* (Geneva: Women's International League for Peace and Freedom, [1919]), 248. Important groundwork was also laid by Britain's Margaret Bondfield, who met independently with George Barnes on March 11, 1919. See Carol Riegelman Lubin and Anne Winslow, *Social Justice for Women: The International Labor Organization and Women* (Durham, N.C.: Duke University Press, 1990), 21.

25. "We could not have gotten along": Anderson, *WW*, 123; *Charte internationale du travail*, 17–24; and Cobble, "The Other ILO Founders," 32.

26. "Dear American comrades": cited in Cobble, "The Other ILO Founders," 32. Jouhaux's toast is in Schneiderman, *All for One*, 134; and Anderson, *WW*, 123.

27. Lubin and Winslow, *Social Justice for Women*, 15–16.

28. "The establishment" and "why not": Schneiderman, *All for One*, 134. On Macarthur, see Lubin and Winslow, *Social Justice for Women*, 16.

29. "To assume responsibilities": The First International Congress for Working Women, Call, August 5, 1919, 7MGF/A/203. Cobble, "A Higher Standard," 1064–65.

30. M.G.B. (Bondfield), "Report of the International Women's and the Labour Conference," *Woman Worker* (February 1920): 1–2. See also Ulla Wikander, "Demands on the ILO by Internationally Organized Women in 1919," in *ILO Histories: Essays on the International Labour Organization and Its Impact on the World During the Twentieth Century*, ed. Jasmien van Daele (New York: Peter Lang, 2010), 78.

31. Margaret Dreier Robins to the Executive Board, July 30, 1919, RSP, Reel 114; Cobble, "The Other ILO Founders," 33; and Lara Vapnek, "The 1919 International Congress of Working Women: Transnational Debates on the 'Woman Worker,'" *Journal of Women's History* 25, no. 4 (spring 2013): 164. Gertrude Hanna of the *Allgemeiner Deutsche Gewerkschaftsbund* had been chosen to serve as female advisor to the ILO Conference, but the Germans learned belatedly that they could participate and were unable to secure passage in time. See Maud Swartz, circular letter to the delegates of the first International Congress of Working Women, June 1, 1920, 4–5, WILPF, First Accession, IV-6-10.

32. "Memorial to the National Women's Trade Union League of America, from Representative Negro Women of the United States," reproduced in "First International Conference of Working Women, National Museum, Washington, D.C., November Fourth, 1919, Afternoon Session, Sixth Day," 35–38, in *Women and Social Movements, International—1840 to Present*, ed. Kathryn Kish Sklar and Thomas Dublin (Alexandria, Va: Alexander Street Press, 2012). On the protest, see Vapnek, "The 1919 International Congress," 166. On the WTUL and black women workers, see Payne, *Reform, Labor, and Feminism*, 54; and Dumenil, *The Second Line of Defense*, 162–66.

33. Bouvier, *MM*, 124–26.

34. Bouvier, *MM*, 124–26.

35. "I was deeply moved": Bouvier, *MM*, 128. "Of course": "Mount Vernon," *Woman Worker* (February 1920): 4.

36. Anderson, *WW*, 125–26.

37. "Washington Labour Conference," *Jus Suffragii*, December 1919, 47. The final Women's Congress resolution was slightly less restrictive, requiring only government and labor to appoint a female delegate. National Women's Trade Union League of America (hereafter NWTULA), "Resolutions Adopted by First International Congress of Working Women, Washington, U.S.A., October 28 to November 6, 1919," 2, FJB, Box 23.

38. On the women who doubled as ILO advisors and Women's Congress delegates, see Cobble, "The Other ILO Founders," 38–39.

39. Mrs. Raymond Robins, "Address of Welcome," First International Congress of Working Women, in *Women and Social Movements, International*.

40. Rachel Fuchs, "The Right to Life: Paul Strauss and the Politics of Motherhood," and "France in Comparative Perspective," in *Gender and the Politics of Social Reform*, ed. Elinor Ann Accampo, Rachel Ginnis Fuchs and Mary Lynn Stewart (Baltimore: Johns Hopkins University Press, 1995), 82–105, 157–88; Alice Kessler-Harris, "Gendered Interventions: Exploring the Historical Roots of U.S. Social Policy," in *Gendering Labor History* (Urbana: University of Illinois Press, 2007), 208–21; and Grayzel, *Women's Identities at War*, 119.

41. On Mulon and Thuillier-Landry, see Bouvier, *MM*, 130.

42. "To my great joy": Bouvier, *MM*, 130. Thuillier-Landry's sister, Marguerite Pichon-Landry, held leadership positions in both the French Union for Women's Suffrage and the National Council for French Women. Kerstin Hesselgren wrote in her 1919 diary that Macarthur took the conference "like a storm." Cited in Cobble, "The Other ILO Founders," 40. On the Women's Congress's maternity resolution, see NWTULA, "Resolutions Adopted by First International Congress of Working Women," 4–5.

43. "Projet de convention pour la protection de la maternité, FJB, Box 23; Bouvier, *MM*, 245–245; and Vapnek, "The 1919 International Congress," 172.

44. Wikander, "Demands on the ILO," 86; and Cobble, "The Other ILO Founders," 41. For the ongoing pressure in the United States to adopt ILO maternity standards, see Dorothy Sue Cobble and Mona Siegel, "America Once Led the Push for Parental Rights. Now It Lags Behind," *Washington Post*, February 8, 1919, https://www.washingtonpost.com/outlook/2019/02/08/america-once -led-push-parental-rights-now-it-lagsbehind/?fbclid=IwAR3hiiUaoudLd UomQRKeZNnmLwxqEAH7ChNL9xQqgjEefb3myiee1WWshuB8&utm _term=.d9a989fda66b.

45. On night-work prohibitions in Europe, see Karen Offen, *European Feminisms, 1700–1950: A Political History* (Stanford, Calif.: Stanford University Press, 2000), 162. A second international convention adopted in 1906 prohibited the use of white phosphorous in matches.

46. "Weary" cited in Alice Kessler-Harris, "The Paradox of Motherhood: Night-Work Restrictions in the United States," in *Gendering Labor History* (Urbana: University of Illinois Press, 2007), 222–36.

47. "That protective measures": Maria Vérone, "À la conférence de la paix," *Le Droit des Femmes*, April 1919, 53–55. See also Wikander, "Demands on the ILO," 71; Offen, *Debating the Woman Question*, 230, 444; and Kessler Harris, "The Paradox of Motherhood," 234.

48. On the Swedish and Czech statements, see First International Conference of Working Women, National Museum, Washington, D.C., November Fourth,

1919, Afternoon Session, Sixth Day," 22, 26. Schneiderman cited in Vapnek, "The 1919 International Congress," 170. See also NWTULA, "Resolutions Adopted by First International Congress of Working Women," 6.

49. Dorothy Sue Cobble provides the most complete accounting of Tanaka Taka's role in the 1919 ILO Conference to date: Dorothy Sue Cobble, "Japan and the 1919 ILO Debates Over Rights, Representation and Global Labour Standards," in *The ILO from Geneva to the Pacific Rim: West Meets East*, ed. Jill M. Jenson and Nelson Lichtenstein (New York: Palgrave Macmillan, 2016), 55–79.

50. *The Kanegafuchi Spinning Company Limited: Its Constitution; How It Cares for Its Employees and Workers* (Osaka: Sanseisha, October, 1919), ii–iii, https://babel .hathitrust.org/cgi/pt?id=coo1.ark:/13960/t4cn7ps7g;view=1up;seq=1. For Mutō's statement before the commission, see "Commission du travail des femmes, Exposé de M. Muto, Délégué patronal, Japon," typescript, translation office of the ILO, FJB, Box 23. See also Cobble, "Japan," 55–56.

51. "Very bad conditions": Anderson, *WW*, 128. "Physically and mentally": cited in Cobble, "Japan," 57.

52. "Deranged": cited in Cobble, "Japan," 57. "Always together": Anderson, *WW*, 128.

53. Anderson, *WW*, 129; and Cobble, "Japan," 66–68.

54. International Labour Office, *The Labour Provisions of the Peace Treaties* (Geneva: 1920), 13, https://www.ilo.org/public/libdoc/ilo/1920/20B09_18_engl.pdf.

55. Bouvier, *MM*, 132–34.

56. ILO, *The Labour Provisions of the Peace Treaties*.

57. I am using here Dorothy Sue Cobble's formulation of "labor feminism." See Cobble, "The Other ILO Founders," 28. On the International Federation of Working Women and its relation to the international trade union movement, see Christine Bolt, *Sisterhood Questioned? Race, Class and Internationalism in the American and British Women's Movements, c. 1880s–1970s* (New York: Routledge, 2004), 116; Geert Van Goethem, "Protection ou égalité? Les femmes dans le mouvement syndical international (1919–1938)," in *Femmes et relations internationales au XXe siècle*, ed. Jean-Marc Delaunay and Yves Denéchère (Paris: Presses Sorbonne nouvelle, 2006), 287–90; and Cobble, "A Higher Standard," 1070.

58. Circular letter to the delegates of the first International Congress of Working Women, July 7, 1920, 4, FJB, Box 23.

59. Mary Sheepshanks, cited in Leila J. Rupp, *Worlds of Women: The Making of an International Women's Movement* (Princeton, N.J.: Princeton University Press, 1997), 144. On American hostility between labor feminists and equal rights feminists, see Nancy F. Cott, *The Grounding of Modern Feminism* (New Haven, Conn.: Yale University Press, 1987), 117–42; and Katherine M. Marino, *Feminism*

for the Americas: The Making of an International Human Rights Movement (Chapel Hill: University of North Carolina Press, 2019).

60. "Time": Bouvier, *MM*, 137. Alice Kessler-Harris, "Problems of Coalition Building: Women and Trade Unions in the 1920s," in *Gendering Labor History* (Urbana: University of Illinois Press, 2007), 52–70; Van Goethem, "Protection ou égalité," 290; Deborah Thom, "Gender and Work," in *Gender & the Great War*, ed. Susan Grayzel and Tammy M. Proctor (Oxford: Oxford University Press, 2017), 46–66.

61. Kessler-Harris, "Rose Schneiderman," 86.

62. Lubin and Winslow, *Social Justice for Women*, 40–45; Cobble, "The Other ILO Founders," 47; and Cobble, "A Higher Standard," 1082–83.

63. Lubin and Winslow, *Social Justice for Women*, 48; Cobble, "The Other ILO Founders," 48.

64. Japanese Worker Delegation to Bouvier, Geneva, November 4, 1921, FJB, Box 23; Bondfield to Bouvier, December 31, 1923, FJB, Box 17; Anderson to Bouvier, July 11, 1936, FJB, Box 17; Lublin and Winslow, *Social Justice for Women*, 33.

65. Bouvier, *MM*, 132–33.

66. "Where men": Bouvier, *MM*, 137 and 47. On Bouvier's dismissal from her leadership position in the CGT, see Secrétaire fédéral de la Fédération de l'habillement au Camarade Jouhaux, February 26, 1923, FJB, Box 17. Bouvier aired some of her grievances against Jouhaux in a letter dated October 21, 1923, which is printed in annex to her memoir, *MM*, 259–61. She also complained that after supporting a twelve-week maternity standard in Washington, Jouhaux and the French Confédération général du travail endorsed an eight-week standard in the union program. See Jeanne Bouvier, *Deux époques, deux hommes* (Paris: Éditions Radot, 1927), 164, 231.

67. International Labour Organization, "Gender Equality," https://www.ilo.org /global/topics/equality-and-discrimination/gender-equality/lang—en/index .htm. On women and the ILO from the 1920s through the 1980s, see Lubin and Winslow, *Social Justice for Women*. On women and trade unionism in the United States after World War II, see Dorothy Sue Cobble, *The Other Women's Movement: Workplace Justice and Social Rights in Modern America* (Princeton, N.J.: Princeton University Press, 2004).

Epilogue: Rome, 1923

1. "Rome," *Time*, May 19, 1923;, and Helen Fraser, "Forward," *Report of the Ninth Congress of the International Woman Suffrage Alliance, Rome, Italy, May 12th to 19th, 1923* (Dresden: B. G. Teubner, 1923), 24.

2. Rosa Manus to Clara Hyde, cited in Leila J. Rupp, *Worlds of Women: The Making of an International Women's Movement* (Princeton, N.J.: Princeton University Press, 1997), 194; and "After Mrs. Catt," *Time*, May 24, 1923.

3. On Corbett Ashby, see Johanna Alberti, *Beyond Suffrage: Feminists in War and Peace, 1914–28* (London: Macmillan, 1989).

4. Aleka Boutzouvi, "Theodoropoulou, Avra (Born Drakopoulou), 1880–1963," in *Biographical Dictionary of Women's Movements and Feminisms: Central, Eastern, and South Eastern Europe, 19th and 20th Centuries*, ed. Francesca de Haan, Krassimira Daskalova, and Anna Loutifi (New York: Central European University Press, 2005), 569–74; and Charlotte Weber, "Nationalism and Feminism: The Eastern Women's Congresses of 1930 and 1932," *Journal of Middle East Women's Studies* 4, no. 1, Special Issue: Early Twentieth-Century Middle Eastern Feminisms, Nationalisms, and Transnationalisms (Winter 2008): 83–106.

5. Cynthia Jeffress Little, "Moral Reform and Feminism: A Case Study," *Journal of Interamerican Studies and World Affairs* 17, no. 4, Special Issue: The Changing Role of Women in Latin America (November 1975): 386–97.

6. *Report of the Ninth Congress of the International Woman Suffrage Alliance*, 35–36; and Katherine M. Marino, *Feminism for the Americas: The Making of an International Human Rights Movement* (Chapel Hill: University of North Carolina Press, 2019), 14–25, 34–39.

7. Alice La Mazière, "Après le Congrès de Rome," *Journal des débats du dimanche*, June 3, 1923. On Lutz, see Marino, *Feminism for the Americas*, 198–224. Indian women had already participated in the Alliance's congress in Geneva in 1920, but in 1923 the Women's Indian Association became formally affiliated. Sumita Mukherjee, *Indian Suffragettes: Female Identities and Transnational Networks* (New Delhi: Oxford University Press, 2018), 121–30.

8. On Tcheng and the 1920 congress, see "Les femmes d'Orient et d'Extrême-Orient ont envoyé des délégués," *Le Matin*, June 13, 1920. On the November 1922 demonstration, see "Une manifestation internationale à la Sorbonne pour le suffrage des femmes," *Le Petit Parisien*, November 17, 1922.

9. "Promote the conception": *Report of the Ninth Congress of the International Woman Suffrage Alliance*, 6.

10. *Report of the Ninth Congress of the International Woman Suffrage Alliance*, 26.

11. La Mazière, "Après le Congrès."

12. To suffragists' disappointment, the Government of India Act of 1919 did not mandate female suffrage, leaving women's political rights to be determined at the provincial level. In British India, Madras (April 1921) and Bombay (July 1921) were the first to adopt women's suffrage on the same terms as men, including a steep property qualification. In the princely states, both Travancore (1920) and Jhalwar (1921) followed suit. Mukherjee, *Indian Suffragettes*, 26–76. On Turkey, see Arzu Öztürkmen, "The Women's Movement under Ottoman

and Republican Rule," *Journal of Women's History* 25, no. 4 (2013): 255–64. On Latin America, see Marino, *Feminism for the Americas*, 97. For a global overview of women's suffrage, see Jad Adams, *Women and the Vote: A World History* (Oxford: Oxford University Press, 2014).

13. Victoria de Grazia, *How Fascism Ruled Women: Italy, 1922–1945* (Berkeley: University of California Press, 1992), 36–37.

14. Figures are drawn from the UN Women website. On the number of female parliamentarians, see http://www.unwomen.org/en/what-we-do/economic-empowerment/facts-and-figures. On comparative figures on men's and women's wages, see http://www.unwomen.org/en/what-we-do/economic-empow erment/facts-and-figures. On child marriage, see http://www.unwomen.org /en/what-we-do/economic-empowerment/facts-and-figures. On women's participation in peace processes, see http://www.unwomen.org/en/what-we -do/economic-empowerment/facts-and-figures. "Progress": Bernard Kouchner cited in Nicholas D. Kristof and Sheryl WuDunn, *Half the Sky: Turning Oppression Into Opportunity for Women Worldwide* (New York: Knopf, 2009), xx.

15. On the push to secure women's rights as human rights after World War II, see Jan Herman Burgers, "The Road to San Francisco: The Revival of the Human Rights Idea in the Twentieth Century," *Human Rights Quarterly* 14, no. 4 (November 1992): 447–77; Kenneth Smiel, "The Recent History of Human Rights," *American Historical Review* 109, no. 1 (February 2004): 117–35; Stefan-Ludwig Hoffman, "Introduction: Geneologies of Human Rights," in *Human Rights in the Twentieth Century*, ed. Stefan-Ludwig Hoffman (Cambridge: Cambridge University Press, 2011), 1–28; Leila J. Rupp, *Worlds of Women*, 222–25; and Marino, *Feminism for the Americas*, 170–97.

16. Margot Badran, *Feminists, Islam, and Nation: Gender and the Making of Modern Egypt* (Princeton, N.J.: Princeton University Press, 1995), 210–13; Mona Siegel, "Feminism, Pacifism and Political Violence in Europe and China in the Era of the World Wars," *Gender & History* 28, no. 3 (November 2016): 641–59; Mona Siegel, "The Dangers of Feminism in Colonial Indochina," *French Historical Studies* 38, no. 4 (October 2015): 661–89; Jessie Fauset, "Nationalism and Egypt," *Crisis*, April 1920, 310–16; and "Les grandes figures féminines de l'orient," *L'Égyptienne*, October 1927, hors texte.

17. Badran, *Feminists, Islam, and Nation*, 238–46; Francesca Miller, "Latin American Feminism and the Transnational Arena"; and Angela Woollacott, "Inventing Commonwealth and Pan-Pacific Feminisms: Australian Women's International Activism in the 1920s–30s," in *Globalizing Feminisms, 1789–1945*, ed. Karen Offen (London: New York: Routledge, 2010), 193–203, 217–31; Marino, *Feminism for the Americas*, 13–66, 113; Weber, "Nationalism and Feminism," 83–106; Sumita Mukherjee, "The All-Asian Women's Conference 1931: Indian Women and Their Leadership of a Pan-Asian Feminist Organization," *Women's History*

Review 26, no. 3 (2017): 363–81; and Marie Sandell, *The Rise of Women's Transnational Activism: Identity and Sisterhood Between the World Wars* (New York: I. B. Tauris, 2015).

18. UN Women, *Equality in Law for Women and Girls by 2030: A Multistakeholder Strategy for Accelerating Action* (New York: UN Women, 2019), http://www .unwomen.org/-/media/headquarters/attachments/sections/library/publica tions/2019/equality-in%20law-for-women-and-girls-en.pdf?la=en&vs=5600.

19. Information on UN Women can be found at http://www.unwomen.org/en. Kristof and WuDunn, *Half the Sky*, 255–58, offers a list of global organizations supporting women in developing countries.

Index

Note: Chinese and Japanese names are alphabetized by family name, followed by given name. Arabic names use standard English transliteration. Arabic family names beginning with al- are alphabetized under the element that follows the al-.

and, 23; Women's Congress and, 217,
218–22, *220*

boycott movement, in Egypt, 121, 122, 123

breastfeeding, 222, 223, 224

Brest-Litovsk Treaty, 145, 154

Brigode, Jane, 26, 29, 31

British forces, in Egypt, 107; women's
confrontations with, 92, 108–9,
112–14, 117–18, 120, 127, 161

British Protectorate in Egypt, 5, 7, 92,
109, 128; independence movement
and, 92–93, 106–7, 116–17; Wilson's
recognition of, 116

British Union of Women's Suffrage
Societies, 2, *27*

British WILPF, 88–89

British Women's Trade Union League,
215, 216

Brougham, H. Bruce, 22

Cabrini, Laura Casartelli, 241–42

Calmann-Lévy, Madame Paul, 72

Cambon, Jules, 36

Catt, Carrie Chapman, 1–2, 3, 4, 16, 29,
125–26, 232, 239; Egypt and, 125,
126; Luisi and, 239; Nineteenth
Amendment and, 21, 238; Orientalist
rhetoric of, 241; at Rome Congress,
238, 239, 244; M. Schlumberger and,
21; successor, 41, 238; support for
WWI of, 20; M.C. Terrell and, 58

Cavell, Edith, 92, 109, 117

CCP. *See* Chinese Communist Party

Cecil, Robert, 42–43, 45, 155

Central Powers, 79, 92, 138; Allied food
blockade and, 142–44; famine in,
142–44, 159–60; Inter-Allied
Women's Conference and, 29;
recruitment of China against,
173–74; women delegates from
Allied and, 130; Women's Congress

absence of delegates from, 218;
Zurich Congress and, 8, 79, 130,
138–40, 149–54

charitable work, of women, 16, 59, 102;
during WWI, 18, 64–65, 74; WILPF
decision not to limit itself to, 161

Cheng Yongsheng, 180

Chiang Kai-shek, 195

Chiang Kai-shek, Madame, 187, 197

Chicago Evening Post, 156, 157

Chicago Tribune, 22, 40, 46, 139, 146, 147,
150

China, 218; Allied betrayal of, 178–81;
Communist revolution of 1949, 198;
feminism in, 8, 10, 50, 127, 170–71,
184–86, 191; feminism-nationalism
ties in, 184–86; Japanese invasion of,
183, 197–98; Modern Woman in,
185–89; National Assembly (Nanjing)
of, 170; Nationalist Party in, 164,
174, 175, 184–86, 195–98, 237;
Orientalist beliefs about, 163–4;
peace delegation of, 5, 32, 33, 164,
174, 175, 179–84; republican Civil
Code of, 197; Revolutionary
Alliance for, 168–70, 171; Tcheng
representation of "young," 186;
Tcheng war recruitment in, 173–74;
U.S. recognition of new Republic of,
175; Woman Question in, 189–91;
women's emancipation in, 165, 188,
192, 196, 198; women's rights in,
184–86, 191–99; WILPF and, 79, 87,
162; WWI and, 173; WWII and, 198.
See also May Fourth Movement;
Shandong; Soumay Tcheng

Chinese Communist Party (CCP), 198

Chinese Society for International Peace,
180

Christianity, 15, 35, 37, 117, 134, 187,
206–7

Church, Louisa Ayers, 55
Church, Mary Eliza. *See* Terrell, Mary
    Church
citizenship status, marital laws and, 48,
    68, 148
civilizing mission, 33, 61–63, 73, 172
civil rights, 86, 197, 247–48
Clemenceau, Georges, 13, 38, 155,
    212; Inter-Allied delegates
    meeting with, 36, 39; Labor
    Commission and, 212; Versailles
    Treaty and, 144
clothing, symbolism of women's, 31;
    Tcheng fashion choices and, 164,
    168, 185–88, 196. *See also* veiling
colonialism (imperialism), 50, 54, 110,
    172; colonial soldiers of WWI, 65,
    76; French, 61, 75–6, 88–89, 172;
    I. G. Hunt on racism and, 61–63;
    Japanese, 178, 183; mandate system
    and, 83; Middle Eastern feminism
    and, 127, 128; petition for Rhineland
    removal of soldiers, 88–89; post-
    peace conference struggles against,
    237; U.S., 175; Wilson on, 92–93.
    See also civilizing mission
Colored American, The, 60
Commission for International Labor
    Legislation (Labor Commission),
    Paris Peace Conference, 31, 40–41,
    201, 214, 226; Bouvier and, 210;
    Inter-Allied women and, 210–15;
    night work ban and, 226–27;
    recommendations of, 213; request for
    women delegates at conference, 214;
    Schneiderman and, 206; women's
    exclusion from, 212
Commission on the Status of Women,
    UN, 234, 240
Commission on War Responsibilities,
    Paris Peace Conference, 36

Commission on Women's Employment,
    ILO, 222, 223, 227
communism, 116, 139, 184, 187, 189,
    190, 195, 198, 237
compassionate diplomacy, 158, 162
concubinage, 50, 95, 167, 190, 197
contraception, 19
Crisis, The, 64, 70, 73, 85, 247–48;
    H. Shaarawi featured in, 127
Crowdy, Rachel, 47–48, 242
Curtis, Helen, 74

Daily Mail, 6–7, 163, 164, 189
Davis, Richard Harding, 138
Declaration of Human Rights, UN, 247
democracy: Chinese claims to, 165, 173;
    178; industrial, 219; feminists' claims
    to, 3, 4, 13, 20–1, 40, 46, 53, 90, 93,
    124; men's limited vision of, 9, 48,
    123, 178; Paris Peace Conference and,
    245–46; popular sovereignty and, 44,
    145, 256; racial discrimination and,
    68, 81, 83, 90, 220–21; Wilson on, 3,
    20, 53, 175, 179
Democratic Party, antisuffrage bloc of
    American, 20
Despard, Charlotte, *140*, 146
Dewey, John, 179
Diagne, Blaise, 71–73, *73*, 74, 76
divorce: Amin on, 101; Chinese Civil
    Code on, 197; Egyptian feminists on,
    124; Tcheng legal cases on, 195–96
Divorcees, The (Rushdi), 99
doctors, women, 43–44, 135, 193, 223
Doctors without Borders, 245
Doll's House, A (Ibsen), 190
dressmaking, 207
Drexel, Constance, 40, 45–46, 139, 146,
    147, 150; lobbying advice from, 22
Du Bois, W.E.B.: Diagne and, 71–72;
    French "color-blindness" and, 75;

Marcus Garvey and, 85; I.G. Hunt and, 63, 64, 70–71, 74–75, 85, 86; Pan-African Congress and, 54, 70–75, 73; Pan-African movement and, 85, 86; suffrage support of, 59; M.C. Terrell and, 86; WWI and, 70

Duchêne, Gabrielle, 208, 209, 213, 214–15; human rights ideas of, 204; Inter-Allied women's labor subcommittee and, 209–12, 215; Labor Commission and, 212–13; night work ban debate and, 226

Dutch feminists, 135, 139; the 1915 Hague Conference and, 136, 209; support for League of Nations of, 147. See also Aletta Jacobs

Eastern Women's Congresses, 127, 248

education, 167–68, 172–73, 187; African American women and, 53, 54, 55–56; in Egypt, 95–97, 101, 102, 103, 124–25; reforms in Chinese, 189–90; M. C. Terrell on, 80; Zurich Congress resolution on race and, 80

Egypt: domestic seclusion of women in, 91, 94–95, 99, 100; education in, 96–97, 101, 102, 103, 124–25; gender equality and, 93–94, 124; partial independence of, 122; polygamy in, 95, 101, 102–3, 125; prior to WWI, 92, 99, 103–7; WILPF protest against British rule of, 161; women's awakening in, 50, 99–103; women's rights in, 118, 124; WWI and, 92, 105. See also British Protectorate; Egyptian Revolution of 1919; Wafd

Egyptian Feminist Union, 124–27, 240; international feminist organizations and, 125–26, 238, 240, 247–48; pan-Arab feminist organizations and, 127

Egyptian Mail, 112–13, 118–19

Egyptian Revolution of 1919: boycott of British goods, 121, 122, 123; female victims of, 107, 115; independence movement and, 106–7, 110, 116–17, 120–23, 237; male view of feminism in era of, 110, 118–20, 121–23; militant female activists in, 115–16; Paris Peace Conference and, 5, 116–17; Wafd leadership and, 116–17; Wilson and, 92–93; 110; women's nationalism and, 91–92, 106–12; women's rights and, 118. See also Egyptian women's demonstrations

Egyptian women's demonstrations (women's march in Cairo), 10, 91–92, 108–9; British policy of sexual harassment towards, 114; journalists portrayal of, 111–13, 118–19; Margueritte portrayal of, 117–18; Milner Commission and, 120–21; nationalism and, 87, 110–11, 118; Russell, perception and portrayal of, 113–15; Wafd and, 117, 118, 123; Wilson and, 111; women bystanders, response to, 111. See also Egyptian Feminist Union

electoral laws, 122, 244

emancipation, of women: in China, 165, 184, 188, 189–91, 192, 196, 198; in Egypt, 101, 107, 110, 184; national independence tied to, 110–12, 184; Western suffragists pursuit of, 110

Emancipation Proclamation, 84

Entente, 79

Equal Nationality Treaties, 249

equal pay, 40, 213, 227, 245

Equal Rights Treaties, 249

Espionage and Sedition Acts, 156

Europe, James Reese, 66

famine, 142–44, 159–60, 237

fascism, 2, 49, 244

Fawcett, Millicent Garrett, 2, 4, 16–17, 26, *27*, 33, 39, 41, 238–39; Wilson and, 31–32

Federation of Clothing Workers, French, 207–8

female journalists, 22, 40, 45–46, 123, 150, 207; Tcheng-Viollis interview, 163–64, 182, 185, 288n1

feminism (female activism): central demand of, 245; charity as channel for, 16, 18, 64–65, 102; definition of, 263n13; divisions in, 81, 88–9, 230, 232, 233; emotion cited in critiques of, 157; imperialism and, 37, 50, 128; nationalism and, 106–7, 110–12; pacifism ties to, 151–54; pan-Arab, 127; Paris Peace Conference era, 4, 50; prior to WWI, 3, 263n13; pronatalism and, 19; social class and, 200–202; Tcheng's nationalism and, 184–86, 188; universal appeal of, 9, 245; Western, 19, 49, 110. *See also* international feminist organizing; global feminism; labor feminism; *specific topics*

Figaro, Le, 188

food blockade, Allied, 142–44, 146, 150, 154, 159

footbinding, 166, 167, 190

France: African American women in, 74, 274n47; anti-famine work of WILPF in, 160; battlefields of Northern, 51–53, 75–78, 82–83; bridge-building between Germany and, 149–54; Egyptian women's march, response of, 112; German occupation of, 150–51; government resistance to suffrage in, 243; Hague Congress delegates from, 136;

marriage laws in, 208; maternity leave in, 223; myth of "color-blind," 75–76; suffrage struggle in, 12–14, 17–18, 25–26, 243; Tcheng 1927 return to, 196; Zurich Congress delegates from, 139

Franco-Prussian War, 15, 19

French colonies, 54, 56, 60–62, 71, 73, 76, 172; German Rhineland and troops from, 88–89

French General Confederation of Labor, 208, 212, 235–36

French journalists: all-women newspaper, 207; on Tcheng 1928 return to France, 196; on Wilson's 1918 suffrage statement, 21; Tcheng portrayal by, 163–64, 176, 183, 186, 188, 209, 288n1; on Wilson's 1918 suffrage statement, 21

French Office for Women's Interests, 209

French Socialist Party, 151

French Union for Women's Suffrage, 16–18, 20–21, 151, 297n42; demonstrations, *17*, 17–18; I. G. Hunt collaboration with, 64; Inter-Allied Women's Conference and, 25, 26; meeting with Wilson, 12–14, 22, 25–26; Mélin collaboration with, 151–52; M. Schlumberger as president of, 16, 152

Fronde, La, 207

Garvey, Marcus, 85

Gaulois, Le, 31

Gazette de Lausanne, 153

gender equality: for African American women, 53, 241; CCP and, 198; Egyptian women and, 93–94, 124; global stability role of, 9; human rights and, 209; male apprehension of, 156; under Nationalist rule in China, 197–98; night work ban and, 232; Pan-American treaty on, 47; Paris Peace Conference and, 2–3, 8–9; peace based on, 249; political parity and, 222; term use, 261n4; victimhood strategy and, 37

gender solidarity, 37

Geneva, 161; Hesselgren in, 234; IFWW meeting in, 231; ILO conference in, 234; ILO office in, 230–31; IWSA meeting in, 232, 240, 242; WILPF headquarters in, 132, 152, 158, 159

Genoni, Rosa, 137, 139, *140*

George, David Lloyd, 2, 13, 144, 212

Germany: Addams-Hamilton postwar tour of, 159–60; Alsace, surrendered by, 6, 15; Belgian occupation by, 29, 64–65; Brest-Litovsk Treaty, 145, 154; feminists in, 16, 29, 43, 68; France occupation by, 150–51; Hague Congress delegates from, 136; ILO conference, absence from, 218, 296n31; Schneiderman passage through, 204; Shandong territory claim by, 174; surrender of, 6; M.C. Terrell in, 58; Versailles Treaty and, 144–46, 155; WILPF in, 160; Zurich Congress and, 139, 149–54; Zurich delegates from, 68, 79; WWII and, 14. *See also* food blockade, Allied

Ghana, independence of, 89–90

Girard-Mangin, Nicole, 43–44

Global feminism, 239–40, 241; Paris Peace Conference spawning, 4, 7–11; term use, 9, 263n13; women's appeals to peacemakers, 37. *See also* feminism; international feminist organizing; labor feminism

Gompers, Samuel, 40, 212–13

Government of India Act, 243, 300n12

Great Britain, armistice and, 3; Bondfield, Minister of Labor in, 234; mandate system and, 147; Opium Wars and, 168; peace negotiations and, 5, 13, 178; Schneiderman in, 215–16; suffragettes in, 17; suffragists in, 2, 16, 21, 146; WILPF delegates from, 79; women's suffrage in, 49. *See also* British Protectorate in Egypt

Great Depression, 233

Greek League for Women's Rights, 239

Grinberg, Suzanne, 26, *28*, *31*, 32, 46; League of Nations Commission addressed by, 44, 45

Guizot, François, 15

Hague Congress. *See* International Women's Conference, at The Hague

Haiti: American occupation of, 87; WILPF fact-finding mission to, 87, 161–62

Hamilton, Alice, 52, 140, *140*, 141, 143; Addams and, 159

Hamilton-Gordon, Ishbel Maria (Lady Aberdeen), 37–38, 41–42, 43, 267n27

harem, 7, 95, 98–99, 107, 114, 118, 185

Harlem Hellfighters, 66

Harriman, Florence Jaffray, 27, 30–31

Hertzka, Yella, 241

Hesselgren, Kerstin, 221, 234, 297n42

Heymann, Lida Gustava, 136, 139, *140*, 157; Mélin-Heymann embrace at Zurich, 153, 154

Hoover, Herbert, 138, 159

Hua Mulan, 167, 188–89, 195, 199

Huang Dinghui, 180

Hull House, 130, 140

human rights, 48, 149, 247; gender equality as fundamental, 209

Hunt, Ida Gibbs, 8, 200; anti-colonialism of, 62–63; Du Bois and, 63, 64, 70–75, 85; French feminists and, 64; League of Nations disillusionment of, 83; in Madagascar, 54, 61–64, *62*; marriage, 60; Pan-African movement and, 85–87, 241; on racism and colonialism, 61–63; M. C. Terrell and, 53–54, 65, 84; NAWSA and, 60, Pan-African Congress (1919) and, 70–75, *73*; refugee aid during WWI, 64–65; teaching position of, 60; upbringing and education, 56; WILPF and, 87
Hunt, William Henry ("Billy"), 60, 61, 63–64; Diagne and, 72
Hunton, Addie Waites, 74, 161–62
Hu Shi, 190, 191

Ibsen, Henrik, 190
ICW. *See* International Council of Women
ILO. *See* International Labor Organization
ILO Commission on Women's Employment, 222, 223, 227
ILO Conference, Washington D.C.: feminist lobbying and, 47, 221–30; International Labor Conventions adopted by, 230–31; key concerns of, 201–2; Maternity Protection Convention of 1919, 221–25, 231; night work debate and policy of, 225–30; nonvoting female advisors to, 222; Women's Congress and, 214, 216–22, 224–25
India, 300n7; female activism in, 7, 87; IFWW membership of, 232; peace delegates from, 38; Rome Congress, participation in, 238; WWI soldiers

from, 65; Women's Congress, participation in, 218; women's suffrage in, 243, 300n12
industrial home work, 226
inheritance rights, 9, 97, 197
Intellectual Association of Egyptian Women, 103
Inter-Allied Women's Conference, 8, 13, 14, 26–32, *30*, 56; Central Powers excluded from, 29; date of, 29; dress styles and, 31; individual self-determination and, 44–45; international participation resulting from, 47–48; Labor Commission addressed by delegates of, 40–41; labor subcommittee of, 210–11, 215, 223; League of Nations Commission addressed by delegates of, 40–45, 49–50; League of Nations Covenant and, 148; limited knowledge of other cultures, 50; list of delegates to, 266n27; location of, 26; meeting with Clemenceau, 39; meetings with peace plenipotentiaries, 32–35; secretary, *28*; suffrage demands of, 14, 44; suffrage gained by some delegates to, 49; violence against women angle of, 34–35; Western superiority and, 49–50; WILPF compared with, 51, 68; WILPF membership contrasted with, 51; Wilson and, 25, 31–32, 38; women as peacemakers and, 46–7; Women's Commission proposal and, 31–32; Yesayan and, 35–37
International Committee of Women for Permanent Peace, 137, 138, 271n1
International Congress of Women. *See* Women's International League for Peace and Freedom; Zurich Congress

International Congress of Working Women of 1919 (Women's Congress), First, 8, 41; African American absence from, 218–19; American organization of, 216–18; countries not represented in, 218; delegates to, 218; delegates' union work and careers following, 233–36; first day of, 221–22; ILO Conference and, 216 21, 216–22, 224–25; Japanese delegates of, 229; labor feminism organization created out of, 231–32; maternity leave policy and, 223; Mt. Vernon outing of, 219–21, 220; night work ban debate and policy of, 225–30; welcome card, 217

International Congress of Working Women of 1921, Second, 232

International Congress of Working Women of 1923, Third, 232, 234, 242

International Council of Women (ICW), 41, 46, 212–13

International Council of Women of the Darker Races, 89, 241, 248

International Federation of Trade Unions, 232

International Federation of Working Women, 231, 241–42; members of, 232

International feminist organizing, 239–40, 241, 247–48; Addams on new, 159; Egyptian women and, 126–27; international agreements and, 47; new hierarchies in, 242–44; labor and, 230–36, 242; League of Nations and, 47–8, 246; media and, 249; United Nations and, 47; women's appeals to peacemakers, 37. *See also* feminism; global feminism; labor feminism; organizations, of women; *specific topics*

International Labor Conference. *See* ILO Conference, Washington D.C.

International Labor Office, in Geneva, 213–14; 230–31

International Labor Organization (ILO), 10, 40–41; Bondfield and, 216, 234; female advisors to, 246; women staff at office of, 213–14; Versailles Treaty establishing, 201

International Woman Suffrage Alliance: Addams neutral meeting letter to, 135–36; Corbett Ashby presidency of, 41, 238; Catt presidency of, 16, 20, 41; decision not to meet in 1919 of, 29; Egyptian affiliation with, 125–26; French Union affiliation with, 16; Geneva congress of 1920, 232; Mussolini and, *243*; Rome Congress of 1923, 11, *125*, 125–27, 237–44

International Women's Conference, at The Hague, in 1915, 133, 135–37; delegates, 136–37; Duchêne's endorsement of, 209; Heymann and Mélin at, 153–54; Kulke at, 142, 143; Mélin's inability to attend, 152; resolutions, 137, 283n20; suffragists across enemy nations attending, 209

Islam, 97, 101, 123, 124, 126; British depiction of, 116; suffrage and, 243

Italy: peace negotiations and 5, 13; labor feminists from 212, 218, Mussolini dictatorship of 11, 49, 237; suffragists from 21; WILPF members from, 79, 137; women's suffrage and, 49, 243–44. *See also* Rome Congress of 1923

Jacobs, Aletta, 135, 140; Addams and, 136; Duchêne and, 209; Hague Conference of 1915 and, 133, 135–37, 152; Zurich Congress and, 138–39, 140; world tour, Catt and, 125

Modern Woman, construct of, 117,
185–89, 199
motherhood: labor feminism, maternity
leave and, 222–23; maternalist
rhetoric, 81, 157; as paid labor,
224–25; pronatalism and, 18–19
Muhammed Ali (Pasha), 92
Muller v. Oregon, 226
Mulon, Clothilde, 223
Musa, Nabawiya,103, 116, *125*, 126
Mussolini, Benito, 11, 49, 237, *243*,
243–44
Mutō Sanji, 227–28, 229

NAACP. *See* National Association for
the Advancement of Colored People
Nabarawi, Saiza, *125*, 126, 128
NACW. *See* National Association of
Colored Women
Nasif, Malak Hifni (Bahithat
al-Badiyah), 102–3, 105
Nasser (General), 124
National American Woman Suffrage
Association (NAWSA), 1–2, 20,
58–59, 60
National Association for the
Advancement of Colored People
(NAACP), 64, 70, 86, 134
National Association of Colored
Women (NACW), 59–60
National Consumers League, 140
National Council of French Women, 74,
208, 212, 267n27
National Council of Negro Women,
89–90
Nationalism, feminism and: in China,
184–86, 188; in Egypt, 91–92,
106–12, 120; in Europe, 135
Nationalist Party, in China
(Guomindang), 174, 175, 195, 237;
Tcheng appointed peace delegate by,

174, 184; Tcheng appointed envoy by,
196; Tcheng appointed to Yuan by,
197; women's rights under, 196–98
National Recovery Administration
Labor Advisory Board, 202–3,
233–34
National Union of Women Workers,
Great Britain, 215
National Women's Trade Union League
of America (NWTULA), 134, 202,
205–6, 216, 217–19, 233;
representatives sent to Paris, 211
NAWSA. *See* National American
Woman Suffrage Association
Nazis, 14
New Culturalists, in China, 189–91
New York Times, 2, 5–6; on French
Union meeting with Wilson, 22;
Tcheng interviewed by, 176; Tcheng
photo in, *186*; on women's hearing
before League of Nations
Commission, 46; on Zurich
Congress, 139–40, 141, 144
New Zealand: delegate to Inter-Allied
Women's Conference, 27; suffrage in,
49
Night-Work Convention of 1919,
229–30
Nineteenth Amendment, 21, 140–41,
238
Nkrumah, Kwame, 89–90
Nobel Peace Prize, 8, 132, 231, 241, 249
North-China Herald, 179
NWTULA. *See* National Women's
Trade Union League of America

Oberlin College, 55, 56
Opium Wars, 168, 175
Orientalism, 33, 114, 163, 184
Ottoman Empire, 1, 3, 92, 104, 147, 237;
persecution of Armenians in, 35–36

pacifism, 37; Addams work and leadership in, 132–38; anti-suffragists on Addams, 138; as broadly defined, 129–30; criticism of, 137–38; government hostility towards, 139; Hague Congress and, 136–37; racial justice and, 81; Schlumberger warning against, 18; social ostracism due to, 129–30, 137–38; in wartime France and Germany, 151–54, 209; Zurich Congress and, 146

Pan-African Congress of 1919: delegates, 34, 73, *73*, 74; I. G. Hunt and, 54, 70–75, 82; sexism and, 85–86; women delegates, 74, 161–62

Pan-Africanism, 85–86, 89–90; and feminism, 8, 89, 248; Third Pan-African Congress, 241

Pan-Americanism, 47, 239, 248

Pan-Pacific Women's Association, 248

Paris Peace Conference, 1919: African American women and, 53, 63; China's seat at, 174; disillusionment over, 83; Egyptian appeals and treatment, 116–18; gender equality and, 2–3, 8–9; global events following, 237–38; history, women's rights and, 245; international feminism spawned by, 7–11, 262n12; Labor Commission formed during, 201, 210–15; labor women representatives at, 206; League of Nations Covenant and, 146–49; legacies of, 94, 244–49; lone female delegate at, 33, 163–65, 174, 184; meetings with Inter-Allied women, 32–33; opening day of, 12; overlooked legacies of, 84; participants in, 5; proclamations and failures of, 244–45; race issues not addressed by, 54, 71; racial equality controversy, 77–78; retrieved documents telling of women's role in, 14–15; Shandong award to Japan, 177–81, 183; Wafd leaders appeals to, 116–17, 120; WILPF conference coinciding with, 67; Wilson on goal of, 3–4; women's aspirations and appeals, 4–7, 14; women's labor charter presented to, 209, 294n14; women's organizational legacy of, 89; Zurich delegates and, 155–58. *See also* Labor Commission; League of Nations Commission; plenipotentiaries; Supreme Council; Tcheng, Soumay; Versailles Treaty

passports, *42*, 68–69, *69*, 71, 74, 77, 136, 139, 152, 204

paternalism, 34, 105, 112, 228

patriarchy, 57, 115, 122–23

patriotism, 15, 19, 20, 238; of Egyptian women demonstrators, 110–11, 118; racial equality and, 70, 83; suffrage and, 49. *See also* nationalism

peacemaking, women roles in, 4–5, 132, 157, 162, 245

Pethick-Lawrence, Emmeline, 135

Petit Parisien, Le, 173, 176

plenipotentiaries, Paris Peace Conference, 5, 25; Chinese, 8, 164, 174, 175–76, 181; female attaché for Chinese, 164; international women's appeals to, 37; racism and, 54, 71, 77–78; Women's Commission and, 32; women's meetings with, 41–42

polygamy, 50; in Egypt, 95, 101, 102–3, 124, 125

Portugal, suffragists from, 21

pronatalism, 18–19

protective labor legislation, 8; ban on women's night work, 225–30, 232; feminist divisions over, 232, 233

Qing dynasty, 164, 166, 175–76, 189–90;
    fall of, 168–70; Tcheng description
    of, 176; Tcheng's father and, 167, 168
Qiu Jin, 170
Quaker relief work, 159–60

race: American racial segregation, 53,
    59–60, 66, 90; feminist racism, 33,
    59, 88, 241; Paris Peace Conference
    not addressing, 54, 246; racial
    discrimination, 52–53, 54, 82; racial
    justice and feminism, 53, 79, 82, 84,
    246; racial stereotypes, 33, 87–88,
    184, 185, 221; racial uplift activism,
    57–60; racism of peace delegates, 54,
    71, 77–78; suffrage movement issue
    of, 59; racism of Wilson, 66
Rankin, Jeanette, 140–41, 156–57
Red Cross, 27, 31, 52
Red Scare, in United States, 237
Red Summer, of 1919, 83–84
religion: *See* Christianity; Islam;
    Judaism; Quaker relief work
Republic of China, U.S. recognition of,
    175
Robins, Margaret Dreier, 205, 206, 211;
    return to Europe in 1923, 232;
    Tanaka and, 228–29; Women's
    Congress and, 216, 217–18, *220*, 222
Rome Congress of 1923, 11, *125*, 125–27,
    239–44; global scope and participation
    of delegates in, 239–40, 241;
    hierarchical procession to, 242–44
Roosevelt, Eleanor, 202, 218
Roosevelt, Franklin Delano, 202–3, 233–34
Roosevelt, Theodore, 138
Russell, Thomas, 109, 113–15

Save the Children Fund, 160
Schlumberger, Marguerite de Witt, 4, 8,
    17, 200, 238; Bouvier and, 209;

charitable work by, 18; death of, 49;
    as French Union leadership of, 16,
    152; I.G. Hunt and, 64; Inter-Allied
    Women's Conference and, 26–32, 39,
    148; League of Nations Commission
    and, 40, 44–45, 148; legacies of,
    46–47, 49; marriage and children,
    15–16, 18; maternalist feminism of,
    19; pronatalism of, 19; "people's
    peace" strategy of, 25; politics and
    background, 15–16, 18; Rome
    Congress and, 283; Tcheng and, 240;
    Thomson and, 22–23; Wilson and, 4,
    12–14, 19–21, 24–26, 31–32, 38
Schlumberger, Paul, 15–16
Schneiderman, Rose, 8; activism of
    Bouvier and, 201–3; childhood
    poverty of, 203–4; garment worker,
    204; first union experiences and
    leadership, 204–6; ILO Conference
    and, 222; immigration to America,
    204; as labor advisor to F. D.
    Roosevelt, 202–3, 233–34;
    International Federation for Working
    Women and, 232; in London, 215–16;
    message to Wilson from, 214;
    NWTULA presidency of, 233;
    representing NWTULA in Paris,
    206, 211, 214–15; return to Europe in
    1923, 232; social class of Bouvier and,
    200–201, suffrage and, *205*; support
    for night-work ban of, 227; Wilson
    and, 214; at Women's Congress, 217,
    218, *220*
Schwimmer, Rosika, 135
seclusion, of women, 91, 94–95, 100.
    See also harem
self-determination: individual and
    national, 9, 15, 184, 246; Wilson's
    articulation of national, 92–93, 106,
    117, 145; women's appropriation of,

Wilson, Woodrow, 1, 2, 5–6; Addams and, 135; African Americans and, 66–67; as "apostle of peace," 23; bas-relief sculpture inscribed to, 23, 24; British Protectorate support from, 116–17; Chinese betrayal and, 179, 180; Egyptian independence movement and, 111; "Fourteen Points" of, 3, 137, 145, 175; French suffragist meetings with, 3, 24–26; French women's delegation meeting with, 22–24, 210; French WILPF message to, 160; Inter-Allied Women's Conference and, 31–32; Japanese leverage over, 178; labor women and, 214; League of Nations and, 45, 146; message to WILPF on food blockade, 144; national self-determination principle of, 92–93, 106, 117, 145; on peacemakers goal, 3–4; racial equality clause rejected by, 77–78, 81, 83, 178; Red Summer and, 84; Republic of China recognized by, 175; Versailles Treaty and, 144–46; Women's Commission proposal and, 31–32, 38–39; women's suffrage viewed by, 3, 12–14, 23–24

Woman Worker, 220

"Women's Charter," Zurich Congress creation of, 8, 148–49

Women's Commission proposal, 31–35; Lady Aberdeen efforts for, 37–38; objections to, 38; strategy for winning support for, 36–37; Wilson and, 31–32, 38–39

Women's Congress. *See* International Congress of Working Women

Women's International League for Peace and Freedom (WILPF), 152; Addams in, 78, 155; anti-famine work of, 159–61; battlefields visit by, 52, 75–76;

Black Horror on the Rhine campaign and, 87–88, 89; British, 88–89; in China, 196, 240; delegates, 51, 75, 76; fact-finding missions of, 87; French WILPF message to Wilson, 160; foundations laid by, 158–62; Inter-Allied Conference compared with, 51, 68, 241; interwar decades work of, 160–62; labor feminism and, 233; League of Nations and, 159; membership, 158; mission to Asia, 247; at Paris Peace Conference, 155–56; permanence and wide reach of, 132; plan of action after Zurich, 158–59; racial stereotypes within, 87–88; at Rome Congress, 241; Tcheng and, 162, 240; Terrell and, 79–81, 80, 141. *See also* International Committee of Women for a Permanent Peace; Zurich Congress

Women's Motor Corps, Red Cross, 27

Women's Peace Party, U.S., 135

Women's Refinement Union, Egyptian, 103

women's rights: in China, 184–86, 191–99; colonial divide and, 128; in Egypt, 118, 124; League of Nations and global, 45–50; under Nationalist Party in China, 196–98; night work ban threat to, 230; pan-Arab feminism and, 127. *See also specific topics*

women's work, 206, 211, 232; during WWI, 6–7; industrial home work, 226. *See also* labor feminism; maternity leave; protective labor legislation

World Disarmament Conference in Geneva, 161

World War I (WWI), 1–2, 25; Addams pacifism during, 130; Cavell

COLUMBIA STUDIES IN INTERNATIONAL AND GLOBAL HISTORY
Cemil Aydin, Timothy Nunan, and Dominic Sachsenmaier, Series Editors